CONTAINING DIVERSITY

Containing Diversity

Canada and the Politics of Immigration in the 21st Century

YASMEEN ABU-LABAN, ETHEL TUNGOHAN, AND CHRISTINA GABRIEL

UNIVERSITY OF TORONTO PRESS
Toronto Buffalo London

© University of Toronto Press 2023
Toronto Buffalo London
utorontopress.com

ISBN 978-1-4426-0905-1 (cloth)   ISBN 978-1-4426-0907-5 (EPUB)
ISBN 978-1-4426-0904-4 (paper)   ISBN 978-1-4426-0906-8 (PDF)

All rights reserved. The use of any part of this publication reproduced, transmitted in any form or by any means, electronic, mechanical, photocopying, recording, or otherwise, or stored in a retrieval system, without prior written consent of the publisher – or in the case of photocopying, a licence from Access Copyright, the Canadian Copyright Licensing Agency – is an infringement of the copyright law.

Library and Archives Canada Cataloguing in Publication

Title: Containing diversity : Canada and the politics of immigration in the 21st century / Yasmeen Abu-Laban, Ethel Tungohan, and Christina Gabriel.
Names: Abu-Laban, Yasmeen, 1966– author. | Tungohan, Ethel, author. | Gabriel, Christina, author.
Description: Includes bibliographical references and index.
Identifiers: Canadiana (print) 20220175764 | Canadiana (ebook) 20220175918 | ISBN 9781442609051 (cloth) | ISBN 9781442609044 (paper) | ISBN 9781442609075 (EPUB) | ISBN 9781442609068 (PDF)
Subjects: LCSH: Immigrants – Government policy – Canada. | LCSH: Multiculturalism – Canada. | LCSH: Citizenship – Canada. | LCSH: Canada – Emigration and immigration – Political aspects.
Classification: LCC JV7225.2.A28 2023 | DDC 305.9/069120971 – dc23

We welcome comments and suggestions regarding any aspect of our publications – please feel free to contact us at news@utorontopress.com or visit us at utorontopress.com.

Every effort has been made to contact copyright holders; in the event of an error or omission, please notify the publisher.

We wish to acknowledge the land on which the University of Toronto Press operates. This land is the traditional territory of the Wendat, the Anishnaabeg, the Haudenosaunee, the Métis, and the Mississaugas of the Credit First Nation.

University of Toronto Press acknowledges the financial support of the Government of Canada and the Ontario Arts Council, an agency of the Government of Ontario, for its publishing activities.

We dedicate this book to our parents:

Baha Abu-Laban and Sharon McIrvin Abu-Laban,
Leonides and Arlene Tungohan,
and
Keith and Betty Gabriel.

We are inspired by their collective strength and resilience as newcomers who adapted and contributed to the country said to be named after the Huron-Iroquois word kanata.

Contents

Acknowledgments   ix

Introduction   1

Part I

1 Mapping Containing Diversity   13
2 Contextualizing Containing Diversity: Historic and Contemporary Policies   28

Part II

3 Controlling "Global Citizens": Refugees, International Obligations, and Security   69
4 Seeking Citizens: "Skilled" Immigrants as Ideal Neoliberal Citizens   104
5 Making Non-citizens: Temporary Workers and the Production of Precarity   137
6 Family Migrants as "Undesirable"? Sponsoring New Citizens amid New Restrictions on Family Immigration Policies   179

Part III

7 Redefining Membership and Belonging: Contestations over Citizenship and Multiculturalism   221
8 Towards a Politics of Global and Social Justice   264

Conclusion and Future Directions   299

Select Podcast and Documentary Suggestions   315

Index   321

Acknowledgments

The completion of this book benefitted from the support of many individuals and organizations.

From University of Toronto Press, we would like to particularly thank Michael Harrison for his vision and encouragement of this project early on, as well as Mat Buntin, Stephen Jones, and Marilyn McCormack for their support and guidance at different junctures.

We benefitted from supports given by our respective departments of political science at the University of Alberta, Carleton University, and York University, as well as the Canada Research Chairs Program. Additionally, various colleagues commented on portions of this manuscript at meetings of the International Conference on Public Policy, the Canadian Political Science Association, the Canadian Ethnic Studies Association and other events, including one sponsored by the Canadian Institute for Advanced Research. We thank in particular Alexandra Dobrowolsky, Keith Banting, Irene Bloemraad, Will Kymlicka, Leah Levac, Dagmar Soennecken, and Luc Turgeon for comments on various portions of the manuscript at different phases.

We sincerely thank our four anonymous reviewers for their careful and constructive suggestions and comments, and the time they took to support the peer review process.

We are also very appreciative of Salina Abji for her expert, timely, and dedicated editorial support.

For capable and contributory research assistance we thank Margot Chalborn, Myka Jaymalin, Nariya Khasanova, Angela Natial, Nicole Lugosi, Mycah Panjaitan, and Bea Seardon.

A big thank you is extended to artist Ahmad Farid for his generosity in sharing an image of his work "Cultural Migration" for the cover of this volume.

We are especially grateful to our families. We completed this book during the COVID-19 pandemic and like so many others experienced an intensification of work, family, and care responsibilities in this period, made all the more poignant by global health inequities as well as painful loss. We would like to thank our families: Wayne Chu; Winifred and Georgina Tungohan-Chu; William and Zoë Walters; Zachary Jericho Couture; Baha, Riyad, and Max Abu-Laban; Carol Shaben; and Sharon McIrvin Abu-Laban. They all provided loving support and much more throughout this time and over the course of this project.

Introduction

On March 11, 2020, the novel coronavirus known as COVID-19 was declared a global pandemic by the World Health Organization (WHO). On that day, the director-general of WHO, Dr. Tedros Adhanom Ghebreyesus, asserted that in order to deal with the deadly virus all countries were called on to "activate and scale up ... emergency response mechanisms," cautioning at the same time that "all countries must strike a fine balance between protecting health, minimizing economic and social disruption, and respecting human rights" (UN WHO 2020). A common response by governments, however, was to assert control over migration policy. By March 20, 2020, more than 130 countries had implemented border closures, travel restrictions and bans, as well as enhanced screening measures. In many cases, these measures reactivated historic tendencies to blame migrants for the public health concerns of the day by treating migrants and refugees as threats to containing COVID-19 (Banulescu-Bogdan et al. 2020). As a consequence of some 75 per cent of the world's countries implementing border closures to new entrants in short order, vulnerable irregular migrants and refugees were made even more so (Reidy 2020). Consequently, leading migration policy experts began to raise alarm bells about governments using the unprecedented crisis as a rationale to push through exceptionally restrictive migration legislation (Reidy 2020). At the same time, however, countries like Canada and the United States informed their citizens abroad to return home.

They additionally endeavoured to keep migration flows open to some temporary foreign workers who, despite being denied citizenship, were deemed essential to maintaining agriculture and food production and other essential work (Malbeuf 2020; Sewer 2020). Migrant workers and minority citizens on both sides of the 49th parallel also had to deal with new forms of racist and violent attacks, especially directed at those of Asian origin erroneously blamed for spreading the disease with derogatory terms like "Wuhan virus" or "Chinese virus" (Marcos 2020).

If the COVID-19 pandemic has exposed our vulnerabilities as humans interconnected globally, the responses to the pandemic also provide an unprecedented window on the power of the state to regulate the movement of citizens and non-citizens. Of course, the long-term political, social, and economic impacts of the COVID-19 pandemic promise to play out in the years and decades ahead. Yet the immediate response to the pandemic was notable because re-assertions of state control over migration and entry unfolded amid complex discussions concerning work, perceptions of threat, and expressions of racism. As such, the immediate pandemic response captures key elements of a broader process we call *containing diversity*, which involves the racialization and control of specific groups, alongside contradictory impulses exhibited between closure to threatening outsiders and openness to valued workers and citizens. Racialization intersects with religion, gender, country of origin, class, and citizenship status in manifold ways in both discourse and individual experiences. In this volume, we examine the shifts that have taken place in immigration, citizenship, and multiculturalism in Canada in the period 2001–21 to illustrate how *containing diversity* finds expression in the current conjuncture.

We mobilize the tools of social science to assess broad patterns in migration, citizenship, and cultural pluralism (multiculturalism) by attending to Canada within comparative frames of reference attuned to other Western countries. The connection and balance between immigration, citizenship, and multiculturalism has been characterized as a three-legged stool by Will Kymlicka (2003) to capture how each leg reinforces (or lessens) the other two. Writing in 2003, Kymlicka argued that the Canadian case, in contrast to the British situation, showed strong state support of immigration and multiculturalism that has "defused or pre-empted" (202) concerns about citizenship. Our project in this book is to ask if Canada's strong support for immigration, multiculturalism, and citizenship is still the case today. Recent shifts reflecting the process we call containing diversity necessitate that we think more closely about the changing nature of immigration and citizenship policy and multicultural practice in Canada. While our focus is on the twenty-first century, we also consider the history and evolution of Canada as a settler colony built on the expropriation of land from Indigenous peoples and repeated waves of immigrants, starting with settlers from France and Britain. This attention makes clear that the political, policy, and ethical considerations involved are multifaceted and tied to an ongoing process of national boundary construction.

In Canada, immigration policy and practice has long been implicated in a process of national boundary construction, where Canada selects "potential" citizens while simultaneously keeping those deemed less desirable or undesirable out (Abu-Laban and Gabriel 2002). As well, different values and visions of Canada may underlie differing understandings of who ideal citizens are. For example, the 2015 federal election can be characterized as a watershed moment insofar as it was marked by public debates about migration, citizenship, and multiculturalism that reflected on competing values and visions of Canada. A comparison of election speeches by the leaders of the two main Liberal and Conservative parties is instructive. In his victory speech, incoming Liberal Prime Minister Justin Trudeau spoke about immigration and citizen diversity as a key part of Canada's history and strength imploring:

> We know in our bones that Canada was built by people from all corners of the world who worship every faith, who belong to every culture, who speak every language.
>
> We believe in our hearts that this country's unique diversity is a blessing bestowed upon us by previous generations of Canadians, Canadians who stared down prejudice and fought discrimination in all its forms. (*Maclean's* 2015a)

In contrast, outgoing Conservative Prime Minister Stephen Harper in his concession speech remarked on the importance of jobs, trade, and the unique role of the military in supporting other Canadian citizens:

> Our country stands tall today. We have built a Canada that is stronger than ever. Our economy is growing and new jobs are being created. The budget is balanced and federal taxes are at their lowest in 50 years. We – we are poised to seize the opportunities that come with free trade access to Europe, to the Americas, and now to the Asia Pacific. Our men and women in uniform have the tools to do the jobs and the steadfast support of their fellow citizens. (*Maclean's* 2015b)

As the different themes expressed by Trudeau and Harper in their short speeches might suggest, there was a lot going on during the lead-up to the 2015 election. Canadians were moved by the plight of Syrian refugees and many were critical of Harper's apparent lack of response to the refugee crisis. Throughout the country the Harper administration's attempt to block Muslim women wearing the *niqab* (a head and face cover) as they took the oath of citizenship, and its proposal to introduce a RCMP tip line to allow Canadians to report on the "barbaric cultural practices" of their co-citizens and neighbours proved divisive. There were ongoing challenges to legislation that introduced citizenship revocation. Broadly, then, the 2015 election was one in which issues of immigration, multiculturalism, and citizenship raised questions about what kind of national community Canadians wished to embrace and the extent to which it would be open or closed to diverse others (Abu-Laban 2020).

We consider how these issues and questions were taken up in the period 2001–21. This time period is flanked by two key events with global repercussions: 9/11 and COVID-19. Indeed, long before the pandemic of 2020, the September 11, 2001, attacks on Washington, DC and New York as well as US President George W. Bush's "global war on terror" ushered in another form of identifying danger buoyed by specific policies as well as popular expressions of a particular form of racism. The post-9/11 emphasis on the potential terrorist threats posed by Muslims (or those who were perceived to be Muslims) in turn gave way to new forms of surveillance, popular, and partisan expressions of anti-Muslim racism and more generalized policy debates about values, immigration, and citizenship (Abu-Laban 2002). We argue that changes to citizenship and immigration are shifting the ideal from that of a multicultural community built on immigration and diversity towards a gated community insulated from "risk" and "threat" purportedly posed by "others," be they citizens or non-citizens.

We make this argument as three immigration scholars whose engagement with migration and citizenship is marked by a number of intellectual referents. Central to our approach to understanding the dynamics associated with *containing diversity* is the concept of intersectionality. Initially developed by Kimberlé Crenshaw (1989), this approach forces us to think about the way in which social relations, including gender, race, ability, and class, intersect to produce complex and shifting patterns of inequality (see also Dhamoon, 2011; Irvine, Lang, and Montoya 2019). We also build on the insights of critical political economy, most notably its attention to issues examining how political and economic forces structure our lives. As Wally Clement puts it, "to know how societies are, and can be, transformed is the primary goal of political economy" (1997, 6). Additionally, feminist political economists have focused on the critical importance of social reproduction, its intersection with production, and the gendered and racialized assumptions which underpin it (Luxton 2018). Lastly, and relatedly, our engagement draws on the insights of feminist scholarship on care. In relation to this volume, our interest in care is twofold. First, we highlight the relevance of care work undertaken by migrants, often racialized women from developing countries, as well as the salience of unpaid care work undertaken within families (see R.H. Brown 2016; Francisco-Menchavez 2018). Second, the insights of care ethics have prompted us to reflect on the need to treat phenomena like immigration not merely as an empirical issue (facts) but also in relation to ethical concerns about values (Gilligan 1982, Tronto 2013). Our approach to immigration as a matter of ethics allows us to consider not only existing trends but what ought to be.

OUTLINE OF THE BOOK

In *Containing Diversity*, we focus on the main dimensions of Canadian immigration policy and its relationship to citizenship within a comparative frame of reference. While our discussion focuses on the period 2001–21, as noted, we also consider relevant historical practices and touch on some more recent developments, like the 2022 Russia–Ukraine war and its significance for producing refugees.

In chapter one, "Mapping Containing Diversity," we outline the framework that structures our analysis. We first identify some key international trends that characterize international migration most notably: the growing number of refugees worldwide, the valorization of high-skilled migration, the growth of temporary migration, and efforts to reduce family migration. Second, we highlight two distinct and contradictory processes – neoliberalism and criminalization. Both of these dynamics are found within contemporary immigration processes and are implicated in discursive understanding of "desired" and "undesired" immigrants.

In chapter two, "Contextualizing Containing Diversity: Historic and Contemporary Policies," we emphasize that the dynamics and tendencies associated with *containing diversity* are not restricted to the current conjuncture but in fact have a long history in Canada. However, their expression varies in different historical moments reflecting changing politics, configurations of power, and struggles for recognition. Thus we map some key periods in immigration history to demonstrate how these dynamics and tendencies have manifested and their associated inclusions and exclusions. This examination allows us to position Canada's trajectory within a comparative and global frame of reference.

In chapter three, "Controlling 'Global Citizens': Refugees, International Obligations and Security," we consider how wealthy countries like Canada should respond to growing numbers of refugees. Analysing responses over two decades, our findings suggest that Canada's policy has re-emerged under the period of the Trudeau Liberals to place more emphasis on humanitarian considerations than that of the previous Harper Conservative government. Nonetheless, there are several indications that the government remains locked into controlling refugees through criminalization and threat discourses, particularly as concerns unofficial entry points on the border between Canada and the United States. This dimension was especially acute in relation to bilateral Canadian and US responses to the COVID-19 pandemic and management of the US–Canada border.

In chapter four, "Seeking Citizens: 'Skilled' Immigrants as Ideal Neoliberal Citizens," we turn to the heart of the preferred category of immigrants with needed skills. As we show in our examination of skilled labour migration, this is an area of interest for employers as well as provincial governments. However, as we also show, the "provincial nominee system" has been beset with controversy and overall has fostered the entrenchment of a market model that ties Canadian immigrant selection to economic rationales and ideas associated with neoliberalism.

Chapter five, "Making Non-citizens: Temporary Workers and the Production of Precarity," analyses the trend towards temporary migration and related problems besetting Canada's Temporary Foreign Worker Program (TFWP). Our analysis illustrates how, despite differences in discourse, the Trudeau Liberals have employed very similar approaches as the previous Harper Conservatives. The continued embrace of temporary migration serves to render Temporary Foreign Workers with limited voice and increase their vulnerability to exploitation by employers. We also examine the important role played by Temporary Foreign Workers in the context of COVID-19, with reference to special procedures the Canadian government put in place to maintain Canada's food production while simultaneously legislating travel bans and border closures.

In chapter six, "Family Migrants as 'Undesirable'? Sponsoring New Citizens amid New Restrictions on Family Immigration Policies," we analyse the shifting restrictions pertaining to family migration in Canada. We illustrate how Canada has followed trends in other countries with respect to family migration. These trends include problematic discourses that prioritize neoliberal economic rationales undervaluing care work and reinforce criminalizing concerns over "fraudulent" migration.

Chapter seven, "Redefining Membership and Belonging: Contestations over Citizenship and Multiculturalism," addresses trends in naturalization (the process of extending citizenship to immigrants) and multiculturalism (a policy tied to recognizing and valuing diversity in Canada's ongoing evolution as a settler colony). This chapter shows that both naturalization and multiculturalism have been subject to considerable debate, as well as symbolic and substantive policy tweaking over the period of examination from 2001 to 2021. As such, naturalization and multiculturalism have also been implicated in xenophobic populist discourses which cast immigrants, especially Muslim immigrants, as outsiders. In this way, the case of Canada reflects some striking similarities to themes evident in the backlash directed at immigrants and multiculturalism also evident in other Western locales.

In chapter eight, "Towards a Politics of Social and Global Justice," the focus turns to summarizing themes in the book as well as engaging consideration of ethical issues through a review of some of the key debates and approaches. By making use of feminist care ethics, we aim to draw attention both to the value of paid and unpaid labour and relations of care in and outside of families, as well as outline the questions and conditions wherein a more just approach to immigration may emerge. Part of this reflection involves more conscious awareness of ethical debates on the legitimacy borders, and the kind of world we want, as well as Indigenous rights in the context of Canada's colonial past and colonial present.

The substantive chapters of this book highlight how racialized and exclusionary trends – the hallmarks of containing diversity – find expression in immigration, multicultural practice, and the politics of citizenship in the period 2001–21. We emphasize the importance of thinking and confronting these trends through an ethical frame. Our concluding chapter sums up our major findings in these areas and looks to the future by flagging a number of challenges that scholars, officials, and concerned publics will have to address in the near future.

BIBLIOGRAPHY

Abu-Laban, Yasmeen. "Liberalism, Multiculturalism and the Problem of Essentialism." *Citizenship Studies* 6, no. 4 (2002): 459–82.
– "The Two Canadas as a Story without an End: Institutional Choices and the State of the Federation." In *Canadian Federalism and its Future*, edited by Alain G. Gagnon and Johanne Poirier. Montreal: McGill-Queen's University Press (forthcoming).
Abu-Laban, Yasmeen, and Christina Gabriel. *Selling Diversity: Immigration, Multiculturalism, Employment Equity, and Globalization*. Peterborough, ON: Broadview Press, 2002.

Banulescu-Bogdan, Natalia, Meghan Benton, and Susan Fratzke. "Coronavirus Is Spreading across Borders, but It Is Not a Migration Problem." Migration Policy Institute, *Commentaries*. www.migrationpolicy.org/news/coronavirus-not-a-migration-problem.

Brown, Rachel H. "Re-examining the Transnational Nanny: Migrant Carework beyond the Chain." *International Feminist Journal of Politics* 18, no. 2 (2016): 210–29.

Clement, Wallace. "Introduction: Whither the New Canadian Political Economy?" In *Understanding Canada: Building on the New Canadian Political Economy*, edited by Wallace Clement, 4–18. Montreal and Kingston: McGill-Queen's University Press, 1997.

Crenshaw, Kimberlé Williams. "Demarginalizing the Intersection of Race and Sex: A Black Feminist Critique of Antidiscrimination Doctrine, Feminist Theory and Antiracist Politics." *University of Chicago Legal Forum* 1, no. 8 (1989): 139–67.

Dhamoon, Rita. "Considerations on Mainstreaming Intersectionality." *Political Research Quarterly* 64, no. 1 (2011): 230–43.

Francisco-Menchavez, Valerie. 2018. *The Labor of Care: Filipina Migrants and Transnational Families in the Digital Age*. Chicago: University of Illinois Press.

Gilligan, Carol. *In a Different Voice: Psychological Theory and Women's Development*. Cambridge, MA: Harvard University Press, 1982.

Irvine, Jill, Sabine Lang, and Celeste Montoya, eds. *Gendered Mobilizations and Intersectional Challenges*. Colchester, UK: Rowman & Littlefield, 2019.

Kymlicka, Will. "Immigration, Citizenship, Multiculturalism: Exploring the Links." *The Political Quarterly* 74, no. s1 (2003): 195–208.

Luxton, Meg. "The Production of Life Itself: Gender, Social Reproduction and IPE." In *Handbook of the International Political Economy of Gender*, edited by Juanita Elias and Adrienne Roberts, 37–49. London: Edward Elgar Press.

Maclean's. "Justin Trudeau, for the Record: We Beat Fear with Hope." *Maclean's* (October 20, 2015a), www.macleans.ca/politics/ottawa/justin-trudeau-for-the-record-we-beat-fear-with-hope/.

– "Stephen Harper, for the Record: 'It Has Been an Unbelievable Honour." *Maclean's* (October 20, 2015b), www.macleans.ca/news/canada/stephen-harper-for-the-record-it-has-been-an-unbelievable-honour/.

Malbeuf, Jamie. "'It's a Complicated Situation': Temporary Foreign Workers Allowed into Canada, but There Are Hurdles." CBC News (April 7, 2020), www.cbc.ca/news/canada/edmonton/temporary-foreign-workers-alberta-1.5523916.

Marcos, Christina. "Asian American Lawmaker Warns of Fear of Racism over Coronavirus Stigma." *The Hill* (March 30, 2020), https://thehill.com/homenews/house/490261-asian-american-lawmaker-warns-of-fear-of-racism-over-coronavirus-stigma.

Reidy, Eric. "The COVID-19 Excuse? How Migration Policies Are Hardening Around the Globe." *The New Humanitarian* (April 17, 2020). www.thenewhumanitarian.org/analysis/2020/04/17/coronavirus-global-migration-policies-exploited.

Sewer, Adam. "The Sinister Logic of Trump's Immigration Freeze." *The Atlantic* (April 29, 2020). www.theatlantic.com/ideas/archive/2020/04/trump-order-immigration/610822/.

Tronto, Joan C. *Caring Democracy: Markets, Equality and Justice.* New York and London: New York University Press, 2013.

United Nations, World Health Organization (UN WHO). "WHO Director-General's Opening Remarks at the Media Briefing on COVID-19, 11 March 2020." UN WHO (2020), www.who.int/dg/speeches/detail/who-director-general-s-opening-remarks-at-the-media-briefing-on-covid-19---11-march-2020.

PART I

CHAPTER ONE

Mapping Containing Diversity

The first two decades of the twenty-first century have been marked by numerous shifts and changes in immigration, citizenship, and multiculturalism that have seen a disturbing retreat from the premises that guided these policies between the 1970s and the 1990s. We argue that changes to citizenship and immigration are shifting the ideal from that of a multicultural community built on immigration and diversity towards a gated community insulated from "risk" and "threat" purportedly posed by "others," be they citizens or non-citizens. As noted, we call this process containing diversity because it involves the racialization and control of specific groups based on perceived or actual differences relating to race and ethnicity and their intersection with religion, gender, country of origin, class, and citizenship status in manifold ways in both discourse and individual experiences.

In this chapter we do three things. First, we map the international context and identify the key trends in which we situate Canada and its changing immigration, multiculturalism, and citizenship policies. Second, we address more closely the paradox between Canada's openness to some alongside newer measures aimed at controlling the movement of others across borders and into the political community. Our discussion shows the contradictory interplay between neoliberal-inspired attempts that liberalize migration provisions for the "skilled" and "highly skilled" and, by contrast, policy developments that reflect on national boundary construction. The latter involve efforts to control movement and increasingly criminalize migrants and diasporic communities. Criminalization draws on themes of danger and threat to security and safety. Criminalization also works to associate foreigners and racialized citizens with fraud, law-breaking, and the undermining of community norms and values. The chapter concludes with a review of our theoretical framework.

THE SHIFTING LANDSCAPE OF INTERNATIONAL MIGRATION POLITICS: CURRENT TRENDS

This section briefly considers the global picture and broad trends that characterize international migration. All of these trends, as we demonstrate in this volume, find expression in the Canadian context.

The number of people on the move has seen accelerated growth since 2005. In 2019, international migrants accounted for 272 million people – or 3.5 per cent of the world's population – an increase of 80 million from 2005 and 119 million from 1990 (UN DESA 2019, 3–5). Migration impacts all world regions: both the Global South and the Global North receive migrants (UN DESA 2017, 1). Approximately 57 per cent of the world's migrants are in developed countries and 43 per cent in developing regions (UN DESA 2017, 1). The majority of international migrants live in countries of Europe (82 million) and North America (59 million). Countries in Northern Africa and Western Asia come next, with some 49 million international migrants (UN DESA 2019, 6).

Countries of Europe and North America receive migrants from countries of both the Global North and the Global South. While overall countries of the European Union (EU) receive the most migrants, the United States was the leading destination country for permanent international migrants in 2017, followed by Germany, the United Kingdom, Spain, and Canada (OECD 2019, 21). In 2017, the top five origin countries for new immigrants to OECD countries were China, Romania, India, Poland, and Vietnam (OECD 2019, 41). Likewise, the leading origin countries for refugees to OECD countries in 2017 were Afghanistan and Syria, followed by Iraq and Venezuela (OECD 2019, 19). Women and girls accounted for about 48 per cent of all international migrants worldwide (UN DESA 2019, i). As migration scholars have observed, women are increasingly moving as independent migrants as opposed to trailing spouses (Castles 2014, 194).

Rates of migration are framed by a number of important contemporary trends. First on the list of trends is that there are *growing numbers of refugees worldwide*. Between 2005 and 2019 the number of refugees worldwide doubled (UN DESA 2019, 17). A related feature of this trend, however, has involved *a decline in the numbers of people seeking asylum in more wealthy countries*. Stephen Castles has characterized refugees and asylum seekers as the "most disadvantaged of all in the new global migration hierarchy" because in the past "they were seen as worthy of international protection; now entry rules have been tightened up to the point where it is virtually impossible to enter most northern countries to make a protection claim" (2014, 195). Recent data indicates that refugees are primarily located in countries of the Global South: in fact, among high-income countries, refugees only accounted for 2.7 per cent of migrants, whereas in middle-income countries they accounted for 22.5 per cent of migrants, and in low-income countries they accounted for 44.5 per cent of migrants (UN DESA 2019, 18). Moreover, despite growing numbers of people seeking refuge from conflict, violence, and persecution worldwide, wealthy OECD member countries actually experienced a 34 per cent decline in asylum applications after record highs in 2015 and 2016 (OECD 2019, 13).

Increasingly, then, countries in the Global North have been less open to asylum seekers, even though there have been international efforts to create more equitable responsibility sharing. For example, in December 2018, the majority of member states in the United Nations General Assembly, including Canada, voted in support of two global compacts, one concerning safe and orderly international migration, and the other concerning refugees (UN DESA 2019, v). However, it is unclear what impact the Global Compact on Refugees will have on the distribution of refugees globally, and indeed the United States, important as a global power, voted against both compacts in 2018 when Republican Donald Trump was president. In December 2021, the Democratic administration of President Joseph Biden offered a revised statement on the Global Compact for Migration endorsing its overall vision (US State Department 2021).

A second trend is that *economic considerations are at the fore of many OECD member country immigration policies*. There is a specific focus on skills, with a number of countries adopting measures to attract highly skilled migrants. For example, Germany has adopted measures that give family members of skilled foreign workers unrestricted access to the labour market. In an effort to attract skilled workers, the French government proposed a new "passport of expertise" to replace the existing permit system for skilled workers (OECD 2015, 41). However, while skilled workers are still wanted, the OECD has also observed a shift to more selective targeting (OECD 2015, 11). This is particularly true in the case of Australia, New Zealand, and Canada, where there have been concerns about the labour market outcomes of immigrants as evidenced by declining earnings, unemployment, and underemployment. In an effort to improve outcomes through selective targeting, Australia and New Zealand adopted an Expression of Interest (EOI) system whereby potential migrants must use an online tool to enter their details. Following an initial pre-screening by the state, an individual's profile is made available to prospective employers who then assess for available job vacancies. In 2015, Canada implemented a similar model called "Express Entry," where employers, provinces, and territories were involved in choosing immigrants that corresponded to existing labour market needs (Akbari and MacDonald 2014, 808–9).

Many countries in the Global North are engaged in an effort to attract high-skilled migrants and thereby enhance their competitive advantage in a globalizing world (Abu-Laban and Gabriel 2002; Shachar 2006). This development has been characterized by Ayelet Shachar as a "race for talent" and is often coupled with the extension of citizenship. In this way, citizenship is characterized as a recruitment incentive – "talent-for-citizenship exchange" to attract highly skilled migrants. Shachar suggests that skilled migrants are seeking better economic opportunities in receiving states, but they are also motivated by non-economic factors, such as "the security and prosperity that is attached to membership in a stable, democratic, and affluent polity (the citizenship factor)" (2006, 164).

In contrast to the pathways of the highly skilled, citizenship status is not usually extended to temporary migrants. This is despite the fact that temporary and circular migration remains an important phenomenon in international migration (OECD 2015) and, in fact, witnessed a significant increase between 2016 and 2017 alone (OECD

2019, 13). In Canada, analysts have observed how, in the period we examine in this volume, the number of temporary foreign workers has even sometimes exceeded those individuals admitted as immigrants and refugees. For example, this was the case in both 2010 and 2011 in Canada (Alboim and Cohl 2012, 45). As the Global Commission on International Migration notes, temporary migrants often bring important skills, allow receiving states to respond quickly to short-term labour shortages, and provide an important source of remittances to sending states (GCIM 2005). Additionally, such programs may be preferred by governments, both because there are fewer integration costs and the perception that they may be more attractive to domestic populations (Castles 2014, 193). However, the status of these workers can render them vulnerable to labour market abuse and exploitation. Agricultural workers such as those in Canada's Seasonal Agricultural Worker Program (SAWP), for example, do not have a path to permanent residence, experience limited worker mobility, and often experience poor living and working conditions (Hennebry and Preibisch 2012).

A third major trend is that of *immigration restrictions on family migration*. While rates of skilled and temporary labour migration are increasing and prioritized, an overall trend of restriction characterizes the family class category (OECD 2019, 19). In recent years, efforts to constrain family migration included such policy changes as higher income obligations for sponsors, stronger language requirements, and the introduction of measures designed to address so called marriages of convenience. Such restrictions were introduced in Norway, Canada, Korea, the Netherlands, and Ireland (OECD 2015, 48), although with the Trudeau government in Canada, there have been efforts to facilitate family migration, such as increasing the age limit of dependents from nineteen to twenty-two and implementing new processes to facilitate the arrival of grandparents that were introduced in 2019 (OECD 2019, 62). However, while there is some variability in responses to family class migration, the continued emphasis on economic (skilled) migration in the face of broader immigration controls remains an issue in Canada and elsewhere.

Speaking to the case of Canada, the privileging of the economic class has led scholars to note that "Canada's immigration policies and programmes give little recognition of how families contribute to integration and, indeed, tend to portray families as 'burdens' on the state and unworthy of support ... immigrant families are frequently constructed as 'problems' to be effectively managed" (Creese, Dyck, and McLaren 2011, 141–2). Although there are few large-scale comparative studies on the impact of family reunification on the integration of immigrants, preliminary data from several OECD countries suggests family reunification plays an important role in the integration of immigrant children (OECD 2019, 201). It should also be noted that states play a key role in family migration by institutionalizing particular family forms through their policies, practices, and legislation. Indeed, "a certain concept of family and family life has been an essential part of the conception of what constitutes a good citizen" (Kofman et al. 2011, 13).

THE PARADOXICAL IMPACT OF NEOLIBERALISM AND CRIMINALIZATION

Building from the three trends we highlighted around growing numbers of refugees, the primacy of economic considerations, and family restrictions, we turn in this section to consider broad tendencies, specifically neoliberalism and criminalization.

On neoliberalism, it can be noted that Canadian immigration policymaking in the post-war period has always been informed by human capital considerations. However, this emphasis has become much more marked with the ascendency of neoliberal policy frameworks from the 1980s onward. Neoliberalism has been problematized in various ways, but many scholars have reflected on its different configurations (Brodie and DeGagne 2014; Dobrowolsky 2009; Larner 2000). For instance, Tejaswini Ganti (2014) draws attention to four main referents associated with neoliberalism:

- a set of economic policies ... which are concerned with the deregulation of the economy, the liberalization of trade and industry and the privatization of state-owned enterprises;
- a prescriptive development model that defines very different political roles for labor, capital and the state compared with prior models;

- an ideology that values market exchange as "an ethic in itself, capable of acting as a guide to all human actions and substituting for all previously ethical beliefs" (Treanor 2005); and
- a mode of governance that embraces the idea of the self-regulating free market, with its associated values of competition and self interest (91).

Policy responses to criminalization are in evidence in relation to the treatment of undocumented or unauthorized migrants and asylum seekers. These take the form of increased practices evident across countries of the West of border control, detention, and deportation (Kretsedemas and Brotherton 2017). Indeed, immigration and border control policies have been coupled with security and surveillance measures in relation to undocumented people (Abu-Laban 2019, 5). Such policies also both fan and feed anti-immigrant attitudes, a phenomenon in evidence when American President Donald Trump kicked off his 2015 bid for the presidency in front of a "Make America Great Again" sign. His speech negatively stereotyped Mexicans and other immigrants and drove a wedge between them and "Americans" of non-Mexican or non-immigrant origins. In Trump's words:

> When Mexico sends its people, they're not sending their best. They're not sending you. They're not sending you. They're sending people that have lots of problems, and they're bringing those problems with us. They're bringing drugs. They're bringing crime. They're rapists. And some, I assume, are good people.
>
> But I speak to border guards and they tell us what we're getting. And it only makes common sense. It only makes common sense. They're sending us not the right people.
>
> It's coming from more than Mexico. It's coming from all over South and Latin America, and it's coming probably – probably – from the Middle East. But we don't know. Because we have no protection and we have no competence, we don't know what's happening. And it's got to stop, and it's got to stop fast. (annotated by Philips 2017)

Donald Trump's words conflate immigrants with criminals and threats; his rhetoric went hand in hand with his call to build a wall along the US southern border with Mexico. Trump's electoral win in 2016 underscores as well the power of xenophobic populism in electoral and party politics (Inglehart and Norris 2016).

Neoliberalism and criminalization may be understood as two clashing tendencies. These tendencies clash because neoliberalism, in valorizing the market, rests on a logic of openness to global markets. In contrast, criminalization rests on casting immigrants as dangerous criminals and threats, and therefore embraces border closure. The tension between these tendencies has been observed by a number of scholars in relation to security and border control in North America (see Cote-Boucher 2014; Gilbert 2012; Sparke 2006), but Katja Franko Aas captures it well when she writes:

> An essential part of the globalizing condition is precisely the creation of mechanism [sic] for distinguishing between "good" and "bad" mobilities ... Contemporary governments seem to be caught between two contradicting impulses: on the one hand, the urge toward increasing securitization of borders, and on the other hand, the awareness of the importance of global flows for sustaining the present world economic order. (2007, 292)

We argue that developments within the fields of citizenship and immigration can be broadly understood through the paradoxical clashing dynamics of neoliberalism and criminalization.

In illuminating dynamics of criminalization, we join scholars concerned with how migrants and refugees are increasingly associated with crime as well as threat and danger (Chan and Chunn 2014). This criminalization often feeds into xenophobic populist movements and their electoral success, albeit in different ways in different countries (Fukuyama and Gocek 2019). We focus on the association of migrants and refugees with crime, threat, and danger in Canada and how this intersects with neoliberal rationales to produce different forms of inclusion and exclusion in the main period under examination from 2001 to 2021. Neoliberalism, as Mathew Sparke puts it, "represents an extraordinarily messy mix of ideas and practices that have been developed and deployed in different ways with different names in different places" (2006, 154). Our concern is how certain rationales find expression in immigration, citizenship, and multiculturalism in the twenty-first century.

As Abu-Laban and Gabriel (2002) analysed in *Selling Diversity*, neoliberal assumptions framed many changes that came with the 2002 Immigration and Refugee Reform Protection Act (IRPA) and related changes in the areas of multiculturalism and citizenship. Highly skilled immigrants, for example, were constructed as sources of comparative advantage within a global context (2002, 79). Now, as then, harnessing the economic benefits from immigration remains a priority in Canadian policy. However, there has been a shift from a broadly conceived notion of human capital to more targeted selection (Akbari and Macdonald 2014). Equally important are policy debates where the values associated with neoliberalism – entrepreneurship, self-sufficiency, individual responsibility, choice, voluntarism – are implicated. While Abu-Laban and Gabriel (2002) noted the use of temporary workers, this development has become more prominent in recent decades. Other matters have also come to the fore, including the decentralization of immigration policymaking, where neoliberal premises inform the workings of various Provincial Nominee Programs (PNPs) at the subnational level (Dobrowolsky 2013), and more recently in 2018 a pilot program known as the Economic Mobility Pathway Project designed to facilitate the entrance of high-skilled refugees to meet labour market needs.

While our examination of new policy directions focuses on neoliberal referents, we recognize that this is by no means a straightforward and inexorable process. As many have noted, neoliberal projects are not necessarily coherent and are often beset by a host of contradictions (Brodie 2008; Dobrowolsky 2009; McBride and Whiteside 2011). To see contradictions, we have only to recognize the rapidity with which governments, including Canada's, developed new programs of public spending to support citizens in the wake of social distancing and isolation measures enacted in response to stemming COVID-19. Moreover, we suggest that recent developments cannot only be understood through neoliberal ideas and imperatives alone.

Over the period we are examining, between 2001 and 2021, policy developments in the field of immigration and citizenship have also been coupled with an increasing concern with crime and security that is enacted in a twofold manner through law and criminalization.

This development is not necessarily new. Dhamoon and Abu-Laban (2009) remind us that Canadian history is replete with instances where the national state has targeted and constructed citizens who are members of racialized and minority groups as "dangerous internal foreigners." Here, attention has been focused on the internment of the Japanese Canadians in the Second World War; the use of the War Measures Act against Quebec nationalists and separatists; and police actions against Mohawks at Oka in 1990. In the post-9/11 period, the figure of the "dangerous foreigner" is intimately linked to national security with particular racialized groups, such as Muslim Canadians and Arab Canadians, constructed as threats (Abu-Laban 2014; Chan and Chunn 2014; Cote-Boucher 2014). And while refugees have long been associated, in varying degrees, with security concerns, the Harper administration (2006–15) especially relied on a set of crime and security tropes to justify its policy reforms within many areas of immigration and citizenship, as we discuss in more detail in this volume.

The prominence of crime and security discourses within immigration policy formulations is not unique to Canada. Juliet Stumpf's term "crimmigration," for instance, draws attention to how criminal law and immigration law in the United States are increasingly connected: "Immigration law today is clothed with so many attributes of criminal law that the line between them has grown indistinct. Scholars have labeled this the 'criminalization of immigration law'. The merger of the two areas in both substance and procedure has created parallel systems in which immigration law and the criminal justice system are merely nominally separate" (2006, 376). Stumpf (2014) identifies three salient aspects of crimmigration in the United States. First, she notes that there are immigration consequences in situations where non-citizens are involved in the commission of a traditional crime referring to the possibility of deportation because of a criminal conviction. Second, criminal law is increasingly implicated in migration regulation and control. She asserts, "The main feature of this aspect of crimmigration law is the legislative construction of migration related acts [such as illegal entry, working without authorization,] as criminal rather than administrative violations" (241). The third aspect she flags is the use of police powers to control unlawful immigration. Here she highlights the use of networks of surveillance and technology databases that track data on travellers and migrants. She notes: "the entry of information into these databases is contingent not on a criminal conviction or immigration proceeding, but merely on whether the individual has contact with the government agency that administers the database" (242).

In Canada, scholars have drawn attention to crimmigration at play in the areas of deportation and detention: "In Canada, just under 150,000 people were deported between January 2004 and the end of June 2014, more than 70% were failed asylum seekers. Last year [in 2013] the Canada Border Services Agency detained almost 10,000 people – including refugee claimants, permanent residents and other non-citizens ... non-citizens designated as 'security threats' face the prospect of indefinite detention on the basis of secret evidence and limited rights of appeal or due process" (Aiken et al. 2014, i). Others have also noted the increasing securitization of citizenship policy through the introduction of measures like Bill C-24, the *Strengthening Canadian Citizenship Act*. The Bill went into effect in June 2015 and included provisions for citizenship revocation (Macklin 2014). While elements of this controversial measure were repealed by the Trudeau Liberals in October 2017, it is now clear that citizenship may be defined differently depending on the government of the day.

The connection between migration and security is also in evidence in the framing of immigration through the lens of criminality. People with irregular status, for example, are often constructed as "illegal migrants" and by extension a threat to national security. Chan and Chunn (2014) explain how "racialized groups of immigrants and refugees have been increasingly constructed as unworthy and criminal, and as illegitimate border crossers" (134). They and others have noted how former Minister of Immigration (subsequently Alberta's premier) Jason Kenney, linked terms such as "bogus," "queue jumpers," and "fraudsters" to Canada's refugee claimants (see also Côté-Boucher 2014, 79). In other instances, the Harper Conservative government engaged in a concerted campaign against "fraudulent" citizenship applications. Such portrayals are not limited to state officials but also find expression in media representations of immigrants and racialized Canadians (Roberts and Mahtani 2010, 252).

We focus on neoliberalism and criminalization as two distinct processes that are nevertheless intertwined in the contemporary context of immigration in Canada. While both have different logics and operate in distinct ways, examining their interplay can help us to understand how categories of "desired" and "undesired" immigrants are being produced in public discourse. Likewise, to understand how meanings of citizenship are shifting – including what it means to be a "good" or "bad" citizen – requires that we understand both the neoliberal and criminalizing discourses of immigration that permeates policy and public debates in Canada.

While neoliberalism tends to champion the disembodied individual who is not connected to any particular identity, addressing the interplay of neoliberalism with criminalization forces a consideration of the ways in which social relations of power, including those of gender, race, class, and citizenship status, constitute individuals as members of groups.

Additionally, we are interested in considering the ethical debates that have played out over borders and their functions over the past twenty years. Migration scholars and citizens in the Global South have long recognized that state borders and boundaries mitigate against the movement of people. In the context of the COVID-19 pandemic this reality was also felt around the world. Given this heightened sensitivity to the role borders play in limiting human movement, we find the returning to the border debate significant.

BIBLIOGRAPHY

Aas, Katja Franko. "Analysing a World in Motion." *Theoretical Criminology* 11, no. 2 (2007): 283–303.
Abu-Laban, Yasmeen. "Liberalism, Multiculturalism and the Problem of Essentialism." *Citizenship Studies* 6, no. 4 (2002): 459–82.
– "Citizenship and Foreignness in Canada." In *Routledge Handbook of Global Citizenship Studies*, 274–83. London and New York: Routledge, 2014.
– "Immigration and Settler-Colonies Post-UNDRIP: Research and Policy Implications." *International Migration* (International Organization for Migration) (December 30, 2019): 1–17.
– "The Two Canadas as a Story without an End: Institutional Choices and the State of the Federation." In *Canadian Federalism and its Future*, edited by Alain G. Gagnon and Johanne Poirier. Montreal: McGill-Queen's University Press.

Abu-Laban, Yasmeen, and Christina Gabriel. *Selling Diversity: Immigration, Multiculturalism, Employment Equity, and Globalization*. Peterborough, ON: Broadview Press, 2002.

Aiken, Sharryn, David Lyon, and Malcolm Thorburn. "Introduction." *Queens Law Journal* 40, no. 1 (2014): 1–12.

Akbari, Ather H., and Martha MacDonald. "Immigration Policy in Australia, Canada, New Zealand and the United States: An Overview of Recent Trends." *International Migration Review* 48, no. 3 (2014): 801–22.

Alboim, Naomi, and Karen Cohl. *Shaping the Future: Canada Rapidly Changing Immigration Policies*. Toronto: Maytree Foundation, 2012. https://maytree.com/wp-content/uploads/shaping-the-future.pdf.

Boyd, Monica. "Recruiting High Skill Labour in North America: Policies, Outcomes and Futures." *International Migration* 52, no. 3 (2014): 40–54.

Brodie, Janine. "We Are All Equal Now: Contemporary Gender Politics in Canada." *Feminist Theory* 9, no. 2 (2008): 145–64.

Brodie, Janine, and Alexa DeGagne. "Neo-Liberalism." In *Critical Concepts: An Introduction to Politics*. Fifth Edition, edited by Janine Brodie, Sandra Rein, and Malinda Smith, 60–76. Toronto: Pearson Canada, 2014.

Castles, Stephen. "International Migration at a Crossroads." *Citizenship Studies* 18, no. 2 (2014): 190–207.

Chan, Wendy, and Dorothy Chunn. *Racialization, Crime and Criminal Justice in Canada*. Toronto: University of Toronto Press, 2014.

Côté-Boucher, Karine. "Bordering Citizenship in 'an Open and Generous Society' the Criminalization of Migration in Canada." In *The Routledge Handbook on Crime and International Migration*, edited by Sharon Pickering and Julie Ham, 75–90. London and New York: Routledge, 2014.

Creese, Gillian, Isabel Dyck, and Arelene Tiger McLaren. "The Problem of Human Capital: Gender, Place and Immigrant Household Strategies of Reskilling in Vancouver." In *Gender, Generations and the Family in International Migration*, edited by Albert Kraler, Eleanore Kofman, Martin Kohli, and Camille Schmoll, 141–62. Amsterdam: Amsterdam University Press, 2011.

Dhamoon, Rita, and Yasmeen Abu-Laban. "Dangerous (Internal) Foreigners and Nation-Building: The Case of Canada." *International Political Science Review* 30, no. 2 (2009): 163–83.

Dobrowolsky, Alexandra. "Introduction." In *Women and Public Policy in Canada. Neo-liberalism and After?*, edited by Alexandra Dobrowolsky, 1–24 Toronto: Oxford University Press, 2009.

– "Nuancing Neoliberalism: Lessons Learned from a Failed Immigration Experiment." *Journal of International Migration and Integration* 14, no. 2 (2013): 197–218.

Fukuyama, Francis, and Naz Gocek. "Immigration and Populism in Canada, Australia, and the United States." Working Paper. Stanford

University: Center on Democracy, Development and the Rule of Law (July 2019). https://cddrl.fsi.stanford.edu/publication/immigration-and-populism-canada-australia-and-united-states.

Ganti, Tejaswini. "Neoliberalism." *Annual Review of Anthropology* 43 (2014): 89–104.

Gilbert, Emily. "Borders and Security in North America." In *North America in Question*, edited by Jeffrey Ayres and Laura Macdonald, 196–217. Toronto: University of Toronto, 2012.

Global Commission on International Migration (GCIM). *Migration in an Interconnected World: New Directions for Action*. Geneva: Global Commission on International Migration, 2005. www.iom.int/jahia/webdav/site/myjahiasite/shared/shared/mainsite/policy_and_research/gcim/GCIM_Report_Complete.pdf.

Hennebry, Jenna, and Kerry Preibisch. "A Model for Managed Migration? Re-examining Best Practices in Canada's Seasonal Agricultural Worker Program." *International Migration* 50, no. s1 (2012): 1–33.

Inglehart, Ronald, and Pippa Norris. "Trump, Brexit and the Rise of Populism: Economic Have-Nots and Cultural Backlash." *Harvard Kennedy School Faculty Research Working Paper Series* 16–026 (August 2016).

Kofman, Eleonore, Albert Kraler, Martin Kohli, and Camille Schmoll. "Introduction – Issues and Debates on Family-Related Migration and the Migrant Family: A European Perspective." In *Gender, Generations and the Family in International Migration*, edited by Albert Kraler, Eleonore Kofman, Martin Kohli, and Camille Schmoll, 13–54. Amsterdam: Amsterdam University Press, 2011.

Kretsedemas, Philip, and David C. Brotherton, eds. *Immigration Policy in the Age of Punishment: Detention, Deportation and Border Control*. New York: Columbia University Press, 2017.

Larner, Wendy. "Neo-liberalism: Policy, Ideology, Governmentality." *Studies in Political Economy* 63, no. 1 (2000): 5

Macklin, Audrey. "Citizenship Revocation, the Privilege to Have Rights and the Production of the Alien." *Queens Law Journal* 40, no. 1 (2014): 1–55.

McBride, Stephen, and Heather Whiteside. *Private Affluence. Public Austerity.* Halifax: Fernwood, 2011.

OECD. *International Migration Outlook 2015*. Paris: OECD Publishing, 2015. www.oecd-ilibrary.org/social-issues-migration-health/international-migration-outlook-2015_migr_outlook-2015-en.

– *International Migration Outlook 2019*. Paris: OECD Publishing, 2019. www.oecd-ilibrary.org/social-issues-migration-health/international-migration-outlook-2019_c3e35eec-en.

Phillips, Amber. "'They're Rapists': President Trump's Campaign Speech Two Years Later, Annotated." *The Washington Post* (June 16, 2017). www.washingtonpost.com/news/the-fix/wp/2017/06/16/theyre-rapists-presidents-trump-campaign-launch-speech-two-years-later-annotated/.

Pickering, Sharon, and Julie Ham, eds. *The Routledge Handbook on Crime and International Migration*. London and New York: Routledge, 2014.

Roberts, David J., and Minelle Mahtani. "Neoliberalizing Race, Racing Neoliberalism: Placing 'Race' in Neoliberal Discourses." *Antipode* 42, no. 2 (2010): 248–57.

Sewer, Adam. "The Sinister Logic of Trump's Immigration Freeze." *The Atlantic* (April 29, 2020). www.theatlantic.com/ideas/archive/2020/04/trump-order-immigration/610822/.

Shachar, Ayelet. "The Race for Talent: Highly Skilled Migrants and Competitive Immigration Regimes." *New York University Law Review* 81, no. 1 (2006): 148–206.

Spade, Dean. "Intersectional Resistance and Law Reform." *Signs* 38, no. 4 (2013): 1031–55.

Sparke, Matthew B. "A Neoliberal Nexus: Economy, Security and the Biopolitics of Citizenship on the Border." *Political Geography* 25 (2006): 151–80.

Stumpf, Juliet. "The Crimmigration Crisis: Immigrants, Crime, and Sovereign Power." *American University Law Review* 56, no. 2 (2006): 367–419.

— "Crimmigration: Encountering the Leviathan." In *The Routledge Handbook on Crime and International Migration*, edited by Sharon Pickering and Julie Ham. London and New York: Routledge, 2014: 237–50.

Townsend-Bell, Erica. "What Is Relevance? Defining Intersectional Praxis in Uruguay." *Political Research Quarterly* 64, no. 1 (2011): 187–99.

United Nations, Department of Economics and Social Affairs (UN DESA), Population Division. *International Migration 2017: Report*. Ref: ST/ESA/SER.A/404. New York: United Nations, 2017. www.un.org/en/development/desa/population/migration/publications/migrationreport/docs/MigrationReport2017_Highlights.pdf.

— *International Migration 2019: Report*. Ref: ST/ESA/SER.A/438. New York: United Nations, 2019. www.un.org/en/development/desa/population/migration/publications/migrationreport/docs/InternationalMigration2019_Report.pdf.

United Nations, World Health Organization (UN WHO). "WHO Director-General's Opening Remarks at the Media Briefing on COVID-19, 11 March 2020." UN WHO, 2020. www.who.int/dg/speeches/detail/who-director-general-s-opening-remarks-at-the-media-briefing-on-covid-19---11-march-2020.

United States State Department. "Revised National Statement of the United States of America on the Adoption of the Global Compact for Safe, Orderly, and Regular Migration." (17 December 2021), https://www.state.gov/wp-content/uploads/2021/12/GCM.pdf.

CHAPTER TWO

Contextualizing Containing Diversity: Historic and Contemporary Policies

The history of Canadian immigration is marked by varied practices of inclusion and exclusion of potential newcomers that are historically specific and socially constructed. These practices shed light on what we dub "containing diversity," which involves the racialization and control of specific groups and contradictory impulses of closure to outsiders deemed threatening, and openness to workers and citizens that are deemed valuable. Our conception of diversity moves beyond enumerating points of difference per se to a consideration of how difference is implicated in the way power and resources are allocated at any given moment (Abu-Laban and Gabriel 2002, 13). A resource we are especially concerned with in this chapter is membership – both access to membership in the polity and the ability to determine membership in the polity.

This chapter maps key policies shaping Canadian immigration over time, as well as current trends and issues that will be taken up in more extensive detail in the chapters ahead. As we show, the contradictory dynamics that constitute containing diversity involve discrimination on the basis of social locations of race, gender, and class (among others) and are also deployed by reference to health and security. As such, the racialization and control of specific groups have been animated through different policies and discourses; however, exclusion and inclusion in access to membership (along with differential forms of inclusion) have been an enduring aspect of historic and contemporary immigration practices.

In this chapter we argue that the process of containing diversity is not just a feature of the current moment but in fact has a long history within Canada's foundation and trajectory as a white settler colony. In illuminating this argument, we take a threefold approach. First, we cover historical trends from before Confederation in 1867 to 1967. Second, we address the modern immigration policy, which was formalized in 1967, and its emphasis on skills. Last, we discuss current dynamics and highlight the continued relevance of containing diversity, as well as the sovereignty of the Canadian state when it comes to membership.

PART ONE: HISTORICAL LEGACIES – PRE-CONFEDERATION TO 1967

Canada marked 150 years of Confederation in 2017, and in this national narrative marking the foundation of the Canadian state, immigration plays a central role. Indeed, "Canada is often referred to as a *land of immigrants* because, over the past 200 years, millions of newcomers have helped to build and defend our way of life" (CIC 2012, 12). But Canada's history as a white settler colony is a complicated narrative that defies the easy characterization of a "nation of immigrants." The white settler construct, as Daiva Stasiulis and Radha Jhappan observe, draws our attention to the particularities of Canada's development. They point out that Canada and other white settler colonies, such as Australia and New Zealand, were given liberal democratic government and a measure of political autonomy unlike other colonies in Africa, Asia, and the Caribbean. Thus in white settler colonies "the dominant culture, values and institutions of the society mimic those of the 'mother' country" (1995, 97). However, they also note the construct's explanatory limitations: it overlooks the role and struggles of Indigenous peoples in the face of settlement; immigration and settlement were much more diverse than the construct implies; and many of its assumptions "are not only racist but also androcentric" insofar as it emphasizes the activities of men in the public realm of work and politics and associates women with their reproductive roles, whereas "in reality, however, women played multiple, complex roles, depending on their own racial/ethnic, class and marital statuses" (1995, 99).

These insights are the starting point for our reading of history. The trajectory of nation building in Canada is marked by many and varied processes of membership inclusion and exclusion that are historically specific and socially constructed and as such resonate with our concept of containing diversity. We can roughly situate historic immigration practices in relation to pre-Confederation, Confederation, and the early decades following the Second World War.

Pre-Confederation

Patterns of settler colonization and early immigration to Canada set the stage for subsequent policy developments and practices. At this time, the territories that would become Canada were already populated by distinct Indigenous nations engaged in various livelihoods: "This way of life, based on regulated patterns that had evolved over thousands of years, grew out of an intimate knowledge of resources and the best way of exploiting them" (Dickason 2008, 17). In the early period of European colonization Indigenous peoples were recognized as nations through treaties such as the Royal Proclamation of 1763 (Ladner 2003, 46). The Proclamation outlined that Indigenous lands could only be turned over to the Crown and not individuals and this had to be secured with the consent of the relevant Indigenous nation affected (Jhappan 2008, 31). Despite this, land dispossession became the hallmark of European and Indigenous interactions. It has been observed by historians that "the encounters need not all have been violent and warlike to have contributed to land dispossession, because the gradual settlement and the establishment of British North America in the 18th century altered Indigenous ways of life in some areas to near extinction" (Pellerin 2019, 6). And it is against this context that Canadian immigration history and current practices must be considered.

Following John Cabot's landing in Newfoundland in 1497, the two imperial powers, France and England, initially paid little attention to establishing settlements, preferring to maintain small trading posts (Kelley and Trebilcock 2000, 57). Nevertheless, this period has been characterized as an early wave of immigration insofar as it sees the arrival of merchants, skilled workmen, soldiers, and members of religious orders. In fact, 1663–73 is recognized as "the one period in history of pre-1760 Canada when immigration figured prominently in its development" as some 2,000 settlers were sent from France. They were almost all single men. Subsequently, unmarried women were recruited from France, *filles du roi*, and sent to the colony at the king's expense (Knowles 1997, 10–11).

The situation changed in 1760 with the Conquest of New France. Almost instantly French immigration came to an end. The British also moved to expel the Acadians, French-speaking settlers, on the basis that they were a security risk, from New Brunswick, Nova Scotia, and Prince Edward Island. This forcible removal, from 1755 to 1762, has been characterized as "a means for the British to structure the ethnic and political makeup of the Maritimes into one more amicable and supportive of the military goals of the empire" (Molinaro 2018, 2). Subsequently, the first groups of Scottish settlers came to Canada. Initial attempts were made to assimilate French in Quebec through the Royal Proclamation Act of 1763, but ultimately social and religious institutions persisted. Additionally, the Act was premised on the assumption that there would be more English-speaking settlement that would overwhelm the French-speaking population. This did not immediately happen (Knowles 1997, 18–19).

However, "A total of some 40,000 to 50,000 Loyalists flocked to British North America between 1775, when hostilities broke out, and 1784" (Knowles 1997, 20). The Loyalists included "political refugees" and individuals serving in Loyalist regiments – British and Hessian soldiers. The group also included members of the Indigenous tribes that supported the British cause and free Blacks (Knowles 1997, 20–5). In this period, they had a powerful impact on Nova Scotia, were instrumental in the birth of New Brunswick and were behind the division of Quebec into Lower Canada and Upper Canada (Ontario). Importantly, it has been observed that while subsequent migrant flows surpassed that of the Loyalists, the latter's arrival ensured that Canada would maintain its colonial ties with Britain and that its political institutions would follow the British model and not that of the United States (Knowles 1997, 26).

Immigration in the period 1846–54 saw the arrival of more than 400,000 people who left Great Britain for British North America (Knowles 1997, 44). The majority of these newcomers were Irish whose unfortunate socio-economic circumstances prompted their journey. Most notably, Irish landowners consolidated their lands and adopted new farming practices. As a result, many evicted their tenants. This development was coupled with the failure of the potato crop that began in 1845 and the subsequent resulting famine (Horner 2018, 259). The migrants coming to Canada were often poor and suffered through difficult conditions on cramped ships. Consequently, many contracted diseases such as typhus. Famine migrants were discursively constructed as "outsiders, not as prospective citizens or members of a community ... these migrants saw themselves cast as social problems" (Horner 2018, 275). Notably, it is at this time that quarantine becomes more established as a means to regulate entry to new provinces of Canada.

The roots of several elements of Canada's immigration legislation are found in early quarantine and public health provisions (Hanes 2009, 97). Officials first adopted quarantine and inspection measures in response to the threat posed by infectious disease. Ships were, as early as 1720, subject to these measures in an effort to address the threat of plague. By 1848, the admission of immigrants was subject to medical inspection (Vineberg 2015, 280–3). Quarantine procedures were contested during the period of Irish migration, just as they were to be during the COVID-19 pandemic. In the case of Irish migration, on the one hand, some members of the public wanted more restrictive measures. On the other hand, quarantine rules found little favour with Montreal merchants, many of whom were concerned that the process would impinge on the flow of goods across the Atlantic and affect their profits (Horner 2018, 270).

It was the *Act to Consolidate the Laws Relative to Emigrants and Quarantine* (1853) which came to institute a set of standard regulations directed at all vessels. All ships' passengers were subject to a quarantine process at Grosse Ile before they were allowed to move down the St. Lawrence to Quebec, Montreal, Kingston, and Toronto. As Fogarty states, the policy "stretched beyond the control of cholera and typhus as medical inspectors surveyed for physical disability, mental illness and moral depravity," and she goes on to point out that "health inspection of immigrants was used as a principal tool for selecting members of an ideal Canadian society" (2020, 2). With the exception of "contagious people or people suspected of being contagious" there were few bars to entry to Canada in this period (Hanes 2009, 97, quoting *Canada in the Making*).

Confederation and "Nation Building"

The British North America Act outlined that immigration was a shared responsibility between the federal government and the provinces. However, in practice, the former soon assumed responsibility for immigration matters particularly as emphasis centred on "settling" Western Canada (Whitaker 1991, 4). This period is marked by a familiar imperative – policies and regulations designed to attract the "right" kinds of settlers to the new country while simultaneously keeping those constructed as "unwanted" out even as immigration to the new country was widely promoted. For instance, the 1869 *Act Respecting Immigration and Immigrants*, which kept earlier medical controls, included additional restrictive provisions directed at the poor and the physically and mentally infirm. It also outlined the parameters of "excessive demand" in relation to dependence, that is, if a "person is, in the opinion of the Medical Superintendent, likely to become permanently a public charge" (Hanes 2009, 98). Later amendments also blocked entry of "criminals" and members of the "vicious classes" (Knowles 1997, 49). "This pattern of expanding the categories of undesirables by steadily augmenting and adding to the list of banned mental disabilities" became a hallmark of subsequent immigration policy (Chadha 2008, n.p.). This period also sees the introduction of more formal deportation measures directed at those deemed unsuitable "on the basis of 'race,' political radicals, the socially undesirable (including women deemed 'immoral') and 'foreign' industrial workers" (Wright 2013, 38). Immigration was central to the colonial white settler project, and social relations, including class, gender, race, and ability, were central to the process of nation building.

During the late nineteenth century, the number of immigrants arriving in Canada ranged from 6,300 to 133,000. By the turn of the century, as Canada encouraged western settlement, these numbers rose sharply. In 1913 more than 400,000 people came to Canada as immigrants – the highest ever recorded (Statistics Canada 2018, 3). In 1871 the Canadian Census indicated that the majority of these immigrants (83.6 per cent) came from the British Isles. The United States (10.9 per cent), Germany (4.1 per cent) and France (0.5 per cent) accounted for the next four top immigrant source countries. New immigrant groups from Eastern Europe – Russians, Poles, and Ukrainians – as well as people from Western Europe and Scandinavia arrived between the late 1800s and early 1900s (Statistics Canada 2018, 5). The dominance of immigrants from Great Britain, which continued until the post-war period, was the outcome of deliberate policy choices that sought to consolidate a white and British settler project.

John A. Macdonald's government embarked on an ambitious set of initiatives known as the National Policy in an effort to spur economic growth and development. Immigration, railway construction, and western expansion were key elements of this initiative (Brodie 1990). These initiatives were framed by a particular ethno-racial project which valorized characteristics and traits associated with white, Anglo-Saxon Protestants (Stasiulis and Jhappan 1995, 97). This is illustrated in Methodist minister and founding member of the Co-operative Commonwealth Federation (CCF) J.S. Wordsworth's work *Strangers within Our Gates* (1909). In it he captured prevailing societal views when he outlined a hierarchical immigration classification. The book flagged "desired" immigrant groups – notably those from Great Britain, then the United States, followed by Scandinavians. The "non preferred" immigrants groups included "the Jews, portrayed as though they were a single geographic group; the Italians ... and finally, the most alien of all, 'the Orientals' and the 'Negro' and the [East] Indian" (Valverde 2008, 110). As Stasiulis and Jhappan note, immigration policy functioned not just to attract people to provide capital and labour but also "entailed facilitating the development of a morally and physically healthy settler population, and later a citizenry based on 'love and loyalty to Canada and the British Empire'" (1995, 97, citing Roberts 1979, 186).

The federal government did not immediately assume a key role in directing immigration and recruitment in the post-Confederation period despite the critical importance of immigration to economic development and the nation-building project. Rather, it chose to partner with private-sector groups such as the Canadian Pacific Railway (CPR). The CPR was not only engaged in railway construction but was also active in immigration and settlement activities. These activities were hardly neutral and are deeply implicated in internal colonization and Indigenous land dispossession. For example, "in 1870 and 1885, federal forces were used ruthlessly to suppress the Metis and Native armed rebellions against incorporation into federal state control"

(Stasiulis and Jhappan 1995, 114). In 1881, the federal government, as part of the *Canadian Pacific Contract*, transferred 25 million acres of prairie land to the CPR. These lands functioned as a means to finance the railway and to attract settlers (Whitaker 1991, 6). "The enclosure of the lands – forced transfers from Indigenous nations to the railway corporation – served as the prime asset through which the CPR was able to raise money in the London financial markets" (Cowen 2020, 474). The CPR also embarked on a marketing campaign to attract settlers to the west and by the turn of the century was spending more than the federal government on recruiting migrants (Cowen 2020, 474). This effort was not particularly successful, and many new immigrants left Canada to move to the United States (Vineberg 2012, 10).

The arrival of Wilfrid Laurier's Liberal government in 1896 has been characterized as a "turning point in the history of immigration" (Whitaker 1991, 6). Under the leadership of Clifford Sifton, Minister of the Interior, and his "Last Best West" campaign, large numbers of immigrants arrived in Canada attracted by the promise of free land (Vineberg 2012, 11). Sifton prioritized agriculturalists over other groups and directed his recruitment efforts first on the United States. Black Americans, however, were not welcomed and were actively excluded. For instance, Black farmers experiencing racism and segregation in Oklahoma sought to move north. Opposition to their settlement in Alberta was fuelled by a "sex-race panic" as Black men were "perniciously portrayed as 'over-sexed' and potential rapists" (Stasiulis and Jhappan 1995, 113). Black settlement was discouraged initially by the refusal of Canadian agents to provide immigration materials and increased border security (Shepard 1983, 6). The cabinet also passed a 1911 Order-in-Council that banned "any immigrants belonging to the Negro race, which race is deemed unsuitable to the climate and requirements of Canada" (cited by Shepherd 1983, 13). Additionally, the government took action to halt immigration at the source. It sent a Black doctor to Oklahoma to discourage Black Americans from moving to western Canada (Shepard 1983, 9–13). While the Order-in-Council was subsequently repealed, it suggests just "how serious Canada was about keeping the northern plains white" (Shepard 1983, 13).

Sifton also focused recruitment campaigns in Central and Eastern Europe. As he famously said, "I think that a stalwart peasant in a sheepskin coat, born to the soil, whose forefathers have been farmers for ten generations, with a stout wife and a half-dozen children, is good quality" (cited by Knowles 1997, 68). This forms the start of Canada's now large Ukrainian diaspora whose long history and contributions to Canada, and identification with their ancestral homeland, drew international attention and Canada's sympathy following the February 2022 invasion of Ukraine by Russia (Cecco 2022). However, in Sifton's time, this attempt to draw on those deemed "foreigners" was controversial, and he was careful to continue to encourage British immigration even if this group did not include agriculturalists. This was "deemed politically necessary since English Canadians took it for granted that the government would do everything possible to retain the British character of the country" (Knowles 1997, 70). In this initial period of nation building, "the adopted strategies of recruitment contained a certain vision of what immigrants should be and do. Europeans were recruited for settlement, with the promises of land and ownership ... [thus connecting] immigration opportunities in Canada with access to land, as if they were only occupants to this land" (Pellerin 2019, 7). Railroad construction, western expansion, and aggressive recruitment of the "desired" immigrants went hand in hand with land dispossession of Indigenous peoples.

"Non preferred" immigrant groups, notably South Asians and Chinese, were simultaneously included in and excluded from Canada. On the one hand they provided much needed labour, but on the other hand they were constructed as too "alien" or too "foreign" to be desired members of the new nation and were often cast as threats. Unlike "preferred" groups, who were wooed with promotional literature and promises of free land, Asians were recruited as workers. Indeed in 1885 the Royal Commission on Chinese Immigration characterized them as "living machines" (Avery 1995, 45). Chinese, South Asian, and Japanese groups were subject to a range of exclusionary measures, including restrictions on entry, residence, denial of political rights, and bans on spousal immigration. These measures in effect were designed to engender a "white" country.

The experience of the Chinese migrants offers a case in point and indicates how deeply rooted anti-Asian racism is in Canada. The California Gold Rush saw the arrival of Chinese on North America's west coast. Some of these men moved north to Canada, but it was the labour demands of railway construction that saw large-scale recruitment of workers from China. In a pattern that presages the regulation of temporary workers today that we discuss in greater detail later in this book, Chinese men were often recruited through private labour agencies who would organize their employment and transportation. The cost of their passage was deducted from their wages (Kelley and Trebilcock 1998, 94). Between 1881 and 1885, an estimated 10,000 Chinese workers came to British Columbia (Avery 1995, 46). They were particularly attractive to railway contractors because they could be paid 30–50 per cent less than white workers (Kelley and Trebilcock 1998, 94). They were often relegated to the most dangerous jobs, such as blasting tunnels, and had little recourse if they became injured or sick. Some 1,000 workers died during the CPR construction (Babad 2012). Chinese workers were essential for the completion of the railway, a fact recognized by John A. Macdonald, who told detractors "either you must have labour or you can't have the railway" (Kelley and Trebilcock 1998, 95). But the prime minister also pledged to the House of Commons that once the CPR was completed, he would "join to a reasonable extent in preventing a permanent settlement in this country of Mongolian and Chinese immigrants" (Kelley and Trebilcock 1998, 95). When the railway project was completed, efforts were made to send Chinese men home. Their treatment was intimately linked to the prevailing views of Chinese people in general. "Racist fear of the 'yellow peril' pervaded all classes of the British population, but was most emphatically organized within the white, male working class where cheap and coerced Asian labour provoked fear of undercutting and strike-breaking" (Stasiulis and Jhappan 1995, 112).

Macdonald established a Royal Commission on Chinese Immigration in 1884 with a mandate to examine the possibility of restricting immigration to Canada. Of the fifty-one witnesses that appeared in hearings in San Francisco and across British Columbia, only two were Chinese (Larsson 2020). The Commission heard testimony that Chinese could never belong to Canada because they were uncleanly, lived in overcrowded conditions, and were responsible for the spread of contagious disease (Kelley and Trebilcock 1998, 94–5). While the Royal Commission agreed with employer groups that Chinese workers were important to the Canadian economy, it did support more restrictive measures based on the rationale that Chinese people could not be integrated into the larger white community and there was too much hostility directed at them by white residents (Kelley and Trebilock 1998, 97). By 1885 the government had introduced an *Act to Restrict and Regulate Chinese Immigration* into Canada "legally defining immigration from China as different than that from Europe" (Dua 2007, 452). Its regulations included a $50 "head tax" that was imposed on all Chinese immigrants. This amount steadily increased to $500 by 1923 when all immigration from China was banned under the *Chinese Immigration Act* (1923), with the exception of diplomats, students, children born in Canada, and merchants.

Through this period, Asians and their communities were linked to disease and "myths of genetic inferiority framed 'race' as being a form of disability" (Fernando and Rinaldi 2017, 14). Chinese migrants, for example, were also portrayed as sources of disease. "In the Royal Commission Report it was a common belief that syphilis, leprosy and especially smallpox were 'communicated to the Indians and the white population' from Chinese communities" (Larsson 2020). Amendments to the Immigration Act in 1902 barred the landing of any individual "suffering from any loathsome, dangerous or infectious disease of malady" and marked the entry of medical officials into Canadian immigration practice. It was also the first time "explicit health-related prohibitions targeted certain classes of persons from entering Canada" (Chandha 2008). Quarantine officers at Canadian ports were directed to inspect all Chinese-origin passengers. These historic instances are indicative of how the "language of disease is often encoded with racial prejudice" (Larsson 2020).

Like the Chinese, other "non preferred" groups, such as South Asians and Japanese, were also targeted by specific immigration measures. "These changes transformed the status of Asian male residents from members of the colonial formation to aliens in the emerging national formation" (Dua 2007, 447). It was the CPR that again played a major role in the recruitment of these Asian workers to British Columbia. It not only operated profitable shipping lines between the countries concerned and Canada but also had considerable interests in mining and fruit farming. After restrictions were placed on the entry of Chinese to Canada, the CPR expanded its operations with Japan and the Indian subcontinent using a system of steamship agents to bring workers to British Columbia (Avery 1995, 46–7). The Trades and Labour Congress called on the government to exclude "certain nationalities and classes of people who, either by temperament, non-assimilative qualifications, habits, customs or want of any permanent good their coming brings to us" (Vineberg 2015, 286). As opposition to Asian migration grew, the government introduced new restrictions. In 1908, the Canadian government negotiated a "Gentlemen's Agreement" to control the numbers of Japanese coming to Canada. Under its terms the Japanese government agreed to voluntarily limit the number of passports issued to workers and domestic servants to 400 (Pier 21). In the same year, the government moved to restrict the entry of South Asian immigrants by imposing a "continuous journey regulation." It mandated that all immigrants coming to Canada had to arrive directly from their country of origin by continuous journey on a ticket purchased in that country. While this measure "did not require that Canada resort to the distasteful and the increasingly unacceptable practice of designating 'undesirable immigrants' by race or nationality" (Knowles 1997, 93), it did largely affect only individuals from Japan and the Indian sub-continent who could not access a direct shipping route, thus ensuring the aims of a white settler project.

The Asian workers who came to Canada in the late nineteenth and early twentieth century were overwhelmingly men. For instance, in the case of the Chinese, in the period 1885–1924, 40,000 Chinese men arrived in Canada but only 1,100 Chinese women (Chu 2006, 393). Men were recruited as labour, and their low wages dictated that they could not afford the costs of bringing family members to Canada or to support them once they were in the country even in the absence of restrictive immigration measures. In many instances this led to painful family separation. As Ena Dua has pointed out, it was assumed that the absence of family made it less likely that these workers would stay in Canada, thus reinforcing the perception that they were temporary workers (2007, 451). There was little appetite for permanent communities of "non preferred" group members. Measures were directed at keeping Asian women out through tools such as the head tax and continuous journey. The imposition of a head tax restricted entry but also created a situation where "married Chinese women's migration to Canada depended significantly on their husband's race, financial status and occupational classification" (Chu 2006, 398).

But at the same time, as Dua details, some elements advocated for Asian female migration as there were concerns that men would not be able to control their sexual appetites and in the absence of Asian women the spectre of miscegenation was raised, as well as concerns that white women would be led into depravity (Dua 2007, 446). Asian women were located at the intersection of these contradictions.

In addition to immigration regulations designed to exclude or limit on the basis of racial criteria, the state moved to formalize other exclusions and extend the ambit of deportation. Deportation was formalized in 1907, though it was practised informally for many years prior (Wright 2013, 38). Molinaro characterizes deportation as a "nation building mechanism" and points out "many immigrants were deported if authorities viewed them as upsetting accepted racial, gender, political, religious or class norms" (Molinaro 2018, 1). Deportation, like immigration, has its roots in quarantine acts "which were designed to keep out the sick and poor ... Authorities, including medical professionals believed the poor were lazy and ignorant and that such qualities contributed to their propensity to become ill and be a burden" (Molinaro 2018, 3).

The grounds for deportation grew during this time and often linked medical grounds to national origin reflecting a eugenics logics. For instance, the 1906 Act "barred entry of feeble-minded, idiot, epileptic, insane or pauper immigrants 'likely to become a public charge'" (Fogerty 2020, 4). However, some groups, it was believed, were more likely to suffer from these deficiencies. "Italians, for example, were considered more prone to emotional instability and violent outbursts ... it was [also] believed Jews were physically inferior and even harmful to society" (Fogerty 2020, 4). In 1935, sixty-five Chinese immigrants at a British Columbia asylum were deported on the grounds that their lunacy, which required twenty-four-hour care, was a burden on tax payers. "Medical records attributed their Cantonese language to 'speaking in tongues' and a signifier of 'some unseen pathology'" (Fernando and Rinaldi 2017, 15, citing Menzies 2005). Between 1903 and 1909, 1,481 people were deported for being a "public charge" (Molinaro 2018, 5). Stereotypes about Black women were also mobilized to deny entry of Guadeloupean women domestics to Quebec in 1911. Immigration officers believed that these domestic workers "were likely to become a public charge because they were single parents. The immigration officer surmised that they were likely to become pregnant again and would probably become a drain on the public purse."

Consequently, the scheme that recruited women from Guadeloupe was closed to applicants on the basis that these women were "morally and physically unfit" (Calliste 1993–4, 134).

The 1910 Immigration Act added "political radical" to the list of potential deportees (Molinaro 2018, 7). While "public charge" and "medical inadmissibility" were the two most frequently used reasons for exclusion, the years 1914–30s saw the systematic deportation of people on the basis of being radicals, labour unionists, and activists (Wright 2013, 39). One of the key targets for the government before the First World War were the Industrial Workers of the World (IWW) activists. The IWW was attempting to organize all workers into one big union, and its long-term goal was to dismantle capitalism through a series of widespread general strikes (Molinaro 2018, 8). Following the 1919 Winnipeg General Strike, the government introduced further measures. As such, "any non-citizen, or anyone whose citizenship had been acquired through nationalization, advocating the overthrow of constituted authority or associating with a group advocating the overthrow of government, could be deported" (Whitaker 1991, 11).

Morality, while not an official category (Molinaro 2018, 6), was also used as a basis to deport immigrants. Women immigrants charged with prostitution also faced expulsion, as they were perceived as "perpetrators of degenerating immorality as well as reservoirs of sexually transmitted infection" (Fogarty 2020, 5). But additionally, women who did not adhere to conventional female roles were sometimes excluded. Single immigrant mothers came under scrutiny because of societal expectations that women should be supported by male wage earners. Those that tried to take paid work were sometimes subject to deportation (Molinaro 2018, 6). Masturbation could also constitute grounds for deportation, for both men and women, because of the perception that this activity was linked to insanity (Molinaro 2018, 7).

The two decades following the Second World War mark the culmination of historic practices, as well as a period of greater immigration, which was greatly slowed during the Depression. The 1941 census indicated that Canada's immigrant population numbered two million people. However, from the 1950s on, the foreign-born population in the country continued to increase. While immigration from Britain remained privileged, the period 1950–70 also saw the arrival of immigrants from Western Europe and Southern Europe, including Germany, the Netherlands, Italy, and Greece. Consequently, "at the time of the 1971 Census, 28.3% of immigrants were born in the United Kingdom and 51.4% were born in another European Country" (Statistics Canada 2018). In many ways, this period marked an era of transition from the prevailing rationales that had characterized Canadian immigration to the system we are more familiar with today. And it has been suggested that these years were characterized by "a sense of economic optimism" following the Depression and war that engendered "a momentary consensus that an expansive future would need a more expansive immigration policy" (Whitaker 1991, 14). Nevertheless, many hierarchies remained in place.

The continuing dominance of British immigrants reflected the ongoing efforts of the Canadian government to privilege this group over others in the period 1940–50 (Stasiulus and Jhappan 1995, 117). In 1947 Prime Minister Mackenzie King told the House of Commons: "the people of Canada do not wish, as a result of mass immigration, to make a fundamental alteration in the character of our population. Large-scale immigration from the orient would change the fundamental composition of the Canadian population ... The government, therefore, has no thought of making any change in immigration regulations which would have consequences of the kind" (Mackenzie King, May 1, 1947). Nevertheless, the government signalled that it was prepared to use immigration as a means to expand the population and spur economic growth. The government moved to admit displaced persons from Europe; however, they were still selectively recruited. It sent immigration teams, comprising immigration, medical, security and labour officials, to Europe to evaluate an immigrant's potential economic contribution to Canada. Young, able-bodied men who could do manual labour in primary industries were preferred because of labour shortages in these areas (Knowles 2000, 69). However, this was not the only criteria, as once again ethno-racial preferences came into play. While "the category of 'race' does not appear in post-war immigration control regulations ... what does appear are the categories of 'colour' and 'coloured person,' euphemisms for 'race,'" and these groups of people could only enter if they were "close relatives of Canadian citizens" and in cases "of exceptional merit" (Satzewich 1988, 289). Similarly, as during the war, Jewish people were still consistently rejected despite their war-time experiences of genocidal targeting by Nazis. An applicant's political leanings were also considered. The RCMP was responsible for security vetting, and because of its "strong right-wing bias, the label 'undesirable' was all too often applied to applicants regarded as left wing ... Communists being the ultimate pariahs during the Cold War" (Knowles 1997, 133). In the immediate years after the war the government moved very cautiously to open the country to new immigrants.

Canada's role in the war and its war-time industrial production prompted a new-found confidence in the country and its place in the world. This sense of identity is linked to the passage of the 1947 *Canadian Citizenship Act* (Knowles 2000, 64–5). Previously, Canadians had British subject status. In his speech to the House of Commons, Cabinet Minister Paul Martin Sr. stated: "For the national unity of Canada and for the future and greatness of this country, it is felt to be of utmost importance that all of us, new Canadians or old, have a consciousness of a common purpose and common interest as Canadians; that all of us are able to say with pride and say with meaning: 'I am a Canadian citizen'" (cited in Knowles 2000, 65). The new legislation created Canadian Citizen as a distinct status given to people born in the country and those who naturalized. With this new Act "Canada became the first Commonwealth country to create its own class of citizenship separate from that of Great Britain" (Knowles 2000, 66). The new elements of the act have been characterized as "perfunctory" insofar as they only specified that every Canadian citizen has a right to enter the country, a residency requirement, circumstances for revocation of citizenship, and a new oath of allegiance (Brodie 2002, 50). It should be noted that at this time the Liberals, prompted in part by the new UN Charter and the beginnings of the human rights revolution, also moved to repeal the Chinese Immigration Act of 1923 and announced that Chinese persons in Canada would be eligible to apply for naturalization.

It was also during this period that the government underscored its commitment to permanent immigration as the cornerstone of nation building. "Guest worker programs were rejected and temporary migration was 'modest and limited'" and Canada developed settlement programs and a path to citizenship for permanent migrants (Walsh 2014, 588). Nevertheless, there are some noteworthy examples of temporary migration during this time. Vic Satzewich details how different groups of people were recruited for farm labour – Polish veterans, displaced persons from Eastern Europe, and immigrants from a range of European countries, including Germany, Holland, Italy, and Portugal. He points out that most of these groups were admitted as "free immigrants" but others entered as contract labour. Polish veterans and displaced persons were recruited for particular jobs, such as farm labour, and had to remain in these positions for two years before they earned the right to remain in the country and freely circulate in the labour market (Satzewich 1988, 286). In 1955, the government also recruited women from Jamaica and the Barbados to work as domestics when it was unable to draw on workers from Europe. Under this arrangement the costs of recruiting, training, and medical inspection of workers was borne by the sending country. To be eligible applicants had to be between twenty-one and thirty-five and commit to work as a domestic worker for twelve months with an assigned employer. "Through tests for pregnancy and the emphasis on women's single status, the Canadian government wanted to ensure that this group would be in Canada solely for the purpose of filling a labour requirement; it was assumed that there would be no sponsorship of spouses and children" (Arat Koć 1997, 75).

While the Immigration Act (1952) became the first new immigration legislation since the 1910 Act, it did not contain many new legislative directions but merely coded practices that were already in place (Kelley and Trebilcock 1998, 324). For example, this reform still included a preferred immigrant classification based on origin. "At the top were unsponsored British subjects from the United Kingdom and the white Commonwealth, as well as those of American and French origin ... at the bottom was a residual category designed to restrict Asians to sponsored close relatives without indicating that intention openly" (Whitaker 1991, 17–18). The Act, as many scholars have observed, also gave the minister and cabinet considerable discretionary powers over immigration matters (Whitaker 1991, 18). For example, Jack Pickersgill, Minister of Immigration and Citizenship (1954–7), used these powers to allow the admission of "epileptics whose condition could be controlled by drugs," people with TB, and those with histories of mental illness on the proviso that they would pose no threat to the community and were adequately supported (Knowles 1997, 138). He also used discretionary powers to admit thirty-nine Palestinian Arab heads of family and their dependents in 1956 following their becoming refugees after 1948, and later thousands of Hungarian refugees in 1957 (Knowles 1997, 139). As Whitaker puts it, "these refugee movements did not conform to any legislatively created category: they were made possible by the mass issuing of ministerial permits" (1995, 18). There was also considerable emphasis on listing the groups of applicants that should be barred from entry and an elaboration of powers of exclusion, arrest, and detention (Whitaker 1991, 17).

The Canadian government also began promoting a new form of immigration – "sponsored" immigrants. Under the terms of this stream, relatives agreed to sponsor and support newcomers. During the 1950s and 1960s this sponsored stream, the family class, accounted for 37 per cent of total flows. This stream, as Reg Whitaker observes, tended to favour the growth of ethnic groups already in Canada "with strong kinship ties; it helped foster, especially in major cities, strong ethnic pressure groups with political leverage, which seek to maintain and expand the system" (Whitaker 1991, 16).

The 1952 legislation more clearly enumerated the grounds upon which a person would not gain entry to the country. Section 5 of the Act contained prohibitions directed at persons classified as "idiots, imbeciles, morons," diseased persons, physically defective persons, and persons medically certified as unable to work due to a physical or mental abnormality (Hanes 2009, 109). In this respect the legislation did not depart significantly from the previous Immigration Act of 1910. "There remained the age-old concerns pertaining to social dependence as well as age-old stigmatization of people with disabilities as noncontributing citizens" (Hanes 2009, 110).

The 1952 Act also specifically prohibited the entry of homosexuals to Canada. As Philip Girard notes, this was the first time the term "homosexual" appeared in immigration legislation. Prior to this, legislation barred people convicted of "moral turpitude" and denied admission to "prostitutes and women and girls coming to Canada for any immoral purpose and pimps or persons living on the avails of prostitution" (Girard 1987, 6). The ban on persons categorized as "homosexual" stemmed from Cold War politics (Girard 1987). As Gary Kinsman and Patriza Gentile elaborate, "in national security discourse homosexuals were constructed as suffering from an unreliable

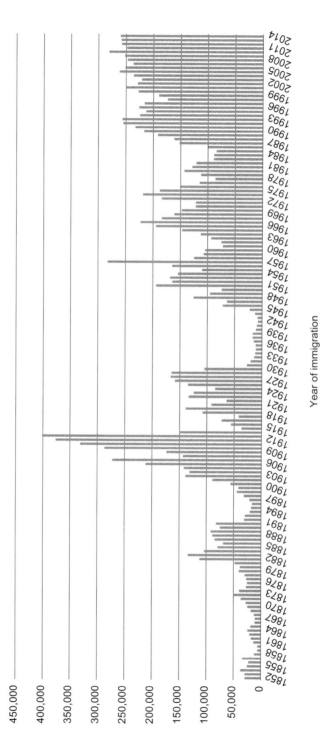

Figure 1. Number of immigrants who landed annually in Canada, 1852–2014

Source: Statistics Canada 2018. "150 Years of Immigration in Canada," www150.statcan.gc.ca/n1/pub/11-630-x/11-630-x2016006-eng.htm.

and unstable character," which rendered them a threat to national security (2010, 7). The RCMP and the Department of National Defence played a role in inserting this prohibition into the new Act as opposed to other government departments or the Canadian public at large. The RCMP were influenced by developments in the United States where "by the end of 1950s, the homosexual witch-hunt in the U.S. had been underway for several months" (Girard 1987, 8). The provision in the 1952 Immigration Act paralleled surveillance and national security campaigns against lesbians and gay men in what Kinsman and Gentile (2010) term "the war on queers" that took place in the Canadian public service and military from the 1950s on.

Though the post-war period shared much with earlier periods, the two decades following the Second World War also pre-figured the transformation towards Canada's modern immigration system. The modern immigration system was to become officially non-discriminatory in relation to race/ethnicity but also attuned to specific categories: skilled workers, family, and refugees.

PART TWO: THE MODERN IMMIGRATION ENVIRONMENT – SKILLS, CATEGORIES, AND POINTS

In 2017 Immigration, Refugees and Citizenship Canada (IRCC) reported that India, the Philippines, and China were the three top source countries of permanent residents admitted in 2017 (IRCC 2018). This contemporary fact can only be understood by considering the changes which took place from the late 1960s, a decade which marked a critical moment in immigration history and where we root the modern immigration system. This transformation was related to the reordering of the inclusionary and exclusionary rationales that underpinned immigration policy and the emergence of new practices of classification, most notably the introduction of a "points-based system" and the establishment of the broad immigration categories that are in place today, namely, economic, family, and humanitarian streams.

In the 1960s, Canada's immigrant population became increasingly diverse as immigrants from Asia and other "non-traditional" source countries grew and the government introduced many reforms to immigration policy, including the introduction of a new points-based selection model. These changes reflected a number of concerns. First, the frameworks that guided immigration at the turn of the century, with their emphasis on racial and ethnic criteria and valorization of values and morals associated with white Anglo-Saxon Britain were no longer tenable. As Triadafilos Triadafilopoulos puts it, "the discrediting of scientific racism, integral nationalism and white supremacy, and the simultaneous emergence of human rights after the war problematized discriminatory policies" (2013,18). Second, and relatedly, Canadian politicians, policymakers, and some interest groups were looking to skilled workers and professionals as the Canadian economy was becoming more reliant on technology as opposed to primary sectors like agriculture (Avery 1995, 176–7).

It is against this context in 1962 that the federal government introduced amendments to the 1952 Immigration Act. Subsection 31(a) clearly emphasized human capital criteria insofar as it "called for a person to be admitted to Canada 'who by reason of his education, training, skills or other special qualifications is likely to be able to establish himself successfully in Canada' and has either sufficient means to support himself or has secured employment" (cited in Kelley and Trebilcock 1998, 332). This was the first step towards eliminating explicit discriminatory measures in the policy and was hailed as "a long overdue and radical reform that virtually abolished the White Canada immigration policy" (Knowles 1997, 152). This said, it should be noted that immigration officers still had the authority to determine which skills were important, and this discretionary power was not removed until the points system was implemented (Kelley and Trebilcock 1998, 332). Additionally, racial restrictions still applied to the sponsored class. Canadian citizens from Europe and Western Hemisphere countries could sponsor a wide range of family members, including adult children, married children, siblings and their families, and unmarried nieces and nephews under the age of twenty-one. But citizens from non-European and non-Western nations were limited to a much narrower group of relatives (Triadafilopoulos 2013, 25).

In a major innovation, the federal government developed a new points-based selection model in 1967, which was presented as a neutral and objective means to evaluate potential immigrants to Canada. This selection model was directed at independent applicants in the economic stream, and applicants were awarded points on the basis of education, skills, and occupation. Initially applicants had to secure fifty points out of a maximum of one hundred points to be successful. The points-based model has been hailed as "a novel and influential set of admission criteria for the highly skilled" (Shachar 2006, 171). It has been emulated by other settler colonies, such as Australia, which initiated its system in the late 1970s and formalized it in the 1980s. More recently President Trump also extolled the virtues of the points-based system, which he referred to as "merit based" and sought to pursue a similar initiative in the United States.

In many ways the points-based model reflects the assumptions of the post-war Keynesian welfare state, namely that the state can and should play a major role in the management and direction of the economy. This found expression in immigration policy insofar as the state determined immigrant flows with an eye to the needs of the economy. "This meant that in times of economic slowdown the immigration tap should be turned down, or off. These were essential terms upon which labour was drawn into the new consensus" (Whitaker 1991, 15). This role was markedly different to the situation that characterized immigration at the turn of the twentieth century. But the points-based system, with its emphasis on human capital, also proved amenable to more neoliberal governance directions that emerged in the 1990s.

It has been observed that points-based systems, such as the Canadian model, on the one hand appeal to policymakers because they convey clear human capital standards and demonstrate to the broader public that states can manage the admission of economic migrants in a fair and transparent manner. But on the other hand, it has been observed that "the greatest single flaw of the traditional points-based model is that immigrants arrive without a job offer and there is no guarantee that they will find work easily at their skill level" (Papademetriou and Sumption 2011, 3). Additionally, Canada's points-based model itself is premised on a set of class, gender, and racial hierarchies. For instance, in terms of gender, the points-based system valorized activities in the public realm by awarding points for formal education, vocational educations, and job experience. Such opportunities vary by country, and additionally women, depending on gender relations in sending countries, may have had more difficulty than men in meeting these criteria (Abu-Laban and Gabriel 2002, 50). Others have noted that the points system did not address the discriminatory provisions that applied to people with disabilities (Hanes 2009, 113). Nevertheless, the skills-based model was popularly celebrated as a move away from the discriminatory practices within Canada's immigration policy. However, as Walsh importantly observes, "while race and nationality were eliminated as admissions criteria, as the country's migration program evolved it became clear restrictiveness was being reordered rather than erased" (2014, 588).

The 1976 Immigration Act marked the first time that immigration legislation specified the goals of the policy – "Sub-section 3(i) specified the need to 'maintain and protect the health, safety and good order of Canadian society'" (Vineberg 2015, 289). In an important departure with past practice, it mandated the federal government to consult with the provinces after which the Minister of Immigration would present an annual plan to Parliament outlining the number of immigrants the government proposes to admit (Knowles 1997, 169). The Act also recognizes three groups of people who are eligible for landed immigrant status:

- *family class*, which includes the immediate family and dependent children, and parents and grandparents of any Canadian or permanent resident who agrees to provide for lodging, care, and maintenance of his or her family members for a period of up to ten years;
- *humanitarian class*, which includes (a) refugees who fit the definition of refugee contained in the 1951 UN Convention and the 1967 Protocol relating to refugees ... (b) persecuted and displaced persons who do not qualify as refugees under the rigid UN definition but who are members of a specially designated class created by the cabinet for humanitarian reasons;
- *independent class*, i.e., individuals who apply for landed immigrant status on their own initiative and who are selected on the basis of the points system. (Knowles 1997, 169–70)

Notably, the act also outlined amended grounds for medical inadmissibility. People would be denied admission if (i) "They are likely to be a danger to public health or to public safety," or (ii) "their admission

Table 1. Permanent residents admitted to Canada, 2019

Immigration Category	Number
Economic Total	196,658
Family Total	91,311
Refugees and Protected Persons	48,539
Humanitarian and Other	4,681
TOTAL 2019	341,180

Source: IRCC, CDO, Permanent Resident Data as of March 31, 2020, from Immigration, Refugees and Citizenship Canada, *2020 Annual Report to Parliament on Immigration*, p. 35.

would cause or might reasonably be expected to cause excessive demands on health or social services" (cited in Fernando and Rinaldi 2017, 17). The 1976 Immigration Act provides the framework for contemporary immigration policy, and the three broad categories remain in place today.

For the year 2019, a year not impacted by the border and travel restrictions relating to COVID-19, permanent residents admitted to Canada comprised just over 341,000, with the vast majority admitted under the economic category, followed by family. The refugee and other humanitarian category consistently comprises the smallest number, as was also the case for 2019.

It was also during the 1970s that the government moved to outline and consolidate its temporary worker programs under the Non-Immigrant Employment Authorization Program (NIEAP) introduced in 1973. While Canada did not open its doors to a full-fledged temporary worker program along the lines of a European guest worker system, Canadian agriculture and domestic worker programs shared many similar features to those in other countries (Avery 1995, 207). Further, and importantly as Nandita Sharma has asserted, "Those given 'temporary foreign worker' status are generally cheaper to hire than people with citizenship or permanent resident status. Indeed, their relative 'cheapness' is *legislated* by the state to the benefit of employers" (Sharma 2019, 222). Initially, temporary entries were proportionately low, but their subsequent growth belies the claims that Canada is a place where everyone who migrates becomes a member in the polity. In 2019, a year not impacted by COVID-19-related travel and border restrictions, Canada issued over 404,000 temporary work permits through the temporary foreign worker and international mobility programs (Immigration, Refugees and Citizenship Canada 2020, 3) a number that exceeded those admitted for permanent residence.

PART THREE: CONTEMPORARY DYNAMICS AND SOVEREIGNTY IN THE CANADIAN SETTLER COLONY – COMPARATIVE, INTERNATIONAL, AND ETHICAL CONSIDERATIONS

In many ways Canada's historically exclusionary immigration policy, an outcome of its foundation as a white settler colony as well as the exertion of state sovereignty, has reverberations in the present. Below we consider some of these dynamics to situate Canada and issues of membership inclusion/exclusion in a comparative and global frame of reference.

Membership Inclusion/Exclusion

Today dynamics of inclusion/exclusion play out on a qualitatively distinct terrain marked by different sensibilities and evolving discourses and policies that are more pluralist and inclusionary in ethos. Canada's post-war commitment to human rights, as noted, led in 1967 to the formal prohibition of discrimination on the basis of race/ethnicity in Canada's immigration policy. It also led to an official policy of multiculturalism within a framework of English and French bilingualism since 1971, as well as greater embrace of Indigenous self-governing arrangements (Abu-Laban 2018). These more inclusionary impulses were themselves the outcomes of struggles of marginalized groups, including Francophones, racialized minorities, and Indigenous peoples, who also continue to make demands for equity, fairness, and in the cases of Francophone Quebecers and Indigenous Peoples forms of self-rule (Abu-Laban 2018). One way these more inclusionary impulses have impacted immigration is seen in the fact that Quebec has come to be granted more say in the selection of immigrants, and attention is paid by the federal government to the impact of immigration on official language minorities (such as Francophone communities in provinces outside Quebec). However, it is important to note that ultimately admissions remain in the control of the Canadian state, suggesting the sovereignty of the Canadian state and its power to determine who gets in is largely unfettered, just as it was historically.

More recently, the 2015 final report of the Truth and Reconciliation Commission of Canada's (TRC) described the impact of historically state-run residential schools on Indigenous children as "cultural genocide" (Truth and Reconciliation Commission of Canada 2015a). By 2021 this diagnosis was further amplified by the identification, with ground-penetrating radar, of the remains of over 1,000 children (of an estimated 10,000–15,000) in unmarked graves on the grounds of several residential schools across Canadian provinces (Austen 2021). As a result of the TRC, there has been greater attention to reconciliation between Indigenous Peoples and non-Indigenous Canadians, which is understood to involve at a minimum attention to the TRC's ninety-four calls to action directed at transforming governmental, societal, and educational institutions (Truth and Reconciliation Commission of Canada 2015b).

However, growing discussion of reconciliation (and even in some circles decolonization) has not fundamentally altered the fact that it is the Canadian state (and not Indigenous peoples) which not only regulates borders but also membership. In other words, it is the Canadian state that exerts sovereign control by determining who is allowed to enter Canada and who is granted Canadian citizenship. Analysts attuned to Indigenous issues also suggest that the prevailing settler-colonial culture means many incoming immigrants follow the lead of the non-Indigenous Canadian born in their views of Indigenous peoples and the land. This is what helps lead to the perpetuation of a settler identity and inequitable structures *vis à vis* First Nations, Metis, and Inuit peoples (Lowman and Barker 2015).

In relation to other real-world states, Canada's approach to immigration has been widely viewed by many scholars and policymakers as both open as well as supportive of integration. This is because it is one of the few states that in 2021 and 2022 planned increases in the overall numbers of immigrants and because there are also relatively extensive resources put into place to support settlement services and integration; not least there is a clear pathway for immigrants (other than temporary foreign workers) to receive citizenship or membership (Esses et al. 2021, 8). As well, when compared to the two decades following the Second World War, the contemporary more pluralist ethos has clearly given rise to more openness towards prospective immigrants from around the world (rather than just Europe), and in turn Canada has a more demographically diverse population. Indeed, until the COVID-19 pandemic's border closures dramatically impacted immigration intake from outside of Canada, over the course of the 2000s Canada had come to welcome some 300,000–350,000 immigrants annually. Moreover, in light of the impact of travel restrictions and border closures resulting from the COVID-19 pandemic on dwindling the expected intake of immigrants, in April 2021 the Liberal Minister of the Department of Immigration, Refugees and Citizenship Canada announced a new pathway to permanent residence for non-citizens with temporary status already in the country. Specifically, non-citizens working in "essential" jobs in health and other areas, as well as international graduates of the last four years from Canadian postsecondary institutions who were proficient in English and/or French were given the opportunity to apply for permanent residence (Jones 2021).

Despite this 2021 announcement and opening to select workers deemed essential and its success in maintaining high levels of immigration, the vast majority of non-citizens in Canada were not given a pathway to citizenship. In fact, Canada's immigration policy and selection system has and continues to be primarily economically driven and attuned to perceived labour market and regional development needs as well as the implications of an aging population (Esses et al. 2021, 8). As with other countries of the global North, this has resulted, as noted, in a decided preference for newcomers with skills. What is notable is that there are instances when this preference is also even exhibited in relation to humanitarian admissions. For example, among recent policy pilots, the Economic Mobility Pathways Pilot focuses on granting skilled refugees access to permanent residence through existing economic immigration programs. This project began in 2018–19 in partnership with the United Nations High Commissioner for Refugees (UNHCR) and seeks to identify "additional ways for refugees, who have skills that Canadian employers need, to find a home in Canada while contributing to our country's economic growth" (Immigration, Refugees and Citizenship Canada 2021).

As we noted, the net result of Canada's approach to immigration, marked as it is by the preference for skilled immigrants, is not neutral. But it is important to note that this is also the case when it has been pursued elsewhere in other countries like Australia. Analysts have identified informal biases that creep into the process of skilled immigrant selection that differentially impact applicants on the basis of country of location (and by extension race/ethnicity), by socio-economic position or class, as well as by gender (Abu-Laban and Gabriel 2001; Boucher 2016). With respect to gender, Boucher sums the various points at which discriminatory outcomes facing women immigrants are evident in a policy emphasizing skills:

> They arise in the political discussions through which immigration policies are negotiated and designed in ways that often advantage male applicants and disadvantage female applicants. They also come into the selection stage when immigrants choose to apply as skilled immigrants, based upon assessment of selection criteria. Policy design often overlooks the different life course experiences of women and men, for instance whether part-time work or career breaks are acknowledged within skilled immigration design. Skilled immigration policies frequently perpetuate a stereotypical divide between an autonomous male breadwinner and an accompanying (implicitly female) spouse. Joint worker-carer models are absent from policy design. Finally, as regards actual immigration outcomes, women disproportionately enter as accompanying family members of skilled immigrants rather than as principal skilled immigrants in their own right. (2016, 2–3)

The term "brain drain" has long been applied to policies aimed at attracting skilled immigrants, particularly from parts of the developing world to countries of the West. Equally significantly, in all countries that have pursued skilled migration policies and engaged in the global talent race by joining forces with business, there have been issues in relation to foreign credential recognition (Guo and Shan 2013). Because the previous training and education of many immigrants is often not recognized, immigrants frequently end up in jobs for which they are overqualified, with negative implications for earnings. In the case of Canada, this trend towards the underutilization of immigrant skills has been especially evident since the 1990s and has been dubbed a "brain waste" along with being a major source of disappointment and frustration for immigrants to Canada since there is little difference between provinces on this issue (Reitz, Curtis, and Elrick 2013, 1).

Not least, after more than fifty years of having an official policy of multiculturalism, issues around racism remain stubbornly persistent and often harken back to earlier tropes associating immigrants with risk and danger and fuelling racism. The September 11, 2001, attacks in Washington and New York, and the ensuing "war on terror" exacerbated concerns around security in migration and in particular refugees, casting those fleeing persecution as threats, and giving rise to various refugee-excluding exhibitions of sovereignty by states particularly, though not exclusively, in countries of the Global North (Abu-Laban 2016; Adamson and Tsourapas 2020). In this context, those that are, or are perceived to be, Arab and/or Muslim have faced significant forms of surveillance and discrimination in both state policy and civil society in Canada and other Western polities (Abu-Laban 2016; Ragazzi 2016). The tragic shootings of six worshippers at the Islamic Cultural Centre, a mosque in Saint-Foy Quebec City in 2017, along with the horrendous 2021 attack on a Muslim family in London, Ontario, which left four dead, are widely understood to be examples of anti-Muslim racism (sometimes called Islamophobia) (Ann 2021). Such attacks have occurred elsewhere, including two consecutive attacks during Friday prayers in March 2019 at mosques in Christchurch, New Zealand, which left fifty-one dead. Chillingly, the Christchurch shooter's guns sported the name of the Quebec City shooter, suggesting the global reach of violent white supremacist movements (Elliott 2019). As well, the Christchurch shooter's gun made reference to the United Nations compact on migration (this Compact is discussed further below) (Elliott 2019).

Harkening to longstanding quarantine practices, both the 2003 SARS outbreak in Toronto, as well as more recently the 2020 COVID-19 pandemic, drew on older tropes associating immigrants and minorities with disease with language like "Chinese flu" in the case of SARS, or "Chinese virus" in relation to COVID-19. Linking disease with a country or ethnic group clearly fuelled racism in the 1800s, and likewise it did so in the 2020s, with violent incidents targeting

Chinese Canadians and more broadly Asian Canadians (Keil and Ali 2006; Go 2021). In June 2020, a survey of Chinese Canadians released by Angus Reid found half were called names or insulted during the pandemic, and 43 per cent reported being threatened. The majority, 61 per cent, changed their routine to avoid conflict. Only 13 per cent of those surveyed felt that others consistently saw them as Canadian (Zeidler 2020). Added to this the impact of the pandemic was to exacerbate extant inequities for migrant workers and racialized groups in relation to higher rates of COVID-19 infections due to housing and employment conditions in specific sectors, as well as higher rates of unemployment (Go 2021). As vividly summed by Avvy Go in 2021: "With the development of vaccines, there is hope that the pandemic will soon be over. But the virus of racism will likely go on, ravaging the lives of people of colour and Indigenous peoples in Canada and beyond. While scientists may be able to cure COVID-19 with a dose or two of the vaccine, combating racism takes a lot more concerted effort from all of us."

In a world made up of states, the movement of people across borders by definition involves more than a single state and brings to the fore issues of sovereignty and control, as well as international cooperation. In the aftermath of the Second World War the relevance of the newly formed United Nations to the working out of conventions in relation to refugees (1951) or stateless persons (1954) draws attention to the possibility of international cooperation. Moreover, deepening forms of regional integration in the European Union and the advance of an EU Citizenship in 1992 allowing for the free movement of nationals of member states belonging to the EU, and new forms of cooperation around the entry of non-EU nationals, suggest how the governance of migration may also take regional continental forms.

Global Governance and Sovereignty

In the contemporary period, the year 2015 marks a pivotal turning point in the discourse used by media and political elites in northern states, particularly in Europe, when refugee flows came to be called a "crisis." While it is true that a new record number of 1.3 million claims were made in Europe that year, the crisis was in fact primarily constructed and understood from the vantage point of northern states having to deal with an influx of unwanted asylum seekers (Hyndman and Reynolds 2020, 66). In other words, the refugee crisis was not treated in relation to the conditions giving rise to violence and displacement in countries like Syria (Hyndman and Reynolds 2020, 66), or what former United Nations Secretary-General Ban Ki Moon insisted was a crisis of solidarity in terms of responses (UNHCR 2016, 5). Some seven years later, the comparatively quick, as well as generous, response of European and other states, including Canada, to Ukrainian refugees fleeing the Russia–Ukraine war which began in February 2022 also drew attention. This was because it was deemed by many critics to reveal a double standard rooted in racism on the part of Western media and political elites. Such depictions of Ukrainians as being "civilized" as having "blonde hair and blue eyes," and fighting for freedom by "throwing Molatov cocktails," were seen to contrast with Syrians and other groups who were treated as uncivilized potential terrorists (Øverlid 2022).

Notwithstanding the contested nature of the "crisis" discourse in relation to refugees, as well as lingering charges of inconsistent humanitarian responses to refugees depending on country of origin and race, 2015 was a turning point. Specifically, the increased concern among northern states with numbers of refugee claims, alongside newspaper reports concerning boats capsizing and people drowning in the Mediterranean while trying to seek refuge and a better life, did capture the concern of policymakers internationally and specifically in the United Nations (Koslowski 2020, 5). As a consequence, in September 2016, the UN General Assembly unanimously adopted the New York Declaration on Migrants and Refugees, committing all 193 UN member states to work to more equitably share responsibilities towards refugees as well as strengthening international cooperation in relation to both migrants and refugees (United Nations General Assembly 2016). As spelled out in Article 11:

> We acknowledge a shared responsibility to manage large movements of refugees and migrants in a humane, sensitive, compassionate and people-centred manner. We will do so through international cooperation, while recognizing that there are varying capacities and resources to respond to these movements. International cooperation and, in particular, cooperation among countries of origin or nationality, transit

and destination, has never been more important; "win-win" cooperation in this area has profound benefits for humanity. Large movements of refugees and migrants must have comprehensive policy support, assistance and protection, consistent with States' obligations under international law. We also recall our obligations to fully respect their human rights and fundamental freedoms, and we stress their need to live their lives in safety and dignity. We pledge our support to those affected today as well as to those who will be part of future large movements. (United Nations General Assembly 2016, Article 11)

The New York Declaration in turn led to several intergovernmental conferences over the next two years, out of which came two global compacts in December 2018: one dealing with migration and the other dealing with refugees. A striking feature that stands out is that negotiations for these compacts took place in a climate of unusually high levels of opposition to immigration. Importantly, this also included one of the world's most powerful and influential countries, the United States, where Donald Trump was inaugurated as president in 2017 (Ferris and Donato 2020, 17–25). Indeed, under Trump the United States withdrew from negotiations of both compacts, suggesting both an absence of committed global leadership and a less-than-robust form of international agreement – or multilateralism – guiding the compacts (Ferris and Donato 2020). As noted in chapter one, in December of 2021, the administration of Democrat Joe Biden signalled their endorsement of the Global Compact on migration, suggesting a (re)embracing of the role of the United States as a key player in multilateral institutions and migration governance.

At the same time that President Trump was rejecting the compacts, it is interesting to note that north of the US border, the government of Justin Trudeau, and Canadian representatives, responded differently in pursuing a more multilateral approach in migration. A 2019 report produced for the Library of Parliament is indicative of the Canadian role and endorsement of the Global Compacts on migration and refugees. The report makes clear that even prior to the New York Declaration Canada worked with the countries of Jordan, Fiji, Kenya, Lebanon, and Turkey in leading international efforts to ensure greater cooperation around refugee and migration practices (Chesoi and Naef 2019, 4). Moreover, it was Canadian jurist Louise Arbour, appointed special representative of the United Nations Secretary-General for International Migration, who was critical in steering the adoption of the Global Compact for Migration after the New York Declaration of 2016 (Chesoi and Naef 2019, 2). Political scientist James Milner also specifically highlights the role of Canada in relation to the Global Compact on Refugees, showing how Canadian leaders acted as norm entrepreneurs on issues relating to gender inclusion in the Compact as well as being a bridge builder in facilitating dialogue with like-minded states and civil society actors throughout the process (Milner, 2021).

Given the recency of both the Global Compact for Safe, Orderly and Regular Migration (GCM) and the Global Compact on Refugees (GCR), it will take time to fully assess their impact in creating conditions of greater international cooperation, responsibility sharing of refugees, and a commitment to human rights. However, it is fair to note that the compacts have been criticized on a number of grounds, including for decentring the voices of migrants and refugees in favour of states, including states that are hostile to human rights (Ferris and Donato 2020, 100–22; Hyndman and Reynolds 2020, 66). Most critically, the fact that provisions are non-binding means that state claims of sovereignty in either support or opposition to the wording and spirt of the compacts will be exerted.

In light of the fact that there are clearly choices in relation to how state and civil society actors approach immigration, in the pages that follow we are also concerned with addressing ethical approaches attuned to "what ought to be," in addition to outlining developments in Canada from 9/11 to the COVID-19 pandemic within a comparative frame of reference. To do this, we pay special attention to issues relating to gender and care in our discussion of refugees, economic immigrants, family immigrants, temporary foreign workers, and citizenship. We also draw attention to ongoing normative debates about whether borders should be more or fully open. As the pandemic unfolded and vaccines developed, such questions about international borders gained global resonance in the context of new discussions of having to have documented evidence or proof of having received vaccination against COVID-19 (sometimes also referred to as a "vaccine passport") to travel across state borders. Of course, proof of vaccination requirements, and other pandemic measures, were also a domestic issue in countries like Canada, as seen in the weeks-long

"Freedom Convoy" protests in Ottawa and other cities in 2022. Given global COVID-19 vaccine inequity which disadvantages countries in the Global South, such requirements to travel internationally could be seen to further fuel inequities that can feed new forms of what we call containing diversity.

CONCLUSION

As this chapter has argued, there is a way in which the process we label containing diversity is not confined to particular leaders or particular times, but rather has resonance in Canadian history and its formation and evolution as a settler colony. However, as we also show, the specific dynamics animating the racialization and control of specific groups, alongside contradictory impulses exhibited between closure to threatening outsiders and openness to valued workers and citizens, differs. Although issues relating to security came to be heavily defined around "terrorism" in the 2000s, it is notable that since the start of the COVID-19 pandemic there has been a shift to a greater emphasis on health and the mitigation of disease. As we also illuminated in the chapter, this theme echoes much earlier emphases in Canadian immigration policy.

In subsequent chapters we address each of the key classes of immigration relating to Canada's current policy: refugees, economic, and family. We also consider temporary foreign workers. In these chapters we trace details of specific debates from 9/11 to the COVID-19 pandemic and illuminate recent policy turns and their possible implications. In our final three chapters, we will return to the discussions begun here on issues relating to multiculturalism and citizenship as well as the ethical debates over borders in light of Canada's foundation as a settler colony, reconciliation, and decolonization.

BIBLIOGRAPHY

Abu-Laban, Yasmeen. "The Political Economy of International Migration and the Canadian Example." In *International Political Economy*, edited by Greg Anderson and Christopher J. Kukucha, 476–91. Don Mills: Oxford University Press, 2016.

- "Recognition, Re-distribution and Solidarity: The Case of Multicultural Canada." In *Diversity and Contestations Over Nationalism in Europe and Canada*, edited by John Erik Fossum and Birte Siim, 237–61. London: Palgrave Studies in European Sociology, 2018.
Abu-Laban, Yasmeen, and Christina Gabriel. *Selling Diversity*: Immigration, Multiculturalism, Employment Equity, and Globalization. Peterborough, ON: Broadview Press, 2002.
Adamson, Fiona B., and Gesasimos Tsourapas. "The Migration State in the Global South: Nationalizing, Developmental and Neoliberal Models of Migration Management." *International Migration Review* 54, no. 3 (2020): 853–82.
Ann, Virginie. "Hate is Still Present: Quebec City Mosque Co-founder Reacts to London Attack." *Canadian Press* (June 8, 2021). https://globalnews.ca/news/7930597/quebec-city-mosque-london-attack-reaction/.
Arat-Koc, Sedef. "From 'Mothers of the Nation' to Migrant Workers." In *Not One of the Family: Foreign Domestic Workers in Canada*, edited by Daiva Stasiulis and Abigail Bakan, 53–79. Toronto: University of Toronto Press, 1997.
Austen, Ian. "The Indigenous Archeologist Tracking Down the Missing Residential Children." *The New York Times* (July 30, 2021). www.nytimes.com/2021/07/30/world/canada/Indigenous-archaeologist-graves-school-children.html.
Avery, Donald H. *Reluctant Host: Canada's Response to Immigrant Workers. 1896–1994*. Toronto: McClelland and Stewart, 1995.
Babad, Michael. "A Quiz for Joe Oliver: How Many Died Building the CPR?" *Globe and Mail* (January 10, 2012). www.theglobeandmail.com/report-on-business/top-business-stories/a-quiz-for-joe-oliver-how-many-died-building-cpr/article1357931/.
Boucher, Anna. *Gender, Migration and the Global Race for Talent*. Manchester: Manchester University Press, 2016.
Brodie, Janine. *Political Economy of Regionalism*. Toronto: Harcourt-Brace, 1990.
- "Three Stories of Canadian Citizenship." In *Contesting Canadian Citizenship*, edited by Robert Adamoski, Dorothy Chunn, and Robert Menzies, 43–66. Peterborough, ON: Broadview Press, 2002.
Calliste, Agnes. "Race, Gender and Candian Immigraton Policy: Blacks from the Caribbean, 1900–1932." *Journal of Canadian Studies*. 28, no. 4 (1993-4): 131–48.
Canada, Immigration, Refugees and Citizenship Canada. "Economic Mobility Pathways Project: Backgrounder." (June 18, 2021). www.canada.ca/en/immigration-refugees-citizenship/news/2021/06/economic-mobility-pathways-pilot.html.
Cecco, Leyland. "In Canada, World's Second Largest Ukrainian Diaspora Grieves Invasion." *The Guardian* (3 March 2022). https://www

.theguardian.com/world/2022/mar/03/canada-ukraine-diaspora-relief-efforts-russia-attack

Chadha, Ena. "'Mental Defectives': Not Welcome: Mental Disability in Canadian Immigration Law, 1859–1927." *Disability Studies Quarterly* 28, no. 1 (Winter 2008). https://dsq-sds.org/article/view/67/67.

Chesoi, Madalina, and Brendan Naef. "Primer on the *Global Compact on Refugees and the Global Compact for Safe, Orderly and Regular Migration*." Ottawa: Library of Parliament, May 30, 2019. (Publication No. 2019-21-E).

Chu, Sandra Ka Hon Chu. "Reparation as Narrative Resistance: Displacing Orientalism and Recoding Harm for Chinese Women of the Exclusion Era." *Canadian Journal of Women and Law* 18, no. 2 (2006): 387–438.

Citizenship and Immigration Canada (CIC). *Discover Canada: The Rights and Responsibilities of Citizenship*. Ottawa: CIC, 2012. www.canada.ca/content/dam/ircc/migration/ircc/english/pdf/pub/discover.pdf.

Cowen, Deborah. "Following the Infrastructures of Empire: Notes on Cities, Settler Colonialism, and Method." *Urban Geography* 41, no. 4 (2020): 469–86.

Dickason, Olive Patricia. "Canada When Europeans Arrived." In *The History of Immigration and Racism in Canada*, edited by Barrington Walker. Toronto: Canadian Scholars' Press, 2008; 17–26.

Dua, Ena. "Exclusion through Inclusion: Female Asian Migration in the Making of Canada as a White Settler Nation." *Gender, Place and Culture* 14, no. 4 (2007): 445–66.

Elliott, Josh K. "New Zealand Shooter Covered Weapons with Names of Andre Bissonnettee, Other Killers." *Global News* (March 18, 2019). https://globalnews.ca/news/5059136/christchurch-shooter-guns-names-new-zealand/.

Esses, Victoria, Jean McRae, Naomi Alboim, Natalya Brown, Chris Friesen, Lea Hamilton, Aurélie Lacassagne, Audre Macklin, and Margaret Walton-Roberts. *Supporting Canada's COVID-19 Resilience and Recovery through Robust Immigration Policy and Programs*. Ottawa: Royal Society of Canada, 2021.

Fernando, Shanti, and Jen Rinaldi. "Seeking Equity: Disrupting a History of Exclusionary Immigration Frameworks." *Canadian Ethnic Studies* 49, no. 3 (2017): 7–26.

Ferris, Elizabeth G., and Katharine M. Donato. *Refugees, Migration and Global Governance: Negotiating the Global Compacts*. London and New York: Routledge, 2020.

Fogarty, Clare. "Sanitation, Sanity, and (Moral) Suitability: The History of the Medical Inadmissibility of Immigrants into Canada" Commentary. *McGill Journal of Medicine* 18, no. 7 (2020). https://mjm.mcgill.ca/article/view/169.

Girard, Philip. "From Subversion to Liberation: Homosexuals and the Immigration Act 1952–1977." *Canadian Journal of Law and Society* 2 (1987): 1–87.

Go, Avvy. "Tracing Racism in COVID-19." *Active History* (June 22, 2021). http://activehistory.ca/2021/06/tracking-racism-in-covid-19/.

Guo, Shibao, and Hongxia Shan. "The Politics of Recognition: Critical Discourse Analysis of Recent PLAE Policies for Immigrant Professionals in Canada." *International Journal of Lifelong Education* 32, no. 4 (2013): 464–80.

Hanes, Roy. "None Is Still Too Many: A Historical Exploration of Canadian Immigration Legislation as It Pertains to People with Disabilities." *Developmental Disabilities Bulletin* 37, nos. 1–2 (2009): 91–126.

Horner, Dan. "A Population Takes Flight: The Irish Famine Migration in Boston, Montreal, and Liverpool, and the Politics of Marginalization and Criminalization." In *The Criminalization of Migration: Context and Consequences*, edited by Idil Atak and James C. Simeon, 257–79. Montreal-Kingston: McGill-Queens University Press, 2018.

Hyndman, Jennifer, and Johanna Reynolds. "Beyond the Global Compacts: Reimagining Protection." *Refuge* 36, no. 1 (2020): 66–74.

Immigration, Refugees and Citizenship Canada. *Annual Report to Parliament on Immigration.* 2018. www.canada.ca/en/immigration-refugees-citizenship/corporate/publications-manuals/annual-report-parliament-immigration-2018.html.

– *Annual Report to Parliament on Immigration.* 2020. www.canada.ca/content/dam/ircc/migration/ircc/english/pdf/pub/annual-report-2020-en.pdf.

Jhappan, Radha. "The 'New World': Legacies of European Colonialism in North America." In *Politics of North America: Redefining Continental Relations*, edited by Yasmeen Abu-Laban, Radha Jhappan, and Francois Rocher. Peterborough, ON: Broadview Press, 2008: 27–50.

Jones, Ryan Patrick. "Ottawa Opens New Pathway to Permanent Status for Temporary Essential Workers and Graduates." CBC News (April 14, 2021). www.cbc.ca/news/politics/pathway-permanent-residency-essential-workers-1.5987171.

Keil, Roger, and Harris Ali. "Multiculturalism, Racism and Infectious Disease in the Global City: The Experience of the 2003 SARS Outbreak in Toronto." *Topia: Canadian Journal of Cultural Studies* 16 (2006): 23–49.

Kelley, Ninette, and Michael Trebilcock. *The Making of the Mosaic: A History of Canadian Immigration Policy.* Toronto: University of Toronto Press, 1998.

Kinsman, Gary, and Patrizia Gentile. *The Canadian War on Queers: National Security as Sexual Regulation.* Vancouver: University of British Columbia Press, 2010.

Knowles, Valerie. *Strangers at Our Gate: Canadian Immigration Policy, 1540–1997.* Toronto: Dundurn Press, 1997.

– *Forging Our Legacy: Canadian Citizenship and Immigration 1900–1977.* Catalogue Ci51-93/2000E. Ottawa: Public Works and Government Services, 2000.

Koslowski, Rey. "Introduction to the Symposium on the Global Compact on Migration." *Newsletter of the American Political Science Association Section on Migration and Citizenship* 7, no. 2 (2020): 8–9.

Ladner, Kiera. "Rethinking Aboriginal Governance." In *Reinventing Canada. Politics of the 21st Century*, edited by Janine Brodie and Linda Trimble, 43–60. Toronto: Pearson Hall, 2003.

Larsson, Paula. "Anti-Asian Racism during Coronavirus: How the Language of Disease Produces Hate and Violence." *The Conversation* (March 31, 2020). https://theconversation.com/anti-asian-racism-during-coronavirus-how-the-language-of-disease-produces-hate-and-violence-134496.

Mackenzie King, William Lyon. Statement of the Prime Minister as to Immigration. May 1, 1947. The Linked Parliamentary Data Project. www.lipad.ca/full/1947/05/01/1/.

Milner, James. "Canada and the UN Global Compact on Refugees: A Case Study of Influence in the Global Refugee Regime." In *International Affairs and Canadian Migration Policy*, edited by Yiagadessen Samy and Howard Duncan, 41–63. (Canada Among Nations 2019). Cham: Palgrave MacMillan, 2021.

Molinaro, Dennis. *Deportation from Canada*. Ottawa: The Canadian Historical Association, Immigration and Ethnicity in Canada Series No. 36. 2018.

Øvelid, Veronica. "Is the Welcome to Ukrainian Refugees Unusually Generous or Racist?." *The Conversation* (16 March 2022). https://theconversation.com/is-the-welcome-to-ukrainian-refugees-unusually-generous-or-overtly-racist-178819

Papademetriou, Demetrios G., and Madeleine Sumption. *Rethinking Points Systems and Employer Selected Immigration*. Washington, DC: Migration Policy Institute, 2011.

Pellerin, Hélène. "Indigenous Peoples in Canadian Migration Narratives: A Story of Marginalization." *Aboriginal Policy Studies* 8, no. 1 (2019): 3–24.

Pier 21. "Gentlemen's Agreement 1908." https://pier21.ca/research/immigration-history/gentlemens-agreement-1908.

Ragazzi, Francesco. "Suspect Community or Suspect Category: The Impact of Counter-Terrorism as 'Policed Multiculturalism.'" *Journal of Ethnic and Migration Studies* 42, no. 5 (2016): 724–41.

Reitz, Jeffrey G., Josh Curtis, and Jennifer Elrick. "Immigrant Skill Utilization: Trends and Policy Issues." *Journal of International Migration and Integration* 15, no. 1 (2014): 1–26.

Satzewich, Vic. "The Canadian State and the Racialization of Caribbean Migrant Farm Labour 1947–1966." *Ethnic and Racial Studies* 11, no. 3 (1988): 282–304.

Shachar, Ayelet. "The Race for Talent: Highly Skilled Migrants and Competitive Immigration Regimes." *New York University Law Review* 81, no. 1 (2006): 148–206.

Sharma, Nandita. "Citizenship and Borders." In *Power and Everyday Practice*, edited by Deborah R. Brock, Rebecca Raby, Mark P. Thomas, and Aryn E. Martin, 234–55. Toronto: University of Toronto Press, 2019.

Shepard, R. Bruce. "Diplomatic Racism Canadian Government and Black Migration from Oklahoma, 1905–1912." *Great Plains Quarterly* No. 1 (Winter 1983): 5–16.

Stasiulis, Daiva, and Radha Jhappan. "The Fractious Politics of a Settler Society: Canada." In *Unsettling Setter Societies: Articulations of Gender, Race, Ethnicity and Class*, edited by Daiva Stasiulis and Nira Yuval Davis, 95–131. London: Sage, 1995.

Statistics Canada. "150 Years of Immigration in Canada." *The Daily* (2018) www150.statcan.gc.ca/n1/pub/11-630-x/11-630-x2016006-eng.htm.

Triadafilopoulos, Triadafilos. "Dismantling White Canada: Race, Rights, and the Origins of the Points System." In *Wanted and Welcome*, edited by Triadafilos Triadafilopoulos, 15–37. New York: Springer, 2013.

United Nations General Assembly. "Resolution Adopted by the General Assembly on 19 September 2016 (New York Declaration for Refugees and Migrants). A/RES/71/1. https://documents-dds-ny.un.org/doc/UNDOC/GEN/N16/291/97/PDF/N1629197.pdf?OpenElement.

United Nations High Commissioner for Refugees (UNHCR). *Global Trends: Forced Displacement in 2015*. UNHCR, 2016. www.unhcr.org/576408cd7.

Valverde, Mariana. *The Age of Light, Soap, and Water: Moral Reform in English Canada, 1885–1925*. Toronto: University of Toronto Press, 2008.

Vineberg, Robert. *Responding to Immigrants' Settlement Needs: The Canadian Experience*. Netherlands: Springer, 2012.

– "Healthy Enough to Get in: The Evolution of Canadian Immigration Policy Related to Immigrant Health." *International Migration and Integration* 16 (2015): 279–97.

Walsh, James. "From Nations of Immigrants to States of Transience: Temporary Migration in Canada and Australia." *International Sociology* 29 no. 6 (2014): 584–606.

Whitaker, Reg. *Canadian Immigration Policy Since Confederation*. Ottawa: Canadian Historical Association, 1991.

Wright, Cynthia. "The Museum of Illegal Immigration: Historical Perspectives on the Production of Non-Citizens and Challenges to Immigration Controls." In *Producing and Negotiating Non-Citizenship. Precarious Legal Status in Canada*, edited by Luin Goldring and Patricia Landolt, 31–54. Toronto: University of Toronto Press, 2013.

Zeidler, Maryse. "New Poll Reveals Chinese-Canadians Experiences with Racism." CBC News (June 22, 2020). www.cbc.ca/news/canada/british-columbia/new-poll-reveals-chinese-canadians-experiences-with-racism-1.5621261.

PART II

CHAPTER THREE

Controlling "Global Citizens": Refugees, International Obligations, and Security

To illustrate the frontlines of the containing of diversity, in this chapter we examine policy responses to refugees in Canada. As noted in chapter two, the humanitarian stream (made up largely of refugees) form a small component of Canada's annual immigration intake; however, they are particularly relevant for illuminating the contours of containing diversity over the 2000s. Our analysis demonstrates the growing attention paid by governments to security and threat following the September 11, 2001, attacks in New York and Washington as well as the impact of neoliberal cuts and exclusionary rationales in the two decades under examination. In analysing refugee policy as a harbinger of contemporary forms of containing diversity, we pay special attention to the implications of detention/deportation practices, the US-Canada safe third-country provisions and other measures to control the flow and selection of refugees. As we detail, Canada's policy responses effectively sidestep the spirit of the legal principles and obligations flowing from the 1951 *United Nations Convention Relating to the Status of Refugees* and the 1967 *Protocol*. Specifically, we call attention to the government's valorization of exclusionary practices through discourses of state sovereignty, state security, as wel as public health responses in the wake of the COVID-19 pandemic.

"Refugees" are typically distinguished from other migrants because they have been forced to flee from their home country and cannot safely return to the state they may hold citizenship in.

People who are forced to flee but remain within their home country are referred to as "internally displaced people." Some refugees may be legally stateless, a situation many Palestinian refugees are in. However, not all stateless people are refugees, just as not all refugees are stateless. Refugees who seek protection in another country are referred to as "asylum seekers" in many parts of the world, although in Canada the term of choice has been "refugee claimants." In Canada, refugee claimants go through a process of determination regarding their status. This involves decision-making from the Immigration and Refugee Board, and studies have shown that such decisions, as well as appeals, can at times be highly dependent on who is deciding them rather than the legal merits of a claim (Rehaag 2012). A successful claimant may potentially be offered a permanent new home, becoming a "resettled refugee." Additionally, refugees may be referred to Canada from abroad by the United Nations High Commissioner for Refugees, and a Canadian visa officer determines eligibility and admissions.

As we discuss further, the legal definition of a refugee that Canada and many other countries employ has been derived from the 1951 United Nations *Convention Relating to the Status of Refugees*, and those who meet the definition are referred to as "Convention refugees." However, it can be noted that before this Convention came into force, the United Nations also played a role in providing an operational definition of "Palestine refugees" stemming from the violent events that led Palestinian Arabs to flee Palestine (then under a British mandate) prior to the creation of Israel in 1948 (Abu-Laban 2021).

Theorizing the unique situation of refugees fleeing across national borders, it has been argued that they are the archetypical "global citizens" in so far as they draw attention to both rights and obligations at the global level (Hassner 1998). Bearing this in mind, this chapter considers issues of rights, and we are also interested in highlighting the ethical issues that surround obligations to refugees, which require consideration of normative or ethical principles in both public and policymaking discussions. Drawing from the work of liberal and non-liberal political philosophers, we outline the case for a feminist ethic of care: both as a moral orientation in its own right, as well as an underexamined lens from which to critique how the contemporary refugee regime works to exclude refugees from entering liberal states.

The contemporary context is one that is especially stark when it comes to refugees. Imploring countries of the world to respond, in 2014 then United Nations High Commissioner for Refugees (UNHCR) António Guterres described the rapidly increasing numbers of refugees from Iraq and Syria as a "mega crisis" (Morello 2014). Since that time, Guterres went on to become UN secretary-general, and the numbers of refugees worldwide further increased. In their annual reporting for the year 2018, the UNHCR indicated 70.8 million forcibly displaced people worldwide, of which 25.9 million were refugees living outside their country of origin, 41.3 million were internally displaced within their country of origin, and 3.5 million were asylum seekers in a third country (UNHCR 2019, 2). Of the 25.9 million refugees living outside their country of origin, 20.4 million fell under the mandate of the UNHCR, with two-thirds of them coming from five countries in the developing world: Syria (6.7 million), Afghanistan (2.7 million), South Sudan (2.3 million), Myanmar (1.1 million), and Somalia (0.9 million) (UNHCR 2019, 3). An additional 5.5 million Palestinian refugees fall under the mandate of a different UN organization, the United Nations Relief and Works Agency (UNRWA). UNRWA was created one year before UNHCR, and operates in five areas – Jordan, Lebanon, Syria, West Bank, and Gaza. UNRWA provides services and relief to "Palestine refugees," the term given to those Palestinian refugees who are registered with the organization (see Abu-Laban 2021).

We know from a special online data portal set up by UNHCR that within the first five weeks of the Russia–Ukraine war, which began in February 2022, more than four million refugees fled Ukraine to neighbouring countries, with still many more becoming internally displaced (UNHCR 2022). In the case of refugees fleeing horrible violence in Ukraine, the Trudeau government's response marked a departure by allowing for an unlimited number of Ukrainian nationals (though not nationals from other countries) to apply to Canada to stay for at least two years as they assess their future. While this approach drew support from Ukrainian-Canadians and refugee supporting groups, it did also raise questions about whether and how permanent pathways to Canadian citizenship might eventually be offered (Garnier, Lieu, and Labman 2022). It was an approach that also contrasted with that towards Syrian refugees in its rapidity, as well as the way by which their plight registered with the Canadian public and in policy.

In the case of Syrian refugees, it took a photo of a dead child to humanize the numbers and raise profound moral questions. It was the image of a lifeless Alan Kurdi, a three-year-old Syrian boy who drowned trying to reach the shores of the Greek island of Kos with his family in September 2015, that seemed to resonate with the global public and draw firm attention to the inadequacy of the responses of wealthy states to refugees fleeing for safety (Edwards and King 2015). The photographer who captured the chilling image of young Alan called it a "silent scream" (Virtue 2015). But it was Alan's Canadian aunt, Tima Kurdi, who gave the image voice in the media interviews that followed. Recounting her own bureaucratic difficulties in getting family members who fled Syria to safety in Canada, she beseeched the world to "step in and help the refugees" (quoted in Edwards and King 2015). As legal scholar Audrey Macklin poignantly noted in an op-ed in the *New York Times*, "the moral distance between Syrian refugees and Canada evaporated with the revelation that Alan Kurdi's Canadian aunt made an urgent and futile application to sponsor family members to Canada" (Macklin 2015).

It was also in this exact period that major Canadian newspapers shifted their coverage from stories addressing Syrian refugees in relation to an external conflict with little bearing on Canada, to one that had implications for Canadians within a tradition of resettlement of refugees (Wallace 2018). The sluggish response of the Harper Conservative government to Syrian refugees was beset by unusual practices which fed into the idea that they posed a threat to Canada, especially if they were Muslim. In 2014–15, the Harper Conservatives made culturalist arguments that seemed to favour refugees from Syria who were "religious minorities," i.e., non-Muslims, likely Christians. In the name of security, the Conservatives also required that Syrian refugees referred by UNHCR be vetted by the Prime Minister's Office (PMO), as opposed to the normal vetting practice by Canadian immigration officials. This unusual move prompted accusations that the PMO was actually vetting "cultural" suitability and propensity to support the Conservatives (Martin 2015). This led the former head of the Canadian Arab Institute, Raja Khouri, to decry both the limited numbers of refugees from Syria actually making it to Canada and the discriminatory criteria for prioritizing. In his words:

> Worse [than the low numbers arriving], the government now inexplicably wants to prioritize any Syrian refugees it relocates based on

their being from a religious minority, instead of based on need. The UNHCR follows a thorough process to prioritize the most vulnerable, including women and children at risk, survivors of violence or torture, refugees with medical needs or disabilities, and those at risk due to sexual orientation, among other factors. Agency policy requires resettlement programs to be needs-based and non-discriminatory. (Khouri 2014)

In combination with the questions raised by the Kurdi image, Stephen Harper's highly unusual and direct intervention in vetting Syrian refugees became a new issue of partisan division and electoral debate (*Guardian* 2015). When Liberal leader Justin Trudeau won the 2015 election, he did so by pledging to bring in 25,000 Syrian refugees in short order, a promise he made good on between November 2015 and February 2016.

Many scholars and Canadians themselves see Canada as having a long and proud tradition of welcoming refugees. Indeed, the United Empire Loyalists are frequently upheld as Canada's first major wave of refugees (see Dirks 1977). Canadians now widely condemn the xenophobic and anti-Semitic responses that conditioned a "none is too many" rejection of Jewish refugees fleeing Nazi persecution during the Second World War (Abella and Troper 1982). This condemnation is also reflected in the 2010 decision of the federal government to fund a monument entitled "The Wheel of Conscience" at Halifax's Pier 21, home to the Canadian Museum of Immigration, under the auspices of the Harper government's Community Historical Recognition Programme. The monument reflects on Canada's historic response to Jewish refugees fleeing Nazi violence who arrived on the ship M.S. *St. Louis*. These refugees were denied entry to Canada and ultimately turned back, many to death camps. In contrast to this historic example, Canada's subsequent resettlement of refugees is readily pointed to as exemplifying a tradition of welcoming refugees. This tradition includes, for example, the resettlement of approximately 37,000 Hungarians in 1956, 11,000 Czechs in 1968, 7,000 fleeing Uganda in 1972, 7,000 from Chile in 1973, 60,000 Vietnamese between 1978 and 1980, and 5,000 Kosovars in 1999 (Macklin 2015).

Indeed, in 1986, Canada was the first *country* to be awarded the United Nations Nansen Medal, established by the UNHCR in 1954 and named in honour of Norwegian Nobel laureate Fridtjof Nansen, who served as the first high commissioner for refugees under the

League of Nations, the forerunner to the United Nations. This annual award is given to an individual, organization, or group in recognition of extraordinary service to refugees. The award was given to the people of Canada in 1986 in recognition of Canada's innovative system of private sponsorship involving the Canadian public, along with the role played by various levels of government in supporting Indochinese refugees in the late 1970s (Molloy et al. 2017, 3–4). Canada's system of private sponsorship that was pioneered in the 1970s is still in operation today (see Labman and Cameron 2020). Under current rules, eligible refugees may find initial support through sponsorship, usually of a year, by organizations like churches and mosques or groups of five or more Canadians. Alternatively, refugees may be solely sponsored by the government, and in some cases both government and private sources will sponsor. While the Canadian government may admit refugees from abroad, as noted, claims for asylum can also be made upon entering Canada. Canada was also the first country in the world to develop guidelines relating to gender-based persecution of refugees in 1993.

While this tradition of welcoming and openness resonates with Canadian popular discourse, in this chapter we argue for a different perspective grounded in recent immigration trends. Since 2002, Canadian policy responses to refugees have also exemplified in the rawest form an exclusionary and racialized immigration trend that we identify as "containing diversity." Refugees, we suggest, have served as the harbinger of sweeping immigration controls fortified by neoliberalism and criminalization and justified by rationales that reinforce racialized exclusion. In other words, exclusionary refugee controls have, in different ways, extended past the category of refugees on to other groups of newcomers.

In the first part of the chapter, we analyse the United Nations legal framework that has evolved in relation to refugees, along with the normative insights of select political philosophers. In the second part of the chapter we examine "safe third country" agreements in Europe and North America. Taking the case of Canada, we illustrate how this agreement has dramatically reduced refugee claims. The chapter ends with a discussion of the value of a normative lens and illustrates how a feminist ethic of care offers an alternative to containing diversity.

PART ONE: INTERNATIONAL LAW, POLITICAL THEORY, AND REFUGEES

Writing of the period between the First and Second World Wars, Hannah Arendt poignantly highlighted the connection between states and rights, and in the process raised questions about the inalienability of human rights as understood in the UN's 1948 Universal Declaration of Human Rights. As she famously put it, a person's "right to have rights" is contingent on political community, and more specifically on one's membership in a state (Arendt [1951] 2004). The decades following the Universal Declaration saw the emergence of a strong human rights discourse and international agreements, including ones addressing the rights of migrants (Soysal 1994). Tellingly, however, the right to emigrate (leave a country) was not accompanied by its corollary, the right to immigrate (enter a country), even in the Universal Declaration (Benhabib 2004, 11; Pécoude and de Buchteneire 2009). Thus, the centrality of the state persists, particularly when it comes to the exercise of mobility rights. This is also seen within academic and popular discussions of globalization since the 1990s, which retain nation-states as the basic organizing unit (Held et al. 1999), as well as in the twenty-first century, where states continue to decide whom to include or exclude from the territories they claim sovereignty over. The fact that the state remains central to the reception of immigrants is also perhaps why social analysts continue to find the nation-state concept so critical to understanding immigration (Wimmer and Schiller 2002).

Refugees form an especially compelling case for understanding rights and responsibilities at a global level (Hassner 1998; Nyers 2006). The United Nations has played a critical role in legally defining who is entitled to asylum and by extension the legal responsibility of states. Two important agreements are the 1951 United Nations Convention Relating to the Status of Refugees, which focused on European refugees from before the year 1951, and the 1967 Protocol, which removed all geographic and temporal restrictions in discussing refugees. Through the former Convention, as amended by the latter Protocol, a refugee is defined as someone who is outside his or her country and unable or unwilling to return "owing to a well-founded fear of being persecuted for reasons of race, religion, nationality, membership of a particular social group or political opinion" (UNHCR 2010, 14).

As of 2015, 142 countries, including Canada, were parties to both the 1951 Convention and the 1967 Protocol and were expected to work with the UNHCR in ensuring that the rights of refugees were protected. The UNHCR definition of a refugee has also been important in legal jurisprudence (Dauvergne 2016, 47–50). For instance, both Canada and the United States have incorporated this definition of refugee into their domestic laws and therefore have agreed to the principle of *non-refoulement*, where a refugee will not be returned to a country where his or her life or freedom is in danger (Macklin 2003, 1). Yet, the fact remains that the spirit of the Convention and Protocol can be easily evaded by states. In addition to the uncertainty of Convention rights being protected, it is also possible for refugees, or other groups like those whose births are not registered, to be stateless without citizenship anywhere. All these realities recall the concerns of Arendt about the unevenness of the right to have rights.

When combined, the uncertainty of rights and the possibility of statelessness suggests the need not only for a legal framework but also a moral frame of reference to guide human action in the twenty-first century. By a moral framework, we mean a frame of reference that is based on considerations of justice, not simply of utilitarianism. In chapter eight we take up in greater depth the question of whether there should be states and borders. This question has engaged scholars from many traditions and has come to involve Indigenous thinkers concerned with settler colonialism. Suffice it to say here, however, that traditionally much of the normative debate over immigration was understood as a tension between communitarianism and the right to exclude others in the name of the community on the one hand (see Walzer 1998; and at the extreme, Masters 2001) and liberalism and the call for (semi-)open borders on the other hand (see Carens 1998; 2013). Yet framing the debate as between communitarians and liberals does not fully capture the range of approaches, which we would characterize more broadly as reflecting a tension between universalism (all people being treated the same) and particularism (some people being more equal than others). One example of this universalism–particularism tension can be seen in the debates between nationalism and cosmopolitanism that emerged in the 1990s (see, for example, Kymlicka and Walker 2012). Benhabib's (2004) contribution, *The Rights of Others: Aliens, Residents and Citizens*, for instance, calls for moral universalism and cosmopolitan federalism as an alternative to (particular) nationalism, echoing Immanuel Kant (Benhabib 2004, 220–1).

Limiting the ethical debates about immigration to a struggle between communitarianism and liberalism likewise fails to capture how universalism may be approached outside the liberal tradition. For example, universalist perspectives on migration have been addressed from the standpoint of Marxist (Brown 1992; Castles and Kosack 1973) and natural law scholars (Dummett 1992). With the latter, a particularly important component of natural rights stems from religious insights, such as those based on contemporary Catholic social thought (O'Neill and Spohn 1998). Such perspectives are important given the role of religious organizations in advocating for refugees.

In addition to taking seriously the range of ethical frameworks, our purpose here is also to bring forward a feminist ethic of care as an equally valuable ethical framework for migration (Abu-Laban 2012). Much contemporary work on the ethics of care stresses the importance of care in relation to individual and collective moral obligations, and in relation to human interdependence (Engster 2005; Hankivsky 2004; Sevenhuijsen 1998). In addition to offering an ethical orientation, a feminist ethic of care might suggest the value of being attuned to gender and to care, and therefore provides another means to critically assess government responses (Hankivsky 2004, 2).

By cutting across these traditions and adding care ethics into the mix, we have identified three emergent themes that can guide a more principled response to immigration, specifically in the treatment of refugees (Abu-Laban 2012). First, given that a feminist ethic of care recognizes that humans are interdependent, this renders problematic the communitarian logic of reducing claims to discrete bounded communities. In fact, a care ethic encourages the reshaping of obligations at local, state, and even global levels (Robinson 2005). This sensitivity to the global level may potentially be in keeping with cosmopolitanism (Benhabib 2004), but it does not rule out attention to other levels, including in relationships of care.

A second theme involves attention to gender, which is a hallmark of the ethic of care, along with intersectional approaches. A gender-based, intersectional analysis illuminates how refugees who are the most mobile – and thus able to make claims – tend to be relatively advantaged males (Hyndman 1999; Valji et al. 2003). Thus, policy prescriptions need to address not only rights but also the vulnerability of marginalized groups, including refugee women and children, among others. Marginalized groups are typically hampered in their ability to exercise rights. More broadly, a critical ethic of care perspective examines global inequity produced by the capitalist system – a feature highlighted in Marxist accounts. Finally, the care tradition asserts an ethical obligation to care: a feature that shares some scope with notions of humanitarianism, which also involves the liberal tradition.

Third, the framework of liberalism highlights states' special obligation to refugees, not only for humanitarian reasons or for reasons of rights but also because states themselves are directly involved in the production of refugees. In other words, the state system itself creates refugees and hence preserving the state system requires an ethical response to refugees (Carens 1991; 2013, 195–6). Arguably, the state system may be viewed by some as worthy of preservation since rights may be seen to stem from the state. Yet, as we show in our discussion of refugee policies in Canada and other Western states, the spirit of the Convention and Protocol have not only been evaded at times by states, but there has also been a sidestepping of other, normative principles by states. These sidestepped principles are drawn from normative traditions such as the obligation to care, attention to gender and difference in policymaking, and the unique obligations of states to refugees given that states produce refugees. When this evasion of moral obligations happens, the assertion of state sovereignty and security is often used to justify exclusionary practices, that is, actions rationalized in the name of protecting national security, public health, public order, or the law. Such exclusionary practices are evident in the growing number of safe third-country agreements between countries of the West, which work to deny refugees from being able to make claims if they arrive from a country deemed "safe," and in the general transformation of the post–Second World War refugee regime into a regime of non-entry in the post–Cold War period.

PART TWO: THE REGIME OF NON-ENTRY AND THE CASE OF NORTH AMERICA

Canada and the United States have foundational histories as "countries of immigration" and, notwithstanding COVID-19 travel bans and border closures in the wake of the 2020 pandemic, both countries still seek immigrants. Recent developments, however, suggest that policymaking is becoming more bilateral rather than strictly national. In particular, the bilateral US and Canada Smart Border Declaration was issued in December 2001, during the aftermath of the September 11 attacks. This now landmark thirty-point plan has been trumpeted by Canada as foundational to facilitating by 2014 approximately one million dollars every minute in trade across the US–Canada border (Government of Canada 2014). The Declaration set in motion joint management of the border through enhanced cooperation in areas such as refugee determination, visa policies, the sharing of passenger information, and an immigration database. The impact of this accord should not be underestimated for understanding the evolving relationship between Canada and the United States. It illustrates how the two countries have grown closer after the 1994 North American Free Trade Agreement (NAFTA) went into effect, an agreement also involving Mexico.[1]

When it comes to historical shifts in Canada's response to refugees, the era of the Cold War (roughly 1946–91) elicited a distinctive response from Western states as compared to the post–Cold War period. The offering of asylum took on a different political meaning before and after 1991. A core component of the international refugee regime is the 1951 UN Convention, which emerged from the context of the forty million Europeans displaced after the Second World War, as well as the Cold War. During the Cold War period, offering asylum to those fleeing Communist persecution served to boost the propaganda arsenal of the liberal-democratic advanced capitalist countries of West over the Soviet bloc (Castles 2002, 178). However, as refugees increased from countries of the Global South, particularly once the Cold War ended, the response of Western states altered. Since the collapse of the Soviet Union in 1991, the refugee regime of the Global North "shifted from a system designed to welcome Cold War refugees from the East and to resettle them as permanent exiles in new homes to a 'non-entrée regime' designed to exclude and control asylum seekers from the South" (Castles 2002, 181).

The non-entry refugee regime, we would suggest, in effect works to exclude or control movement of predominantly non-white refugees from entering the West. Indeed, today's refugees primarily come from countries in the developing world, and as noted in chapter one, refugees are likewise more likely to reside in countries of the developing world. In 2018, the majority of refugees (78 per cent) were in protracted situations as defined by UNHCR, meaning they had been in exile for at least five years, and oftentimes longer (UNHCR 2019, 22). As noted in chapter two, it remains to be seen whether the United Nations Global Compact on Refugees can achieve its promise of greater solidarity with, and more equitable responsiveness to, refugees (UNHCR 2019, 17).

As it stands, however, the non-entry regime has been justified by states in the Global North through a discursive shift wherein refugees are "securitized" (Buzan et al. 1998). As Aiken describes: "the refugee has been reconceived as the 'bogus asylum seeker,' illegal migrant, and even worse, criminal or terrorist" (2001, 9). Of course, the securitization of refugees has roots that can be traced back prior to September 11, 2001. In particular, the discourse around "international terrorism" came to the fore in American policies in the 1980s, often associated with countries of the Middle East seen to be tied to the Soviet bloc/Cold War (Abu-Laban and Bakan 2011). It was also in this context that terrorism became a consideration in the treatment accorded to non-citizens in immigration and refugee discussions and policies (Abu-Laban and Bakan 2011). For example, in the 1980s, Canadian politicians began talking about refugees as a potential security threat, although the linkage has been heightened between terrorism and migration since the events of September 11, 2001, including the migration of refugees. Indeed, after 9/11, in the name of combating terrorism, even greater focus has been placed by countries of the West on non-citizens, including refugees (Abu-Laban 2004; Abu-Laban and Bakan 2011; Bigo 2005; Van Selm 2005).

The non-entry regime is also backed by an arsenal of policies. In fact, there are widespread and creative ways in which Western states have worked to prevent refugees from even being able to make rights claims at all. The plethora of measures taken which work to deny rights claims by refugees has led Gibney (2004, 152) to refer to "a thousand little Guantanamos," alluding to the infamous US detention centre which represents a space in which the law offers no recourse to rights abuses. One example of this provided by Gibney is evidenced in Switzerland, France, Germany, and Spain declaring parts of domestic airports an "international" zone strictly off limits to asylum claims (Gibney 2004, 150).

The numerous policies which animate the non-entry regime are both domestic and international. Along with the Global North, countries of the South have increasingly fortified and patrolled borders (Aiken 2001, 9), as have non-EU countries like Ukraine and Russia, which for different reasons sought good relations with the European Union (Zhyznomirska 2008; 2011). In addition to the erection of fences and the fortification of borders which has produced a "wall around the West" (Andreas and Snyder 2000), the spirit of the Convention and Protocol have increasingly been sidestepped through other policy measures. This includes the selective use of visa requirements, which serve to bifurcate the experience of citizens from countries of the North – who typically do not need them – with those of the South, who do (Salter 2003, 2). For example, between 2009 and 2016 Canada imposed visa requirements on Mexican visitors in a concerted effort to reduce the number of refugee claimants from Mexico (Bell 2018). They also include increased use of detention, or what Alison Mountz (2020) has called the death of asylum. Detention amounts to prison, and in the case of Canada, legal scholars have noted how problematic it is that Canada has no time limits on this when it comes to detaining refugee claimants (Arbel and Davis 2018). Sidestepping also includes governments' use of restrictive policy concepts in regional agreements, among which policymakers in the EU have taken the lead (Hentges 2002, 118). Restrictive policy concepts include terms suggesting that there are states that do not engage in persecution, such as "non-persecuting state" or "safe country of origin." A related concept is that states can be deemed safe with respect to the practice of returning an asylum seeker, or "safe third country."

The safe third country principle, for example, has been incorporated into EU law (Soennecken 2014, 108). This principle suggests that an asylum claim may be viewed as inadmissible if the claimant arrives via another country deemed to respect refugee rights (a safe third country). The practice has been controversial because it may risk access to asylum claims and violate *non-refoulement* according to both the UNHCR and refugee scholars (Cortinovis 2018, 9). In 2016 both EU and Turkish officials agreed that Greece, an EU member state, could refuse to accept an asylum claim for individuals crossing from Turkey – deemed a safe third country – to Greek islands. Such individuals would be found to be irregular migrants and removed back to Turkey, despite evidence of political instability and human rights abuses in Turkey. Indeed, critics have raised important questions about whether Turkey is actually "safe" for refugees (Cortinovis 2018, 8). A similar issue has emerged in relation to the Safe Third Country Agreement between Canada and the United States, which we discuss below as part of our analysis of North American regional agreements.

It should, however, be noted that, when compared to North America, the case of Europe is distinct. Deepening regionalism over the 1980s and 1990s brought with it the call not only for the free movement of goods, capital, and services but also for people. The free movement of people, meaning nationals of EU member states, was backed by a rights framework evident in the passage of the Maastricht Treaty in 1993. Maastricht ushered the "European citizen" into being; a EU citizen was to be able to move, live, study, work, or retire in any EU country of their choice. The free movement of people necessitated opening internal borders to the flow of people. This led, perhaps paradoxically, to the fortification of external EU borders through the 1990 Schengen Convention. During this period, attention also came to centre on refugees. The 1990 Dublin Convention, which came into force in 1997, created criteria for determining the country in which a refugee had to make their claim, generally the country where they first arrived. Legislators justified this provision by claiming it prevents so-called asylum shopping. But in reality, the provision has allowed EU countries to potentially circumvent the UN Convention and Protocol (Hentges 2002, 118). As van Selm (2005) notes of the EU Dublin Convention and its successor the Dublin Regulation:

> States see a need to prevent 'asylum shopping' – the suggestion that some individuals may try to seek protection either in the state in which they believe they are most likely to be granted it, or in the state which is most generous in welfare benefits, for example, or in

multiple states – playing the system to see which one offers the best deal. These assumptions about potential refugee behaviour undermine the very notion that protection is the same everywhere – and also demonstrate that governments seem to presume that asylum seekers generally are seeking a better life and not safety. (21)

Indeed, it is striking how refugee legislation, and the debates they engender, seldom make central issues of safety and security from the vantagepoint of refugees themselves.

Ultimately, the impact of European integration and the Dublin Convention was to bolster the refugee regime of non-entry. Numbers of asylum seekers admitted to EU member states dropped steadily during this time (Bhabha 1999, 18). According to UNHCR statistics, the number of asylum seekers arriving in the EU halved from 1992 to fewer than 400,000 a year by the early years of the twenty-first century (Commission of the European Communities [CEC] 2002). By 2012, there was a total of 335,895 asylum applications to the EU, despite the EU's growth to twenty-seven countries (CEC 2014). It was against this backdrop that the total number of people forcibly displaced reached 51.2 million in 2014, described then as "the largest humanitarian crisis" since the end of the Second World War. About 16.7 million of those forcibly displaced were defined by the UN as refugees, with the remaining numbers comprising people internally displaced as a result of conflict within their countries of origin (Migration Policy Institute 2014).

In response to the humanitarian crisis and growing number of refugees, some EU countries have been relatively generous with respect to asylum seekers, such as Germany under the Christian Democratic Party led by former Chancellor Angela Merkel. Other EU countries have been less so. Prime Minister Victor Orbán of Hungary, for example, has engaged in xenophobic populist rhetoric and amplified efforts at detaining of refugees. Hungary, along with Poland and the Czech Republic, were also found by the European Court of Justice in 2020 to have failed in their obligations as EU member states to take in refugees in order to distribute them more evenly within the EU (BBC News 2020). This was when refugees were largely from outside Europe, in fact Poland, and to a lesser extent Hungary, officially welcomed Ukrainian refugees in 2022.

As has been suggested, border control, discursive and policy shifts, and the idea of a safe third country characterize general international developments, including in the European Union. As we will show, these find echoes in the case of North America, and the budding refugee regime that emerged in the wake of September 11.

Fortress (North) America: Smart Borders and the Safe Third Country Agreement

Although Canada and the United States are not party to an arrangement quite like what has developed in the continent of Europe, the two countries became increasingly close as a result of the 1989 Canada–US Free Trade Agreement. The tenets of this agreement were subsequently expanded to include Mexico with the North American Free Trade Agreement (NAFTA) in 1994. NAFTA ushered in a new phase of continental economic integration between Mexico, the United States, and Canada. In 2014, on the twentieth anniversary of the agreement, it was clear that trade had accelerated between the NAFTA partners, with Canada established as the largest trade partner of the United States, and Mexico the third largest (Villarreal and Fergusson 2014, 2). For both Canada and Mexico, the United States is their most important trade partner (Andreas 2003, 12). However, in contrast to the EU's creation of regional political institutions, national governments in North America exist in an asymmetrical relationship with one another; one that is increasingly shaped by constitution-like restrictions. Moreover, unlike the greater mobility of EU citizens that accompanied the free movement of goods, capital, and services in Europe, this has not been the case in North America. In fact, border controls grew dramatically between the United States and Mexico from the time NAFTA was passed. America's border controls were in part a response to the politicization of so-called illegal immigrants from Mexico. The term is problematic since only actions (not people) can be illegal and also because major sectors of the US economy continue to exert a demand for migrant labour, irregular or not (Abu-Laban 2005). It can further be observed that irregular migrants provide business with an especially exploitable pool of cheap labour. After the inauguration of President Donald Trump in 2017, his call for "the wall" became a striking image suggestive of unchecked migration across America's southern border. But in fact, in 2018 Mexicans comprised only 26 per cent of all US immigrants, down from 30 per cent in 2000. The emigration rate from

Mexico had likewise been fairly steadily low since the recession of 2009 (Zong et al. 2018, 8–9). Moreover, apprehension rates of unauthorized immigrants at the border were lower in 2015–16 than in the late 2000s, with Mexican nationals constituting about half (Zong et al. 2018, 21–2).

In contrast to the US–Mexico relationship, citizens of Canada and the United States have traditionally enjoyed visa-free travel between the two countries, marked as they were by the "world's longest undefended border." This openness was challenged with the attacks on September 11, 2001. This is because of the empirically faulty, yet politically salient, construction of Canada's immigrant population as presenting a security risk to the United States in the form of terrorism. This construction relies on racialization: those that are, or are perceived to be, Muslim and/or Arab are targeted by state immigration and security personnel (Abu-Laban 2004; 2005). More recently, the openness between Canada and the United States was challenged by Canada's response to the COVID-19 pandemic. In March 2020, Prime Minister Trudeau announced the suspension of all non-essential inbound travel to Canada, with the exception of the traffic of goods carried by truckers from the United States to Canada and for select people, such as seasonal workers from countries like Mexico who were needed in areas of agriculture (Macklin 2020).

Debates following the September 11 attacks oscillated between creating a "fortress America," understood as a unilateral fortification of US border controls, or whether the "Europeanization" of border controls akin to the EU's *Schengen* arrangement should occur between NAFTA countries, or at the very least between Canada and the United States (Andreas 2003, 14–15). Neither image, however, fully captures what actually happened. Following September 11, "smart borders" were embraced through bilateral agreements between the United States and Canada and between the United States and Mexico. Smart borders are enabled by "adding personnel, detection equipment and getting advance information in automated form to risk manage who you question and what you inspect" (Bonner 2003, 4–5). Less glossily, smart borders may be seen as part and parcel of a trend towards intensified regional as well as global surveillance. The introduction of smart borders raises profound questions regarding both privacy as well as social justice (Broeders 2007; Bennett et al. 2014, 105–28). Smart border agreements were signed between Canada and the United States in

December 2001 and between Mexico and the United States in March 2002. In addition to the overall trend towards increased surveillance, "new world" arrangements like smart borders are a far cry from the creation of a "North American citizenship" akin to that of the EU's *Schengen* arrangement.

The 2001 US-Canada Smart Border Declaration is a thirty-point plan that, as we go on to show, securitizes refugees and immigrants in new ways distinct from the Cold War era. For instance, during the Cold War, ideological criteria were used by both the United States and Canada to bar those refugees or immigrants perceived to have Communist sympathies, as well as to facilitate the entry of refugees fleeing communism (Whitaker 1987, 13–54). Following September 11 the focus was to create, in the words of former Canadian Prime Minister Jean Chrétien, "a border that is open for business, but closed to terrorists" (Chrétien 2002).

In examining the role of the Canadian government in fortifying the US–Canada border, the provisions for refugees like the Safe Third Country Agreement are particularly telling. Unlike other aspects of the Smart Border Accord, there is considerable evidence that the Canadian government was the one that pushed for this provision relating to refugees (DeVoretz and Hanson 2003, 2). In other words, Canadian officials exerted their (perceived) national interest and Canadian sovereignty through refugee provisions. This finding counters common assumptions that "Fortress America" is fuelled primarily by US unilateralism. Further, it challenges the idea that Canadian sovereignty is often undermined in relation to the United States. As DeVoretz and Hanson (2003) note, it also refutes the idea, bandied about in the Canadian media at the time, that with the Safe Third Country Agreement Canada was simply trying to "appease American politicians' complaints that Canada's wide-open refugee system presented a security risk" (2003, 2). In fact, a provision for designating the United States as a safe third country for refugees made its way into Canadian legislative debates as early as the 1980s and indeed appeared in 1989 refugee legislation, although it was not enacted (Bissett 2002, 36). The full embrace of the safe third country idea – or what Soennecken dubs a "European turn in Canadian refugee policy" – needs to be seen in relation to policy sharing and even discourse sharing around the idea of a safe third country (Soennecken 2014, 110–13). To better understand

Canada's motivation for embracing the idea of a safe third country, we situate this embrace in broader trends of refugee exclusion that are occurring and the logic and implication of the Safe Third Country Agreement that came into force on December 29, 2004.

A primary way in which refugee exclusion has been enacted discursively by the Canadian state relates to the more frequent use of themes of security, public safety, crime, and fraud – or what Anna Pratt (2005) terms "criminality." In her examination of detention and deportation in Canada, Pratt shows how the invocation of "criminality" shifted from being one of many justifications used historically to exclude refugees, to becoming the single guiding rationale of policy by the 1990s and 2000s (Pratt 2005, 220). Indeed, in this period denials of permanent residency to refugees grew (Keung 2005), as did the possible grounds by which permanent residency can actually be removed (Alboim and Cohl 2012, 35). Discourses of fraud informed the adjudication of refugee claims, putting a higher burden of proof for groups such as LGBTQ2+ asylum seekers to "prove" their queer identity to show that they are truly at risk of persecution in their home countries (Gaucher 2018). As Pratt notes, exclusion based on criminality is both in keeping with liberal democratic norms, since exclusion cannot take overtly racist forms, and also serves to "construct the state and the public, not the refugee, as the victim" (Pratt 2005, 221). For many Canadians, discourses around criminality may present seemingly reasonable grounds for not honouring international instruments like the 1951 UN Convention on Refugees, or for welcoming refugees.

The 2004 Safe Third Country Agreement also carries implications in relation to the UN Convention and Protocol. In policy terms, what the Agreement says is that an asylum seeker must make their claim in the country where they first arrive (i.e., Canada or the United States). This applies to land border ports of entry only, with specified exceptions, such as claims relating to a family member being present in the state where the claim is made or claims made by an unaccompanied minor. As Macklin noted in the wake of its passage:

> Between 1995 and 1997 Canada tried to persuade the US to enter into a safe-third country agreement, and ultimately failed. This agreement would have covered inland claims. One reason the present Agreement does not apply inland is the impossibility of determining whether

inland claimants arrived via the US. Refugee claimants who wish to pursue their claim in Canada have no incentive to disclose that they passed through the US, and every reason to conceal it. The task of establishing a person's route into Canada or the US is obviated when the person concerned is literally standing at the Canada-US border. (2003, 2–3)

In other words, by focusing on official border crossings between the United States and Canada, a person's entry from one or the other country would be immediately apparent.

In strictly numerical terms, it is clear that prior to the Safe Third Country Agreement there were more refugee claimants arriving from the United States to Canada to make claims than the inverse. For example, in 2001 there were 13,497 claimants who arrived from or through the United States to Canada, in comparison with only a few hundred who came from Canada to make claims in the United States (DeVoretz and Hanson 2003, 4). Many argued the benefits of the Safe Third Country Agreement's potential reduction in the number of asylum seekers. Former Canadian Ambassador James Bissett suggested that the Agreement would save Canadian taxpayers money and increase security, themes in keeping with neoliberal and securitization rationales (Bissett 2003, 37).

Critics of the Safe Third Country Agreement tended to be refugee advocacy groups on both sides of the border. Advocates "challenged the contention that the US is always a safe country for refugees, denounced the purpose and effect of reducing the number of refugees who can seek Canada's protection and predicted that the Agreement would lead to an increase in smuggling and irregular crossing at the border" (Canadian Council for Refugees 2005, i). Notably as well, the Agreement was further criticized for not sufficiently accounting for gender and the vulnerable position of female and LGBTQ2+ refugees in particular who might make claims reflecting gender-based persecution. For instance, some suggested Canada, a country that had pioneered gender-based persecution guidelines for the world, also applied them more liberally than the United States (Macklin 2003, 15–17). Importantly, this analysis amplified the gendered implications of the Safe Third Country Agreement if Canada was rendered off limits to claims.

More broadly, analysts pointed to how the Agreement might undermine the spirit of Canada's international legal commitment not to *refoule* a refugee and/or return a person to a country when torture is the likely outcome (Macklin 2002, 18; see also Hyndman and Mountz 2020; Arbel 2013). Put differently, Canada could potentially avoid admitting refugees, while technically not being seen to evade its international obligations as spelled out in the Convention and Protocol, and assuming a legal distinction between avoidance and evasion (Macklin 2003, 5). To date, the courts have not yet proven to be a definitive stumbling block for the Safe Third Country Agreement in relation to The Canadian Charter of Rights and Freedoms. For example, initial attempts to challenge the Agreement on grounds that it violates Charter rights were unsuccessful. Specifically, the Canadian Council for Refugees (CCR), Amnesty International, and the Canadian Council of Churches (CCC) argued that the Agreement violates Charter rights by potentially denying refugees the right to make a claim in Canada (CCR 2009). As will be discussed further, after Trump's election to office in the United States, a new legal claim was launched concerning whether the United States should be considered safe for refugees. While initially successful in 2020, this was then successfully appealed by the Canadian government in 2021 on technical grounds. This was appealed, and in December 2021 it was announced by the coalition CCR, CCC, and Amnesty International that the Supreme Court of Canada would review the constitutionality of the Safe Third Country Agreement which the coalition sees as violating Section 15 gender equality rights for its negative impacts on women fleeing gender-based persecution (Amnesty International 2021).

Notably, nothing in the Safe Third Country Agreement commits either Canada or the United States to better support refugees, who, as noted, reside primarily in camps and in countries of the developing world. Assessing the full impact of the Agreement since it has been in place is difficult since some consequences may be invisible to the media and public (CCR 2005, ii). Nevertheless, in the months and years following its passage, the Safe Third Country Agreement went hand in hand with reducing the overall number of claims made in Canada. As a 2005 report by the CCR that examined the first six months of the Agreement's operation indicated, Canada was set to receive the lowest number of claims since the mid-1980s (i). On average, 29,680 annual claims were accepted by Canada between 1989 and 2004. In contrast, in 2005 the annual figure was down to 19,935, and by 2010 it was 9,041 (Alboim and Cohl 2012, 30). The reduced number of asylum claims made in Canada was also linked with a reduction in the overall intake of refugees, particularly in the period when Conservative leader Stephen Harper was prime minister (2006–15). As Alboin and Cohl (2012) note of the period of the mid-2000s to 2010s: "Refugees admitted to Canada form a smaller proportion of the total immigrant flow than they have in the past. Within the refugee class, the numbers of government-assisted refugees have remained fairly constant, privately sponsored refugees have increased and the number of successful refugee claimants has decreased dramatically" (30).

Assessing the impact of the Harper Conservatives from 2005 to 2015 also requires centring major refugee legislation that came into effect in 2012. In particular, Bill C-31 of the Protecting Canada's Immigration System Act and the Balanced Refugee Reform Act further transformed the refugee system in Canada. Under this legislation, refugee determination would depend on a claimant's country of origin and how they arrived, i.e., alone or with assistance. Widely deemed to be problematic by analysts (see, e.g., Labman and Liew 2019), the legislation left it up to ministerial discretion whether a country produced refugees and also introduced automatic detention for "irregular" arrivals in what was akin to a medium security prison (see Alboim and Cohl 2012, 30–40). This period was also notable for the June 2012 decision by the Harper government to cut and deprive health care to privately sponsored refugees and asylum claimants, although this support was reinstated by the Trudeau government in 2016. While the 2012 cuts to refugee health care were in keeping with neoliberal demands to reduce state spending, and justified by the Harper Conservatives by saying it was directed at "bogus" refugees, in fact the cuts impacted the majority of refugees (Gulli 2015). Moreover, the cuts were deemed by Canadian physicians to significantly compromise the health care and safety of refugees and, in the case of pregnant women, their children, who would be Canadian at birth (Ubelacker 2012).

Upon assuming office, the Trudeau government also engaged in other changes that have provided important substantive and symbolic support for refugees and immigration. As previously noted, in the early days in office the Trudeau Liberals supported the resettlement of over 25,000 Syrian refugees, a move that a 2017 survey found was supported by a majority (68 per cent) of Canadians (Nanos 2017). Additional support was advanced globally through

Canada's active engagement with the United Nations Global Compact on Refugees in 2018. The Trudeau government also raised the levels of immigration across all categories, including for refugees, although in keeping with trends in Northern states and Canada that we identified in chapter one and we discuss further in chapter four, Canada's preference in immigration intake overall was given to skilled immigrants. Refugees by comparison were the smallest category (Abu-Laban 2019).

In keeping with the tenets of the Global Compact on Refugees, and a longstanding preference for skilled entrants, Canada also in April 2018 worked with the UNHCR to quickly resettle skilled refugees from the Middle East and elsewhere. This involved developing an additional avenue beyond those referred by UNHCR on the basis of need. The pilot project, known as the Economic Mobility and Pathways Project (EMPP), was described as follows:

> In testing labour mobility pathways for refugees through the EMPP, Canada is exploring bringing together the two worlds of humanitarian and economic immigration. More specifically, Canada is testing to what extent a protection lens can be applied to its economic programs in order to be sensitive and more responsive to the circumstances of forced displacement while preserving the ability of Canada's economic immigration system to support economic growth and prosperity in Canada. (Canada and United Nations High Commissioner for Refugees 2019, 3)

While the EMPP program is still in its infancy, the program's rationale for identifying refugees "with high human capital and/or who meet Canadian labour market needs" (2019, 4) is a clear articulation of the valorization of the market, which is a hallmark of neoliberalism.

Overall, however, it is telling that the Trudeau government has kept the Harper-era refugee legislation of 2012 intact along with the Safe Third Country Agreement, even while engaging in high-profile statements in support of refugees that served as a contrast to the Trump administration. Indeed, in the wake of the January 2017 US travel ban on select Muslim-majority states announced by President Trump, Prime Minister Trudeau famously tweeted, "to those fleeing persecution terror & war, Canadians will welcome you regardless of your faith. Diversity is our strength" (Paling 2017).

In more recent years, the Safe Third Country Agreement has not worked in the same way to reduce the number of asylum seekers arriving from the United States. Coinciding with the rise to power of the Trump administration in the United States, once President Trump threatened withdrawal of protective measures extended to specific groups, there was a new surge of refugee claimants attempting perilous journeys from the United States to Canada entering through *unofficial* points (Bilefsky 2018). Importantly, these unofficial points, such as the Roxham Road crossing in Quebec, where some 50,000 attempted crossing between 2017 and 2019, were points not covered by the Safe Third Country Agreement (Ormiston 2019). Trump's withdrawal of protective measures was ultimately realized in November 2017 for Haitians and in January 2018 for Salvadorans.

As the number of asylum seekers coming from the United States via unofficial points of entry rose, it resulted in a more aggressive campaign on the part of the Trudeau Liberals designed to deter potential asylum seekers arriving from the United States. For example, Trudeau's former Minister of Immigration, Refugees and Citizenship Canada (IRCC), Ahmed Hussen, made it clear that these refugee claimants were not wanted, stating: "We don't want people to illegally enter our border, and doing so is not a free ticket to Canada. We are saying, 'You will be apprehended, screened, detained, fingerprinted, and if you can't establish a genuine claim, you will be denied refugee protection and removed'" (quoted in Bilefsky 2018).

More recently, with the COVID-19 travel bans and border closures to all but essential workers and the transport of goods in March 2020, the border control went even further. Specifically, it was announced that asylum seekers entering at unofficial points of entry would either be returned immediately to the United States or put in detention for fourteen days and then sent back, leading Alex Neve of Amnesty International Canada to raise concerns about this "unexpected and shocking reversal" of Canada's obligations under the UN Convention and Protocol (quoted in Ling 2020).

In relation to the Safe Third Country Agreement, with good reason the Canadian Council for Refugees early on asked with respect to the Agreement: "how few claimants is few enough for the Canadian government? And more fundamentally, is this goal an acceptable one, when Canada already accepts so few of the world's refugees, when there are so few places where refugees can find protection and when the consequences of closing the door on refugees means that their fundamental rights might be violated?" (2005, 26). This moral appeal is instructive because it is premised on the sense that legal instruments have failed thus far to challenge the status quo of the Safe Third Country Agreement. Indeed, while the Safe Third Country Agreement required that the UN High Commissioner for Refugees monitor the Agreement after the first year, the role of the UNHCR was confined to ascertaining whether the Agreement was correctly applied (rather than impact), and it had no role in monitoring thereafter, nor was there any schedule for further review of the Agreement beyond the first year (Canadian Council for Refugees 2005, 6–7). This was the backdrop to the December 2017 announcement of the Canadian Council for Refugees (CCR), the Canadian Council of Churches (CCC), and Amnesty International Canada announced that they would once again challenge the designation of the United States as a safe third country in the federal court, especially in light of Trump's policies (CCR 2017). In July 2020 the federal court ruled the agreement to be unconstitutional and in violation of Section 7 (life, liberty, and security of the person), but following an appeal by the Trudeau government which has continually defended the Canada–US Safe Third Country Agreement, as noted the Federal Court of Appeal overturned the decision (Immigration and Refugee Board of Canada, 2021). The Trudeau government has also worked to defend the logic of "safe third countries" beyond the United States. Specifically, with no public discussion, and tucked in an omnibus budget bill in April 2019, the Liberals introduced a new provision which would prevent asylum claimants from making a claim in Canada if they had done so previously in any other countries making up the security and intelligence Canada partners within the "Five Eyes" (i.e., the United States, the United Kingdom, Australia, and New Zealand) (Harris 2019).

In the face of these limitations as concerns legal obligations and rulings, it becomes evident why an appeal to ethical considerations in the field of migration, and in relation to refugees specifically, is also what needs to be considered by policymakers and publics alike. Clearly legal humanitarian considerations may be crowded out in the face of security and public health, as the COVID-19 pandemic revealed. They may also be sidelined by culturalist considerations (for example, favouring Christian over Muslim refugees as Stephen Harper wished to do). They may also be tempered by economic considerations.

Indeed, while Canada was once criticized by the international community for only taking "the best and brightest" refugees that served perceived economic interests, over the 2000s Canada's intake became more clearly in line with the United Nations High Commission for Refugees and the international community in terms of embracing the needs of refugees for protection, as well as resettlement (Pressé and Thomson 2008, 95–6). Still, as illustrated, neoliberal policy rationales have continued to exert influence, accounting for cuts between 2012 and 2016 to the health care benefits extended to asylum claimants, as well as a return to the use of economistic criteria in refugee selection via the 2018 Economic Mobility and Pathways Project, albeit with the support of UNHCR and the Global Compact on Refugees, which allows for such ventures.

For the record it can be noted that studies show refugees to Canada (as compared to other immigrant categories) may struggle more in relation to employment than other categories of newcomers, yet this situation improves over time (Yu, Ouellet, and Warmington 2007). It is equally of note that far from being distant from cultural values, refugees are especially keen to receive Canadian citizenship and place a high value on Canada's political stability and peaceful resolution of conflict (Yu, Ouellet, and Warmington 2007, 26). Finally, the fact that Canadians are generally supportive of refugees is noteworthy. A 2019 Angus Reid survey shows that 38 per cent of Canadians believe Canada's current refugee intake is "about right," with 23 per cent of Canadians holding that Canada should actually increase the number of refugees it accepts annually (Angus Reid 2019).

CONCLUSION: THE PROMISE OF ADDRESSING ETHICS AND REFUGEES

This chapter has overviewed the shifting international refugee regime from one in which Cold War refugees were made welcome by Western receiving states to one in which refugees fleeing persecution from countries of the South have encountered a non-entry regime. Budding regional migration initiatives in the continent of North America, and in particular the Safe Third Country Agreement signed between Canada and the United States, have created a new way the non-entry regime is exercised. The manner in which this has occurred suggests the very real limits of international law, and the continued necessity of thinking not only legally, but morally – i.e., in relation to principles of obligation and justice.

While there may indeed be grounds for legitimate exclusion of migrants/refugees, the task of understanding the grounds for inclusion needs more work. Much existing scholarly work on immigration is empirically based, thus there is a need for greater scholarly engagement with normative questions. Attention to ethics of care and cosmopolitan perspectives underscore the manner in which we are interdependent and the obligations that can exist at local, national, and global levels; liberal perspectives can attune us to the obligation of states in a world divided into states; not least care perspectives also draw attention to gender inequality. Yet, the provisions of the Safe Third Country Agreement pay little attention to these factors, and indeed its net impact to date has been to exclude, and to encourage dangerous crossing of the US–Canada border. As such, policymakers and publics might also benefit from greater explicit consideration of the normative – what ought to be.

Over seventy years ago Hannah Arendt identified the way lack of membership in a state can serve to deny some "the right to have rights." In this context, refugees form a particularly compelling example, and indeed this is a grouping where there is, arguably, the greatest moral claim on states, and relatively less legal scope to deny entry in light of international agreements (Benhabib 2004, 137). As the crisis in Syria reminded the world when the image of Alan Kurdi went viral in 2015, the refugee problem shows no signs of abating in the twenty-first century. Indeed, the global circulation of Alan Kurdi's image in the midst of the 2015 Canadian federal election campaign propelled a new discussion of the Harper Conservative's responses to refugees; moreover, the perception that they were not doing enough played a role in eventually toppling former Conservative Immigration Minister Chris Alexander's own re-election in Ajax, Ontario (Blackwell 2015).

Since states of both the South and the North have been increasingly erecting barriers to the entrance and rights of refugees fleeing persecution, and since states still form the basic organizing unit of our world, there is every reason to continue the task of thinking through alternatives to the problem Arendt identified. However, as we will continue to detail in the chapters that follow, in many ways the restrictions which characterize policy towards refugees since 2002 in Canada find echoes in the difficulties other groups are encountering in immigrating to Canada and acquiring citizenship. It is in this sense that refugees have served as a forerunner and harbinger to containing diversity.

NOTE

1 In 2020, NAFTA was replaced with the ratification in all three countries of what is now called the United States-Mexico-Canada Agreement (USMCA) in the United States but is called the Canada-United States-Mexico Agreement (CUSMA) in Canada, and *Tratado entre México, Estados Unidos y Canadá* (T-MEC) in Mexico.

BIBLIOGRAPHY

Abella, Irving, and Harold Troper. *None Is Too Many: Canada and the Jews of Europe 1933–1948*. Toronto: Lester and Orpen Dennys, 1982.

Abu-Laban, Yasmeen. "The New North America and the Segmentation of Canadian Citizenship." *The International Journal of Canadian Studies* 29 (2004): 17–40.

– "Regionalism, Migration and Fortress (North) America." *Review of Constitutional Studies* 10, nos. 1, 2 (2005): 135–62.

– "A World of Strangers, or a World of Relationships? The Value of Care Ethics in Migration Research and Policy." In *Rooted Cosmopolitanism: Canada and the World*, edited by Willi Kymlicka and Kathy Walker, 156–77. Vancouver: University of British Columbia Press, 2012.

– "Immigration and Settler-Colonies Post-UNDRIP: Research and Policy Implications." *International Migration* December 30, 2019 (Early View): 1–17. https://doi.org/10.1111/imig.12685.

– "Re-defining the International Refugee Regime: UNHCR, UNRWA and the Challenge of Multigenerational Protracted Refugee Situations." In *Research Handbook on the Law and Politics of Migration*, edited by Catherin Dauvergne, 310–22. Cheltenham and Northampton: Edward Elgar Press, 2021.

Aiken, Sharryn J. "Of Gods and Monsters: National Security and Canadian Refugee Policy." *Revue québécoise du droit international* 14, no. 2 (2001): 1–51.

Alboim, Naomi, and Karen Cohl. *Shaping the Future: Canada Rapidly Changing Immigration Policies*. Toronto: Maytree Foundation, 2012. https://maytree.com/wp-content/uploads/shaping-the-future.pdf.

Amnesty International. "Supreme Court Decision to Hear Safe Third Country Appeal is a Promising Step for Refugee Rights." December 16, 2021, https://amnesty.ca/news/supreme-court-decision-to-hear-safe-third-country-agreement-appeal-is-a-promising-step-for-refugee-rights/.

Andreas, Peter. "A Tale of Two Borders: The U.S.-Canada and U.S.-Mexico Lines after 9–11." In *The Rebordering of North America*, edited by Peter Andreas and Thomas J. Biersteker, 1–23. New York and London: Routledge, 2003.

Andreas, Peter, and Timothy Snyder, eds. *The Wall around the West: State Borders and Immigration Controls in Europe and North America*. Lanham, MD: Roman and Littlefield, 2000.

Angus Reid. "Immigration: Half Back Current Targets, but Colossal Misperceptions, Pushback over Refugees, Cloud Debate." October 7, 2019. https://angusreid.org/election-2019-immigration/.

Arbel, Erfrat. "Shifting Borders and the Boundaries of Rights: Examining the Safe Third Country Agreement between Canada and the United States." *International Journal of Refugee Law* 25, no. 1 (2013): 65–86.

Arbel, Erfrat, and Ian C. Davis. "Immigration Detention and the Problem of Time: Lessons from Solitary Confinement." *International Journal of Migration and Border Studies* 4, no. 4 (2018): 326–44.

Arendt, Hannah. *The Origins of Totalitarianism*. New York: Schocken Books, [1951] 2004.

BBC News. "EU Court Rules against Three States Over Refugees." April 2, 2020. www.bbc.com/news/world-europe-52133906.

Bell, Stewart. "Mexico Again among Canada's Top Sources of Refugee Claims after Visa Requirement Lifted." *Global News* (February 23, 2018). https://globalnews.ca/news/4042075/mexico-refugee-claims-spike-visa-lift/.

Benhabib, Seyla. *The Rights of Others: Aliens, Residents and Citizens*. Cambridge: Cambridge University Press, 2004.

Bennett, Colin J., Kevin D. Haggerty, David Lyon, and Valerie Steeves. *Transparent Lives: Surveillance in Canada*. Edmonton: Athabasca University Press, 2014.

Bhabha, Jacqueline. "Belonging in Europe: Citizenship and Post-National Rights." *International Social Science Journal* 51, no. 159 (1999): 11–23.

Bigo, Didier. "From Foreigners to 'Abnormal Aliens': How the Faces of the Enemy Have Changed Following September the 11th." In *International Migration and Security: Opportunities and Challenges*, edited by Elspeth Guild and Joanne van Selm, 64–81. London and New York: Routledge, 2005.

Bilefsky, Dan. "Migrants Fleeing to Canada Learn Even a Liberal Nation Has Limits." *The New York Times* (January 13, 2018). https://www.nytimes.com/2018/01/13/world/canada/quebec-immigrants-haitians.html.

Bissett, James. "A Defense of the "Safe Country" Concept for Refugees." *Policy Options* (September 2002): 36–8.
Blackwell, Tom. "Syrian Story Adds New Twist to Tight Race in Immigration Minister Chris Alexander's Riding." *The National Post* (September 3, 2015). http://news.nationalpost.com/news/canada/canadian-politics/syrian-refugee-story-adds-new-twist-to-tight-race-in-immigration-minister-chris-alexanders-riding.
Bonner, Robert C. "Remarks of Commissioner Robert C. Bonner, Customs and Border Protection." Keynote Address. Center for Strategic and International Studies Conference on Safety and Security in North American Trade. July 16, 2003.
Broeders, Dennis. "The New Digital Borders of Europe: EU Databases and the Surveillance of Irregular Migrants." *International Sociology* 22, no. 1 (2007): 71–92.
Brown, Chris. "Marxism and the Transnational Migration of People: Ethical Issues." In *Free Movement: Ethical Issues in the Transnational Migration of People and of Money*, edited by Brian H. Barry and Robert E. Goodin, 127–44. Hemel Hempstead: Harvester Wheatsheaf, 1992.
Buzan, Barry, Ole Waever, and Japp de Wilde. *Security: A New Framework for Analysis*. Boulder and London: Lynne Reinner Publishers, 1998.
Canadian Council for Refugees (CCR). "Closing the Front Door on Refugees: Report on Safe Third Country Agreement 6 Months after Implementation." December 2005. https://ccrweb.ca/sites/ccrweb.ca/files/static-files/closingdoordec05.pdf.
– "Supreme Court Denial of Leave on Safe Third Regretted." February 5, 2009. https://ccrweb.ca/en/bulletin/09/02/05.
– "Why We Are Challenging the USA as a 'Safe Third Country' in the Federal Court of Canada." December 2017. http://ccrweb.ca/en/safe-third-country-challenge-explanation.
Carens, Joseph. "States and Refugees: A Normative Analysis." In *Refugee Policy: Canada and the United States*, edited by Howard Adelman, 18–29. Toronto: Center for Refugee Studies, York University, 1991.
– "Aliens and Citizens: The Case for Open Borders." In *The Immigration Reader: America in a Multidisciplinary Perspective*, edited by David Jacobson, 365–87. Malden, MA: Blackwell, 1998.
– *The Ethics of Immigration*. Oxford: Oxford University Press, 2013.
Castles, Stephen. "The International Politics of Forced Migration." In *Fighting Identities: Race, Religion and Ethno-nationalism*, edited by Leo Panitich and Colin Leys. London: Merlin Press, 2002.
Castles, Stephen, and Godula Kosack. *Immigrant Workers and Class Structure in Western Europe*. London: Oxford University Press, 1973.
Chrétien, Jean. "Remarks by the President and Prime Minister Chretien on U.S.-Canada Smart Borders." September 9, 2002. https://georgewbush-whitehouse.archives.gov/news/releases/2002/09/text/20020909-4.html.

Citizenship and Immigration Canada (CIC). *Annual Report on the Operation of the Canadian Multiculturalism Act 2009–2010*. Ottawa: Minister of Public Works and Government Services Canada, 2011.

Commission of the European Communities. "Communication from the Commission to the Council and the European Parliament: Integrating Migration Issues in the European Union's Relations with Third Countries." Brussels. March 12, 2002.

– "Common European Asylum System." 2014. http://ec.europa.eu/dgs/home-affairs/what-we-do/policies/asylum/index_en.htm.

Cortinovis, Roberto. "Asylum: The Role and Limits of the Safe Third Country Concept in EU Asylum." Discussion Brief. *Research Social Platform on Migration and Asylum*, July 2018.

Dauvergne, Catherine. *The New Politics of Immigration and the End of Settler Societies*. Cambridge: Cambridge University Press, 2016.

DeVoretz, Don J., and Philip Hanson. "Sourcing out Canada's Refugee Policy: The Safe Third Country Agreement." Commentary Series No. 03–06. Vancouver: Vancouver Centre of Excellence for Research on Immigration and Integration in the Metropolis, November 2003.

Dirks, Gerald. *Canada and Refugees: Indifference or Opportunism?* Montreal and Kingston: McGill-Queen's University Press, 1977.

Dummett, Ann. "The Transnational Migration of People Seen within a Natural Law Tradition." In *Free Movement: Ethical Issues in the Transnational Migration of People and of Money*, edited by Brian H. Barry and Robert E. Goodin, 169–80. Hemel Hempstead: Harvester Wheatsheaf, 1992.

Engster, Daniel. "Rethinking Care Theory: The Practice of Caring and the Obligation to Care." *Hypatia* 20, no. 3 (2005): 50–74.

Garnier, Adèle, Jamie Chai Yun Liew, and Shauna Labman. "Is Canada's Welcome to Fleeing Ukrainians a New Era of Refugee Policy?" *The Conversation* (March 9, 2022), https://theconversation.com/is-canadas-welcome-to-fleeing-ukrainians-a-new-era-of-refugee-policy-178501.

Gibney, Matthew J. "'A Thousand Little Guantanamos': Western States and Measures to Prevent the Arrival of Refugees." In *Displacement, Migration, Asylum*, edited by Kate E. Tunstall, 139–69. Oxford: Oxford University Press, 2006.

Gilligan, Carol. *In a Different Voice: Psychological Theory and Women's Development*. Cambridge: Cambridge University Press, 1982.

Government of Canada. "Perimeter Security and Economic Cooperation." 2014. http://actionplan.gc.ca/en/page/bbg-tpf/canada-us-border-cooperation.

Government of Canada and the United Nations High Commissioners for Refugees (UNHCR). "The Economic Mobility Pathways Project—Policy Principles and Lessons Learned: A Canadian Perspective on Complementary Pathways for Admission." June 2019. www.unhcr.ca/wp-content

/uploads/2019/07/The-Economic-Mobility-Pathways-Project-Policy-Principles-and-Lessons-Learned-June-2019.pdf.
The Guardian. "Canada's PM Office Ordered Delay on Syrian Refugee Claims Processing." October 8, 2015. www.theguardian.com/world/2015/oct/08/canada-stephen-harper-processing-syrian-refugees?CMP=twt_gu.
Hankivsky Olena. *Social Policy and the Ethic of Care.* Vancouver: University of British Columbia Press, 2004.
Harris, Kathleen. "Don't Blame Trump: New Study Explores Canada's Surge in Asylum Seekers." CBC News (December 12, 2019). www.cbc.ca/news/politics/trump-immigration-trudeau-asylum-seekers-roxham-road-1.5393071.
Hassner, Pierre. "Refugees: A Special Case for Cosmopolitian Citizenship?" In *Re-Imagining Political Community: Studies in Cosmopolitan Democracy*, edited by Daniele Archibugi, David Held, and Martin Kohler. Stanford, CA: Stanford University Press, 1998: 252–72.
Held, David, Anthony G. McGrew, David Goldblatt, and Jonathan Perraton. *Global Transformations: Politics, Economics and Culture.* Stanford, CA: Stanford University Press, 1999.
Hentges, Gudrun. "Refugee and Asylum Policy Influenced by Europeanisation." In *Europe's New Racism? Causes, Manifestations and Solutions*, edited by Ellen Preckler. New York and Oxford: Bergahn Books, 2002: 105–29.
Hyndman, Jennifer. "Globalization, Immigration and the Gender Implications of *Not Just Numbers* in Canada." *Refuge* 18, no. 1 (1999): 26–31.
Hyndman, Jennifer, and Alison Mountz. "Seeking Safe Haven in Canada: Geopolitics and Border Crossings after the Safe Third Country Agreement." In *Haven: The Mediterranean Crisis and Human Security*, edited by John Morrissey, 110–28. Cheltenham, UK: Edward Elgar, 2020.
Immigration and Refugee Board of Canada. "Government of Canada Appeal Allowed on Safe Third Country Agreement." 2021. https://irb.gc.ca/en/news/2021/Pages/appeal-allowed-safe-third-country-agreement.aspx.
Keung, Nicholas. "Refugee Files Lawsuit over States." *The Toronto Star* (November 9, 2005). www.pressreader.com/canada/toronto-star/20051109/281900178609437.
Khouri, Raja. "What's the Holdup on Syrian Refugees?" *The Globe and Mail* (December 22, 2014). www.theglobeandmail.com/globe-debate/whats-the-holdup-on-syrian-refugees/article22163219/.
Kymlicka, Will, and Kathy Walker, eds. *Rooted Cosmopolitanism: Canada and the World.* Vancouver: University of British Columbia Press, 2012.
Labman, Shauna, and Geoffrey Cameron, eds. *Strangers to Neighbours: Refugee Sponsorship in Context.* Montreal: McGill-Queen's University Press, 2020.
Labman, Shauna, and Jamie Chai Yun Liew. "Law and Moral Licensing in Canada: The Making of Illegality and Illegitimacy along the Border." *International Journal of Migration and Border Studies* 5, no. 3 (2019): 188–211.

Ling, Justin. "The Dark Side of Canada's Coronavirus Response." *Maclean's* (March 20, 2020). www.macleans.ca/news/canada/the-dark-side-of-canadas-coronavirus-response/.

Macklin, Audrey. "The Value(s) of the Canada-US Safe Third Country Agreement." Paper. Caledon Institute of Social Policy, December 2003.

– "Canadians Have a Decision to Make That Will Affect Syrian Refugees." *The New York Times* (September 15, 2015). www.nytimes.com/roomfordebate/2015/09/15/what-can-countries-do-to-help-refugees-fleeing-to-europe/canadians-have-a-decision-to-make-that-willaffect-syrian-refugees.

– "In Canada: Who Is Really Essential?" *Open Democracy* (May 6, 2020. www.opendemocracy.net/en/pandemic-border/canada-who-really-essential/.

Martin, Don. "Short-pants PMO People Shouldn't Be in the Refugee Business." CTVNews (2015). www.ctvnews.ca/politics/don-martin-s-blog/short-pants-pmo-people-shouldn-t-be-in-the-refugee-business-1.2603728.

Masters, Michael W. "Ecology, Ethics and Immigration: The Writings of Biologist Garrett Hardin." *The Social Contract* (Fall 2001): 5–12.

Migration Policy Institute. "Top 10 of 2014: Issue #1: World Confronts Largest Humanitarian Crisis Since WW2." http://migrationpolicy.org/article/top-10-2014-issue-1-world-confronts-largest-humanitarian-crisis-wwii.

Molloy, Michael J., Peter Duschinsky, Kurt F. Jensen, and Robert J. Shalka. *Running on Empty: Canada and the Indochinese Refugees, 1975–1980*. Montreal: McGill-Queen's University Press, 2017.

Morello, Carol. "Refugee Wave from Syria and Iraq Now a 'Mega Crisis' UN Official Says." *The Washington Post* (November 17, 2014). www.washingtonpost.com/world/national-security/refugee-wave-from-syria-and-iraq-now-a-mega-crisis-un-official-says/2014/11/17/ebc5ee50-6eab-11e4-893f-86bd390a3340_story.html.

Mountz, Alison. *The Death of Asylum: Hidden Geographies of the Enforcement Archipelago*. Minneapolis: University of Minnesota Press, 2020.

Nanos Survey. "Canadians' Impression of the Government's Response to Syrian Refugee Crisis." May 1, 2016. www.nanos.co/wp-content/uploads/2017/07/2016-832A-Globe-April-Omni-Syrian-Refugees-w-tabs-R.pdf.

Nyers, Peter. *Rethinking Refugees: Beyond State of Emergency*. London and New York: Routledge, 2006.

O'Neill, William R., S.J., and William C. Spohn. "Rights of Passage: The Ethics of Immigration and Refugee Policy." *Theological Studies* 59 (1998): 84–106.

Ormiston, Susan. "How Thousands of Asylum Seekers Have Turned Roxham Road into a De Facto Border Crossing." CBC News (September 29, 2019). www.cbc.ca/news/canada/the-national-roxham-road-immigration-border-1.5169249.

Paling, Emma. "Trudeau Tells Refugees: Canada Will Welcome You." *The Huffington Post* (January 29, 2017). www.huffingtonpost.ca/2017/01/28/trudeau-refugees_n_14461906.html.

Pécoude, Antoine, and Paul de Buchteneire, eds. *Migration without Borders: Essays on the Free Movement of Peoples*. New York: Berghahn Books and UNESCO, 2009.

Pratt, Anna. *Securing Borders: Detention and Deportation in Canada*. Vancouver: University of British Columbia Press, 2005.

Pressé, Debra, and Jessie Thomson. "The Resettlement Challenge: Integration of Refugees from Protracted Refugee Situations." *Refuge* 24, no. 2 (2008): 94–9.

Rehaag, Sean. "Judicial Review of Refugee Determinations: The Luck of the Draw?" Comparative Research in Law & Political Economy. Research Paper No. 9/2012, 2012. http://digitalcommons.osgoode.yorku.ca/clpe/7.

Robinson, Fiona. "Care, Gender and Global Social Justice: Toward a Moral Framework for Ethical Globalization." Paper. Annual Meetings of the Canadian Political Science Meetings. London, June 2–4, 2005.

Salter, Mark. *The Passport in International Relations*. Boulder, CO, and London: Lynne Reinner Publishers, 2003.

Sevenhuijen, Selma. *Citizenship and the Ethics of Care: Feminist Considerations on Justice, Morality and Politics*. London and New York: Routledge, 1998.

Soennecken, Dagmar. "Shifting Up and Back: The European Turn in Canadian Refugee Policy." *Comparative Migration Studies* 2, no. 1 (2014): 101–22.

Soysal, Yasemin Nuhoglu. *Limits of Citizenship: Migrants and Postnational Membership in Europe*. Chicago: University of Chicago Press, 1994.

Ubelacker, Sheryl. "Doctors Group Calls on Ottawa to Rethink Cuts to Refugee Health Program." *The Vancouver Sun* (September 28, 2012). www.vancouversun.com/health/Doctors+group+calls+Ottawa+rethink+cuts+refugee+health+program/7310620/story.html.

United Nations High Commissioner for Refugees (UNHCR). *Convention and Protocol Relating to the Status of Refugees*. Geneva: UNHCR, 2010. www.unhcr.org/3b66c2aa10.html.

– *Global Trends: Forced Displacement in 2018*. Geneva: UNHCR, 2019. www.unhcr.org/statistics/unhcrstats/5d08d7ee7/unhcr-global-trends-2018.html.

– "Ukraine Refugee Situation." UNHCR Data Portal (2022), https://data2.unhcr.org/en/situations/ukraine.

Valji, Nahla, Lee Anne de la Hunt, and Helen Moffett. "Where Are the Women? Gender Discrimination in Refugee Practices and Policies." *Agenda* 55 (2003): 61–72.

van Selm, Joanne. "Immigration and Regional Security." In *International Migration and Security: Opportunities and Challenges*, edited by Elspeth Guild and Joanne van Selm, 11–27. London and New York: Routledge, 2005.

Villarreal, M. Angeles, and Ian F. Fergusson. "NAFTA at 20: Overview and Trade Effects." Congressional Research Service Report 7–5700, 2014. www.fas.org/sgp/crs/row/R42965.pdf.

Virtue, Rob. "Photographer behind Image of Dead Syrian Boy: 'I Wanted to Express His Silent Scream." *Express* (September 5, 2015). www.express.co.uk/news/world/603140/Aylan-Kurdi-photographer-speaks-out-about-syrian-dead-child-photo.

Wallace, Rebecca. "Contextualizing the Crisis: The Framing of Syrian Refugees in Canadian Print Media." *Canadian Journal of Political Science* 51, no. 2 (2018): 207–31.

Walzer, Michael. "Membership." In *The Immigration Reader: America in a Multidisciplinary Perspective*, edited by David Jacobson, 341–64. Malden, MA: Blackwell, 1998.

Whitaker, Reg. *Double Standard: The Secret History of Canadian Immigration*. Toronto: Lester and Opren Dennys, 1987.

Wimmer, Andreas, and Nina Glick Schiller. "Methodological Nationalism and Beyond: Nation-State Building, Migration and the Social Sciences." *Global Networks* 2, no. 4 (2002): 301–34.

Yu, Soohn, Estelle Ouellet, and Angelyn Warmington. "Refugee Integration in Canada: A Survey of Empirical Evidence and Existing Services." *Refuge* 24, no. 2 (2007): 17–34.

Zhyznomirska, Lyubov. "Security Concerns in the EU Neighbourhood: The Effects of EU Immigration and Asylum Policy for Ukraine." In *The Boundaries of EU Enlargement: Finding a Place for Neighbours*, edited by Joan DeBardeleben, 147–64. Houndmills, Basingstoke: Palgrave Macmillan, 2008.

– "The European Union's 'Home Affairs' Model and Its European Neighbours: Beyond the 'Area of Freedom, Security and Justice'?" *Comparative European Politics* 9, nos. 4–5 (2011): 506–23.

Zong, Jie, Jeanne Batalova, and Jeffrey Hallock. "Frequently Requested Statistics on Immigrants and Immigration in the United States." *Migration Policy Institute* (February 8, 2018). www.migrationpolicy.org/article/frequently-requested-statistics-immigrants-and-immigration-united-states-8.

CHAPTER FOUR

Seeking Citizens: "Skilled" Immigrants as Ideal Neoliberal Citizens

Canada's history as an immigrant-receiving state is at the core of Canada's identity, informing the way the Government of Canada narrates its history as a nation (Government of Canada 2020a). Indeed, immigration is such an embedded part of Canadian national identity that public opinion polls of Canadians that gauge support for immigration show, on the whole, that Canadians remain supportive of Canada's permanent immigration programs: "for almost two decades, Canadians have been more likely than not to reject the idea that their country is taking in too many immigrants, and this perspective continues to strengthen over time" (Environics Institute for Survey Research 2020, 2). A Government of Canada survey in 2019 corroborates this standpoint, with 54 per cent of Canadians surveyed by the telephone stating that they believed there are "the right number of immigrants coming to Canada" (Government of Canada 2020b).

Yet historically, it should be noted that Canadian permanent immigration policy has actually been driven by two competing concerns. There are nation-building imperatives in a settler colony that necessitate the dispersal of immigrants across the country for reasons of family reunification, cultural and linguistic diversity, and humanitarian considerations. There are also economic concerns that compel Canada to seek immigrants who can contribute to the country's economic growth. The degree to which one is privileged over the other has varied historically.

Today, market concerns have prevailed. Canadians themselves tend to see immigration as being favourable because of its positive economic impacts. In 2019, an Environics survey found that 84 per cent of Canadians believe that "immigration has a positive impact on the Canadian economy" (Environics Survey Institute 2020, 3). Such market logic, defined by the belief that countries should prioritize economic growth when constructing policies, means that neoliberal values inform immigration policy. As Abu-Laban and Gabriel (2002) argue, by the 2000s, the Canadian government's desire to be globally competitive increasingly led to immigrants being selected on the basis of their perceived economic value to the country, making family reunification imperatives and its humanitarian obligations secondary and tertiary considerations. When such neoliberal logics are expressed through "administrative depoliticization" – as seen, for instance, through the growing use of "ministerial discretion" in changing immigration policies without the need to consult the public or elected officials – many of these changes go unnoticed, thereby leaving intact the dominance of market concerns in immigration selection (Hiebert 2019, 13). The use of market models in determining immigration selection, in fact, is commonplace across countries in Europe, Asia, and North America, showing that despite variations in immigration regimes, neoliberal logics are dominating (Boucher and Gest 2018). What this means, then, is that market logics supplant other concerns. These allow countries like Canada to use market logics to "have it both ways – effectively sanitizing globalization from its purported ills but exploiting the economic benefits of human movement" (Boucher and Gest 2018, 156).

The goal of this chapter is to discuss the evolution of Canada's economic immigration programs. Specifically, we claim that following the Immigration and Refugee Protection Act (IRPA) – which we note has not been amended since 2002, leaving intact existing definitions – economic immigration programs sought highly skilled, economically self-sufficient immigrants as the ideal candidates for Canadian citizenship. IRPA defines "skilled workers" as "those applicants who may become permanent residents *on the basis of their ability to become economically established in Canada*" (Tolley 2003). This shows how skilled workers are cast as *desired* citizens when compared to family-class migrants, temporary foreign workers, and asylum seekers and refugees. More recently, the move from a human capital approach to immigration to an employment approach to immigration has intensified these neoliberal tendencies. Although both approaches still prioritize human capital, the employment approach downloads immigration decision-making onto other actors, such as prospective employers, thereby decreasing federal oversight over immigration. To illustrate these points, we first address the creation of new federal immigration pathways – most notably, the *Federal Skilled Workers Program*, the *Canadian Experience Class Program*, and the *Express Entry* system. Then, we assess restrictive and neoliberal shifts within *Provincial Nominee Programs*, which the Canadian government dubs the "rising star of Canada's economic immigration programs" (Turner and Smith 2019). Ultimately, we argue that market logic has come to dominate immigration decision-making, to the exclusion of other priorities, as illustrated by skilled economic immigration streams. Canada seeks citizens who are "high-skilled," economically autonomous, and do not present the "threat" of becoming reliant on Canada's welfare state. In other words, the ideal citizen is one who best embodies neoliberalism.

The Canadian government's prioritizing of skilled economic immigration as a guiding rationale is evident in its Immigration Levels Plan for 2018–20. The targeted immigration levels for 2020 are the highest for economic immigration (195,800), followed by family immigration (91,000), and humanitarian immigration (48,700) (Government of Canada 2017).[1] In fact, Canada now has a "marketized immigration model" (Dobrowolsky 2011, 111) that prioritizes immigrants' settlement based on their economic value. This market logic has led to the segmentation of "low-skilled" migrant workers from other permanent migrants, providing fewer opportunities for permanent settlement for these low-skilled migrant workers, as we will discuss in chapter five. The marketized immigration model has also resulted in family immigration becoming less of a priority, as we will address in this chapter.

The marketized immigration model has meant that new economic immigration programs are created to fit Canada's diverse market needs. Currently, Canada has "more than 80 economic class programs – the most in its history," with each program designed to fill labour shortages through specific economic immigration programs (El-Assal 2020). A marketized immigration model also means that immigration selection is increasingly being downloaded from the federal government to other actors, such as provincial and municipal governments, as well as employers. The shift to employers also suggests a privatization of immigration selection, with employers influencing who gets admitted as citizens by providing job offers through Express Entry and Provincial Nominee Programs, which we discuss in this chapter.

The marketization of immigration has concurrently led to centralized modes of immigration security protocol. In order to securitize its borders against potential "criminals," the Canadian government in 2018 made mandatory the use of biometrics for all visitors *and* immigration applicants. The Canadian government defines biometrics as a "measurement of unique physical characteristics such as fingerprints and facial features" used in order to "establish and confirm that you are who you say you are" (Government of Canada 2018a). Scholars have interpreted the use of biometrics in different ways. For example, James Hollifield (2008) argues that the use of security measures such as biometrics is a manifestation of contradictory elements of neoliberal immigration policy. Namely, biometric security measures strive to encourage the free movement of people between borders but also seek to impose limitations on which people can move. In contrast, Btihaj Ajana (2011) argues that the dominance of "biometric citizenship" is a national extension of neoliberal citizenship. Specifically, Ajana (2011) describes how states portray the use of biometrics as a way for individual immigrants and visitors to exercise "more [individual] control" and thus, more freedom: "Biometric citizenship is as such a neoliberal citizenship to the extent that it embodies individuated claims and practices based on the principles of choice, autonomy, flexibility and entrepreneurialism" (856). In applying these insights, we show how, for skilled economic immigrants who are the "ideal" immigrants, the use of biometrics facilitates their entry into Canada, and is thus not a restrictive measure like it is for asylum seekers, refugees, and temporary labour migrants, whose movements are more easily surveilled using biometrics (Pero and Smith 2014). Seen in this light, we argue, the Canadian government's priorities of neoliberalization and criminalization intertwine in the seeking of skilled economic immigrants as "ideal" Canadians.

The Conservative government's prioritization of economic immigration is facilitated in part by what Paquet and Larios (2018) call "venue shopping," whereby the Harper government shifted "sites of decision making" to new non-governmental actors (e.g., employers), to subnational bodies (e.g., provinces, cities) and to the executive branch through the immigration bureaucracy, including the office of the immigration minister. Downloading immigration decisions to other actors and centralizing it within the executive branch (including through the immigration minister) makes it difficult to contest neoliberalization and criminalization. Indeed, because the immigration minister sets the terms for the economic immigration program at their discretion through their use of Ministerial Instructions, economic immigration priorities are set without giving much opportunity for input to elected officials, policymakers from other government bureaucracies, and members of the Canadian public. The centralization of decision-making is concerning because the types of decisions made on economic immigration "come with significant political implications" (Hiebert 2019, 1). There are no opportunities to ask questions about potential human rights abuses under the new programs – as can be seen when private actors such as employers are given more discretion in determining who gets accepted – nor are there opportunities to question nation-building priorities. The high levels of technical knowledge that is oftentimes required to make sense of new program changes acts as a further barrier to questioning economic immigration policies.

FEDERAL IMMIGRATION PROGRAMS: FROM THE POINTS SYSTEM TO EXPRESS ENTRY

In this section we outline Canada's human capital approach to immigrant selection. A Human Capital Approach to Immigration approach is defined as one that sees the recruitment of immigrants on the basis of their education levels, skills, and prior employment experiences and can be contrasted to an approach to immigration prioritizing European immigration or an employment approach, which prioritizes accepting immigrants with concrete job offers. To show how Canada's Human Capital approach developed, we analyse the market logics underpinning shifts in Canada's economic class programs.

To begin, as we discussed in chapter two, it is important to stress that Canada draws most of its immigrants from economic class applicants, who vastly outnumber immigrants entering under family sponsorship and humanitarian classes. For successive Canadian governments, a human capital approach to immigration selection became a way to gain an advantage in the age of neoliberal globalization. Only those with demonstrable skills and qualifications for entry into the labour market are deemed worthy of permanent entry. By contrast, those who work in essential industries but who do not amass sufficient points, such as farm workers or care workers, are deemed unworthy or less worthy of permanent settlement in Canada.

The 2002 Immigration and Refugee Protection Act (IRPA) refined Canada's economic immigration priorities. According to the Canadian government, "the selection system for skilled workers was changed to respond to the dynamic labour market associated with today's knowledge-based, global economy," subsequently leading to the establishment of IRPA's Federal Skilled Workers Program (FSWP) in 2002 (Government of Canada 2010). In contrast to the pre-IRPA points system, which had ten criteria, the FSWP had six criteria, all designed to more closely align immigration selection with the possibility for economic success. More points are placed on education, knowledge of English or French, and experience, with additional points given for "arranged employment" and "adaptability elements" that include "positive arranged employment opinion" (Government of Canada 2010). Indeed, the desire to be economically competitive meant that more points are allocated to education and skill levels in selecting immigrants, with emphasis being put on *"ever-higher levels* of skill and a greater emphasis on education as opposed to specific occupational skills in various trades" (Reitz 2013, 152, emphasis added). The net result of this new emphasis on potential for economic success, according to the Canadian government, is that IRPA Federal Skilled Workers have higher employment earnings and become economically established more quickly, in contrast to their counterparts recruited under the pre-IRPA points system (Government of Canada 2010).

Yet many scholars contend that emphasizing economic success obscures persisting inequalities. Specifically, emphasis on high skills and high education conceals how "education" and "skill" serve "as a proxy, whether intentional or not, for other forms of discrimination based on race, class, gender, or national origin" (Tanner 2011, 1332). There exist numerous examples of how the use of criteria such as education and skill may lead to different forms of discrimination. Women, for one, have a harder time meeting such criteria because the paid and unpaid care work more frequently undertaken by women does not merit as many, if any, points because of their concentration in reproductive forms of labour (see Abu-Laban and Gabriel 2002, 50–1). Different notions of education and skill also invariably lead immigration applications from Global South countries to be discounted because university and college degrees in these states are not considered on par with Canadian university degrees. Bachelor's degrees from the Philippines, for example, only count as two years' worth of university education in Canada. Under FSWP, the majority of permanent immigrants to Canada have had professional work experience and at minimum a university degree. As noted in the introduction, wealthy countries are increasingly competing for workers deemed high skilled. This global competition for talent has led Canada to impose higher qualifications for entry.

Of course, it is worth noting that even when highly educated and high-skilled immigrants from these countries move to Canada, their education and work experience are not always considered as being on par with Canadians who received their credentials in the country. Alboim, Finnie, and Meng's analysis of visible minority immigrants' labour market participation illustrates this point. Their analysis of the "returns" that immigrants and native-born Canadians get on their education shows that "a foreign degree held by an immigrant who belongs to a visible minority group is heavily discounted in the Canadian labour market" (2005, 11). Hence, using education and skill as measures of potential labour market success are flawed because of underlying race, class, and gender biases.

Express Entry as an Example of Market Logics When Seeking Citizens

The mismatch between immigrants' skills and the jobs they obtain in Canada was one of the rationales, at least in theory, for rehauling Canada's economic immigration programs after 2006 (Alboim et al. 2005). Specifically, the desire to "modernize" the immigration system to ensure that immigrants who are selected are the "best" led the Conservative government of Stephen Harper, in power from 2006 until

2015, to push Canadian immigration policy in a new direction. This is not to say that Harper did not continue the economic immigration policies of his Liberal predecessors. Rather, the Harper Conservatives continued down the same path of prioritizing neoliberal immigration policymaking. However, the Conservatives went further to ensure that economic immigration overtook other immigration categories with the exception of temporary labour migration, as will be discussed in chapter five. What was noteworthy about Harper's approach was not only how this dovetailed with the Liberal party's policies under Jean Chretien but also that this represented a significant shift among right-wing conservatives. Prior to the formation of the Conservative party led by Harper in 2006, Canada's right wing comprised two parties: the former Progressive Conservative Party and the Canadian Alliance Party. In an effort to "unite the right" Harper led the merger of the two parties under the banner of the Conservative Party of Canada. Importantly, Harper's efforts to "modernize" Canada's immigration system marked a shift away from the former Canadian Alliance Party's policies, which were highly critical of immigration.

Attempts to modernize Canada's immigration system was likewise influenced by Jason Kenney, the current premier of Alberta as of 2019, who served in Harper's cabinet (2006–15) in both the immigration and multiculturalism portfolios. Kenney's efforts to reach ethnic minority voters who were deemed likely to support the Conservatives informed both policy and discourse at the time. Hence, the Conservative Party's approach towards immigration explicitly drew a contrast between "good" and "bad" immigrants by recasting the party as one that recognizes the value of good, hard-working, economically productive, and talented immigrants (Carlaw 2015, 109). Harper frequently deployed military metaphors to signal Canada's quest for hard-working, economically productive, "legitimate" immigrants (Carlaw 2011, 110). For example, he tellingly declared that Canada is part of a "global war for talent" (Tanner 2011, 1335).

The Conservative government's desire to make Canada more economically competitive resulted in significant changes to Canada's economic immigration programs. These changes were designed to allow policymakers to recruit the "best and the brightest" immigrants with minimal bureaucracy, i.e., through "administrative depoliticization" (Hiebert 2019, 9). These changes also helped ensure that accepted immigrants have sufficient Canadian work experience. Following Australia and New Zealand's "two-step" immigration models (Hiebert 2019, 4), the Harper government moved from a human capital approach to immigration, which previously defined Canada's points system, towards a more privatized, employment-driven approach to immigration already instituted in part within the FSWP. An employment-driven approach to immigration, as we discuss below, downloads immigration decision-making to employers, businesses, and other private actors, thereby "obscuring processes of racial [and other forms of] discrimination that persist through employer-driven immigrant selection" (Bhuyan et al. 2015, 59). Such an approach also magnifies the power that employers have over prospective immigrants since employers hold the possibility of sponsorship and can use this to ensure worker compliance.

Along with the Provincial Nominee Programs (PNPs), the Canadian Experience Class (CEC) program founded in 2008 offered a way for the Harper government to link labour market needs more closely with immigration policies. This approach was subsequently embraced by the Liberal government of Justin Trudeau. Under the CEC, temporary foreign workers who have been employed in a skilled profession and international students who recently graduated and have one year of work experience are eligible to apply for permanent residency. In contrast to the points system and the FSWP that use "observable characteristics to predict labor market success," the CEC uses private actors to determine who enters the country, including employers, who give job offers, and post-secondary institutions, which give offers of admissions to students (Ferrer et al. 2014, 857).

At first glance, the CEC appears to operate objectively, enabling the entry of immigrants from diverse backgrounds. Yet further scrutiny reveals that the CEC *amplifies* the belief that the ideal immigrant is economically independent and self-reliant – someone who does not rely on the state for their settlement needs – by adding the category of "Canadian Experience" as part of the selection criteria. By putting the onus on immigrants to show that they are worthy of permanent settlement in Canada because they have secured employment, immigrants' labour market successes and failures are *individualized*. As a result, there is little regard for how structural factors impede immigrant employment, including factors that stem from the Canadian government's own policies, such as the non-recognition of foreign credentials. The Conservative government *did* try to rectify the common complaint that the non-recognition of foreign credentials presented barriers to job market entry for immigrants by establishing a Foreign Credentials Referrals Office and a Foreign Credential Recognition Program (Sweetman, McDonald, and Hawthorne 2015), which the Government of Canada reports has led to greater "fairness, consistency, timeliness, and transparency of foreign credential recognition." However, the same report notes that these initiatives have not been sufficient in helping immigrants find "positions that are commensurate with their qualifications" (Employment and Social Development Canada 2020).

Moreover, the Conservative government's justifications in establishing the CEC shows how CEC enables the further entrenchment of neoliberal market logics in immigration selection. Neoliberal market logics are evident, for instance, in former Immigration Minister Jason Kenney's insistence that the CEC would allow Canada to use a flexible and fast system for processing immigration applications. A more efficient system would be achieved, he explained, by prioritizing those who, in contrast to the "billions of prospective immigrants" seeking entry into Canada, can show "seamless economic and social transition" (Bhuyan et al. 2015, 58). The underlying logic is that good immigrants are docile, economically self-sufficient neoliberal subjects, whereas bad immigrants are those who have not shown their economic self-sufficiency and are thus "deportable" (Bhuyan et al. 2015, 58). That only temporary foreign workers who have been employed in "skilled" professions can qualify for the CEC illustrates how Canadian immigration policy has heightened the divisions between so-called high-skilled and low-skilled migrants, with the latter being seen as ultimately undesirable and unworthy.

The Express Entry (EE) program, founded in 2015 by the Conservatives and continuing today, further streamlines the Canadian government's move towards employment-driven approaches to immigration. Established in order to "manage the economic class immigration programs more effectively" (Wang 2018, 1060), the Canadian government's stated objectives were to "recruit the best candidates who are most likely to succeed, rather than the first person in line" (Government of Canada 2014). Three immigration programs administered by the federal government were filtered through the EE program, namely, the Federal Skilled Workers Program (FSWP), the Federal Skilled Trades Program (FSTP, which was created in 2013 as an offshoot of the FSWP) and the Canadian Experience Class (CEC). What this means is that applicants who qualify for the FSWP, the FSTP, and the CEC have to place their applications into the EE pool, after which their applications are ranked using a Comprehensive Ranking System (CRS) where applicants are graded relative to other applicants on the basis of their "skills, work experience, language ability, education, and other factors" (Dam et al. 2017, 893). The first step applicants have to take is to fill out an EE profile to show an expression of interest; in so doing, applicants can then determine their eligibility for any of the aforementioned programs and some Provincial Nominee Programs, which we discuss below (Kushal 2019, 100). Those who rank highest under the Comprehensive Ranking System are then given an "invitation to apply" (Wang 2018, 1064).

There are several important differences between the Points System and the old FSWP and EE. A key distinction has to do with immigration quotas. Under EE, immigration applicants need no longer worry about immigration quotas filling up before their application is evaluated, whereas under the old FSWP, all applications are evaluated and processed against each other (Wang 2018, 1069). In contrast to the points system and the old FSWP, where there exists a set number of points that applicants can receive, EE enables flexibility by allowing the Canadian government to add additional criteria that immigration applicants have to meet on top of the criteria each immigration program requires. The EE program thus increases competition between applicants, who not only have to compete against applicants within the immigration program they are applying under – that is, the old FSWP, the FSTP, or the CEC – but also compete with all other economic-class applicants. This places certain immigration applicants at a disadvantage. For example, international students, particularly those who graduate from doctoral programs in Canadian universities, find it harder to qualify through EE because they do not get as much credit for education compared with job experience (Wang 2018, 1071).

The prioritization of Canadian employment over other criteria in immigrant selection is clearly evident in the EE program. Under EE, more weight is given towards offers of employment than education, in contrast to the points system and to the pre-EE FSWP. Likewise, applicants who receive a positive nomination under the PNP or who have "arranged employment [through a program requiring a Labour Market Impact Assessment, such as through the Temporary Foreign Worker Program]" (Wang 2018, 1064) receive the greatest number of points under the Comprehensive Ranking System.

When critics charged that the EE system prioritized employment over other criteria, the Liberal government subsequently modified the points distribution. Under the Liberals, education levels received more points. The Liberals also differentiated between the types of job offers applicants received, with job offers in senior management netting more points compared to job offers in management, professional careers, or technical trades (Kushal 2019, 104). Hence, while the EE system under the Harper Conservative government guaranteed the invitation to apply if applicants have a job offer, under Trudeau's Liberal government, "a job offer may tip the balance, but it is no longer enough to guarantee an invitation" (Kushal 2019, 104). These changes, however, were minute. Under the Trudeau Liberals, employment still trumped other criteria because to score high in the Comprehensive Ranking Regime, one must have a job offer or a provincial nomination (which in many cases still requires a job offer); as such, employers and provinces still retained considerable power in determining which immigrants were successful (Kushal 2019, 104).

Another change the Canadian government under the Conservatives instituted and that the Liberal government subsequently left intact is the entrenchment of a two-step immigration model. This model requires prospective immigrants to enter Canada through one immigration program and subsequently apply to be part of another immigration program in order to get Canadian citizenship. Two-step immigration models require that applicants put their citizenship applications through another immigration program, such as the PNP or CEC. These programs will then vet whether applicants are likely to economically integrate into Canada, seen most commonly through a job offer. That immigrants with prior Canadian employment had greater earnings a year after acquiring Canadian permanent residency compared to other immigrants without Canadian employment experience seems to corroborate the perception that two-step immigration helps ensure that applicants contribute economically (Hou, Crossman, and Picot 2020, 10). To be clear, two-step immigration has long been a part of Canada's immigration programs, as can be seen through the Foreign Domestics Movement and later, the Live-in Caregiver Program where caregivers are "citizens-in-waiting" and can only obtain Canadian permanent residency upon completion of their two-year live-in work contracts. The government's use of two-step immigration within economic immigration programs, however, intensified under Harper's Conservatives. In fact, such immigration programs have ended up involving not just two but rather a series of different steps.

For example, the international graduate student stream under the CEC was eliminated under this government. International students wishing to obtain Canadian permanent residency now had to first get a student visa, then, after their studies, obtain a Post-Graduate Work Permit, which would allow them to work in Canada for three years. Only after their permit expires can they then apply for permanent residency through one of Canada's economic immigration programs (Government of Canada 2019). On this note, the Liberal government upheld the Harper government's belief that international students are the "ideal immigrants" (Scott et al. 2015, 2). As articulated in the Canadian government's "International Education Strategy," developed by the Conservative government in 2015 and amended by the Liberal government in 2018, "international students make excellent candidates for permanent residency: they are relatively young, are proficient in at least one official language, have Canadian educational qualifications and can help address this country's current and pending labour market needs, *particularly for high skilled workers*" (Government of Canada 2019, 5, emphasis added). In addition, that international students would first have to invest in Canadian institutions by paying international student tuition fees, rent, and other expenses before qualifying to apply for Canadian citizenship shows that, regardless of the outcome of international students' citizenship applications, international students provide a net benefit for Canada as revenue generators. Yet immigration researchers have discovered that international students actually do not fare well under this multiple-step immigration model, with experiences of financial and cultural integration difficulties commonplace (Catungal and Tungohan 2021; Scott et al.

2015). In our chapter on temporary foreign work, we discuss further the notion that international students have become Canada's "new" temporary foreign workers.

When contemplating the additional challenges facing migrants who have to follow multiple steps in order to become permanent residents, immigration researchers are divided. There are those who see two-step immigration models as a logical way to ensure that immigrants are economically productive; for them, multiple-step immigration programs have merit because they ensure that immigrants are employed (see, e.g., Hou, Crossman, and Picot 2020). Given that immigrants themselves point to how hard it is to find a job upon coming to Canada, a program that *requires* them to have a job offer and that even has provisions allowing workers to be matched with prospective employers appears beneficial.

Yet there are those who see such logics as putting the onus on *individual* immigrants to economically integrate without looking at structural reasons for why it is difficult for some to do so. Thus, rather than fixing institutions that make it difficult for immigrants to get employed (e.g., through gatekeeping measures imposed by professional associations, through labour market discrimination grounded in racial and gender bias), the problem of economic integration is equated solely with the idea of individual immigrants failing to find jobs. These critics warn that two-step/multiple-step immigration models "should not become the norm, as it is in some other countries" since they create a second tier of residents whose integration into the country gets delayed (Alboim and Cohl 2012, 44). Researchers also warn of the human rights breaches that may occur under multiple-step immigration because potential immigrants have to retain the goodwill of their employers in order to be eligible for citizenship and, in many cases, have to accept substandard working conditions to make their applications competitive. As we address later, similar critiques are made towards the PNPs and the temporary foreign worker program. Ultimately, the shift into a multiple-step immigration model compel immigrants to prove that they are worthy of becoming Canadian citizens by showing their economic contributions. The ideal citizen is thus someone who is economically productive in ways that the government can easily *measure*, leading to a prioritization of "real" skills versus "theoretical" skills such as "leadership potential and interpersonal communication" and thus to a "lack of creativity" in considering the diverse contributions potential citizens can make to the country (Hiebert 2018, 2, 9).

EVOLVING FEDERAL-PROVINCIAL RELATIONSHIPS AND THE RISE OF PROVINCIAL NOMINEE PROGRAMS

In the 1990s, federal-provincial relations underwent important shifts, which ultimately led to the devolution of immigration decision-making from federal to provincial authorities. In this section, we show how evolving federal-provincial relationships contributed to the rise of the neoliberal citizen. Positioned by governments as an ideal economic immigrant, the neoliberal citizen "contributes to national economic growth and either cost less or pay for their own settlement" (Dobrowolsky 2011, 113). By enabling provinces to exercise a greater role in immigration decision-making through Provincial Nominee Programs (PNPs), the mechanics of which we explain below, immigration policymaking further moved away from nation-building and family reunification imperatives towards primarily prioritizing economic, and more specifically neoliberal, rationales for seeking citizens.

Immigration and Evolving Federal-Provincial Relationships

From its founding as a federation, Canada's 1867 Constitution Act defines immigration as an area of concurrent federal and provincial jurisdiction. Since the 1960s, Quebec has led the way in attempting to get more control over selection in order to ensure that incoming immigrants to Quebec are proficient in French. Provinces have not always played a role in selecting immigrants. Although the initial years of Confederation involved active participation by provinces in immigration decision-making, after the Second World War, provinces played a diminished role. In the decades that followed, the federal government continued to take the lead in immigrant selection, although provinces gradually began to assume a bigger role (Vineberg 1987). It was not until 1967, though, when Quebec pressed for greater autonomy in the wake of the province's Quiet Revolution, that the dominance of the federal government in intergovernmental relations was questioned (Cameron and Simeon 2002, 51). Quebec's insistence in assuming a more prominent role in immigration led to the establishment of the Quebec Immigration Department, which placed provincial Quebec immigration officers in Canadian embassies in Rome, Athens, Beirut, and at the *Delegation Générale du Quebec* in Paris, and which gave Quebec the ability to provide integration and settlement services to newcomers (Vineberg 1987, 307).

This new federal–provincial arrangement was a precursor to the following agreements between the federal and Quebec governments: the 1971 Lang-Cloutier agreement, where the federal government promised to expand the "francophone content of the immigration movement"; the 1975 Andras-Bienvenue agreement, which gave Quebec "substantial" input into immigration selection decisions and which formalized a joint federal–provincial committee on immigration information exchange; the 1978 Cullen-Couture agreement that theoretically gave the federal government and Quebec joint decision-making power in immigration selection but in practice gave Quebec the bulk of the power by specifying that any "independent immigrant" landing in Quebec "requires Quebec's prior agreement" (Vineberg 1987, 312–14); and finally, the 1991 McDougall/Gagnon-Tremblay Accord, also known as the Canada-Quebec immigration agreement, which gave Quebec sole authority to select economic immigrants into the province and to provide integration services (Seidle 2013, 4). The Canada-Quebec agreement was a game changer when it came to federal–provincial relations on immigration because "it created conditions that kept in motion the decentralization mechanism," thus incentivizing other provinces to play a bigger role in immigration policymaking (Paquet 2012, 530).

Consequently, outside of Quebec, provincial leaders began to recognize that their priorities might also be better integrated into federal immigration policymaking. For example, in Manitoba in the 1970s, policymakers, business groups, cultural communities, and social justice organizations wanted to increase immigration not only to address labour market needs but also to develop a more diverse population (Leo and August 2009, 496). The demands for increased immigration made by these various groups led to the establishment of federal–provincial bilateral agreements. These did not go so far as to delegate the same powers to provinces outside Quebec as with Quebec, but nevertheless stipulated the importance of constant communication between the two levels of government and the need to receive provincial input when it comes to the settlement of "certain categories of immigrants, such as entrepreneurs, teachers, and invalids" (Vineberg 1987, 315–16). These bilateral agreements, which scholars describe as a form of "asymmetric federalism" (Smith 2005), prioritize greater provincial input into federal decision-making towards immigration policies, thus ensuring that immigration decision-making is no longer solely dominated by federal policymakers. Although provinces, with the arguable exception of Quebec, were ultimately reluctant to assume a more dominant role in immigration policymaking because of "political and financial costs" (Paquet 2012, 521), that bilateral agreements ensured that provinces give the federal government input on immigration policy helped set the stage for further devolution in immigration policymaking, as we will discuss in this chapter.

In the 1990s, the Atlantic and Prairie provinces raised new concerns about federal–provincial relations on immigration. At the time, the majority of economic immigrants were heading to British Columbia, Ontario, and Quebec – and within these provinces, to Vancouver, Toronto, and Montreal. As a result, the Atlantic and Prairie provinces began expressing their desire for policy responsiveness to their specific needs (Seidle 2013, 4). The demographic problems they faced were not solved through federal immigration programs (Ley and Hiebert 2001), leading provinces to lobby for immigration programs that met their needs. These provinces were particularly concerned about how federal economic immigration programs targeted high-skilled workers, which meant that industries needing low-skilled workers were stagnating (Seidle 2013, 5). Competition for workers between these regions also exacerbated regional labour shortages, particularly in the Prairie provinces, where Alberta's economic strengths led workers to head to Calgary, Alberta, over Winnipeg, Manitoba, for example. These regional concerns were promoted by media outlets like the *Winnipeg Free Press* and enshrined the conviction that immigration programs should target specific provincial needs (Abu-Laban and Garber 2005, 535).

Manitoba in particular took on a leading role in proactively seeking policy solutions to the lack of immigrants coming into their province. In 1996, after years of lobbying the federal government for a say in immigrant selection, the federal government signed the

Canada-Manitoba Immigration Agreement. The agreement identified the roles that Manitoba and the federal government would jointly play in immigration selection and settlement-service delivery (Leo and August 2009, 496). Notably, the federal government initially resisted a bilateral agreement with Manitoba because it "mistrusted provincial capacity to administer an immigration program with logic and integrity" (Paquet 2012, 536).

Moreover, Manitoba also signed an agreement with the federal government for the creation of a specific immigration stream to address labour shortages. Following lobbying efforts by garment industry employers, the Manitoba government launched a pilot project in 1996 enabling the recruitment of 200 foreign garment workers as permanent immigrants into the province (Leo and August 2009, 496). The terms of the project were relatively strict, with employers having to assume all sponsorship costs and provide a guarantee that the workers did not avail of unemployment insurance or social assistance. Nevertheless, the Manitoba government lauded their pilot project as a success (Baxter 2010, 18; Leo and August 2009, 496). Consequently, a Provincial Nominee and Settlement Services Annex was added to the Canada-Manitoba Immigration Agreement that gave Manitoba the ability to nominate 200 entrants per year (Leo and August 2009, 496).

In 2003, the federal government and Manitoba signed another agreement that kept intact the existing agreement, with added provisions addressing "regional needs ... the issue of qualifications recognition, and the need to focus on foreign and temporary foreign workers" (Leo and August 2008, 497). Under the new agreement, the 200-nominee limit on nominations was removed, with the federal government and Manitoba agreeing to negotiate annual quotas (Leo and August 2009, 497). Policymakers have considered it evidence of the program's success that Manitoba has the most nominees out of any provinces and recruits the highest number of economic immigrants through a nominee program (Lewis 2010, 246).

Admittedly, the program initially went through some difficulties concerning nominees' ability to adapt to Manitoba and the emergence of a shadow industry of unethical recruiters. Immigrants whose entry was facilitated by unethical recruiters found themselves arriving in the province without real job offers (Leo and August 2009, 501–4). However, Manitoba revised the terms of the program in 2004 to prioritize nominees who could prove pre-existing connections in the province, which helped ensure easier adaptability. The new terms of the program also prioritized applicants who could prove community support, thus reducing the likelihood of migrants falling prey to unethical recruitment practices.

The importance of immigrant adaptation, in fact, is one that many provinces that have PNPs take seriously, leading them to devote many resources to immigrant integration, although it is noteworthy that all provinces devote most of their resources to economic immigrant integration and not to, for example, social or political integration (Paquet and Xhardez 2020).

Overall, these shifts in federal–provincial relationship over time show that provinces challenged federal dominance in immigration policymaking. As the next section shows, the growth of PNPs bolstered the idea that ideal immigrants are those who are neoliberal citizens with clear economic contributions to the communities where they will settle.

Growing Dominance of PNPs

Manitoba's initiative was the impetus needed for other provinces to sign their own nominee agreements with the federal government (Paquet 2012, 537). Different provinces' PNPs have varying nomination criteria. While all provinces allow employers to nominate workers through the "general or employer recruitment streams," provinces can determine other streams through which immigrants can be nominated, such as through "business investor programs, family reunification programs, and international students" (Seidle 2013, 8). Each province is responsible for determining the types of immigrants to be recruited, nominating immigrants, and administering and monitoring PNPs. In turn, the federal government is in charge of screening all nominees, how many nominees each province gets, and which nominees get selected through the department of Immigration, Refugees and Citizenship Canada (IRCC), formerly known as Citizenship and Immigration Canada (CIC) (Carter 2012, 184; Seidle 2013, 5). British Columbia and Saskatchewan signed nominee agreements in 1998, followed by New Brunswick and Newfoundland and Labrador in 1999, Prince Edward Island and the Yukon in 2001, Alberta and Nova Scotia in 2002, Ontario in 2005, and the Northwest Territories in 2009 (Seidle 2013, 5).

Over the years, PNPs have become one of the most important economic immigration programs, with the Canadian government acknowledging the "exponential growth" of the PNP program since its establishment in 1996. Before PNPs became widespread, the federal government was responsible for choosing 90 per cent of all economic immigrants to Canada, with Quebec selecting the remaining 10 per cent (El-Kassal 2019). This figure rapidly changed: whereas PNP immigrants constituted 12 per cent of all economic immigrants in 2007, the share of PNP nominees grew to 25 per cent of economic immigrants in 2012, and 29 per cent in 2017 (CIC 2015a; OECD 2019). Since the first agreements were signed in provinces other than Quebec, an increasing number of economic immigrants have used PNPs to enter Canada. Although the fallout of the COVID-19 pandemic may complicate stated policy goals, the Canadian government intends to welcome 67,800 PNP immigrants in 2020, or 34.6 per cent of all economic immigrants, and 71,300 PNP immigrants in 2021, or 35 per cent of all economic immigrants (Canada 2018b).

It is not difficult to surmise why employers and policymakers laud the PNP. By allowing employers to nominate workers for permanent immigration through PNPs, newcomers immediately have a foothold in the labour market and theoretically experience an easier time transitioning to Canada. This feature of the PNP can assuage the concerns of immigration critics, who see immigrants' inability to find employment in Canada as a major cause for immigrants' settlement and transition difficulties (Picot and Sweetman 2012, 6–7). Moreover, because provinces set which types of economic immigrants are needed to bolster key industries and determine application criteria, labour shortages are immediately alleviated. More importantly, provincial decision-making around immigrant selection can help ensure that immigrant settlement becomes more evenly distributed across Canada, with smaller cities and rural communities availing of the benefits of immigration (Carter 2012, 184). The flexibility generated by PNPs enable the federal government to revise PNP immigration targets such that population growth through immigration is more widely dispersed. For Atlantic provinces, in particular, PNPs are the biggest source of economic immigrants (CIC News 2019). Given the more even distribution of immigrant settlement across regions, PNPs arguably enable long-term settlement. Indeed, provincial nominees are more likely to stay in the province where they first landed compared to economic immigrants recruited through federal streams, as in the case of nominees in British Columbia, Alberta, Saskatchewan, and Manitoba (Pandey and Townsend 2011, 498).

Yet further scrutiny draws some questions about the perceived overall success of PNPs. Writing in the context of Manitoba's PNP, Nathaniel Lewis's (2010) critique of the program can be extended, we suggest, to a critique of PNPs as a whole: "[PNPs] are neoliberal programs that employ competitive and marketized selection and resettlement regimes, download responsibilities to provincial and non-government parties, and recruit particular groups to increase the volume and speed of immigration ... This type of 'rollback' neoliberalism, now a dominant phenomenon in Western countries, is a set of practices under which central services are cut back, deregulated, or privatized, while local institutions and actors are given 'responsibility without power' through a process of 'regulatory dumping'" (249). That PNPs are jointly administered by the federal government, the provincial government and employers/sponsors makes it difficult to track which bodies are ultimately responsible for how PNP immigrants fare. By "rolling back" on the types of services that look after immigrant well-being, PNPs are at risk of overlooking PNP immigrant abuse.

Indeed, the myriad controversies that have emerged with respect to PNPs highlight all too well the validity of Lewis's observations. Dobrowolsky (2011) analyses the shortcomings of Nova Scotia's PNP, pointing to how some of its objectives were not met. For example, there were many cases showing that the requirements were not followed, namely, that migrants entering through its economic stream have a net worth of at least $300,000, have experience in owning or operating a business, and have a six-month placement with a company providing mentorship and job experience (122). Many nominees were placed not in middle-management jobs but were asked to do menial, low-skilled jobs; in extreme cases, nominees arrived in Nova Scotia and discovered that they were given bogus job offers and did not have work at all (Dobrowolsky 2011, 123). An internal audit undertaken by Nova Scotia's auditor-general corroborated these findings. It showed, for example, that twenty out of the forty-six companies surveyed did not have a middle-management position for nominees and that "'the majority of business matches are not *bona fide*'" (Office of Immigration, as quoted in Dobrowolsky 2011, 124).[2] The perception that PNPs exploit nominees is heightened by the fact that nominees were asked to pay a one-time "non-refundable contribution to the provincial economy" of $130,500 in order to be part of the PNP (Dobrowolsky 2011, 122), which led the government of Nova Scotia to issue refunds worth millions of dollars in 2007 (Dobrowolsky 2011, 124).

Critics charge that part of the problem was the Nova Scotia government's decision to offload the administration of the PNP to a private business, Cornwallis Financial Corporation, which made $4 million from their contract. Representatives of the Nova Scotia government defended their actions by stating that they simply lacked the capacity to administer the PNP and so had to delegate administration of the program to a private company because for-profit entities are, by their very definition, more invested in amassing profit than in safeguarding migrants' welfare. But this means that the likelihood of program mismanagement increased; even the Nova Scotia government was forced to concede that Cornwallis "acted 'with a lack of regard for public sector interests and instead emphasized its own commercial interests'" (Massinon, as quoted in Dobrowolsky 2011, 129).

Similar scandals plagued Prince Edward Island's PNP. Like other provinces without major urban centres, PEI needed a strategy to bolster its declining population. Federal economic immigration programs were insufficient in meeting PEI's needs, which meant the PNP was crucial in bringing in more people into the province. In fact, estimates show that the PNP was responsible for 94 per cent of all immigrants, raising the percentage of economic immigrants from 37 per cent in 2001 to 96 per cent in 2010 (Government of Prince Edward Island 2012, 24). Allegations of mismanagement, however, led the federal government to shut the program down in 2008, leading a spokesperson for then Immigration Minister Jason Kenney to state that, "PEI's mismanagement of the Provincial Nominee Program affected the integrity of Canada's immigration system" (Alex Pavlich, as quoted in Tutton 2012). For example, nominees who gave hundreds of thousands of dollars in investment money to a private firm hired by PEI to administer the PNP found their applications rejected by the federal government and their investment money unreturned (Tutton 2012). Other nominees found themselves in PEI without employment; yet others found that they did not have any connections to the businesses they were supposed to have invested in (University of King's College 2012). Unscrupulous agents also took cuts from nominees' and sponsoring businesses' earnings (University of King's College 2012). Even more controversial were allegations that provincial officials responsible for the PNP took bribes from prospective immigrants and approved their applications despite being unqualified (Wright 2011). Some even owned companies that received investment funds from nominees (CBC News 2009). This controversy adversely affected then Liberal Premier Robert Ghiz, whose opponents accused him of being complicit in the bribery scandal (Bissett 2015).

Beyond these scandals, the perception that nominees are taking jobs away from qualified Canadians also heightened the racial tensions surrounding PNPs. Nominees who are asked to make high investments in order to be eligible for Canadian citizenship have become the source of resentment for some Canadians, who see this as evidence that "the extremely wealthy are buying their way into Canada because they can" (Petrescu 2014). In some extreme cases, businesses that ostensibly served new investors entering through PNPs have become the target of racial attacks, as in the case of a real-estate firm's advertisement on a bus stop being defaced with racial slurs and swastikas in Nanaimo, BC, and the case of pamphlets decrying the BC PNPs using racially charged rhetoric being distributed to different Nanaimo neighbourhoods (*Nanaimo News Bulletin* 2015). Such rhetoric mimics xenophobic sentiments that have historically been – and are currently – used to target immigrants from racialized communities. That both affluent economic immigrants and temporary foreign workers are attacked for job theft, even though they enter through different immigration streams and have completely different sets of entitlements, is indicative of persisting xenophobia towards racialized immigrations.

The fact that PNPs are tied to Canada's system of "two-step immigration," as discussed earlier, magnifies the possibility for abuse. This is particularly the case for temporary foreign workers (TFWs) who saw PNPs as one of their sole routes to permanent residency in Canada, prior to program changes announced in 2014 that we discuss further in chapter five (Hennebry 2010). In fact, migrants who entered Canada as TFWs first, with the intention of becoming provincial nominees are more vulnerable than those who came to Canada with permanent residency through their provincial nominations. Employers dangled the possibility of nominating workers for permanent residency through PNPs in order to ensure worker compliance. Consequently, TFWs often have to be strategic about getting nominated for the PNPs by remaining in their employers' good graces so their employers might promote and sponsor them or by finding loopholes in existing policies that will allow them to qualify for a nomination.

TFWs who wished to obtain provincial nominations became more susceptible to unsavory immigration brokers, such as immigration consultants, some of whom charge exorbitant sums of money and provide misleading information. For example, Honorato Peralta and Vanessa Tamondong, two TFWs working for a fast-food chain in British Columbia who sought permanent status through the BC PNP, lost $15,000 in consultancy fees when their applications were rejected. To make matters worse, they also received deportation orders because the immigration consultant they hired had misrepresented their applications (Kane 2014). Quotas on the numbers of nominees that provinces can make annually – which are set by the federal government – mean that not all TFWs who applied to be nominees get approved. Long processing times in 2015 meant that some nominees had to wait up to thirteen months before they received their results (Cheung 2015). In some cases, TFWs, whose contracts had expired but whose applications to become provincial nominees were still pending, were placed in a conundrum because the legality of their status in Canada was in question, yet they were still waiting for the results of their applications. That PNPs are temporary foreign workers' best route to permanent residency heightens the likelihood that employers, immigration brokers, and other stakeholders will take advantage of their desire to settle in Canada.

Problems with the PNP led to the federal government's decision to institute changes to PNPs. Along with allowing provinces to nominate prospective immigrants through "paper-based processes" that structure individual PNPs, the federal government now allows provinces to make "enhanced nominations" through Express Entry (EE) that are processed online within six months (Canada 2018c). "Enhanced nominations" do not count as part of each province's PNP allocations and get an additional 600 points in their Comprehensive Ranking Score (CRS) (Government of Canada 2018c). These added points will likely guarantee that a nominee's EE application will be accepted. The Canadian government's decision to accept both paper-based nominations through individual PNPs and enhanced nominations through EE enables provinces, private industries, and individual employers numerous options to nominate workers. Needless to say, these additional options further enhance the power that private stakeholders have when it comes to immigration decision-making. Neoliberal market logic has therefore shifted how Canada seeks citizens and forms part of containing diversity.

Other Employment-Driven Economic Immigration Programs

Because of the popularity of PNPs, the Liberal federal government subsequently created additional targeted economic immigration programs. The government's focus on "regionalization," for instance, acknowledges that there are some geographic areas that are more in need of immigrants than others. In 2017, the Canadian government created the Atlantic Immigration Pilot program (AIP) to enable the settlement of more immigrants into Maritime provinces. The AIP is completely employer driven, with employers having the responsibility to nominate immigrants into either the Atlantic International Graduate Program, the Atlantic High-Skilled Program or the Atlantic Intermediate-Skilled Program. All nominees who have been accepted receive Canadian permanent residency (Government of Canada 2019). Although still a relatively new program, the AIP has faced criticisms for making prospective immigrants vulnerable to abuse (MacIvor 2019). For example, unauthorized recruiters have charged prospective immigrants "up to $170,000" to get a slot through the AIP; the same recruiters have also paid employers to "hire the person for no pay or to simply forge their payroll" (MacIvor 2019). The absence of safeguards for immigrants under the AIP make them vulnerable to employer and recruiter abuse.

In 2020, the Canadian government also proposed the creation of a Municipal Nominee Program (MNP) that would function similar to the PNP, except that it would be "local communities, chambers of commerce, and local councils" that would select nominees (Harris 2020). Former Immigration Minister Marco Mendicino's mandate letter specifies that 5,000 spots will be given for prospective nominees in 2020, with "smaller and mid-sized communities" benefiting (Harris 2020). At the time of writing, the federal government has yet to release details on which communities would be running the program, and what the federal government, provincial government, and municipalities' respective roles would be in administering the program.

As we have demonstrated, creating more spots through enhanced nominations, increased provincial nominee allocations, and new programs such as the AIP and the MNP does not solve the problem of worker precariousness, a conclusion that researchers and advocates have likewise stressed (Faraday 2012, 32). The arbitrary classification of skill which makes some workers and not others eligible for permanent residency is at issue in this case, as well as the belief that economic immigration should be pursued at all costs. The downloading of immigration decision-making to stakeholders ultimately absolves the federal government from being responsible for immigrant settlement. This downloading has extended not only to provincial and municipal governments but also to private companies, and even families, the latter of whom have to prove their ability to help nominees settle. Although many provincial policymakers stress that there has to be greater flexibility in immigration decision-making to better reflect their specific labour market needs, greater flexibility has come at the cost of increased migrant vulnerability and multiple rights abuses. When immigrants are selected primarily on the basis of their ability to generate economic growth without concurrently providing immigrants with consistent and robust programs that give support for settlement and integration, immigrants face a harder time adjusting to their new communities. Furthermore, when the administration and management of Provincial Nominee Programs, the Atlantic Immigration Pilot Program, and Municipal Nominee Program become offloaded to stakeholders with very little oversight, immigrants can be exploited further.

CONCLUSION

On the surface, Canada's economic programs seem laudable. The government has strived to make Canada globally competitive and responsive to various regions' and provinces' economic needs. A closer analysis, however, shows how key shifts in these programs have further intensified neoliberal market logics. These shifts include giving provinces, employers, and other private stakeholders such as businesses a greater role in immigration decision-making, exposing migrants to abuse at their hands. Immigrants have also become more vulnerable in terms of their right to remain in Canada. If we situate economic programs within broader efforts to "contain diversity," we can see how what is ultimately produced is an ideal neoliberal subject. This subject is held up as the preferred citizen, thereby justifying the poor treatment of other subjects who largely comprise racialized and poor "low-skilled" migrants from the Global South upon whose labour Canada relies but who Canada does not deem worthy of inclusion.

Such shifts in policy and in discourses, of course, do not come uncontested. Migrant advocacy groups have been at the forefront in calling attention to the Canadian government's attempts to contain diversity by highlighting, among many issues, the unsustainability of economic immigration programs that primarily equate immigrants' worthiness with their economic contributions. In July 2021, the Migrant Rights Network, for instance, had a rally in Ottawa calling for permanent residency to be given not on the basis of immigrants' economic contributions but on the basis of immigrants' ongoing *presence* in Canada (Cohen and Chanco 2021). Hence, as we discuss further in our concluding chapter, advocacy organizations create alternate discourses to counter neoliberal understandings of immigration policymaking.

NOTES

1 Notably, these figures were released before COVID-19, when public health concerns led governments to close borders to all but those deemed essential. However, as of spring 2020, the Canadian government has yet to declare updated immigration priorities. Immigration applications, including applications made for Express Entry, are still being accepted despite travel restrictions being in place; the only caveat that the Canadian government issued is that travel to Canada may be delayed (Government of Canada 2020).
2 Other PNPs were charged with insufficiently placing Provincial Nominees with jobs that match their qualifications, refuting the perception that PNPs solve long-standing issues of immigrant deskilling (Juffs and Siemiatycki 2019).

BIBLIOGRAPHY

Abu-Laban, Yasmeen, and Judy Garber. "The Construction of the Geography of Immigration as Policy Problem: The United States and Canada Compared." *Urban Affairs Review* 40, no. 4 (2005): 520–61.

Ajana, Btihaj. "Biometric Citizenship." *Citizenship Studies* 16, no. 7 (2011): 851–70.

Alboim, Naomi, and Karen Cohl. *Shaping the Future: Canada's Rapidly Changing Immigration Policies*. Toronto: Maytree Foundation, 2012. https://maytree.com/wp-content/uploads/shaping-the-future.pdf.

Alboim, Naomi, Ross Finnie, and Ronald Meng. "The Discounting of Immigrants' Skills in Canada." *IRPP Choices* 11, no. 2 (2005): 1–23.

Baxter, Jamie. *Precarious Pathways: Examining the Provincial Nominee Programs in Canada*. Toronto: Law Commission of Ontario, 2010.

Bhuyan, Rupaleem, Daphne Jeyapal, Jane Ku, Izumi Sakamoto, and Elena Chou. "Branding 'Canadian Experience' in Immigration Policy: Nation Building in a Neoliberal Era." *International Migration and Integration* 18 (2017): 47–62.

Bissett, Kevin. "If Ghiz Had National Ambitions, He Isn't Saying as He Leaves PEI Politics." *iPolitics* (February 20, 2015). http://ipolitics.ca/2015/02/20/if-ghiz-has-national-ambitions-he-isnt-saying-as-he-leaves-p-e-i-politics/.

Boucher, Anna, and Justin Gest. *Crossroads: Comparative Immigration Regimes in a World of Demographic Change*. Cambridge: Cambridge University Press, 2018.

Cameron, David, and Richard Simeon. "Intergovernmental Relations in Canada: The Emergence of Collaborative Federalism." *Publius* 32, no. 2 (2002): 49–71.

Carlaw, John. "A Party for New Canadians? The Rhetoric and Reality of Neoconservative Citizenship and Immigration Policy." In *The Harper Record 2008–2015*, edited by Teresa Healy and Stuart Trew, 105–28. Ottawa: Canadian Centre for Policy Alternatives, 2011.

Carman, Tara. "BC Puts Three-Month Freeze on Applications from Prospective Labour Immigrants." *Vancouver Sun* (March 31, 2015). www.vancouversun.com/puts+month+freeze+applications+from+prospective+labour+immigrants/10935374/story.html?__lsa=4d66-577c.

Carreiro, Donna. "Manitoba is 'Open for Business' for Immigrant Investors." *CBC News* (March 4, 2015). www.cbc.ca/news/canada/prince-edward-island/let-auditor-general-talk-about-pnp-opposition-1.796585.

Carter, Tom. "Provincial Nominee Programs and Temporary Worker Programs: A Comparative Assessment of Advantages and Disadvantages in Addressing Labor Shortages." In *Legislated Inequality: Temporary Labour Migration in Canada*, edited by Patti Lenard and Christine Straehle, 178–201. Montreal, QC, and Kingston, ON: McGill-Queens University Press, 2012.

Catungal, John Paul, and Ethel Tungohan. "Racial Narratives on Repeat: Reflections on Collaborative Research on Asian International Students in COVID Times." *Canadian Literature* 245 (2021). https://canlit.ca/article/racial-narratives-on-repeat-reflections-on-collaborative-research-on-asian-international-students-in-covid-times/.

CBC News. "Let Auditor-General Talk about PNP: Opposition." *CBC News* (October 25, 2009). www.cbc.ca/news/canada/prince-edward-island/let-auditor-general-talk-about-pnp-opposition-1.796585.

Cheung, Christopher. "Is It Going to Help My Immigration?" *The Tyee* (June 26, 2015). http://thetyee.ca/News/2015/06/26/BC-Provincial-Nominee-Program/.

CIC News. "Nova Scotia, Alberta and BC Announce Updates to their Provincial Nominee Programs." September 22, 2015. www.cicnews.com/2015/09/nova-scotia-alberta-bc-announce-updates-provincial-nominee-programs-096225.html.

– "Canada's Maritime Provinces Experience 'Fastest' Population Growth in Decades." May 17, 2019. www.cicnews.com/2019/05/canadas-maritime-provinces-experiencing-fastest-population-growth-in-decades-0512301.html#gs.71mlm9.

Citizenship and Immigration Canada (CIC). "Facts and Figures 2014: Immigration Overview – Permanent Residents." Ottawa: Government of Canada, 2015. www.cic.gc.ca/english/resources/statistics/facts2014/permanent/02.asp.

Cohen, Daniela, and Christopher Chanco. "Advocacy Group Hints at Unexplained Immigration Policy Shift." *Toronto Star* (July 29, 2021). www.thestar.com/news/canada/2021/07/29/advocacy-group-hints-at-unexplained-immigration-policy-shift.html.

Dam, Huyen, Joyce Chan, and Sarah Wayland. "Missed Opportunity: International Students in Canada Face Barriers to Permanent Residence." *Journal of International Migration and Integration* 19, no. 4 (2018): 891–903.

Dobrowolsky, Alexandra. "The Intended and Unintended Effects of a New Immigration Strategy: Insights from Nova Scotia's Provincial Nominee Program." *Studies in Political Economy* 87 (2011): 109–41.

– "Bad versus Big Canada: State Imaginaries of Immigration and Citizenship." *Studies in Political Economy* 98, no. 2 (2017): 197–222.

El-Assal, Kareem. "Canadian Immigration in 2020: Expect a Big Year for Provincial and Regional Immigration Programs." *CIC News* (December 31, 2019). www.cicnews.com/2019/12/canadian-immigration-in-2020-expect-a-big-year-for-provincial-and-regional-immigration-programs-1213412.html#gs.71eu17.

– "Canada Now Operates More than 80 Economic Class Immigration Programs – the Most in Its History." *CIC News* (January 29, 2020). www.cicnews.com/2020/01/canada-now-operates-more-than-80-economic-class-immigration-programs-the-most-in-its-history-0113616.html#gs.6d9q4d.

Employment and Social Development Canada. *Evaluation of the Foreign Credential Recognition Program*. Gatineau, QC: ESDC, 2020.

Environics Survey Institute. "Focus Canada Fall 2020: Canadian Public Opinion about Immigration and Refugees Final Report." *Environics Institute for Survey Research* (October 7, 2020). www.environicsinstitute.org/docs/default-source/project-documents/fc-fall-2020---immigration/focus-canada-fall-2020---public-opinion-on-immigration-refugees---final-report.pdf?sfvrsn=bd51588f_2.

Faraday, Fay. "Made in Canada: How the Law Constructs Migrant Workers' Insecurity." Toronto: Metcalf Foundation, 2012. https://metcalffoundation.com/publication/made-in-canada-how-the-law-constructs-migrant-workers-insecurity/.

Ferrer, Anna, Garnett Picot, and William Craig Riddell. "New Directions in Immigration Policy: Canada's Evolving Approach to the Selection of Economic Immigrants." *International Migration Review* 48, no. 3 (2010): 846–67.

Government of Canada. "Evaluation of the Federal Skilled Worker Program." October 28, 2010. www.canada.ca/en/immigration-refugees-citizenship/corporate/reports-statistics/evaluations/federal-skilled-worker-program/section-1.html.

– "Notice: Supplementary Information 2018–2020 Immigration Levels Plan." November 1, 2017. www.canada.ca/en/immigration-refugees-citizenship/news/notices/supplementary-immigration-levels-2018.html.

– "Biometrics: Making Travel Easier While Keeping Canada Safe." May 5, 2018a. www.canada.ca/en/immigration-refugees-citizenship/news/video/biometrics-summer-2018.html.

– "Express Entry via the Provincial Nominee Program." June 26, 2018b. www.canada.ca/en/immigration-refugees-citizenship/corporate/publications-manuals/operational-bulletins-manuals/permanent-residence/express-entry/provincial-nominee-program.html.

– *2018 Annual Report to Parliament on Immigration*. Ottawa: Citizenship and Immigration Canada, 2018c.

– "Building on Success: International Education Strategy 2019–2024. Ottawa, 2019a. www.international.gc.ca/education/assets/pdfs/ies-sei/Building-on-Success-International-Education-Strategy-2019-2024.pdf.

– "Stay in Canada After Graduation." October 10, 2019b. www.canada.ca/en/immigration-refugees-citizenship/services/study-canada/work/after-graduation.html.

– "Canada: A History of Refuge." August 24, 2020a. www.canada.ca/en/immigration-refugees-citizenship/services/refugees/history.html.

– "IRCC Minister Transition Binder 2019: IRCC – Public Opinion Research on Canadians' Attitude towards Immigration." June 11, 2020b. www.canada.ca/en/immigration-refugees-citizenship/corporate/transparency/transition-binders/minister-2019/por.html.

- "Coronavirus Disease (COVID-19): Immigration Applicants." May 7 2020c. www.canada.ca/en/immigration-refugees-citizenship/services/coronavirus-covid19/immigration-applicants.html.
Government of Manitoba. "MPNP For Skilled Workers." www.immigratemanitoba.com/mpnp-for-skilled-workers/eligibility/.
Government of Prince Edward Island. "Prince Edward Island Provincial Nominee Program: Evaluation Result." December 31, 2012. www.gov.pe.ca/photos/original/ISPNPEVALU2012.pdf.
Harris, Kathleen. "Liberals Plan New Program to Allow Communities to Pick Immigrants." *CBC News* (January 2, 2020). www.cbc.ca/news/politics/municipal-nominee-immigration-program-1.5404402.
Hennebry, Jenna. "Who Has Their Eye on the Ball? 'Jurisdictional Futbol' and Canada's Temporary Foreign Worker Program." *Options Politiques*. July 1, 2010: 62–7. https://policyoptions.irpp.org/fr/magazines/immigration-jobs-and-canadas-future/who-has-their-eye-on-the-ball-jurisdictional-futbol-and-canadas-temporary-foreign-worker-program/.
Hiebert, Daniel. "The Canadian Express Entry System for Selection Economic Immigrants: Progress and Persistent Challenges." Washington, DC: Migration Policy Institute, 2019. www.migrationpolicy.org/research/canadian-express-entry-system-selecting-economic-immigrants.
Hollifield, James, Valerie F. Hunt, and Daniel J. Tichenor. "The Liberal Paradox: Immigrants, Markets, and Rights in the United States." *SMU Law Review* 61 (2008): 67–98.
Hou, Feng, Eden Crossman, and Garnett Picot. "Two-Step Immigration Selection: Recent Trends in Immigrant Labour Market Outcomes." Ottawa: Statistics Canada, July 20, 2020. www150.statcan.gc.ca/n1/en/catalogue/11-626-X2020011.
Immigration, Refugees and Citizenship Canada (IRCC). "Canada: Permanent Residents by Category." Ottawa: Government of Canada. September 5, 2019. https://open.canada.ca/data/en/dataset/082f05ba-e333-4132-ba42-72828d95200b.
Jakubowski, Lisa. *Immigration and the Legacy of Racism*. Halifax, NS: Fernwood, 1997.
Juffs, Lorelle, and Myer Siemiatycki. "The Manitoba Provincial Nominee Program: A Gender-Based Analysis." In *The Promise of Migration*, edited by Harald Bauder, 43–51. Toronto: Ryerson University, 2019.
Kane, Laura. "Family of Foreign Workers Facing Deportation over Paperwork Error." *CTV News* (December 30, 2014). http://bc.ctvnews.ca/family-of-foreign-workers-facing-deportation-over-paperwork-error-1.2167499.
Kaushal, Asha. "Do the Means Change the Ends? Express Entry and Economic Immigration in Canada." *Dalhousie Law Journal* 42, no. 1 (2019): 83–124.

Leo, Christopher, and Martine August. "The Multilevel Governance of Immigration Settlement: Making Deep Federalism Work." *Canadian Journal of Political Science* 42, no. 2 (2009): 491–510.

Lewis, Nathaniel M. "A Decade Later: Assessing Successes and Challenges in Manitoba's Provincial Immigrant Nominee Program." *Canadian Public Policy* 36, no. 2 (2010): 241–64.

Ley, David, and Daniel Hiebert. "Immigration Policy as Population Policy." *The Canadian Geographer* 45, no. 1 (2001): 120–5.

MacIvor, Angela. "Inside the Illegal Immigration Scheme Targeting Atlantic Canada." *CBC News* (September 16, 2019). www.cbc.ca/news/canada/nova-scotia/immigration-fraud-jobs-atlantic-canada-aipp-1.5281668.

Morden Immigration. "Morden's Top In-Demand Jobs." www.mordenimmigration.com/#!in-demand-jobs/csul.

Nakache, Delphine, and Sarah D'Aoust. "Provincial/Territorial Nominee Programs: An Avenue to Permanent Residency for Low-Skilled Temporary Foreign Workers?" In *Legislated Inequality: Temporary Labour Migration in Canada*, edited by Patti Lenard and Christine Straehle, 158–77. Montreal, QC, and Kingston, ON: McGill-Queens University Press, 2012.

Nanaimo News Bulletin. "2015 Year in Review: Major Stories Continue into the New Year." *Nanaimo News Bulletin* (December 31, 2015). www.nanaimobulletin.com/news/363845161.html.

Organisation for Economic Co-operation and Development (OECD). "Recruiting Immigrant Workers: Canada 2019." August 13, 2019. www.oecd-ilibrary.org/social-issues-migration-health/recruiting-immigrant-workers-canada-2019_4abab00d-en.

Pandey, Manish, and James Townsend. "Quantifying the Effects of Provincial Nominee Programs." *Canadian Public Policy* 37, no. 4 (2011): 495–512.

Paquet, Mireille. "The Federalization of Immigration and Integration in Canada." *Canadian Journal of Political Science* 47, no. 3 (2014): 519–48.

Paquet, Mireille, and Lindsay Larios. "Venue Shopping and Legitimacy: Making Sense of Harper's Immigration Record." *Canadian Journal of Political Science* 51, no. 4 (2018): 817–36.

Paquet, Mireille, and Catherine Xhardez. "Immigration Integration Policies When Regions Decide 'Who Comes In': The Case of Canadian Provinces." *Regional Studies* 54, no. 11 (2020): 1519–34.

Petrescu, Sarah. "Program Helps Investors Come to Canada: Critics Cite Potential Abuses." *Times Colonist* (May 16, 2014). www.timescolonist.com/business/program-helps-investors-come-to-canada-critics-cite-potential-abuses-1.1063725.

Reitz, Jeffrey. "Closing the Gaps between Skilled Immigration and Canadian Labour Markets." In *Wanted and Welcome? Policies for Highly Skilled*

Immigrants in Comparative Perspective, edited by Triadafilos Triadafilopoulus, 147–63. New York, NY: Springer, 2013.

Scott, Colin, Saba Safdar, Roopa Desai Trilokekar, and Amira El Masri. "International Students as 'Ideal' Immigrants in Canada: A Disconnect between Policy Makers' Assumptions and the Lived Experiences of International Students." *Comparative and International Education* 43, no. 3 (2015): Article 5.

Seidle, Leslie. "Canada's Provincial Nominee Programs: Securing Greater Policy Alignment." IRPP Study 43. Montreal: Institute for Research on Public Policy, 2013.

Smith, Jennifer. "The Case for Asymmetry in Canadian Federalism." *Asymmetry Working Paper Series*. Kingston, ON: Institute of Intergovernmental Relations, Queen's University, 2005.

Smith, Stephen, and Noah Turner. "Canada's Provincial Nominee Program: Key 2018 Changes That Will Be Felt in 2019." CIC News (January 8, 2019). www.cicnews.com/2019/01/canadas-provincial-nominee-program-key-2018-changes-that-will-felt-this-year-0111702.html#gs.71fma5.

Sweetman, Arthur, James McDonald, and Lesleyanne Hawthorne. "Occupational Regulation and Foreign Qualification Recognition: An Overview." *Canadian Public Policy* 41 (Supplement 1, 2015): S1–S13.

Tannock, Stuart. "Points of Prejudice: Education-Based Discrimination in Canada's Immigration System." *Antipode* 43, no. 4 (2011): 1330–56.

Tolley, Erin. "The Skilled Worker Class: Selection Criteria in the Immigration and Refugee Protection Act." *Canadian Issues* (2003).

Tutton, Michael. "Frustrated Chinese Citizens Demand Refunds from PEI after Immigration Rejected." *Globe and Mail* (August 12, 2012). www.theglobeandmail.com/news/national/frustrated-chinese-citizens-demand-refunds-from-pei-after-immigration-rejected/article4477291/.

University of King's College. "Cashing In: Inside PEI's Controversial Immigrant Partner Program." *Huffington Post* (May 9, 2012). www.huffingtonpost.ca/2012/05/09/pei-immigrant-provincial-nominee-program_n_1499502.html.

Vineberg, R.A. "Federal-Provincial Relations in Canadian Immigration." *Canadian Public Administration* 30, no. 2 (1987): 299–317.

Wang, Chen. "Immigration Gridlock: Assessing Whether Canada's Express Entry Is an Effective Immigration System for International Students' Transition into Permanent Residency?" *Journal of International Students* 8, no. 2 (2018): 1059–78.

Welcome BC. "Skills Immigration: Application Intake." *BC PNP News* (November 10, 2015). www.welcomebc.ca/Immigrate/About-the-BC-PNP/About-the-BC-PNP/News-and-Announcements.aspx.

Wright, Teresa. "Informants Accuse Ghiz of 'Dirty Politics.'" *The Guardian* (September 16, 2011. www.theguardian.pe.ca/News/Local/2011-09-16/article-2751663/Informants-accuse-Ghiz-of-dirty-politics/1.

CHAPTER FIVE

Making Non-citizens: Temporary Workers and the Production of Precarity

In 2013, Vicky Venancio, a Filipina woman who came to Canada through the Temporary Foreign Worker Program (TFWP), was on her way to work at McDonald's when she was hit by a car and left quadriplegic. Despite maintaining that she would like to continue working after finishing her medical treatment, the Canadian government issued her deportation papers, with the immigration official in charge of her case reasoning that she was now a burden on Canadian taxpayers. She contested these claims by arguing that she should be allowed to stay in Canada on humanitarian and compassionate grounds. After all, she had lived and worked in Canada for two years and had made significant economic and social contributions. These contributions, she argued, justified her claims for formal citizenship. Many Canadian citizens and temporary foreign workers were sympathetic to her claims and started the "Justice for Vicky" campaign that asked the federal government to give her Canadian citizenship (Tait 2015). Politicians in Alberta from both the provincial NDP and Progressive Conservative parties supported her cause and demanded that she be given medical coverage despite her lack of status, which the former NDP provincial health minister, Sarah Hoffman, eventually granted in June 2015. In July 2015, then Immigration Minister Chris Alexander declined her request for permanent residency but granted her a work permit, which allowed Venancio to stay in Canada legally for two years (Robb 2015). After a period of sustained advocacy, with support from migrant and Filipino community advocates as well as politicians, Venancio eventually received permanent residency on humanitarian and compassionate grounds.

In 2010, Karen Talosig, a Filipina woman who came to Canada through the Live-in Caregiver Program (LCP), completed an application for permanent residency for herself and her daughter, Jazmin. Under the terms of the now defunct LCP, caregivers could acquire permanent residency for themselves and for their spouses and children after completing a two-year live-in work requirement. Talosig's application for permanent residency, however, was declined after Citizenship and Immigration Canada (CIC) decreed that Karen's daughter Jazmin was "medically inadmissible" because she was deaf. Specifically, CIC saw Jazmin as being a financial burden not only because of the health care costs she might accrue but also because funding her "special education would be too costly for the country's public school system" (Tolan 2015). Following a massive, national campaign, which included disseminating a petition and getting letters of support from allies, such as former British Columbia Minister of Education Peter Fassbender, who attested that Jazmin could be accommodated in British Columbia's school system without needing special funding (Carman 2015), CIC reversed its decision and gave the Talosigs permanent residency.

Venancio's and Talosig's cases replicate the denials of permanent residency status faced by immigrant applicants that we detailed in chapter two. The "excessive demand" provision, which still exists, makes clear that the Canadian government does not want people who are perceived as burdens on Canada's welfare state. What distinguishes Venancio's and Talosig's cases was the public pressure put on the Canadian government by their supporters; it is likely that there are many others facing the same circumstances but who did not have the benefit of being able to mobilize politically. In addition, permanent residency denials because of the "excessive demand" provision show the instrumental way the Canadian state views migrants and would-be migrants.

Of course, such denials are particularly heart-wrenching for temporary foreign workers (henceforth known as TFWs). Despite years working and building their lives in Canada and contributing economically and socially to the country, temporary foreign workers (henceforth TFWs) are treated like commodities who are deemed deportable and/or inadmissible when they are no longer useful and present "too much of a burden" on the state (Stasiulis 2020; Vosko 2019). Neoliberal arguments on how the "ideal" immigrant is one who is self-sufficient, "high-skilled" and highly educated, as articulated in chapter three, illustrate how Venancio, Talosig, and other TFWs cannot avail themselves of "citizenship-track immigration" because they are not considered worthy neoliberal subjects (Perry 2012). Rather than recognizing the tremendous labour contributions made by TFWs, the Canadian state constructs them as beneficiaries of the Canadian government's generosity whose presence is only barely tolerated. In fact, during times of economic crisis, all TFWs become convenient scapegoats. Calls for their removal by anti-migrant groups subsequently increase. Responding to public pressure, the Canadian government thus limits TFWs' presence in Canada.

Yet the exact opposite of seeking the removal of TFWs happens when countries face emergencies. During the COVID-19 pandemic, temporary foreign workers took the place of Canadian workers who are unable or unwilling to work in essential industries because of the risks that they face. The Canadian government thus places special measures encouraging TFWs to come to Canada to work, even including the carrot of possible pathways to Canadian citizenship as a further incentive. Paradoxically, despite requiring the labour of TFWs more than ever, governments and employers deem TFWs' "decision" to work during COVID-19 as an individual decision, absolving themselves from responsibility. For example, Jamaican seasonal agricultural workers reported being asked to sign waivers absolving the Jamaican government from "costs, damages and loss from COVID" as a condition of their employment (Mojtehedzadeh 2019). To cite another example, Alberta Health Minister Deena Hinshaw, when asked to explain the spread of COVID-19 among the primarily Filipino immigrant and temporary foreign workforce in the Cargill meatpacking plants, blamed Filipino cultural norms of hard work instead of considering working conditions. That included a clear absence of social distancing accommodations in the plant as well as a lack of personal protective equipment for workers (Mohamed 2020).

In this chapter, we consider how these contradictory policies make sense: how can TFWs be seen both as providing necessary work and as representing a threat to the nation? We highlight how the Canadian government has a neoliberal economic agenda which, much like other countries that are increasingly reliant on temporary foreign worker programs, sees the "free" entry of labour as a precondition to economic growth. Yet the government must concurrently grapple with the reality that, as human beings, temporary migrants are entitled to make human rights claims. In other words, tensions exist between neoliberal imperatives that see the presence of a cheap, flexible workforce as being necessary for economic growth, and a liberal-democratic ethos that sees such temporary residents as being entitled to a given set of rights. The question of which rights to confer TFWs thus becomes a contentious issue. As we show, Canada's temporary foreign worker policies attempt to straddle these tensions by finding ways to maintain a constant and steady presence of TFWs through policies such as "closed" work permits, which prevent TFWs from changing employers, while also providing such workers with a limited set of rights. These policies vary depending on the type of work a TFW undertakes.

In this chapter, we first discuss international labour migration in global and Canadian contexts. Then, we assess the evolution of Canadian immigration policy towards temporary migrants and the ways different groups of temporary migrants are treated. Specifically, we analyse how temporary migrants' situations in Canada are precarious because of the perception that they are both threatening and promoting Canadian interests. Central to our analysis are racialized discourses of migrant "disposability" and migrant "threat" that underlie temporary migrants' precarious situations in Canada. Our analysis illustrates that Canada's policies towards temporary foreign workers produces precarity, with measures such as tied work permits and time-limited employment contracts magnifying the power differentials between workers and employers.

CONTEXTUALIZING TEMPORARY LABOUR MIGRATION

Between 2017 and 2019, the International Labour Organization (ILO) estimated that there were 169 million migrant workers globally, a 3 per cent increase from 2017 (ILO 2021, 11). Migrant workers represent

4.9 per cent of the world's labour force (ILO 2021, 11). Of this number, 58.5 per cent are men and 41.5 per cent are women (ILO 2021, 12). Roughly 46.3 per cent of migrant workers head to affluent countries in North America (22.1 per cent) and Northern, Southern, and Western Europe (24.2 per cent) (ILO 2021, 15). In Canada, there has been a massive increase in the numbers of migrant workers in the country, with estimates in 2022 showing that in recent years, Canada welcomes 100,000 temporary foreign workers each year (CBC 2022). New policies passed by the Liberal government, which we discuss below, provided migrants holding temporary work permits with more opportunities to transition to permanent residence. However, as we outline, such pathways were limited to only a few categories of migrants, leaving others with no such options. This suggests that the Canadian government does not see TFWs as ideal citizens and seeks to contain diversity by limiting their permanent presence in the country.

There are numerous reasons explaining the growth of temporary migration. The lack of economic opportunities in developing countries and the need for labour in developed countries has meant that labour migration is depicted as a win-win-win situation for sending and receiving countries and for migrants and their families (Ruhs and Martin 2008, 249). With migrant remittances amounting to $689 billion in 2018, out of which $529 billion went to low and middle-income countries (World Bank 2019), it is clear that "remittances remain a key source of funding for developing countries, far exceeding official development assistance and even foreign direct investment" (World Bank 2019, 3–4).

Thus, for sending countries, labour migration is a crucial source of revenue. This is why government bureaucracies in countries that are highly reliant on migrant remittances, such as Indonesia, Mexico, and the Philippines are tasked with handling all aspects of international migration. Sending countries have specific government departments in charge of marketing their nationals to prospective employers and to receiving states; overseeing their nationals' welfare overseas; and extracting a portion of migrants' earnings. Described by some scholars as "labour brokerage states," these sending countries have developed a systematic way to "sell" their nationals abroad, encourage and facilitate migration, and obtain migrant earnings (Rodriguez 2010).

Receiving countries, in turn, also have in place systematic structures encouraging the entry of labour migrants. Specific bureaucracies are responsible for setting policies on labour migration, migration management, and migrant welfare. In some cases, receiving countries dispatch government representatives abroad to "sell" their country to prospective migrants. For example, representatives of provinces such as Alberta and Saskatchewan have gone on recruitment tours to sending countries such as the Philippines to entice prospective migrants to work in Canada (Government of Saskatchewan 2008). In a press release, the Saskatchewan government representative described the recruitment tour as "an example of the type of public-private partnerships that are key to increasing immigration, building our communities, and sustaining our economy," highlighting how international migrants are vital to economic and social growth in Canada (Government of Saskatchewan 2008).

Despite the benefits Canada derives from labour migration, the Canadian government has yet to create a consistent labour migration policy framework. Specifically, its policies towards TFWs remain mired in multiple contradictions. Canada's adherence to liberal democratic norms, which stress the importance of individual human rights, rests uneasily with the curtailment of rights associated with different temporary foreign worker programs. As Marsden (2019) puts it, "the increasing presence of non-permanent migrants in Canada, an ostensibly liberal state, highlights liberalism's 'basic dilemma' with regard to non-permanent migration: the contradiction of a liberal democracy maintaining a population with no political voice and with differential access to the social and economic benefits of membership" (chapter 1). Indeed, that the differential treatment of migrant workers is a result of racial hierarchies shows additional violations to Canada's liberal democratic values. Although immigration selection on the basis of racial criteria was supposed to have been eliminated via the institution of the universal admissions policy, or the points system, scholars like Sharma (2006) and Jakubowski (2006) have pointed to how racial preferences still persist in immigration selection. This is seen precisely through the existence of temporary and permanent pathways to Canada. Specifically, these scholars question the racial double standards that allowed previous generations of primarily European, low-skilled immigrants immediate access to Canadian citizenship and that now bar low-skilled workers from Global South countries from accessing these citizenship rights. As we argue below, these low-skilled workers enter Canada through different channels and face different but similar forms of precarity.

"LOW-SKILLED" TEMPORARY LABOUR MIGRATION IN CANADA

There is a distinction drawn between "citizenship-track immigration" and "non-citizenship-track immigration" in Canada. The former includes economic immigration programs permitting the permanent entry of immigrants, while the latter refers to the temporary labour migration programs discussed in the chapter. Economic immigration programs are generally intended for permanent immigrants possessing the "high skills" needed to ensure Canada's economic growth, while temporary labour migration programs are intended for "unskilled" or "low-skilled" migrants who are seen as filling "short-term" labour shortages and are subsequently only given "temporary resident" permits. Yet we debunk the distinction drawn between migrants on the basis of skill and repudiate the perception that certain industries only face labour shortages in the short term. As scholars have shown, the distinction between citizenship track and non-citizenship track immigration creates hierarchies that compound class and racial inequities. Indeed, for Perry (2012), the presence of temporary labour migration programs where workers' work permits are tied to their employers and where labour mobility is curtailed "normalize the concepts of indentured labour and unfree servitude as ideas that are sutured to the very concept of what it means to be a migrant worker in Canada" (199). Put differently, as Vosko (2019) argues, what makes temporary labour migration programs attractive to employers and to the Canadian government is how it entrenches "modalities of deportability" that keep workforces compliant. This is perhaps why there has been a consistent number of temporary foreign worker permits issued in the country; despite a decrease in temporary foreign worker permits issued from 2014 to 2016 in the immediate aftermath of temporary foreign worker scandals of 2013 and ensuing policy changes that were implemented, the number of permits being issued have started to increase again (see figure 2).

Figure 2. Temporary foreign worker program permit holders (in thousands)

— TFWP permit holders (in thousands)

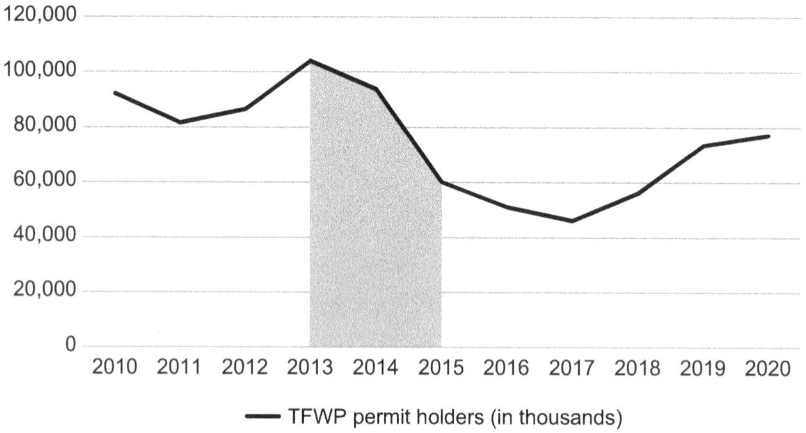

Source: Statista (2022). "Temporary Foreign Worker Program Work Permit Holders in Canada from 2000 to 2020." www.statista.com/statistics/555021/tfwp-work-permit-holders-canada-2000-2014/.

In the ensuing sections, we discuss a range of programs, including the seasonal agricultural workers program (SAWP), Canada's various caregiver programs (CP), the temporary foreign worker program (TFWP), and the International Mobility Program (IMP). Table 1 provides a brief synopsis of these various programs, outlining what type of work falls under each program, when each program started, and, if relevant, when they ceased existing. Our discussion below highlights the way securitization and neoliberalism place migrant workers in Canada in both invisible and hyper-visible positions. Specifically, we show how their labour contributions render them invisible, whereas their status as racialized "others" who are potential economic and security threats render them hyper-visible.

Seasonal Agricultural Workers Program and Migrant Farm Work

The Seasonal Agricultural Workers Program (SAWP) has been a mainstay in Canada's agricultural sector. First established as a bilateral trade agreement between Canada and Caribbean countries in 1966

Table 2. Migrant worker programs in Canada

Type of work	Name of program	Date started/Date ended
Farm work	Seasonal Agricultural Workers Program (SAWP)	1966–present
Care/domestic work	Caribbean Domestics Scheme (CDS)	1955–67
	Foreign Domestics Movement (FDM)	1981–92
	Live-in Caregiver Program (LCP)	1992–2013
	High Medical Needs Stream/In-home Childcare Stream*	2013–19
	In-home Personal Support Work/In-home Childcare Work*	2019–present
"Low-skilled" migrant work	Non-Immigrant Employment Authorization Program (NIEAP)	1973–2002
	Temporary Foreign Workers Program (TFWP)	2002–13
	"Low-Skill" TFWP/International Mobility Program (IMP)	2013–present

*Now requires licensing and language requirements to obtain permanent residency

(Basok 2003, 25), its scope expanded to include trade agreements with Mexico in 1974 (Satzewich 2007). This expansion signified an impending "neoliberal turn" in Canadian immigration policy (see Basok 2003, 8–12; Preibisch 2007), whereby migrants were seen not as potential settlers but as cost-efficient and temporary units of labour. As Preibisch (2007) has explained, "foreign labour is one of the planks of global competitiveness of Canadian horticulture and the industry's comparative advantage rests in part on limiting the rights of foreign workers who cannot move out of the sector" (418–19). With trade liberalization bringing with it more opportunities for the Canadian horticultural industry, SAWP has allowed Canadian growers to maintain their competitive edge in the global market (Preibisch 2007, 425–8).

Conceptualized by international bodies as a "model migration program" (Hennebry and Preibisch 2012, e24), successive Canadian governments and sending states therefore see SAWP as a "win-win" program. SAWP helps curb domestic unemployment in sending states and bolsters their national economies through migrant remittances. Canada, in turn, benefits tremendously from SAWP. It allows Canada to resolve "embarrassing and politically explosive challenges" to its ability to supply workers for Canadian farms by providing employers with a continuous and seemingly unlimited supply of migrant workers (Satzewich 1997).

Since the bulk of the administrative operations associated with SAWP are borne by sending states and employers, another added benefit is its low cost. Canada benefits from having a transient population with minimal claims to permanent residency: time-limited employment contracts mandate that workers can only be in Canada for eight-month contracts, and recruitment procedures specify that only workers who are part of low-income households and who have family in their home countries can be part of the program (Basok 2003; Satzewich 2007). Of course, seasonal agricultural workers may also seek security of status, as will be later discussed. Researchers have shown how the refusal to give seasonal agricultural workers permanent residency is rooted in the logic of white supremacy, whereby: "decisions about whether to allow [e.g., farm workers from the Caribbean] were made in part on assessments of the implications this movement would have on social stability in the country in general and in the workplace in particular, on the likelihood that the Black population would get progressively larger, and the belief that they would be the cause of social problems in the future" (Satzewich 1991, as quoted in Preibisch and Binford 2007, 8). Given the white supremacist logic underlying the program's set up, the extent to which workers also "win" under SAWP is debatable. The ever-present threat of being deported has kept migrant farm workers compliant. Vosko (2019) has described this as the "modalities of deportability," which include "termination without cause, blacklisting and attrition" and that effectively make it hard for workers to fight for their labour rights. Thus, although workers receive economic benefits under SAWP, the balance of power overall is skewed to their disadvantage.

Workers' vulnerability is apparent at all stages of the immigration process, including within recruitment, hiring, and employment policies. Sending states are responsible for recruiting, choosing, and supervising workers. Employers rely on "employer-driven organizations" to assign them workers and are tasked with day-to-day management (Hennebry and Preibisch 2012, e24–5). Because employers are allowed to specify workers' countries of origin and gender but are not permitted to choose workers on the basis of skill level and work experience, seasonal agricultural workers "are treated as interchangeable manual workers" whose "skills are underutilized" (Hennebry and Preibisch 2012, e29). As such, discriminatory hiring practices tend to flourish under this program: reports show, for example, that some employers have opted against hiring women and religious minorities (Hennebry and Preibisch 2012, e29). That such recruitment practices are in violation of Canadian human rights norms and labour practices ultimately does not matter because the organizations doing the recruitment are not subject to Canadian employment legislation (Hennebry and Preibisch 2012, e29).

What this analysis illuminates is how the successes of the program rely on "the employment of workers who are unfree" (Basok 2003, 4). Because it is in sending states' interests to have Canadian employers hire their nationals, sending states seek compliant workers. Foreign consular bodies are supposed to assist workers facing abuse, but workers are often reluctant to report cases of poor treatment because they do not want to be seen as being difficult to work with and risk subsequent removal from the program and from Canada. The systemic pressures to be compliant also mean that the end-of-year report workers complete at the end of their annual work contract becomes "a mechanism for labour discipline" rather than a way for sending states to protect workers' rights (Hennebry and Preibisch 2012, e29).

Workers are additionally disadvantaged by the tremendous amount of control employers have over them. They are given employer-specific work permits restricting their labour mobility, making it difficult for them to leave abusive workplaces. This means that abuse is commonplace. Long working hours beyond what is specified in the employment contract and wage theft are common complaints, as are substandard living and working conditions (see Basok 2003; Preibisch 2007; Otero and Preibisch 2010). Employers' tendency to isolate seasonal agricultural workers from Canadian workers heightens social isolation (Preibisch and Binford 2007). Seasonal workers can also become socially isolated when they are placed in remote housing units that are owned by employers, who may also overcharge them for rent. Importantly, isolated workers have limited access to social networks that could otherwise facilitate their inclusion into their communities or inform them of their workplace rights.

Incidences of racial abuse are also rampant in the SWAP program. Because the vast majority of seasonal agricultural workers are racialized men – which Gabriel and Macdonald (2019) note is not accidental due to previous policies that *barred* women from taking part and/or that specified that only single mothers were allowed – reports have surfaced of workers becoming the "target of racially motivated aggression, both verbal and physical" (Otero and Preibisch 2010, 35, 42). Employers' practices of "country surfing" (Preibisch and Binford 2007, 32) combine neoliberal market imperatives and racial logics, resulting in compliant and unequal workforces. For instance, some employers have indicated that they rank workers on the basis of perceived racial attributes, with some stereotypically deeming Mexican workers more desirable because they are "closer in appearance to the Canadian population" (Preibisch and Binford 2007, 29). Others have problematically expressed a preference for Jamaicans, whom they see as being more capable of doing "physical" work (Preibisch and Binford 2007, 18).

Gender plays a role in perceptions of male versus female workers. Gendered perceptions of men's versus women's work mean that certain responsibilities are assigned on the basis of gender stereotypes, with jobs requiring more patience and a "finer, lighter touch" being assigned to women (Gabriel and Macdonald 2019, 24). In addition, it is noteworthy to see how race interacts with gender when assessing perceptions of workers. Often constructed as sexual deviants, racialized male workers – oftentimes those from Jamaica – have been subject to attacks from white Canadian men for interacting with white Canadian women (Preibisch and Binford 2007, 30). Similarly, racialized female workers – especially those from Mexico – are stereotyped as "sexual transgressors," and have to bear being scrutinized and policed (Encalada 2019, 123). Encalada (2019) shows how female workers face numerous restrictions on their bodies and "comportment" that male workers do not face, with female workers having to withstand numerous instances of "sexual surveillance" (e.g., notices barring male workers from entering female workers' houses). Yet such stereotyping belies consideration of how racialized female workers are actually more vulnerable to sexual harassment. For example, in 2015, an Ontario Human Rights Tribunal ruled in favour of two women from Mexico who filed a suit against their employers for creating a "sexually poisoned work environment," with one woman charging her employer of threatening to fire and deport her if she did not submit to his advances and with both women stating that their employers continuously sexually harassed them (Tungohan 2015). What these examples show are the centrality of gender, race, class, and other social locations in shaping migrant workers' experiences of discrimination and abuse under SAWP.

Workplace accidents are common. Most workers continue to work even when sick and refuse to disclose to their employers their conditions. Those who do report being sick frequently find that their employers either ignore or are indifferent to their requests or take an unreasonably long time to get them the care they need (Otero and Preibisch 2010, 6). Workers' fears of accidents and sickness are warranted because workers who get injured risk being fired and deported. A study conducted between 2001 and 2011 showed that while there were only 4.62 repatriations that took place for every 1,000 workers, 66.8 per cent of workers who were repatriated returned for reasons relating to medical or surgical needs and/or sustained external injuries (Orkin et al. 2014). This study also found that of those repatriated, only 1 in 50 workers went home willingly.

There are also numerous examples showing the connection between sustaining injuries and being fired and given deportation orders for seasonal agricultural workers. The case of Javier Alonzo De Leon, who suffered from a stroke because of a workplace accident, is one such example. After suffering a stroke, his employers fired him, and Canadian officials subsequently deported him to Mexico with a lifelong disability and with no access to medical benefits. His story illustrates not only the everyday occupational health and safety risks that workers face but also how they are deemed as units of labour and not as human beings (Rai et al. 2013).

Policymakers' inaction towards the deaths of seasonal agricultural workers further illustrates the disposability of migrant lives. For example, Ned Livingston Peart, a seasonal agricultural worker from Jamaica, died in 2002 after being injured at work at a farm in Brantford, Ontario. His family unsuccessfully sought a coroner's inquest into his death. There was also the case of eleven Peruvian workers who died in a workplace accident in 2012 in Stratford, Ontario, and whose deaths did not receive a coroner's inquest (Gamble 2013). More recently, the 2015 death of Mexican seasonal agricultural worker Ivan Guerrero in Ormstown, Quebec, which authorities decreed was accidental, angered the seasonal agricultural worker community. Guerrero spoke in a video filmed months before his death decrying the maltreatment he suffered: "it's like I'm the dog and she's my owner," he stated when asked to describe his relationship with his employer. It took three days for his death to be reported, making migrant activists seriously doubt that his death was indeed an accident (CBC 2014).

Practices reflecting disposability and deportability, combined with racialized fears of seasonal agricultural workers as presenting economic and security threats, were heightened following media reports that gave the impression that TFWs were stealing Canadian jobs (Tungohan 2017). These spillover effects have included increased surveillance of seasonal agricultural workers, purportedly to ensure their safety but in practice leading to increased regulation. Farms employing seasonal agricultural workers were exempted from rules setting limits on the numbers of foreign workers that employers could hire because CIC deemed agricultural work as "truly temporary" (IRCC 2015). Nevertheless, workplace inspections and the creation of a worker tip line to report abusive employers have not led to greater workplace protections but instead instilled more precariousness among workers. Because workers who were part of work sites deemed abusive were not given the option of being transferred to a new work site but instead faced contract terminations and deportation, there were no incentives for seasonal agricultural workers – like TFWP workers and caregivers – to be forthcoming about cases of abuse.

There exist other routes for migrant farm workers to enter Canada beyond the Seasonal Agricultural Workers Program. The changes to the Temporary Foreign Workers Program (TFWP), discussed more extensively below, led to the creation of a low-skilled TFWP where workers' employment and immigration visas were tied to their employers. Another program, called the International Mobility Program, included open work permits for workers with higher skills. The creation of these dual programs has led more industries to avail of both. For farmers, this has meant that they no longer have to solely rely on SAWP for migrant farm workers, which, as mentioned above, requires the signing of bilateral agreements between Canada and sending states. Now, farmers can recruit migrant farm workers through the TFWP.

Indeed, as Chartrand and Vosko note (2020), an increasing number of low-skilled TFWs are recruited to work in farms, with most coming from Latin American and Caribbean countries. Regardless of whether migrant farm workers are entering Canada through the SAWP or the TFWP, however, the same working conditions remain.

The realities of the COVID-19 pandemic have exacerbated poor working conditions for seasonal agricultural workers entering through SAWP or TFWP. Not only do some have to sign a waiver asserting that they will not blame the Jamaican government for any negative consequences as a result of COVID-19, as we stated earlier, the absence of stronger protections to safeguard their health makes seasonal agricultural workers more vulnerable (Mojtehedzadeh 2020). There are, at least in theory, rules that are in place to protect them. The Canadian government has also allocated $50 million in funding for farm owners to ensure that protections are in place for farm workers during the pandemic, with the funds being earmarked for the creation of "safe living spaces and working conditions" (Guthrie 2020). Yet these rules are frequently breached. For example, employers are in charge of providing farm workers with food and shelter during their quarantine period and have to pay them a minimum of thirty hours per week while they are in quarantine, but many are finding ways to dock fees from workers' pay cheques. Reports show that in some farms, migrant workers are housed closely together, thus flouting social distancing regulations, with migrant workers even alleging that their employers have refused to sanitize their dwellings (Guthrie 2020). In light of these reports, the resultant outbreak of COVID-19 in farms is both troubling and unsurprising. In Windsor, Ontario, for example, the majority of new COVID-19 cases are among migrant farm workers rather than the general population (CBC News 2020).

Despite the outbreak of COVID-19 cases in Canadian farms, the Canadian government has created a new pilot program that it launched during the pandemic. Canada's agriculture industry, according to the Canadian government, "supports 1 in 8 jobs across the country," with agricultural exports generating $67 billion in 2019 alone (Canada 2020). In May 2020, it began accepting applications for its Agri-Food Pilot Program to "help employers in the meat processing, mushroom and greenhouse production, and livestock-raising industries fill ongoing labour needs" (Canada 2020). Migrant farm workers under this program can apply for permanent residency if they have a job offer from an employer, passed an English or French language test, and have a high school diploma (Keung 2019). Although it is too early to tell what the experiences of migrant farm workers under this program will be, it is not unreasonable to surmise that working conditions will remain the same as it is for other migrant farm workers. The promise of eventually acquiring permanent residency might even increase employers' power over workers, thereby magnifying workers' reluctance to be forthcoming about abuse.

At the same time, the creation of this new program can be seen as a victory for social justice organizations such as *Justicia for Migrant Workers*, who have long been demanding to regularize seasonal agricultural workers' status and provide access to permanent residency. However, the fact that only 2,750 applications are accepted per year, with most applications being accepted "primarily from people already in Canada" (IRCC 2020) leaves open the question of what will happen to the thousands of other migrant farm workers who do not qualify. Hence, it would appear that while the Canadian government recognizes the importance of according citizenship rights to migrant farm workers in recognition of their labour contributions, such rights are only in reality enjoyed by a small number. The uneven application of citizenship rights in this case compounds the "hierarchy of status" within Canadian immigration policies (Marsden 2019). As we have argued, this hierarchy privileges those who best fit the image of the ideal neoliberal immigrant, that is, those who are presumed to not be a drain on the state because they have a job offer, along with the appropriate language and educational qualifications, and are hence deemed most deserving of citizenship. We now turn to a discussion of the CP, which mobilizes a similar logic.

Caregiver Program

Canada's recruitment of domestic workers from abroad has historically been racially segmented. Whereas historically in the early twentieth century, European domestics were seen as "mothers of the nation" and were given immediate access to permanent residency, women from developing countries were initially allowed entry into Canada temporarily. Despite the fact that women from both groups were both doing domestic work, prevailing racial hierarchies depicted European women as "nursemaids" undertaking skilled work, whereas racialized women were seen as "servants" (Tungohan 2012). The classification of skill and by extension who qualified for permanent settlement was based on racial criteria (Arat-Koç 2003).

In many ways, Canada's polices towards migrant domestic workers mirror its policies towards migrant farm work, with Canada initially recruiting domestic workers from Caribbean countries. There were different iterations of domestic worker programs that facilitated the entry of women from developing countries into Canada. In 1911, Quebec accepted 100 domestics from Guadeloupe. Because of public outcry against the perceived immorality of these women, however, subsequent applications from other Caribbean domestics were rejected (Arat-Koç 1997, 74). In 1915, the Caribbean domestics who were in Canada were forcibly deported because the Canadian government feared that they would be a burden to Canada (Arat-Koç 1997, 74).

In 1955, the Caribbean Domestics Scheme (CDS) was established. It was similar to SAWP in that it was deemed a bilateral trade agreement between Canada and Caribbean countries, with the discourse surrounding the program focusing on Canada's supposed generosity in helping "poor," single, unmarried women find employment abroad while typically ignoring that these women's labour allowed Canadian households to flourish. Like SAWP, sending countries were responsible for recruitment, hiring, and employing domestic workers. If workers were deemed "unsuitable" for domestic work – a term left undefined by the Canadian government – then Caribbean countries were obliged to pay for the workers to be deported (Arat-Koç 1997, 75). A crucial difference between CDS and SAWP was that workers could apply for permanent residency. Canadian government representatives later expressed trepidation that this policy did not "lock" women into domestic work and also led to an immigration sponsorship "explosion" that enabled the entry of more people from the Caribbean into Canada. However, the government did not amend the CDS because they feared the rise of protests from the Black Canadian community (Arat-Koç 1997, 75).

Nearly two decades later, the Non-Immigrant Employment Authorization Program (NIEAP) was established in 1973. NIEAP gave migrants who did not qualify for permanent entry into Canada time-limited work contracts (Sharma 2006). These included domestic workers from different countries, which significantly widened the pool from which Canadian employers could hire workers. Domestic workers, feminist and anti-racist organizations, and concerned members of the Canadian public protested the inability of domestic workers to apply for permanent residency. Galvanized by the case of the "seven Jamaican mothers" who came to Canada as domestic workers but later received deportation orders, a widespread social movement on behalf of domestic workers was formed, leading to the slogan that has since been adopted by many other migrant activists and labour unions in Canada: "Good enough to work, good enough to stay" (Arat-Koç 2003). Movement efforts ultimately culminated in the establishment of the Foreign Domestics Movement (FDM) in 1981, allowing domestic workers to apply for permanent residency but only after completing a two-year live-in work contract. The Live-in Caregiver Program (LCP), established in 1992 and in place until 2014, maintained many of the conditions of the FDM, including that caregivers were to live in an employer's home, except it attempted to professionalize domestic work by classifying it as care work and required applicants to demonstrate more educational credentials.

While their efforts seeking permanent status for domestic workers were successful, domestic workers were disappointed that their status was still tied to a single employer and that they still had to go through a two-year period of what many saw as indentured servitude. Much like workers under SAWP, tying their status to employers magnified employers' power over them, with employers able to force domestic workers into compliance by threatening them with termination and deportation. The carrot of potential citizenship kept caregivers compliant, with many reluctant to antagonize their employers because they feared being unable to complete the mandatory two-year live-in work requirement needed for permanent residency. The live-in requirement exacerbated workers' vulnerability because of the lack of privacy and because living with employers made it difficult to enforce set work hours. Cases of employers controlling domestic workers' behaviour, with employers dictating the way they dressed, the food they ate, and their actions during their hours off, also emerged because of the live-in requirement (England and Stiell 1997; Pratt 1997; Tungohan et al.

2015). Moreover, the perception that domestic work was not "real" work and did not deserve financial remuneration was an issue for many (Tungohan et al. 2015).

Caregivers' vulnerability was further heightened by abusive employment agencies that illegally charged individual caregivers recruitment and placement fees, used fraudulent employment contracts, and took illegitimate cuts of caregivers' salaries (Tungohan et al. 2015). Like in the SAWP, employment agents and employers deployed racial stereotypes when making discriminatory hiring decisions. In fact, one reason why Filipino caregivers became more prominent in the LCP compared to Caribbean caregivers can partly be attributed to recruitment agents' and employers' intentional deployment of stereotypes of Caribbean women as being aggressive and lazy in retaliation against Caribbean women's engagement in activism (Bakan and Stasiulis 2005). Such stereotyping, coupled with new policies requiring that caregivers obtained higher education levels in order to qualify for entry, disproportionately disadvantaged Caribbean women (Bakan and Stasiulis 2005).

Adverse living and working conditions have led to highly publicized cases of abuse of migrant care workers. There was the 2011 case of Letitia Sarmineto, who successfully brought human trafficking charges against her employer, Frank Orr, after proving in court that she was asked to work sixteen-hour days and was only paid $500 a month (Luk 2013). Another prominent example of caregiver abuse was the 2009 case involving former Liberal Party Member of Parliament Ruby Dhalla, who hired caregivers Magdalene Gordo and Richelyn Tongson to take care of her elderly mother (Brazao 2009). Gordo and Tongson were not only caregivers but were additionally tasked with cleaning the Dhalla household and other properties owned by the Dhallas. They were made to work twelve to sixteen hours per day while only being compensated $250 a week (Brazao 2009). Gordo and Tongson alleged that their passports were also confiscated, binding them further to their employers.

The Dhalla controversy, so graphic because it involved an elected government official, galvanized domestic worker activists, leading them to vigorously lobby for policy improvements. Such activism prompted the creation of a blacklist for abusive employers. Subsequent reforms passed in 2010 allowed caregivers to count the number of hours rather than the number of years they worked to qualify for permanent residency. This change hastened the completion of the live-in work requirement. Caregivers were also allowed to complete their live-in work requirement within a four-year time frame, enabling caregivers in abusive employment situations to find new employment without worrying about whether their eligibility to apply for permanent residency would expire.

Such reforms, though widely lauded, were still insufficient because the base elements of the program remained unchanged. For example, the provision of an employer-specific work permit, the live-in requirement, and the mandatory two-year work requirement before qualifying for permanent residency remained foundational. As a result, domestic worker activists continued to agitate for improvements to the program. While they were divided on whether the LCP should be reformed or abolished altogether, two issues unified activists: namely, the importance of providing caregivers permanent residency upon arrival and the need to rectify caregivers' arduous experiences of being separated from their families while working (Tungohan 2013).

What is clear from our analysis of the CP over time, is the paradoxical invocations of hyper-visibility and invisibility that define Canada's caregiver program. On the one hand, caregivers' intersecting identities as racialized, working-class women with precarious immigration status place them in hyper-visible positions. Such hyper-visibility can be seen when employers, for example, use hidden "nanny-cams" for surveillance of caregivers (Singh 2012). On the other hand, the substantive elements of the work performed by caregivers remain virtually invisible. Neither the public nor many employers recognize let alone value the actual labour that care work involves. This is of course tied to a larger gendered construction of favouring "paid work," that is, work outside the home, over the unpaid or poorly paid work typically performed by women inside the home (Luxton 1997).

In 2014, a widespread public outcry against the TFWP led to new shifts in public discourse on caregivers. Portrayals of immigrants as economic and security threats, which became prominent during this time, coincided with ongoing discourses promoting caregivers' simultaneous hyper-visibility and invisibility. As such, the Conservative government under Stephen Harper focused new attention on caregivers who were deemed as potential economic drains on Canada's welfare state. The government began rejecting a higher number of caregivers' permanent residency applications through the "excessive demand" provision of the *Immigration and Refugee Protection Act* (IRPA), a policy that the Liberal government under Justin Trudeau has since kept intact but revised slightly in 2017 by raising the requirements for which files counted as causing excessive demand. Examples abound of instances where the Canadian government deems families as causing excessive demand on Canada's welfare system. The case of the Talosigs that we discussed at the start of this chapter involved the rejection of Karen Talosig's application for permanent residency because her daughter was deaf. Luvvy Alicbusan, another caregiver whose permanent residency application got rejected, was likewise turned away because immigration officials deemed her son, who has cerebral palsy and is on the autism spectrum, as causing excessive demand (Adler 2015).

Caregivers were also impacted by new discourses against immigration fraud and the criminalization of immigrants as threats. Inspired perhaps by policymakers' determination to catch "fraudulent" immigrants, the Canada Border Services Agency (CBSA) became fixated on punishing caregivers who violated the terms of their contract, regardless of the individual circumstances that inspired caregivers to do so. The CBSA's "Project Guardian" project launched in 2014 in British Columbia, solicited "tips" from members of the Canadian public to catch and deport caregivers who have "misused" the program (De La Cruz 2016). For many, this exemplified the CBSA's determination to deport errant caregivers. Since its launch, CBSA officials have apprehended forty caregivers, deporting some of them. Natalie Drolet of Migrant Workers Centre BC challenged this characterization of care workers as fraudulent. Speaking on behalf of the domestic workers who came to her organization for help after being apprehended by CBSA, she described how these women were working in "exploitative" conditions and were "forced to work excessive hours, [were] not being paid for overtime, [were] being paid less than minimum wage" and subsequently opted to transfer employers, only to find out that they were unknowingly violating the terms of their contract by working for these new employers before their papers were processed (Ball 2016). Jenny Kwan, NDP Immigration Critic, likewise argued that Project Guardian erroneously portrayed caregivers as violating the program, when the reality was that "unscrupulous employers and agents" were the ones more likely to do so (Tungohan 2016).

Indeed, policymakers justified their decision to "overhaul" the LCP by saying that the program was being "abused" by caregivers who used it as a way to reunify with their families. This logic was upheld despite instances where the ability to live in Canada with their families upon completing their work contracts was within caregivers' rights (Todd 2014). Caregivers, too, were blamed for their and their families' perceived inability to succeed in Canada following the program. Policymakers saw studies showing lower educational achievement rates among children of caregivers as proof of the LCP's failure, thereby justifying the need to place greater restrictions on who can immigrate under the LCP (Todd 2014).

In response to these perceived problems, the Canadian government instituted two "pilot" caregiver programs that gave the government flexibility to fix what they saw as problems to the program: one in 2014 under the Conservatives that divided care work pathways into a "caring for people with high medical needs" stream and into a "caring for children stream" and one in 2019 that amended these pathways into "home support worker" and "home childcare worker" streams under the Liberals. While there were different policies that were in place across various iterations of the two new pilot programs, in essence, the guarantee of Canadian permanent residency that caregivers were given after they finished the terms of the program was revoked. Arguably, positive changes to the program were instituted. The 2014 pilot included the elimination of the mandatory live-in requirement, and the 2019 pilot stipulated that family members could now come with caregivers into the country. However, each of these pilot programs limited the number of caregivers who could acquire permanent residency to 5,500 each year, which meant that caregivers who completed the requirements of the program but whose applications fell outside the cap were not able to acquire permanent residency. Also, the pilot programs created new streams with different language and licensing requirements. The 2014 pilot divided care work into "childcare" and "high medical needs" streams. The 2019 pilot distinguished between "home childcare" and "home support worker" streams.

Ultimately, the Canadian government "killed" the caregiver program by severely limiting which caregivers could get permanent residency. Policies "professionalizing" the program, which were undertaken to make the CP be in compliance with economic immigration programs, prevented an increasing number of caregivers from the Global South from accessing citizenship as caregivers. This is evident in recent figures that show how under the new CP, of the 7,000 caregiver visa holders who could qualify for permanent residency, only 500–600 succeeded (Sanders 2018).

COVID-19 increased the vulnerability of caregivers under the program. The Caregiver Action Centre (CAC) in Toronto, the Caregiver Connections Education and Support Organization (CCESO), the Migrant Workers Alliance for Change (MWAC) and the Vancouver Committee of Domestic Workers and Caregivers Rights (CDWCR) conducted a survey that showed caregivers' experiences during the pandemic (Migrants Rights 2020). Their results showed that caregivers experienced the following: longer working hours, the non-payment of overtime wages, and the expectation that caregivers would be responsible for other domestic responsibilities, such as preparing meals for the entire family, even when their contracts stipulate that the only domestic chores they are required to do are related to the care of children or elderly folks. The pandemic has thus worsened their already abysmal working conditions. In addition, for in-home care providers, social distancing requirements mean that caregivers do not have any respite from their work because they are living in the same households as their employers. For caregivers who provide care for those who have high medical needs, their risks of exposure to COVID-19 are magnified, particularly when they are taking care of individuals who are more susceptible to COVID-19, such as the elderly and those who are immunocompromised.

The vulnerability of migrant care workers as a whole, most of whom are racialized women, has merited some attention during the pandemic. The lack of employers' support of care workers during COVID-19, as seen by the failure to provide access to personal protective equipment (PPEs) at work, highlights the disposability of migrant care workers. Rather than providing migrant care workers with immediate access to permanent residency as a public health measure, migrant care workers still have to "prove" that they are worthy of Canadian citizenship through their completion of program requirements. This shows how neoliberal immigration policies continue to devalue care, refusing to count the jobs undertaken by care workers as high skilled even as the pandemic proves just how essential such care is for the survival of the country and refusing also to acknowledge that the need for care is ongoing. The Canadian government sees migrant care workers as unideal neoliberal subjects who do not directly contribute to the country's economic growth and thus cannot be granted immediate citizenship rights. As we discuss below, there are similar perceptions towards temporary foreign workers under the low-skilled Temporary Foreign Worker Program.

Temporary Foreign Worker Program

The Non-Immigrant Employment Authorization Program (NIEAP), established in 1972, was Canada's first temporary foreign worker program. It provided workers with time-limited and employment-specific work contracts. It curtailed labour mobility by requiring workers to obtain the permission of immigration officials before changing employment and prevented workers from applying for permanent residency. NIEAP's establishment "signaled a shift in Canadian policy from immigration for permanent settlement to temporary foreign workers [and] signaled the increased reliance by employers on unfree labour to perform work that was not attractive to workers who enjoyed freedom in the labour market" (Fudge and MacPhail 2009, 8).

In 2002, the Liberal government under Jean Chretien created a new pilot project following concerted lobbying from employers for the greater availability of "low-skilled" workers in the then booming construction and oil sands sectors, especially in Alberta (Fudge and MacPhail 2009, 22). Coined the "Low Skill Pilot Project" (LSPP), the pilot was similar to NIEAP in that it was an employer-driven program that enabled the entry of TFWs in Canada. Notably, the Canadian government did not set quotas for the LSPP. Employers who proved that they were unable to hire people locally were able to bring as many workers as they needed provided that they were seeking workers for jobs classified under the National Occupation Classification (NOC) category "C," which requires applicants to either have a high school diploma or two years of related work experience, or category "D," which mandates that applicants receive on-the-job training (Fudge and MacPhail 2009, 22).

In November 2006, high employer demand for the program led to an expansion of its use under the Harper Conservative government. The expanded program hastened processing times for applications by reducing the amount of time employers needed to advertise jobs in the Canadian labour market. The "Expedited Labour Market Opinion Pilot Project," launched in 2007, accepted applications for TFWs in twelve "high demand" occupations in Alberta and British Columbia and processed these in five days (Carter 2012, 183). It created a list of "regional occupations under pressure" that initially only applied to select fields but in 2010 expanded to 200 "low-skilled" occupations (Foster 2012, 26). In addition, TFWs' contracts were extended from one to two years, with unlimited contract renewals permitted. Consequently, under the Harper Conservatives, employers' reliance on what became known as the TFWP exploded.

From 2002 to 2011, there were annual increases in the numbers of TFWs (Foster 2012), with more TFWs entering Canada than permanent migrants during this time period. Also during this time period, the number of low-skilled NOC A and NOC D TFWs exceeded that of high-skilled TFWs, with an Alberta government official estimating that in 2008, 60 per cent of all TFWs in Alberta were classified as low skilled (Taylor et al. 2012, 3). The source countries for TFWs also expanded, with low-skilled TFWs coming primarily from Asian and Latin American countries (Nakache and Kinoshita 2012, 6). This meant that the TFWP was irrevocably associated with racialized people "who were seemingly 'naturally' inclined toward work and working conditions that are seen as undesirable by 'Canadians'" (Sharma 2012, 38). Federal and provincial policymakers justified the expansion of the TFWP by stressing that, despite increasing evidence to the contrary, the TFWP was a temporary measure to rectify labour shortages. Moreover, policymakers insisted that Canadian jobs were not being affected and that rights abuses against TFWs were minimal (Barnetson and Foster 2013).

Advocates and researchers sharply contest the latter, arguing that the rapid expansion of the TFWP came at the expense of workers' rights. Some scholars criticize the TFWP by pointing to how Canada's "short-term economic needs" trumped "human rights concerns," arguing that the growth of the program led to minimal government oversight over migrants' rights (Nakache and Kinoshita 2012). Both advocates and scholars have charged that regulations that the Canadian government put into place to protect low-skilled TFWs have been insufficient in curbing abuse, such as the provision of random workplace inspections, stricter measures against unscrupulous recruiters and employers, and the creation of a telephone hotline for TFWs to report abusive employers (see ESDC 2014, 25–6 for further details on the measures). TFWs do not, for example, have an incentive to report instances of abuse because they will not be put in a new place of employment with a new employment contract if their employer is barred from continuing to employ TFWs due to abusive practices.

Although Citizenship and Immigration Canada (CIC), Human Resources and Skills Development Canada (HRSDC), and provincial governments were all responsible for various aspects of the TFWP, it is unclear which of these government bodies were responsible for migrant welfare. This has led to a situation of "jurisdictional football" where different government bodies disavow responsibility for migrant welfare (Hennebry 2010). Similar to seasonal agricultural workers and caregivers, low-skilled TFWs are locked into abusive employment situations because of employer-specific work permits. Examples of TFWs being abused are rampant. For instance, in 2010, TFWs in Edmonton, Alberta, accused Bee-Clean Building Maintenance, Inc. for forcing them to do uncompensated work that was outside the terms of their contracts, such as cleaning their managers' households, and for creating a hostile work environment. Speaking to management about their concerns led some of the workers to be fired (Cotter 2010). Following a highly publicized "Justice for Janitors" campaign, which included community allies and the Services Employees International Union (SEIU), the fired workers were re-instated and wage disputes were resolved (Cotter 2010).

Another prominent case of exploitation involved TFWs who claimed that their employers at the restaurant chain Denny's in Richmond, British Columbia, took cuts from their salaries, stole their wages, did not cover their travel fees as required, and created a hostile work environment (CBC News 2013). Like their counterparts at Bee-Clean, those who complained were fired. Upon filing a class-action lawsuit, the seventy TFWs who were affected received $1.3 million dollars to compensate for their financial losses (CBC News 2013). In 2015, Filipino and Mexican TFWs employed by Tim Hortons in Fernie and Dawson's Creek, British Columbia, alleged that their "race, ancestry, and country of origin" led their employers to refuse payment for overtime work, to place them in "less desirable shifts" compared to Canadian workers, to subject them to "racist and derogatory comments," and to threaten them with deportation (Drews 2015). The BC Human Rights Tribunal refused Tim Hortons request to dismiss the case and heard testimony from both sides (Drews 2015), ultimately resulting in both parties being asked to participate in a formal mediation process (*Chein and others v. Tim Hortons and others* 2015). Some of the TFWs who filed the lawsuit returned to their home countries because their permits expired, yet others stayed in Canada, went through the mediation process, and obtained permanent residency. While these outcomes were not ideal for some, these examples illustrate how, despite the debilitating circumstances migrant workers find themselves in, there are some who use the limited legal resources they have to contest their situations.

Beyond employer abuse of TFWs, however, it is clear that Canada's two-step immigration regime exacerbates workers' vulnerability. Namely, TFWs are lured by the possibility of transitioning from the TFWP to Provincial Nominee Programs (PNPs), which provide pathways to permanent residency, as we discussed in chapter four. Employers keep TFWs compliant by promising that they will nominate them for permanent residency through PNPs, with some employers even encouraging competition between their TFW employees by saying that they will only nominate a select few of them for permanent residency (Polanco 2013). TFWs subsequently feel obliged to accept abusive employment conditions because of the carrot of potential Canadian citizenship. This two-step process has become so commonplace that advocates and researchers question the existence of a policy rationale behind this: "is the TFWP designed to fill short-term labour shortages or is it a pathway to permanent immigration meant to address longer term labour need?" (Hennebry 2010, 62).

In answer to such concerns, in 2011, the Canadian government implemented the "cumulative duration rule," also known as the "four-in, four-out" rule, which holds that TFWs (including live-in caregivers) could only stay in Canada for four years, after which they would have to be out of the country for a further four years before being allowed re-entry (IRCC 2011). What this means is that temporary foreign workers who had been living and working in the country continuously had to make plans to leave if their stay in Canada had exceeded – or would soon reach – the four-year limit. For some TFWs, this rule suddenly meant they were undocumented (Tungohan 2015). It should be noted that while the Liberal government rescinded the cumulative duration rule in 2016, those who were forced to go underground because they lost status were not grandfathered into the program, which meant their situations of precariousness were unchanged (Tungohan 2017).

In 2014, the Canadian government implemented further changes to the TFWP that placed limits on the numbers of TFWs workplaces could hire and that banned the food and hospitality industries from hiring TFWs following the public outcry in the wake of the Royal Bank of Canada (RBC) scandal, during which Canadian employees at RBC were replaced by workers from India. Advocates underscored how the workers from India at the centre of the controversy were not "low-skilled" TFWs but were rather high-skilled "managers" who were being trained in Canada before returning to India to run one of RBC's divisions (Hussan 2015). Despite this clarification, the target of public vitriol were the TFWs in jobs classified by Citizenship and Immigration Canada as NOC C and D. As previously discussed, NOC C jobs are "intermediate jobs that usually need high school and/or job-specific training such as long-haul truck drivers, butchers, and food and beverage servers," whereas NOC D jobs are "labour jobs where on-the-job training is usually given such as cleaning staff, oil field workers, and fruit pickers" (IRCC 2015). Even members of Parliament were vocal about the opposition to what they called foreign job theft, as seen when then Conservative MP John Williamson stated that he opposed the TFWP because "it does not make sense to pay whities to stay at home while we bring in brown people to do these jobs" (Johnson 2015). Such xenophobic statements show the pervasiveness of the perception that TFWs are economically threatening. Paradoxically, such perceptions coincided with discourses that saw TFWs as a drain on the welfare state. TFWs were thus seen as hindering Canadian job security by stealing jobs and as hindering the robustness of Canada's welfare system. Hence, they are both economically *too* productive and not productive enough.

These policies have led to negative consequences for TFWs. Research has shown an increase in hostility towards TFWs (see Knott 2016; Marsden 2019) with TFWs in a recent study indicating that the attention placed on them have led them to feel unsafe. Public markers indicating that TFWs are "unwelcome" in Canada are racialized, as seen, for example, in the visibility of a sticker of a map of Alberta with the words "fuck off, we're full" at the back of vehicles in Edmonton and in the rise of public rallies protesting against the presence of TFWs in Canada (Tungohan 2017).

Because of tremendous public backlash and also burgeoning economic stagnation caused by the decline of the oil and gas industries in Alberta, in 2014 the Conservative government initially implemented a moratorium. This moratorium prevented the food services sector from hiring TFWs before announcing new changes to the TFWP (CIC 2014). It is notable, of course, that when public backlash against the TFWP abated, the Canadian government later reversed some of these restrictions. The Liberal government, elected in 2015, continued such quiet reversals by lifting the cap on the numbers of TFWs who could be employed in seasonal industries, such as seafood plants in Atlantic Canada (CBC News 2016) and hospitality industries in Banff, Alberta, and in Canmore, British Columbia (Dharssi 2016). Such reversals showed, in fact, that the Canadian economy was reliant on TFWs and that economic need trumped other considerations concerning securitization.

In 2014, the Conservative government reorganized Canada's guest worker programs by drawing a distinction between a revamped TFWP and a new program called the International Mobility Program (IMP). The revamped TFWP, like the previous TFWP, was to be regulated by three government units: the Canadian Border Services Agency (CBSA); Immigration, Refugee, and Citizenship Canada (IRCC); and Economic and Skills Development Canada (ESDC), with the latter overseeing the impacts that the employment of TFWs would have on the Canadian job market. Like the previous TFWP, regulations requiring prospective employers to obtain Labour Market Impact Assessments (LMIAs) before hiring TFWs were kept in place, with TFWs' employment and immigration status in Canada still tied to their employers.

The International Mobility Program (IMP), on the other hand, enabled the entry of workers through various streams, such as through Canada's existing free trade agreements, occupations that the Canadian government identified as being in demand, post-graduate work permit holders and young workers under "International Experience Canada," who come to the country on time-limited contracts. While the 2014 announcement of program changes made it appear as though the IMP is a completely new program, in reality, the IMP is a "rebranding of existing subprograms" (Chartand and Vosko 2020, 96). In contrast to the Canadian government's perception of the TFWP as a "program of last resort," it deems the IMP as enabling Canada to acquire a "competitive advantage" in the global economy (ESDC 2014, 27). Because employers hiring foreign workers through the IMP do not have to secure LMIAs, there is no way of tracking impacts on local Canadian job markets. For example, because the IMP allows workers to enter under Free Trade Agreements, Chinese multinational firms are permitted to bring their own workers with them without having to show that efforts were made to recruit Canadian workers first (Nuttall 2017).

Hence, a major difference underpinning the IMP and the TFWP is that LMIAs are not needed to enter Canada through the IMP.[1] This means, first, that there are no quotas to the numbers of workers who could enter under the IMP. Second, this also means that there are even fewer oversights of the IMP compared to the TFWP, leading union leaders and migrant advocates to charge that the absence of government and employer accountability has led to increased instances of worker abuse (Nuttall 2017). In theory, the IMP allows the Canadian government to put into effect its neoliberal agenda of recruiting the best workers who could generate economic growth. Yet in practice, due to the lack of oversight of the IMP in comparison to the TFWP, the IMP creates a condition that "stratifies" worker mobility depending on the permit the worker has, and that makes it harder for workers to access rights and protections, thereby ironically replicating conditions of the TFWP (Chartrand and Vosko 2020, 101).

The direct result of creating two streams of migrant worker programs is that there was a decrease in the use of the low-skilled TFWP and an increase in the use of the IMP (IRCC 2019a; 2019b). Also, source countries for both programs vary. The top five source countries for the

TFWP are countries in the Global South, primarily countries in Latin America, with most workers bound for migrant agricultural work (2019b). The source countries for the IMP, in contrast, has widened to encompass different regions and levels of development (2019a). However, the reality that the majority of IMP migrants are from China and India – which historically have supplied Canada with migrant workers – merits further scrutiny because of what these tell us about "historic relations of expropriation" and Canada's tendency to "sort temporary migrant workers from particular (e.g., colonized and racialized) sources" (Chartrand and Vosko 2020, 91).

One should also note that creating two distinct migrant guest worker programs may result in greater job precariousness for Canadian workers, who may find themselves displaced from high-skilled jobs because of the entry of workers under the relatively unregulated IMP. For example, critics hold that the federal government's decision in 2014 to allow Microsoft to bring workers from abroad into Canada through the IMP reneges on previous promises to make Canadian workers competitive in the job market (Elliot 2014). As immigration lawyer Lorne Waldman stated when asked about this case, "on the one hand, the government is telling us that they are protecting Canadian jobs. On the other hand, they're signing agreements with big corporations to come into Canada to take away jobs that could easily be filled by Canadians" (Elliot 2014).

In short, many critics hold that the changes to the TFWP did not result in "putting Canadians first" because Canadian workers were, for the most part, not interested in getting employment in precarious, low-wage sectors. Instead, the imperatives of economic securitization and neoliberalism ensured that an even more opaque, unregulated program was created through the IMP and that low-skilled TFWs were made more vulnerable. Moreover, advocates have charged that the new changes create an even bigger "revolving door" for TFWs under the TFWP and the IMP (No One Is Illegal 2015, 5) and put into place a more encompassing surveillance regime that heightens migrant vulnerability.

The pandemic exacerbates the vulnerability facing TFWs. The outbreak of COVID-19 among the mostly Filipino immigrant and temporary foreign worker population in the Cargill meatpacking plants in Alberta highlight the absence of labour protections given to essential workers. An investigative report by the *Globe and Mail* revealed that Cargill managers were directly complicit in forcing racialized migrant workers to show up for their shifts, even when feeling ill (Baum et al. 2020). TFWs feel even more pressure to keep working because they have closed work permits, which means that if they get terminated, they risk getting deported. Although the outbreak led Cargill to suspend its operations, the plant re-opened two weeks later, leaving open the question of whether appropriate safety measures had been implemented to ensure worker safety.

The need to fill labour shortages during the pandemic has led the Canadian government to seek new sources of workers. As such, in 2020, the Canadian government lifted restrictions on international students' working hours (previously set at twenty hours per week), allowing international students unlimited hours of work provided that they are employed in an "essential" workplace (Government of Canada 2020c). To be clear, the trend of international students becoming Canada's "new" temporary foreign workers started to emerge in the years before COVID-19. Multiple news reports starting in 2016 point to how employers, for-profit schools, and recruiters take advantage of international students' financial challenges and hire them to perform dirty, dangerous, and demeaning jobs that have nothing to do with their course work and that are oftentimes under-the-table and unregulated (Choise 2016; Zabjek 2017). Yet the reality that international students do not necessarily inhabit "protected" status as potential economic migrants and are also migrant workers who the Canadian state uses as sources of both revenue and labour became especially obvious during the 2020 global health crisis. In fact, migrant worker networks intensified their organizing work with international students during the pandemic in order to help engender recognition for their crucial labour contributions and to fight for their rights to full immigration status (Abbas 2021).

Hence, the pandemic has put into stark contrast the contradictory discourses that inform Canadian society's treatment of TFWs, which as a category can be broadened to also include international students in essential jobs. On the one hand, TFWs' jobs are so essential that they are encouraged to work even after an outbreak that infected and killed workers. On the other hand, their employment in these essential jobs exacerbates the stigma they face. In essence, the pandemic has revealed that temporary foreign workers are simultaneously "good" migrants whose labour contributions are essential and "threatening" migrants who risk contaminating Canadian society. Interestingly, the pandemic seems to have engendered more support from Canadian citizens for temporary foreign workers, with Nanos survey results from 2020 revealing that 80 per cent of Canadians believing not only that temporary foreign workers (especially migrant farm workers) are "essential" to Canada but also that permanent immigration pathways be available to them (Thevenot 2021). This is a marked reversal from Nanos survey results showing respectively that 68 per cent of Canadians in 2012 and 75 per cent of Canadians in 2016 either opposed or somewhat opposed the presence of temporary foreign workers in Canada (Carbert 2016). Perhaps the need to ensure that labour shortages are filled during the pandemic may ultimately lead to lasting support for permanent immigrant pathways for temporary foreign workers, thereby upending previous constructs of migrant workers as necessary threats. In the final analysis, there are multiple processes at work that constitute the construction of TFW, all contributing to their precarity.

CONCLUSION

Migrant workers in Canada, whether they are seasonal agricultural workers, caregivers, or TFWs, are placed in the contradictory situation of being deemed both necessary to Canada and as being threats to the country's safety. Their hidden work harvesting crops, taking care of Canadian families, and working in "low-skilled" jobs make their myriad economic contributions invisible. Yet their social locations as racialized migrants from developing countries make them hyper-visible, particularly in times of duress, such as during economic downturns and during pandemics. The twin logics of neoliberalism and criminalization tend to inspire xenophobic discourses that see migrant workers as cheap and efficient units of labour who can be "sacrificed" for the greater good during the pandemic. However, when they are no longer of use, such as when they are sick and injured, or when they are marked as being too difficult to work with, such as when they raise concerns about workplace matters, they can then be disposed of and deported.

Based on our analysis, we agree with advocates who argue that the best way to respect migrants' rights is not to limit their numbers but to provide all migrant workers with permanent status. For them, the limited pathways to permanent residency given to some migrant workers are insufficient. They see caregiver activists' slogan – that if caregivers are "good enough to work, they are good enough to stay" – as being applicable to all migrant workers, without whom Canadian society would be unable to function (Ramsaroop and Smith 2014). Migrant workers themselves have been at the forefront when making demands for permanent residency and for stronger labour rights, whether through labour unions, through migrants' collectives, or through their own individual lobbying efforts (Gardner, Magsumbol, and Tungohan 2021). Canada has an ongoing need for the types of work that temporary foreign workers perform, and it is hypocritical for the Canadian government to provide barriers to their permanent settlement when previous generations of immigrants doing the same job were able to avail themselves of Canadian citizenship.

Whether Canadian citizenship will ever be given to all TFWs remains to be seen. Because our analysis above shows how the neoliberal and securitized treatment of TFWs fits within the larger pattern of containing diversity in Canada, perhaps the only way for TFWs to gain citizenship is if there exist new ways of being and of belonging, as we discuss in our concluding chapter.

NOTE

1 Although Chartrand and Vosko (2020) note that some IMP subprograms require LMIAs.

BIBLIOGRAPHY

Abbas, Mohsin. "Canadian Migrants Push for Full Immigration Status." *Toronto Star* (June 21, 2021). www.thestar.com/news/canada/2021/06/21/canadian-migrants-push-for-full-immigration-status.html.

Adler, Mike. "Immigration: Temporary Foreign Workers, Two-Tier Citizenship among Election Issues in Toronto." *Toronto.com* (October 8, 2015). www.insidetoronto.com/news-story/5951864-immigration-temporary-foreign-workers-two-tier-citizenship-among-election-issues-in-toronto/.

Arat-Koç, Sedef. "From 'Mothers of the Nation' to Migrant Workers." In *Not One of the Family: Foreign Domestic Workers in Canada*, edited by Abigail Bakan and Daiva Stasiulis, 53–80. Toronto: University of Toronto Press, 1997.

– "Good Enough to Work but Not Good Enough to Stay: Foreign Domestic Workers and the Law." In *Locating Law: Race, Class, Gender Connections*, edited by Elizabeth Comack, 121–51. Halifax, NS: Fernwood Publishing, 2003.

Bakan, Abigail, and Daiva Stasiulis. *Negotiating Citizenship: Migrant Women in Canada and the Global System*. Toronto: University of Toronto Press, 2005.

Ball, David P. "Vancouver Domestic Workers Rally against Project Guardian Raids." *Metro News* (June 16, 2016). www.metronews.ca/news/vancouver/2016/06/16/-domestic-workers-rally-against-project-guardian-raids.html.

Barnetson, Bob, and Jason Foster. "The Political Justification of Migrant Workers in Alberta, Canada." *International Migration and Integration* 15, no. 2 (2014): 349–70.

Basok, Tanya. *Tortillas and Tomatoes: Transmigrant Mexican Harvesters in Canada*. Montreal, QC, and Kingston, ON: McGill-Queen's University Press, 2003.

Baum, Kathryn, Carrie Tait, and Tavia Grant. "How Cargill Became the Site of Canada's Largest Single Outbreak of COVID-19." *The Globe and Mail* (May 3, 2020). www.theglobeandmail.com/business/article-how-cargill-became-the-site-of-canadas-largest-single-outbreak-of/.

Brazao, Dale. "Ruby Dhalla's Nanny Trouble." *The Toronto Star* (May 5, 2009). www.thestar.com/news/investigations/2009/05/05/ruby_dhallas_nanny_trouble.html.

Canadian Council for Refugees (CCR). "Government Overhaul of Temporary Foreign Worker Program: CCR Response to 2014 Changes." November 2014. https://ccrweb.ca/sites/ccrweb.ca/files/ccr_reponse_government_overhaul_en.pdf.

Canadian Press. "Denny's Restaurant Chain Settles Foreign Worker Lawsuit." CBC News (March 6, 2013). www.cbc.ca/news/canada/british-columbia/denny-s-restaurant-chain-settles-foreign-worker-lawsuit-1.1377246.

Carbert, Michelle. "Many Canadians Uneasy about Temporary Foreign Workers." *The Globe and Mail* (September 1, 2016). www.theglobeandmail.com/news/politics/many-canadians-uneasy-about-temporary-foreign-workers-poll/article31656625/.

Carman, Tara. "Deaf Daughter of Caregiver Allowed into Canada." *Vancouver Sun* (June 24, 2015). www.vancouversun.com/news/Deaf+daughter+caregiver+allowed+into+Canada/11163537/story.html.

Carter, Tom. "Provincial Nominee Programs and Temporary Worker Programs: A Comparative Assessment of Advantages and Disadvantages in Addressing Labour Shortages." In *Legislated Inequality: Temporary Labour*

Migration in Canada, edited by Patti Lenard and Christine Straehle, 178–201. Montreal, QC, and Kingston, ON: McGill-Queen's University Press, 2012.

CBC. "Most Canadians Cool to Temporary Foreign Workers." CBC News (December 10, 2012). www.cbc.ca/news/politics/most-canadians-cool-to-temporary-foreign-workers-poll-says-1.1263820.

– "Temporary Foreign Worker Dies in Freak Accident, Leaves behind Chilling Testimony." *Huffington Post* (September 9, 2014). www.huffingtonpost.ca/2014/09/09/ivan-guerrero-foreign-worker-death-canada_n_5790786.html.

CBC News. "Seasonal Employers Relieved about Temporary Foreign Worker Changes." CBC News (March 18, 2016). www.cbc.ca/news/canada/new-brunswick/seasonal-employers-temporary-foreign-worker-changes-1.3497058.

– "CBC Windsor May 25 COVID-19 Update: 36 New Cases Mostly in the Agricultural Sector." CBC News (May 25, 2020). www.cbc.ca/news/canada/windsor/COVID-19-windsor-essex-may25-1.5583090.

– "Expanding Temporary Foreign Workers in Canada Just Means 'More Exploitable Workers.'" CBC News (April 6, 2022). https://www.cbc.ca/radio/thecurrent/the-current-for-april-6-2022-1.6410000/expanding-temporary-foreign-worker-program-just-means-more-exploitable-workers-advocate-1.6410422.

Chartrand, Tyler, and Leah Vosko. "Canada's Temporary Foreign Worker and International Mobility Programs: Charting Change and Continuity among Source Countries." *International Migration* 59, no. 2 (Special Issue, 2020): 89–109. https://doi.org/10.1111/imig.12762.

Chein and others v. Tim Horton's and Others. BCHRT169, CANLII, 2015.

Choise, Simona. "International Student Work Program Creating Low Wage Work Force: Report." *The Globe and Mail* (March 31, 2016). www.theglobeandmail.com/news/national/international-student-work-program-needs-overhaul-report-says/article29463566/.

De La Cruz, Jhong. "Nannies in Canada Warned against Working 'Under-the-Table' Jobs." *Philippine Daily Inquirer* (July 15, 2016). https://globalnation.inquirer.net/141208/nannies-in-canada-warned-against-working-under-the-table-jobs.

Dharssi, Alia. "Banff Businesses Hopeful Eased Restrictions on Temporary Foreign Workers Will Ease Burden." *Calgary Sun* (March 28, 2016). www.calgarysun.com/2016/03/28/banff-businesses-hopeful-eased-restrictions-on-temporary-foreign-workers-will-ease-burden.

Drews, Kevin. "Tim Hortons Loses Bid to Toss out Human-Rights Complaints Lodged by Temporary Foreign Workers in BC." *National Post* (November 10, 2015). http://news.nationalpost.com/news/canada/tim-hortons-loses-bid-to-toss-out-human-rights-complaints-lodged-by-temporary-foreign-workers-in-b-c.

Elliot, Louise. "Foreign Workers: Microsoft Gets Green Light from Ottawa for Foreign Trainees." *CBC News* (December 13, 2014). www.cbc.ca

/news/politics/foreign-workers-microsoft-gets-green-light-from-ottawa-for-foreign-trainees-1.2870289.
Employment and Social Development Canada. "Government of Canada Overhauls Temporary Foreign Worker Program Ensuring Canadians Are First in Line for Available Jobs." Ottawa: Government of Canada, 2014a. www.canada.ca/en/news/archive/2014/06/government-canada-overhauls-temporary-foreign-worker-program-ensuring-canadians-are-first-line-available-jobs.html.
– "Overhauling the Temporary Foreign Worker Program." Ottawa: Government of Canada, 2014b. www.canada.ca/en/employment-social-development/services/foreign-workers/reports/overhaul.html.
Encalada, Evelyn. "Contestations of the Heart: Mexican Migrant Women and Transnational Loving from Rural Ontario." *International Journal of Migration and Border Studies* 5, nos. 1/2 (2019): 118–33.
England, Kim, and Bernadette Stiell. "'They Think You're as Stupid as Your English Is': Constructing Foreign Domestic Workers in Toronto." *Environment and Planning A* 29, no. 2 (1997): 195–215.
Foster, Jason. "Making Temporary Permanent: The Silent Transformation of the Temporary Foreign Worker Program." *Just Labour* 19 (Autumn 2012): 22–46.
Fudge, Judy, and Fiona MacPhail. "The Temporary Foreign Worker Program in Canada: Low-Skilled Workers as an Extreme Form of Flexible Labour." *Comparative Labour Law and Policy Journal* 31 (2009): 101–9.
Gabriel, Christina, and Laura Macdonald. "Contesting Gender Discrimination in the Canadian Seasonal Agricultural Workers Program." *Canadian Ethnic Studies* 51, no. 3 (2019): 17–34.
Gamble, Susan. "Human Rights Case Puts Spotlight on Migrant Workers." *Brantford Expositor* (April 23, 2013). www.brantfordexpositor.ca/2013/04/23/human-rights-tribunal-into-migrant-workers-death.
Gardner, Karl, Dani Magsumbol, Ethel Tungohan. "The Politics of Migrant Worker Organizing in Canada." In *Rethinking the Politics of Labour in Canada*, 2nd ed., edited by Stephanie Ross and Larry Savage, 152-170. Blackpoint, NS: Fernwood Publishing, 2021.
Government of Canada. "Removing Barriers for International Students Working in Essential Services to Fight COVID-19." April 22, 2020. www.canada.ca/en/immigration-refugees-citizenship/news/2020/04/removing-barriers-for-international-students-working-in-essential-services-to-fight-covid-19.html.
Government of Saskatchewan. "Recruiting Skilled Labour Focus of Philippines Trip." Saskatoon, SK: Advanced Education, Employment and Labour, May 20, 2008. www.saskatchewan.ca/government/news-and-media/2008/may/20/recruiting-skilled-labour-focus-of-philippines-trip.
Guthrie, Jade. "COVID-19 Outbreak at Ontario Farm Highlights Deep Problems in Canada's Seasonal Agricultural Worker Program." *Rabble.ca* (May 27,

2020). https://rabble.ca/blogs/bloggers/views-expressed/2020/05/covid-19-outbreak-ontario-farm-highlights-deep-problems.

Hennebry, Jenna. "Who Has Their Eye on the Ball? 'Jurisdictional Fútbol' and Canada's Temporary Foreign Worker Program." *Options Politiques* (July 1, 2010), 62–7. https://policyoptions.irpp.org/fr/magazines/immigration-jobs-and-canadas-future/who-has-their-eye-on-the-ball-jurisdictional-futbol-and-canadas-temporary-foreign-worker-program/.

Hennebry, Jenna, and Kerry Preibisch. "A Model for Managed Migration? Re-Examining Best Practices in Canada's Seasonal Agricultural Workers Program." *International Migration* 50, no. S1 (2012): e19–e40.

Hussan, Syed. "What's Missing from the Coverage of the Amanda Lang-RBC Saga?" *Rabble.ca* (January 13, 2015). https://rabble.ca/blogs/bloggers/hussan/2015/01/whats-missing-coverage-amanda-lang-rbc-saga.

Immigration, Refugees and Citizenship Canada (IRCC). "Backgrounder: Four-Year Limit for Foreign Nationals Working in Canada." Ottawa: Government of Canada. www.cic.gc.ca/english/department/media/backgrounders/2011/2011-03-24.asp.

– "Breaking News: Overhaul of Temporary Foreign Worker Program." Ottawa: Government of Canada, 2014. www.cicnews.com/2014/06/breaking-news-overhaul-temporary-foreign-worker-program-063519.html.

– "Canada – International Mobility Program Work Permit Holders by Country of Citizenship and Year in Which Permit(s) Became Effective." Ottawa: Government of Canada, 2019a. https://open.canada.ca/data/en/dataset/360024f2-17e9-4558-bfc1-3616485d65b9#wb-auto-6.

– "Canada –Temporary Foreign Program Work Permit Holders by Country of Citizenship and Year in Which Permit(s) Became Effective." Ottawa: Government of Canada, 2019b. https://open.canada.ca/data/en/dataset/360024f2-17e9-4558-bfc1-3616485d65b9#wb-auto-6.

– "Agri-Food Pilot Begins Accepting Applications May 15." *News Release* (May 15, 2020). www.canada.ca/en/immigration-refugees-citizenship/news/2020/05/agri-food-pilot-begins-accepting-applications-may-15.html.

– "Find Your NOC," 2022. www.cic.gc.ca/english/immigrate/skilled/noc.asp.

International Labour Organization (ILO). *ILO Global Estimates on International Migrant Workers, 3rd Edition*. https://www.ilo.org/wcmsp5/groups/public/---dgreports/---dcomm/---publ/documents/publication/wcms_808935.pdf.

Jakubowski, Lisa. "Managing Canadian Immigration: Ethnic Selectivity and the Law." In *Scratching the Surface: Canadian Anti-racist Feminist Thought*, 98–124. Toronto: Women's Press, 2006.

Johnson, Kelsey. "Williamson Tweets Apology for 'Offensive and Inappropriate' Language on TFW Program." *iPolitics* (March 7, 2015). http://ipolitics.ca/2015/03/07/mp-and-former-harper-advisor-john-williamson-tfw-program-favours-brown-people-over-whities/.

Keung, Nicholas. "Filipino Canadians Fear End of Immigrant Dreams for Nannies." *Toronto Star* (July 22, 2014). www.thestar.com/news/immigration/2014/07/22/filipino_canadians_fear_end_of_immigrant_dreams_for_nannies.html.
- "New Immigration Program Offers Migrant Farm Workers Pathway to Permanent Residence." *Toronto Star* (July 12, 2019). www.thestar.com/news/canada/2019/07/12/new-immigration-program-offers-migrant-farm-workers-pathway-to-permanent-residence.html.

Knott, Christine. "Contentious Mobilities and Cheap(er) Labour: Temporary Foreign Workers in a New Brunswick Seafood Processing Community." *The Canadian Journal of Sociology/Cahiers Canadiens De Sociologie* 41, no. 3 (2016): 375–98.

Luk, Vivian. "'Please Help Me': Former Vancouver Nanny Tells Human Trafficking Trial She Was Forced to Work 16-hour Days." *National Post* (June 6, 2013). http://news.nationalpost.com/news/canada/please-help-me-former-vancouver-nanny-tells-human-trafficking-trial-she-was-forced-to-work-16-hour-days.

Luxton, Meg. "The UN, Women, and Household Labour: Measuring and Valuing Unpaid Work." *Women's Studies International Forum* 20, no. 3 (1997): 431–9.

Marsden, Sarah. *Enforcing Exclusion: Precarious Migrants and the Rule of Law in Canada.* Vancouver: UBC Press, 2019.

Migrants Rights. *Behind Closed Doors: Exposing Migrant Care Worker Exploitation During COVID-19.* (October 2020), https://migrantrights.ca/wp-content/uploads/2020/10/Behind-Closed-Doors_Exposing-Migrant-Care-Worker-Exploitation-During-COVID19.pdf.

Mohamed, Bashir. "Opinion: Meatpacking Plant Outbreaks Are a Disaster and Dr. Hinshaw Shares Responsibility." *Progress Report* (April 24, 2020). www.theprogressreport.ca/opinion_meatpacking_plant_outbreaks_are_a_disaster_and_dr_hinshaw_shares_responsibility.

Mojtehedzadeh, Sara. "Migrant Farm Workers from Jamaica Are Being Forced to Sign COVID-19 Waivers." *Toronto Star* (April 13, 2020). www.thestar.com/business/2020/04/13/migrant-farm-workers-fear-exposure-to-covid-19.html.

Nakache, Delphine, and Paula Kinoshita. "The Canadian Temporary Foreign Worker Program: Do Short-Term Economic Needs Prevail over Human Rights Concerns?" *IRPP Study No. 5* (May 1, 2010). https://ssrn.com/abstract=1617255.

No One Is Illegal - Vancouver. "Never Home: Legislating Discrimination in Canadian Immigration." 2015. www.neverhome.ca/.

Nuttal, Jeremy. "Increase in Foreign Workers through Federal Program Still a Problem, Says Union." *The Tyee* (July 27, 2017). https://thetyee.ca/News/2017/07/27/Increase-in-Foreign-Workers-Still-a-Problem/.

Otero, Gerardo, and Kerry Preibisch. "Farmworker Health and Safety: Challenges for British Columbians." *WorkSafe BC*. Burnaby, BC: Simon Fraser University, 2010. www.sfu.ca/~otero/docs/Otero-and-Preibisch-Final-Nov-2010.pdf.

Perry, J. Adam. "Barely Legal: Racism and Migrant Farm Labour in the Context of Canadian Multiculturalism." *Citizenship Studies* 16, no. 2 (2012): 189–201.

Pratt, Geraldine. "Stereotypes and Ambivalence: The Construction of Domestic Workers in Vancouver, British Columbia." *Gender, Place, and Culture* 4, no. 2 (1997): 159–78.

Preibisch, Kerry. "Local Produce, Foreign Labour: Labour Mobility Programs and Global Trade Competitiveness in Canada." *Rural Sociology* 72, no. 3 (2007): 418–49.

Preibisch, Kerry, and Leigh Binford. "Interrogating Racialized Global Labour Supply: An Exploration of the Racial/National Replacement of Foreign Agricultural Workers in Canada." *Canadian Review of Sociology* 44, no. 1 (2007): 5–36.

Rai, Nanky, Abeer Majeed, Jim Deutsch, and Brendan Bailey. "Denying Health Coverage to Injured Migrant Workers Is Shameful." *Toronto Star* (September 18, 2013). www.thestar.com/opinion/commentary/2013/09/18/denying_health_coverage_to_injured_migrant_workers_is_shameful.html.

Ramsaroop, Chris, and Adrian Smith. "The Inherent Racism of the Temporary Foreign Worker Program." *Toronto Star* (May 21, 2014). www.thestar.com/opinion/commentary/2014/05/21/the_inherent_racism_of_the_temporary_foreign_worker_program.html.

Robb, Trevor. "Edmonton Woman Facing Deportation Allowed to Stay." *Edmonton Sun* (July 25, 2015). www.edmontonsun.com/2015/07/25/edmonton-woman-facing-deportation-allowed-to-stay.

Rodriguez, Robyn. *Migrants for Export: How the Philippine State Brokers Labour to the World*. Minneapolis: University of Minnesota Press, 2010.

Ruhs, Martin, and Philip Martin. "Numbers versus Rights Trade-Offs and Guest Worker Programs." *The International Migration Review* 42, no. 1 (2008): 249–65.

Sanders, Doug. "For This Generation of Filipino-Canadians, Broken Policies Have Left a Scar." *The Globe and Mail* (June 15, 2018). www.theglobeandmail.com/opinion/article-for-this-generation-of-filipino-canadians-broken-policies-have-left-a/.

Satzewich, Victor. "Business or Bureaucratic Dominance in Immigration Policymaking in Canada: Why Was Mexico Included in the Caribbean Seasonal Agricultural Workers Program in 1974?" *Journal of International Migration and Integration* 8, no. 3 (2007): 255–75.

Sharma, Nandita. *Home Economics: Nationalism and the Making of 'Migrant Workers' in Canada*. Toronto: University of Toronto Press, 2006.

- "The 'Difference' That Borders Make: 'Temporary Foreign Workers' and the Social Organization of Unfreedom in Canada." In *Legislated Inequality: Temporary Labour Migration in Canada*, edited by Patti Lenard and Christine Straehle, 26–47. Montreal, QC, and Kingston, ON: McGill-Queen's University Press, 2012.
Singh, Sandhya. "Domestic Problems." *Herizons* (Fall 2012). www.herizons.ca/node/524.
Stasiulis, Daiva. "Elimi(Nation): Canada's Post-Settler Embrace of Disposable Migrant Labour." *Studies in Social Justice* 14, no. 1 (2020): 22–54.
Tait, Cam. "Tait on Eight: Getting Justice for Vicky." *Edmonton Sun* (June 25, 2015). www.edmontonsun.com/2015/06/25/tait-on-eight-getting-justice-4-vicky.
Taylor, Alison, Jason Foster, and Carolina Cambre. "Temporary Foreign Workers in Trades in Alberta." Edmonton, AB: The Work and Learning Network (WLN), University of Alberta, 2012. http://en.copian.ca/library/research/wln/temporary_foreign/temporary_foreign.pdf.
Thevenot, Shelby. "Most Canadians Support Permanent Immigration Pathways for Temporary Foreign Workers." *CIC News* (January 2, 2021). www.cicnews.com/2021/01/most-canadians-support-permanent-immigration-pathways-for-temporary-foreign-workers-0116530.html#gs.83apff.
Todd, Douglas. "Live-In Caregiver Program Faces Nine Questions." *Vancouver Sun* (May 25, 2014). https://vancouversun.com/news/staff-blogs/canadas-live-in-caregiver-program-nine-debates-video.
Tolan, Casey. "'Canada Denied This Filipina Immigrant Residency Because Her Daughter Is Deaf." *Splinter News* (June 10, 2015). https://splinternews.com/canada-denied-this-filipina-immigrant-residency-because-1793848292.
Tungohan, Ethel. "Debunking Notions of Migrant 'Victimhood': A Critical Assessment of Temporary Labour Migration Programs and Filipina Migrant Activism in Canada." In *Disturbing Invisibility: Filipinos in Canada*, edited by Roland Coloma, Bonnie McElhinny, Ethel Tungohan, J.P. Catungal, and Lisa Davidson, 161–80. Toronto: University of Toronto Press, 2012.
- "Reconceptualizing Motherhood, Reconceptualizing Resistance: Migrant Domestic Workers, Transnational Hyper-maternalism, and Activism." *International Feminist Journal of Politics* 15, no. 1 (2013): 39–57.
- "Need for Reform of Temporary Foreign Worker Program Highlighted by Human Rights Verdict." *Rabble.ca* (June 12, 2015). http://rabble.ca/news/2015/06/need-reform-temporary-foreign-worker-program-highlighted-human-rights-verdict.
- "'Project Guardian' Raids on Caregivers Leads to Calls for Immigration Reform." *Rabble.ca* (March 29, 2016). http://rabble.ca/news/2016/03/project-guardian-raids-on-caregivers-leads-to-calls-immigration-reform.

- "From Encountering Confederate Flags to Finding Refuge in Spaces of Solidarity: Filipino Temporary Foreign Workers' Experiences of the Public in Alberta." *Space & Polity* 21, no. 1 (2017): 11–26.
Tungohan, Ethel, Rupa Banerjee, Wayne Chu, Petronila Cleto, Conely de Leon, Mila Garcia, Philip Kelly, Marco Luciano, Cynthia Palmaria, and Christopher Sorio. "After the Live-in Caregiver Program: Filipina Caregivers' Experiences of Uneven and Graduated Citizenship." *Canadian Ethnic Studies* 47, no. 1 (2015): 87–105.
Vosko, Leah. *Disrupting Deportability: Transnational Workers Organize*. Ithaca, NY: Cornell University Press, 2019.
World Bank. "Record High Remittances Sent Globally in 2018." Press Release (April 8, 2019). www.worldbank.org/en/news/press-release/2019/04/08/record-high-remittances-sent-globally-in-2018.
Zabjek, Alexandra. "Foreign Students Claim They Were Misled about Chances of Staying in Canada." CBC News (November 7, 2017). www.cbc.ca/news/canada/edmonton/foreign-students-edmonton-college-migrante-alberta-1.4392223.

CHAPTER SIX

Family Migrants as "Undesirable"? Sponsoring New Citizens amid New Restrictions on Family Immigration Policies

Family reunification has long been recognized as a central pillar of Canadian immigration architecture. Canadians overwhelmingly support family-class immigration into Canada. A 2019 Angus Reid poll indicates that 53 per cent of Canadians believe Canada is accepting the "right" amount of family-class immigrants, with 11 per cent indicating, in fact, that the country should increase its annual intake (Angus Reid 2019). The government of Canada states proudly that "Canada has one of the most generous family reunification programs in the world" (IRCC 2015, 14) and has indicated that it intends to have between 84,000 and 102,000 family-class immigrants entering Canada in 2020, up from 78,006 family-class immigration admissions in 2016 (IRCC 2018a). To some extent, these figures mask the complexities, contradictions, and debates that have come to be associated with family migration.[1]

Unlike other immigration categories, where economic and humanitarian considerations are used when selecting immigrants, family migration policies are reliant on "the 'moral claims of insiders,' i.e., people living within state borders who ask to be united with their family" (Block 2012, as cited in Bonjour and Kraler 2015, 1412). Since one of the entitlements of citizenship is the ability to live with one's family members (however this is defined), policies and regulations function to give various categories of people – citizens, temporary migrant workers – different rights to family reunification (Bonjour and Kraler 2015, 1412–13).

In this chapter, we argue that the Canadian government's restrictions on family migration highlights how family migrants are not seen as "ideal" migrants. We further argue that attempts to curtail family migration is one manifestation of the Canadian government's efforts to containing diversity. Canadian citizens, permanent residents, and temporary foreign workers all have different entitlements to family reunification. For some of these groups, particularly for temporary foreign workers, family separation is the norm. Despite the economic, political, and social contributions that family-class migrants make to Canadian society, the Canadian government constructs them as the reverse of the ideal neoliberal immigrant subject: they are literally "dependents" on the primary applicant (their sponsors) and are subsequently constructed as potential drains on Canada's welfare state. In privileging production over social reproduction, this construction sidelines the important role family-class members, whether dependent spouses or grandparents, play in providing unpaid care within the home.

The Harper government passed many restrictions on family immigration. While the Trudeau government offers some reprieve from the Conservative Harper government's policies, save a few exceptions, the rationale underpinning the Harper government's justifications to immigration restrictions remain unchanged. Our analysis illustrates the continuing shift in emphasis away from family-class migrants in favour of the economic stream; narrower definitions of "family" tend to exclude members of migrant families, such as grandparents; concerns have arisen about the legitimacy of marriage migration; and temporary labour migrants, particularly caregivers, face restrictions to their ability to acquire permanent residency for themselves and their families.

FRAMES OF REFERENCE – NEOLIBERALISM AND FAMILY FORMS

We focus on two frames of reference typically used in the literature to discuss family migration. We argue that the changes to the family-class stream – including new interpretations of different family forms – need to be contextualized against a broader neoliberal context. The logic of human capital has played a significant role in Canadian post-war immigration policy. However, the embrace of neoliberal rationales and by extension the economic benefits of immigration from the late 1980s on the recruitment of "high-skilled" labour through the federal economic stream and/or just-in-time labour through the expansion of the Temporary Federal Worker Program (TFWP). This dynamic has rendered family migration of a second order. For example, in 1980, the family class accounted for 35.9 per cent of permanent residents and the economic category numbered 34.9 per cent. By 2000 these numbers had shifted. The family category dropped to 26.7 per cent, while the economic category rose to 59.9 per cent (CIC 2003). The global competition for skills (Shachar 2006) reinforced the distinction between immigrants recruited through an economic selection model and those who enter on the basis of family ties. As Kofman (2004) has pointed out, such global competition has resulted in a gendered dichotomy between the economic realm associated with males and the public sphere and the social linked with women and the private realm (256). Yet as she and co-author Meetoo suggest, the two spheres are related insofar as many who enter through family-class provisions end up in the labour market: "There is a clear need to acknowledge the labour force participation of family migrants and to rethink the outdated image of the female and dependent family migrant with little interest in working" (Kofman and Meetoo 2008, 167).

The adoption of an austerity package in Canada following the 2008 financial crisis has exacerbated neoliberal immigration policymaking and also introduced the fear of potential migrants as being potential burdens of the state (Root et al. 2014, 15–16). In particular, the value of family-based migration has been challenged by a discourse that links family migration to a series of problems as Root et al. (2014) lists: "First, abuse of the immigration system through marriages of convenience or so-called bogus marriages; second, welfare state burdens as a result of low rates of labour market participation by marriage migrants; and third, a perception of the 'migrant family' as a patriarchal institution in which unequal gender roles, forced marriages and gender-based violence are prevalent" (16, citing Hampshire 2013). Not surprisingly, calls for measures to restrict family related migration were justified in terms of neoliberal rationales. These calls also deployed discourses of morality and crime through the use of terms such as "bogus" or "fraudulent" (Gaucher 2014). In this manner government officials associated some groups of immigrants with crime and consequently framed them as "less desirable."

At the heart of family migration debates is the question of how to define "family" for the purposes of immigration. For instance, the list of family members who are eligible for sponsorship has shifted over time. The 1976 Canadian Immigration Act recognized a distinct family-class category whose members did not need to meet labour market criteria but were held to sponsorship rules (DeShaw 2006). Under the 2002 Immigration and Refugee Protection Act (IRPA), the family class was broadened and incorporated new persons such as common-law and conjugal partners, including same-sex partners. In the past, these individuals were processed as economic-class immigrants on humanitarian and compassionate grounds (Halpert and Baldwin 2013).

Despite more expansive definitions of who could immigrate under the family-class category under IRPA, changes within the Canadian family stream restrict eligibility to more narrow conceptions of family. Gaucher (2018), for example, notes that conventional notions of conjugality dictate immigration officers' decisions on whether to accept the immigration applications of common-law and married couples. On the one hand, common-law partners are asked to justify why they chose not to get married, with many having to cite financial reasons regardless of their personal beliefs about marriage. Married or engaged couples, on the other hand, frequently have to prove how their marriage traditions are compatible with Western marriage norms to show that their marriage is legitimate. In these cases, the admission criteria for family members "are shaped in fundamental ways by dominant norms about what the roles of men and women ought to be, what marriage ought to be, what parenting ought to be, and what family ought to be" (Bonjour and Kraler 2015, 1411).

Additionally, sponsorship reinforces gender, racialized, and class-based hierarchies. In many ways sponsorship is premised on particular conceptions of family and reinforces a set of dependent relations. Sponsors must meet the eligibility criteria laid out by immigration regulations, including minimum income requirements and an agreement to be responsible for the person sponsored for a required period of time. Sponsors have to provide food and housing for their family members and should also guarantee that sponsored family members will not apply for welfare provisions (DeShaw 2006, 12). Given that women predominate within family migration streams, these unequal relations are also gendered.

Sponsorship also reinforces heterosexist mindsets. For LGBTQ2+ applicants, the burden of proving the legitimacy of their relationships is higher compared to straight applicants. Queer family-class migrants oftentimes feel compelled to "bring their relationship into some frame of apprehendability" by getting married despite not believing in monogamy or in marriage (White 2020). Requirements to supply documents showing the purported authenticity of the relationship through, for instance, photos, phone bills, etc., may be difficult because of the need to "live underground" as a result of pervasive homophobia (LaViolette 2012, 30).

In addition, conventional understandings of family-related migration are also challenged by the phenomenon of transnationalism. With many families residing across different countries, due in part to immigration policies that prevent families from living together in the same country, immigrants have to devise different ways to maintain ties from afar and frequently utilize Skype, WhatsApp, and other forms of information technology to maintain contact. They therefore subvert conventional understandings of the family by showing that family ties can be maintained across borders. Shifting policies alter definitions of who is eligible for sponsorship, as in the case of different definitions of which adult children can be sponsored, as discussed below. This also means that many transnational families, including conjugal and married couples and migrant families who live in different countries, are placed in a state of limbo.

In fact, confusion on what constitutes the "family" and who can be sponsored to come to Canada has led to many sponsors being charged with "immigration fraud" under IRPA section 117(9)(b). Liew (2016) shows that 90 per cent of cases of immigration "fraud" under IRPA section 117(9)(b) on the grounds of the non-disclosure of family members that were brought in front of the Federal Court and the Federal Court of Appeal "could be described as non-fraudulent" (288). This directly refutes the Conservative government's understanding of "fraud," which rests on the notion that sponsors *deliberately* misrepresent who is part of their families. Hence, Liew believes that IRPA section 117(9)(b) should be abolished. The current Trudeau government has recognized that sponsors may not be acting deliberately. While they did not go as far as abolishing IRPA 117(9)(b), they launched the Pilot Project to Sponsor Undeclared Family Members to allow Canadian citizens to apply to sponsor family members whom they did not declare initially (CIC 2020). The Trudeau government's attempts to ameliorate some of the worst excesses of the Harper government's policies on immigration fraud rests on nebulous grounds because it is a *temporary* and not a permanent measure. Family immigrants are still targeted with discourses of fraud.

Using neoliberalism and family forms as our frames of reference, it becomes clear that in the period under review, family-based migration has come under increasing pressure. While the Trudeau government has passed policies mitigating some of the sponsorship restrictions passed by the Harper government, key policies are still left intact. In the remainder of the chapter, we analyse three policy directions that together show the lack of fundamental changes in family immigration: family-class sponsorship, family reunification for live-in caregivers, and family reunification for temporary workers. When analysed together, these policies illustrate how the ability to sponsor potential citizens is impeded by the Canadian government's persisting need to contain diversity.

FAMILY-CLASS SPONSORSHIP IN CANADA: ONE STEP FORWARD, TWO STEPS BACK?

Family reunification was a centrepiece of the Liberal government's 2015 election campaign. There was a pledge to place it at the forefront of immigration policy reform. These promises, however, were still framed by economic rationales. For instance, Justin Trudeau told a Brampton audience, "Making it easier for families to be together here in Canada makes more than just economic sense. When Canadians have added supports, like family involvement in childcare, it helps drive productivity and economic growth" (Spurr 2015). This pledge was a direct response to the many changes implemented by the Conservative government of Stephen Harper to overhaul family-class sponsorship. These included changes to the age of dependents, parent and grandparent sponsorship, and the introduction of conditional spousal visas. At the heart of each these changes, discussed below, is an assumption of what constitutes the definition of family. There has been an attempt by the Liberal administration to address the most egregious of these changes, but the broad tendencies that characterize family-related migration, many of which predated the Conservative government, remain untouched.

Dependent Children

Parents, under the terms of the family-class category, are able to sponsor their dependent children. Children may also enter as dependents in other immigration streams, including the economic, refugee, and caregiver streams. In both situations, the definition of "dependent" plays a key role in these regulations. In 2014, the Harper administration lowered the age of dependency from twenty-one to eighteen. It also removed a provision that extended the definition to include children twenty-two and older if they were financially dependent on their parents and had continually attended school full time before age twenty-two (Meurrens 2017). The government deployed a specifically economic rationale to justify this regulatory change. As the 2013 Regulatory Impact Statement states: "Statistics demonstrate that older dependent children (those who arrive between the ages of 19 and 21) have lower economic outcomes that those who arrive in Canada at a younger age (between 15 and 18 years old) ... Research has demonstrated that older immigrants have a more challenging time fully integrating into the Canadian labour market; this is more evident for immigrants who are not selected based on their own merits (e.g. dependent children)" (Government of Canada 2013, 1173). By gesturing to the global recession and the imperative that immigration contributes to the development of a strong economy, the Canadian government made clear that it saw the need to contain diversity by limiting immigration to those who they saw as being good economic subjects.

The Canadian, Council of Refugees (CCR), a non-profit body, founded in 1978 to promote refugees', immigrants', and migrants' rights (CCR 2021), took exception to this rationale, pointing out that neither family-class immigrants nor refugees were historically selected because of potential economic contributions to Canada. It and other groups also pointed out that young adult children are still part of the family and often continue to need their parents' support (CCR 2013, 1–2).

Early in the Liberal government's mandate, Canada raised the age of dependent children from eighteen to twenty-one. Here again, however, an economic rationale was used: namely, that "increasing the age of dependency will have positive social and cultural impacts and will enhance Canada's economy by making our nation a destination of choice for skilled immigrants who want to keep their families together" (Meurrens 2017). The Liberal government left unchanged the other provision that the Conservatives had implemented, which removed dependent status for children twenty-two or older who were continuously in full-time education (Meurrens 2017).

The emphasis on biological kin relationship was also introduced with the Immigration and Refugee Protection Act regulations. For instance, the definition of dependent child is only applied to biological children and adopted children, not non-biological children. According to IRCC, a biological child includes a child that:

- was born to the parent making the application
- is not genetically related to the parent making the application, but was born to the person who, at the time of the birth of the child, was that parent's spouse, common-law partner, or conjugal partner
- was born through the application of assisted human reproduction technologies. (IRCC 2018b)

It has been suggested that this focus on biological children stands at odds with the more expansive definition of family enshrined in provincial laws, which recognized the legitimacy of non-biological parenthood (Joly et al. 2017, 394).

Canada began the use of biometrics screening in 1993 to track migrants entering and leaving Canada (Pero and Smith 2014). In addition, Canada began the use of DNA testing in 1991 in those instances where documents are not available to establish kinship between applicant and sponsor or where there are doubts about the relationship. The use of the test is characterized as a "last resort" measure, but observers have noted that requests are directed at applications from certain counties, most notably African countries (Moreno et al. 2017, 258–62). Aside from the financial costs of DNA tests, which applicants have to bear, the use of DNA testing may also lead to "economic, physical, and psychological distress for families that were often already in a vulnerable position due to hardships related to immigration or endured in their country of origin or abroad" (Joly et al. 2017, 397). Not surprisingly, DNA tests have been identified as a significant barrier to family reunification for people coming from countries in Africa, Asia, and the Caribbean and for refugees (CCR 2011). The use of DNA testing forces consideration of discriminatory practices to the extent that testing may be disproportionately directed at people from certain countries, privileges certain kinds of family forms over others, and emphasizes biological ties for immigrants but not nationals of receiving countries (Moreno et al. 2017, 267–9). Researchers suggest removing the word "biological" and using a more inclusive definition of "dependent child" to embrace different conceptions of family "as defined in provincial laws, public policies, and international human rights ... and to integrate the often complex psychosocial realities intrinsic to contemporary family relationships" (Joly et al. 2017, 401).

Conditional Permanent Residence for Spouses[2]

Of all the recent changes within the family sponsorship categories, the short-lived conditional permanent residence (CPR) for spouses offers the clearest instantiation of how the discourses of fraud and criminality were mobilized. The CPR was a regulatory change introduced by the Harper government in 2012. Under its terms, newly sponsored partners of permanent residents or Canadian citizens were only admitted on a conditional basis if their "relationship was less than two years" and they had no children in common (Government of Canada 2017). These restrictive measures were explicitly justified as an anti-fraud measure targeted at marriage migrants, whom it was asserted were coming to take advantage of the system. Conditional status was subsequently repealed by the Trudeau government in 2017.

The concern with marriage fraud was on the Conservative's radar as early as 2008, but it was subsequently taken up and politicized by the then Minister of Citizenship and Immigration Jason Kenney (Gaucher 2014, 188). In 2011, the government introduced a "Fraud Tip Line" designed to allow Canadians to report anonymously to Citizenship Immigration Canada (CIC) or Canada Border Services Agency (CBSA) on "suspicious border activity, a marriage of convenience, a person who gives false information on any immigration application" via an online form or e-mail (CIC, as cited in Bhuyan et al. 2018, 358). Kenney subsequently launched a public consultation and introduced the regulatory change in the same year.

The other key change for CPR during this time was implementing a sponsorship bar. This measure prohibited individuals who entered under the sponsorship category from sponsoring a new spouse within five years of becoming a permanent resident. These actions were presented as anti-fraud measures that were necessary to maintain the integrity of the immigration system.

CIC also produced an ad campaign warning Canadians about marriage fraud as part of its 2013 Fraud Prevention Month (Canadian Press 2013). The campaign included a series of videos. In one, viewers are told: "Many Canadians marry people from other countries, but sometimes marriage is a scam to jump the immigration line," and in another, "Marriage Fraud, it could cost you more than a broken heart. Don't be a victim" (Canadian Press 2013). This ad campaign was enacted despite the fact that it was very unclear how many instances of marriage fraud had actually occurred (Gaucher 2014, 195).

Both CPR and the sponsorship bar were pursued in the face of the ongoing concerns of civil society groups about the sponsorship regime itself. These groups had long been concerned that the structure of sponsorship provision exacerbated gender-based inequities and created conditions that rendered immigrant women vulnerable. In cases of domestic abuse, a sponsored woman may not be inclined to leave a relationship for fear of jeopardizing her status. Conditional status further entrenched this dynamic and thus increased risks for abused women. The government did try to respond to advocates' concern by including an exception to the provision "that allows newly sponsored persons who are impacted by the conditional permanent residence measure and who are victims of abuse or neglect to come forward without having to worry they might face enforcement action" (CIC 2013c, 37). The exception proved difficult to realize in practice. In its survey of 142 settlement organizations, legal clinics, and women's shelters, the Canadian Council for Refugees (CCR) reported that many were either unaware of the exception or did not have accurate information about it for women in vulnerable situations (CCR 2015). Additionally, in the first two years of the exception program's operation, only fifty-seven women requested an exception. Of these, 75 per cent were successful (Keung 2017a). The relative failure of this exception in protecting vulnerable women meant that policies on CPR and the sponsorship bar continued relatively unchallenged.

From the outset, it was clear that CPR would have differential effects. CPR affected more women than men since women were disproportionately represented in the family sponsorship category. Its effects were also racialized. For instance, an analysis of the "top nine countries with the highest proportion of immigrants who received conditional PR all have a majority of Muslim and/or racialized populations," in contrast to the United States, "where the percentage of sponsored spouses ... who received conditional status was relatively low" (Bhuyan 2018, 361).

After pledging to remove this provision during the 2015 election, the Trudeau government acknowledged the impacts of CPR on vulnerable spouses. In the IRCC impact statement, for example, they noted: "On balance, the program integrity benefits of conditional permanent residence have not been shown to outweigh the risks to vulnerable sponsored spouses and partners subject to the two-year cohabitation requirement ... The proposed repeal of conditional permanent residence recognizes that the majority of relationships are genuine, and the majority of applications are made in good faith" (Government of Canada 2016). Contrary to the discourses of marriage "fraud" that the Harper government promoted, the Trudeau government saw that the threat of fraud was so minimal that it made no sense to continue this policy. In 2017, former Minister of Immigration Ahmed Hussen formally announced the end of conditional permanent residency status for sponsored spouses. The repeal of CPR is one of the few instances when amendments to family immigration policies "moved forward" by explicitly rejecting discourses of migrant "fraud."

Parent and Grandparent Sponsorship

The sponsorship of parents and grandparents also falls within the family-class stream. In recent years, this program has been the subject of considerable scrutiny by government officials. This stands at odds with the fact that this category accounts for a small proportion of total immigrants (Vanderplaat et al. 2012, 85). In 2017, Canada admitted 286,479 immigrants, and of these parents and grandparents numbered 20,494 (IRCC 2018a, 13–20).

The attention this stream has generated is related to the fact that it often acts as a proxy for critics of what they perceive as shortcomings of the family-class stream as a whole. For instance, in 2013, the Fraser Institute claimed that the focus on this group was related to "the cost to the public purse on the part of those who come here under this category. Since most are retired, or at least unlikely to find very remunerative employment because of their lack of qualifications, they contribute little, if any, of the income taxes required to pay for the benefits they receive" (Collacott 2013, 9). This discourse is underpinned by a clear economic imperative that casts parents and grandparents as "potential burdens" to our system because it is not likely they will make economic contributions and are more likely to strain the social safety net and healthcare systems (Vanderplaat et al. 2012, 82).

The neoliberal discursive construction of the Parents and Grandparents Program (PGP) informed many of the regulatory changes that the Harper Conservative government introduced, including a cap on applications, a PGP visa, and changes in minimum threshold requirements. But in addition to the neoliberal construction, an additional implied criticism of this stream linked the program with fraud. The Fraser Institute Report suggested that this stream "has also significantly encouraged fraudulent applications of one sort or another" (Collacott 2013, 8). Some changes, as discussed below, were justified in terms of fraud prevention.

The Harper Conservative government targeted the PGP through a series of increasingly restrictive changes. In 2011, then Minister Jason Kenney announced Phase I of Canada's Action Plan for Faster Family Reunification. At the time, the department had a backlog of 160,000 applications, and it was estimated that it would require eight years to review them all (House of Commons, Standing Committee

Citizenship and Immigration 2017, 42). The backlog became the justification for a sweeping overhaul of the program. As Minister Kenney stated in a parliamentary speech:

> Friends, the challenge we're facing is a problem of math, it's also a problem of the heart that families are divided, but the backlogs and wait times are a result of math. When the number of applications exceeds the number of people admitted in a particular program, we end up with a growing backlog and longer wait times ...
>
> Notwithstanding our historic high levels of immigration, because there are obvious practical limits to how many people we can admit, particularly those who are not coming through economic streams to contribute directly to the Canadian tax base. We need to change the math. (CIC 2011b)

The development of the backlog, according to the government, rested on the shoulders of the thousands of applicants who overloaded the Canadian system. But Chen and Thorpe (2015) have challenged this premise. By carefully tracing how the backlog developed, they demonstrate how it was the outcome of the actions of successive administrations, where the entry of parents and grandparents were downgraded within the family class as early as the mid-1990s, followed by subsequent intentional administrative delays in the period between 2003 and 2004 (2015, 87–8). Consequently, they argue that "the shunning and rejection of parent and grandparent migrants echoes the earlier culturally biased discrimination against extended family members in Canadian immigration policy" (2015, 88). The Canadian government's limitations on what justifiably constitutes a family shows overt bias against cultures that do not adhere to nuclear family models.

Specifically, Phase I of Canada's Action Plan for Faster Family Reunification included the following four elements:

- Increase the number of parents and grandparents accepted as permanent residents, from nearly 15,500 admissions in 2010 to 25,000 in 2012.
- Parent and Grandparent Visas ... The multiple entry visa will allow parents and grandparents to remain in Canada for up to

24 months at a time without having to renew their status ... These applications will be examined on a case by case basis.
- The government will consult Canadians on how to redesign the parents and grandparents program.
- Addressing the backlog ... A temporary pause of up to 24 months on the acceptance of new sponsorship applications for parents and grandparents will greatly support backlog reduction. (Government of Canada 2011)

The PGP Super Visa (change #2 above) was a new development within Canada's family reunification policy, according to Chen and Thorpe, insofar as "it reinterprets family reunification to mean reunion without immigration." They further assert that PGP Super Visas "discriminatorily responsiblize the family, marketize regulation and maximize the state's control over borders and population" (2015, 90). Under the Super Visa's criteria, families had to provide proof of relationship as well as evidence indicating that they could provide financial support based on minimum necessary income. For example, in order to sponsor visiting parents or grandparents, a family unit of four persons had to have a minimum necessary income of $41,307 in 2015 – an amount that, in 2020, has increased to $47,084 (IRCC 2020). In addition to this requirement, families also had to purchase additional medical insurance for their family members. According to Minister Kenney, the latter condition was designed "to ensure that taxpayers don't have to carry the burden" (CIC 2011b). Parents and grandparents also needed to have an Immigration Medical Examination before a Super Visa was actually issued (CIC 2011a). The requirements to renew the visa every two years ties family reunification to sponsors' continued financial stability and visa holders' good health (Chen and Thorpe 2015, 90).

The Minister of Immigration explicitly drew links between parents and grandparents and the integrity of Canada's social programs. In addition to flagging the apparent backlog, Kenney stated that a redesigned program was required "so that we are admitting a number of grandparents and parents who we can afford to support in terms of our generous public health care system and other social benefits" (CIC 2011b). Consultations on PGP took place online, where respondents were asked whether they agreed or disagreed with the series of proposals. However, as the CCR observed: "The proposals present a certain bias: the starting point is an assumption that parents and grandparents are a burden on Canadian society and that their numbers should be decreased" (2012). This "bias" became apparent in the subsequent rationales presented to justify the regulatory changes.

Phase II of Canada's Action Plan for Faster Family Reunification was announced in 2013 following the public consultations. It included four noteworthy changes. First, the government proceeded to reopen the PGP but capped the number of new applications at 5,000 per year. Consequently, the program re-opened January 1, 2014, and closed February 3, 2014, when it reached the cap (Bragg and Wong 2016, 47). Second, new changes also required that sponsors meet a more stringent minimum necessary income (MNI) threshold: "The current MNI is low ... and provides no cushion if the family encounters an economic setback" (Government of Canada 2013, 1185). The new income requirement was MNI plus 30 per cent (Government of Canada 2013, 1187).

The third noteworthy change involved an increase in the sponsorship undertaking from ten years to twenty years. This extension was defended by the government on the basis that "sponsors and co-signers (if applicable) would be responsible for repaying any provincial social assistance benefits paid to the PGP and the PGPs' accompanying family members throughout the extended 20-year sponsorship undertaking period" (Government of Canada 2013, 1187). The fourth notable change involved documentation. Under Phase II, the only acceptable proof of income eligibility would be those documents issued from the Canada Revenue Agency for the past three consecutive years. Previously, an assortment of documents could be used to determine eligibility, but this was challenged on the basis that the range of documentation "makes it difficult to detect fraudulent documentation" (Government of Canada 2013, 1185).

Official discourses promulgated by the Harper Government tended to equate the sponsorship of PGP as a potential threat to Canada's social programs, especially the health care system. There was a particular concern that people would enter the country and not contribute. This assertion has since been challenged. Drawing from Statistics Canada's Longitudinal Survey data, Vanderplaat et al. (2012) point out that four years after landing, only a third of sponsored parents and/or grandparents are retired and "the other two thirds are making important contributions to the Canadian economy and their families" (87). Likewise, while the government focused on the drawbacks of PGPs, there was little acknowledgement of any possible benefits whether in relation to care labour, social integration, or cultural benefits (Creese et al. 2008; Bragg and Wong 2016; CCR 2013b).

It is against this political context of seeing family immigration as potentially admitting "fraudulent" and/or "unproductive" immigrants that restrictive changes and new income requirements were introduced. CCR among others have observed that the income criteria and period of sponsorship leaves the family reunification to the purview of the wealthy. But in addition to this class dynamic, the Council also importantly points out that "the changes will disproportionately affect racialized communities and women, as they are economically disadvantaged in Canada, and therefore will be less likely to meet the higher income thresholds" (CCR 2013b). When the Canadian government imposes economic rationales on potential family-class citizens, it paradoxically challenges its longstanding belief that *all* Canadian citizens are entitled to live with their families.

Importantly, the election of the Liberal government did not see a widespread roll back of the regulatory changes enacted by the Conservative administration. During the 2015 campaign, Trudeau promised to raise the cap on parent and grandparent sponsorship applications from 5,000 to 10,000. The new government made good on this promise, but the system itself did not change. Applications, which could only arrive by mail or courier, were processed on a first-come-first-served basis. The PGP Program opened to new applications on January 4, 2016, and within three days, by January 7, 2016, the program closed after 14,000 applications were received. Questions were raised about the fairness of the process, as there were reports of people paying high fees to couriers to guarantee they would be at the head of the line (Canadian Press 2016). In an effort to address the situation, the Liberals introduced a lottery system in 2017. Under this system, applicants could apply online and IRCC would assign each application a random number and then take the first 10,000 numbers (Cardoso 2018). To date, this system has proved very unpopular. Reflecting on their personal experience, one applicant quoted in a media report explained that: "The new system is based on unjust and unscientific means – a methodology of gambling with the lives of hard-working

Canadians trying to unite with their loved ones ... I had just completed the whole immigration process file and were approved to begin ... when you decided to change the entire system to a Vegas-like circus of random choice" (Harris 2018).

In the face of public criticism, the Liberal government announced that it was abandoning the lottery system and would return to the first-come-first-served process effective in 2019. The cap on applications was also increased to 20,000 in 2019 (Wright 2018) and was slightly increased to 21,000 in 2020 (El-Assal 2019). However, under the Liberal administration, the PGP quota, although increased, remains in place. Likewise, the Super Visa that was initially introduced as a temporary measure and then made permanent by the Conservatives also remains intact under the Liberals. Thus, family immigration under the Liberal government may have progressed in some respects (e.g., the removal of CPR and the sponsorship ban) but has also moved a few steps back by leaving intact Harper-era policies. The Liberals continue the trend of containing diversity by curtailing the sponsorship of potential citizens. The increasing politicization of the family-class category through the deployment of discourses of "fraud" and "welfare burdens" that we detail is part of the broader trend to contain diversity.

Seasonal Agricultural Workers, Caregivers, Temporary Foreign Workers, and Their Families

The Canadian government's emphasis on neoliberal immigration policy has sidelined family-class migrants in favour of economic migrants. As the previous sections show, and as chapter three discusses further, economic migrants are seen as the drivers of economic growth and are constructed as more deserving of entry into Canada. Other considerations, such as the need to keep migrant families intact and the importance of creating a coherent immigration policy that falls in line with the country's nation-building goals may be set aside.

What happens, however, in the cases of "low-skilled" temporary migrants such as seasonal agricultural workers, caregivers, and temporary foreign workers whose presence the Canadian government deems as being necessary to fill labour shortages but whose permanent settlement it wants to limit? Temporary migrants' situations are both similar and different to skilled economic migrants and family migrants. Like skilled economic migrants, the Canadian government desires their presence because they take jobs in industries that Canadians do not want to fill (Lusis and Bauder 2010, 28). Unlike skilled economic migrants, however, the Canadian government sees them as only being worthy of temporary entry, with minimal claims for permanent settlement for themselves and their families.

Temporary migrants are likewise similar to family-class migrants in that the government sees their entry as potential burdens to Canada's social welfare system, thereby subjecting their applications to heightened levels of scrutiny. Yet they are unlike family-class migrants in that the already limited pathways that exist for them and their families to get Canadian citizenship are becoming even more curtailed, even under the Liberal government of Trudeau.

The question of Canada's obligations towards temporary migrants and their families therefore emerges. Does Canada have a responsibility towards their families? In the previous chapter, we discussed the distinct histories of Canada's various temporary labour migration programs and what these histories show us about the Canadian government's perceptions of which migrants are deserving and are undeserving of Canadian citizenship. In this chapter, we address how temporary migrants and their families fare in terms of family reunification policies. We argue that temporary migrants – specifically seasonal agricultural workers, caregivers, and low-skilled temporary foreign workers – are placed by the government in a grey area, where they are both seen as economically necessary and yet are also depicted as potential economic drains on Canada's welfare state and moreover, as possible criminal and security threats. In other words, they are only tolerated in the country – they have a "minimal right to be present" and are accepted with "gritted teeth," as Bridget Anderson and Vanessa Hughes (2015) describe. In effect, this means that the question of whether they should be permitted to be with their families becomes a difficult policy conundrum. Although Canada, as a liberal democracy, accepts that all residents within a country should be treated equally, temporary migrants – who, by definition, are only meant to be in Canada for a short period of time – are treated as exceptional. In fact, the Canadian government seems to fear that permitting *any* temporary foreign workers to come to Canada with their families bolsters *all* their claims for permanent settlement. Hence, a patchwork of different policies regulate different groups of temporary migrants and their families. In short, we show how family reunification policies are applied unevenly across different groups.

SEASONAL AGRICULTURAL WORKERS

The Seasonal Agricultural Workers Program (SAWP) specifies that workers can only come to Canada for several months at a time before being sent back to their home countries. Most seasonal agricultural workers are men, with estimates from 2016 showing that women consist of 3 per cent of all workers (McLaughlin 2016). The dominance of men in seasonal agricultural work can be explained, in part, by gendered ideologies that compel male workers under the program to prefer working abroad while their wives take care of their children in their home countries (Preibisch and Hermoso Santamaria 2006, 113). This can also, in part, be explained by state policy. For example, sending states ask prospective female farm workers with children to provide a letter specifying who will be taking care of their children while they are away, a requirement which prospective male farm workers did not have to follow (Preibisch and Hermoso Santamaria 2006, 115). Hence, gendered ideologies that depict men as breadwinners and women as caregivers mean that men leaving their families to work abroad is more easily understood.

Perhaps because of such gendered perceptions, seasonal agricultural workers' separation from their families have not received as much attention compared to caregivers' separation from their families. Nevertheless, seasonal agricultural workers and their allies argue that both they and their families should be given permanent residency in Canada on account of the fact that Canada has benefited from their labour contributions (Justicia for Migrant Workers 2018). Moreover, they have argued that the fragmentation of migrant families violates migrants' human rights, contravening transnational human rights documents such as the United Nations Convention on the Rights of Migrant Workers and Their Families, which explicitly state that migrant families should be kept intact.

In addition, the health risks facing seasonal agricultural workers have brought to the fore questions regarding the Canadian government's obligations towards seasonal agricultural workers and their families. Although such workers are "circular" migrants, staying in Canada for part of the year before returning back to their home countries, the health effects they experience as a result of their work is borne by their home communities and their families (Justicia for Migrant Workers 2018). There are many cases of seasonal agricultural workers whose physical and mental health deteriorate. Some have even died. These health effects and risk of death also have substantial implications for the lives of workers' families who are left behind. For example, the widely publicized case of Sheldon Mackenzie, a seasonal agricultural worker from Jamaica, highlights the Canadian government's treatment of seasonal agricultural workers as "disposable" (CBC 2016). Sheldon sustained a head injury while working in a farm in Leamington, Ontario, and later received a removal order because he was unable to work. In response to his removal order, Sheldon's family in Jamaica campaigned to have a temporary stay on his pending deportation to ensure that he could continue receiving medical care in Canada. They were also in the midst of seeking permanent residency for Sheldon on humanitarian and compassionate grounds when he died before the application could be processed. The loss of Sheldon as the family's breadwinner, coupled with the medical bills that he accumulated, was felt intensely by his family. Such cases raise important questions about the obligations that the Canadian government has towards the families of deceased seasonal agricultural workers and their families.

CAREGIVERS

In contrast to seasonal agricultural workers, most caregivers are women. Figures show that 95 per cent of all caregivers from 2008 until 2012 were women (CIC 2015c). Unlike other temporary labour migrants, caregivers can apply for permanent residency for themselves and their families. Under the terms of the 2014 Caregiver Program (CP), which was previously known as the Foreign Domestics Movement (FDM), which was in place from 1981 until 1992, and the Live-in Caregiver Program (LCP), which was in place from 1992 until 2014, caregivers can apply for permanent residency for themselves and their families upon fulfilling a twenty-four-month contract.

Recent policy changes also mandate their completion of language and licensing requirements (CIC 2015a).

The ability to apply for permanent residency under the CP can be explained because of caregivers' concerted activism on this issue. Being able to do so was the result of a hard-earned fight (Tungohan 2013). Domestic worker activists and their allies campaigned vigorously for their right to stay in Canada in the late 1970s, leading to the establishment of policies allowing them to apply for permanent residency after finishing their employment contracts. These campaigns were successful because of domestic workers' ability to point to the hypocrisy of being asked to take care of Canadian families while living apart from their own (Tungohan 2013).

As in the case of seasonal agricultural workers, gendered and racialized ideologies are also in place, albeit leading to the opposite effect. Namely, because of gendered notions of who should do care work, it became unconscionable for the mostly women of colour workers who were part of the CP to be separated from their families for too long. As such, the Canadian government would need to "rescue" caregivers and their families by giving them the benefits of citizenship, but only after they had proven themselves by completing their employment contracts. However, as explained below, these gendered ideologies only go so far, with caregivers still having to undergo prolonged periods of family separation.

Of course, completing caregiver program requirements does not guarantee receipt of permanent residency. Due to increases in the number of permanent residency applications from caregivers, there was from 2009 until 2018 a backlog of caregiver permanent residency applications. This backlog "hit a high of 64 000 in 2014" and took until 2019 to clear (de la Cruz 2018). Delays in the processing of permanent residency applications lengthen the amount of time caregivers are separated from their families, causing much hardship. Figures from 2014 show that some caregivers have to wait for three years for their applications to be evaluated (Mas 2014). Figures from 2015 show that the average waiting time for applications to be processed is fifty months (Keung 2015), a number that has only decreased to forty-seven months in early 2016 (Keung 2016). The delay in processing caregiver permanent residency applications can in part be explained by the Conservative government's desire to weed out immigration fraud (Gaucher

2018). This can be seen when former Immigration Minister Jason Kenney voiced his concerns about the caregiver program going "out of control" because he suspected that applicants were gaining entry into Canada as "caregivers" without actually working in this profession (Hough 2014). Cases of caregivers who have not heard from IRCC on the results of their applications and who have subsequently gone public about the difficulties of being kept apart from their children became widespread. In response, the Liberal government under Trudeau committed to clearing the backlog in caregiver permanent residency applications by the end of 2018 (de la Cruz 2018).

In addition, caregivers, their spouses, and their children eighteen years and under have to undergo medical and criminal record checks during the application process. This may at times prevent caregivers from reunifying with their families. Because medical tests are only valid for a year, caregivers have to pay hefty testing fees for every year that their applications are not processed (de la Cruz 2018). Medical issues that are detected affect the outcome of permanent residency applications, as in the cases of children declared medically inadmissible because of their disabilities. In fact, a source of much outrage among caregivers and their allies involves caregivers whose permanent residency applications were rejected because of section 38 1(c) of the Immigration and Refugee Protection Act (IRPA), which specifies that to qualify for PR, immigrants should not cause "excessive demand" on Canada's welfare system.

At issue for advocates is whether the Canadian government can justifiably restrict family reunification on the grounds of excessive demand, particularly when interpretations of excessive demand rest on ableist grounds. For caregivers and their allies, the idea that the sum total of an individual's contributions to Canadian society can be measured economically, without taking into account their contributions to their families, to their communities, and to society at large, denotes a neoliberal conception of individual worth (Keung 2017b). Moreover, caregivers and their allies contest the idea that disabled individuals are uniformly assumed to be "burdens" to Canadian society (Keung 2017b). They not only dispute the formula set by IRCC estimating the costs that disabled family members will accrue in Canada in terms of health, education, and other welfare support, but also contest the underlying assumption that disabled individuals are "less than" able-bodied individuals or are potential economic threats. The Council for Canadians with Disabilities (CCD) submitted a brief to parliament calling for the repeal of the excessive demand provision, arguing that this policy relies on an outdated medical model that sees people's disabilities as the source of difficulty (2017, 5). Instead, they argued, the Canadian government would do well to adapt a "Social Model" in its immigration policies, "where society's design of the built environment, programs, legislation and services are acknowledged to be the real barriers to equality for persons with disabilities" (2017, 5).

Numerous campaigns seeking the revocation of the excessive demand provision proliferated across Canada. "Justice for Mercedes" was one such campaign. It centred on the case of Mercedes Benitez, who came to Canada in 2008 under the Live-in Caregiver Program (LCP). She promptly finished the terms of the LCP and applied for permanent residency, only to have her application rejected because the Canadian government estimated that her son, Harvey, who had a diagnosed developmental disability, would cause excessive demand on Canada's medical and social services (Keung 2017b). Benitez and her family were granted permanent residency following a massive campaign that involved migrant activist and caregiver groups, disability rights advocates, sympathetic members of Parliament, and academics. Notably, one of the campaign spokespeople was York University professor Felipe Montoya, whose permanent residency application got rejected because his son, who has Down syndrome, was deemed to cause excessive demand and who successfully appealed to have his rejection rescinded on humanitarian and compassionate grounds.

Ultimately, the ensuing outcry surrounding Benitez's case and the cases of other caregivers whose permanent residency applications were rejected because they have family members with disabilities led the Trudeau Liberal government in 2018 to amend the excessive demand provision. Specifically, they raised the cost threshold for immigration applicants. Rather than rejecting applicants whom the Canadian government estimated would accrue health and social welfare costs of $6,655 or higher per person per year, under the amended rules, the government would reject applicants whose health and social welfare costs were estimated to be $19,812 or higher per person per year (Government of Canada 2018b). While raising the cost threshold benefited families, caregivers and their allies were sharply critical of the way this left intact the excessive demand provision. For them, ableist assumptions went unchallenged, with the Canadian government maintaining its adherence to medical models of disability that construct disability as an 'illness' that needs to be overcome.

In June 2019, the Canadian government announced a new "pilot" caregiver program that would, among many changes and as discussed in the previous chapter, create different – and, for many caregiver applicants, confusing – pathways. Currently, there are two available pathways. First, families wishing to hire caregivers overseas may do so as a "home childcare worker" or a "home support worker," which gives caregivers the opportunity to apply for permanent residency after two years of eligible work experience in Canada. Under this pathway, the requirements for permanent residency include passing a language test, satisfying educational requirements, and continued work experience. The biggest change for caregivers on this pathway is that they can now come into the country with their families, thereby responding directly to caregivers' concerns regarding prolonged family separation. Nevertheless, the difficulties of meeting the requirements for permanent residency mean that fewer caregivers qualify.

A second pathway was also created, however, for caregivers who do not meet the criteria to come as home childcare workers or home support workers *and* who are already living in Canada. Unlike the first pathway, these workers can stay as temporary foreign workers. If they do so, they cannot have family members live with them and are likely to be ineligible to apply for permanent residency.

In sum, changes that the Trudeau government implemented respond directly to the needs for *some* caregivers to be with their families. Raising the threshold through which caregivers can sponsor their disabled family members leaves those who do not meet this threshold in a difficult position. Likewise, there remain caregivers who do not qualify for entry under the new pilot programs and continue to live separately from their families. They may in fact find themselves ineligible to apply for permanent residency altogether. Because these changes leave intact the fundamental belief that caregivers should be kept apart from their families (notwithstanding a few exceptions), we see that the Canadian government still deems caregivers and their families as unideal potential citizens.

"LOW-SKILLED" TEMPORARY FOREIGN WORKERS

While SAWP is male-dominated and the CP is female-dominated, there is greater gender balance among low-skilled temporary foreign workers. These workers enter Canada through low-skilled pilot projects under the Temporary Foreign Worker Program (TFWP). Unlike seasonal agricultural workers and caregivers, temporary foreign workers can bring their spouses and children with them. Their spouses can only work if they can get an employer to sponsor their work permits, which requires a Labor Market Impact Assessment (CIC 2015b). Because temporary foreign workers are sponsoring their spouses and children, they have to cover the costs of airfare and lodging for their families. In addition, depending on the school board's policies, they may have to pay international student fees for their children.

As stated in chapters three and five, a large part of the appeal of the TFWP for workers involves the ability to "switch" to a Provincial Nominee Program (PNP) from a temporary migration program. However, research shows that temporary foreign workers may not necessarily be aware of the difficulties of getting accepted into the PNP. Indeed, there are reports of temporary foreign workers being misinformed prior to arriving in Canada that it is easy to become permanent residents (Tungohan 2018a). Many temporary foreign workers withstand the experiences of deskilling in order to ensure the futures of their families.

Changes to the TFWP implemented in 2011 and 2014 led to a drastic reduction in the numbers of temporary foreign workers who could stay in Canada and who were eligible to apply for the PNPs. This has resulted in a loss of status for many temporary foreign workers and their families. These put limitations on their ability to renew their contracts and stay in Canada and place them and their families in a precarious situation where they may become undocumented (Tungohan 2015). While this policy has since been revoked, temporary foreign workers were not grandfathered into new policies and could find themselves undocumented. Hence, temporary foreign workers may be able to live with their families for the duration of their contracts yet risk undergoing a sudden loss in status and a corresponding increase in precariousness.

Becoming undocumented places temporary foreign workers and their families at risk. Research shows that for municipalities without a "don't ask, don't tell" policy, which allows residents regardless of legal status to access city services, workers' ability to survive depends on the goodwill of stakeholders such as employers, school principals, and community members (Tungohan 2018a). Neoliberal rationales that see access to services such as education as only being justifiable if workers are productive and have legal status render negligible the rights of migrant families. Migrant families in this situation experience "feelings of abandonment, symptoms of trauma, fear, isolation, depression, family fragmentation, and economic hardship" and are placed in a "chronic state of vulnerability and insecurity," all of which have negative effects on emotional and physical health (Brabeck et al. 2011, 279).

Whether temporary foreign workers and their families should have the right to apply for permanent residency despite coming to Canada on temporary visas is an ongoing debate among immigration advocates and political pundits. For proponents of the status quo, Canada should prioritize the immigration of "high-skilled" immigrants who have more to contribute to the country, as we discussed in chapter three. For migrant advocates, borrowing the slogan that if one is "good enough to work," they should be "good enough to stay," it is a short-sighted policy to refuse temporary foreign workers the opportunity to become permanent residents. Advocates frequently cite the fact that previous generations of immigrants and their families worked in similar "low-skilled," menial jobs, yet automatically received Canadian citizenship. Immigrants and their families, they attest, are nation-builders.

Trudeau's Liberal government seems to be moving in that direction. As recently as June 19, 2020, Trudeau attested to the Liberal government's desire to provide all temporary foreign workers with "pathways to permanent residency" (Nerenberg 2020). Exactly what these pathways look like remain to be seen. For advocates, such promises are not enough (Nerenberg 2020). They observe that being given "pathways" does not necessarily mean that all temporary foreign workers would be able to become permanent residents; indeed, they suspect that the imposition of economic requirements mean that only those who are seen as providing sufficient economic contributions would be eligible (Nerenberg 2020; Sorio 2020).

COMPARING SEASONAL AGRICULTURAL WORKERS, CAREGIVERS, AND "LOW-SKILLED" TEMPORARY FOREIGN WORKERS

When assessing temporary migrants' situations, we can see how these three different systems are working together to construct TFWs and their family members as unideal potential citizens. Of the three groups, seasonal agricultural workers have no entitlements with respect to family reunification, which places them in a highly undesirable situation. While migrant activists and seasonal agricultural workers are seeking permanent residency because they believe this will ensure more equitable treatment in the workplace and will allow them to bring their families to Canada (Dharssi 2016), whether policy-makers will heed their demands remains to be seen.

Caregivers, in contrast, may not be able to live with their families during their contracts but can sponsor them for permanent residency afterwards. This means, however, that they suffer from prolonged family separation, which is exacerbated by continuously lengthier processing times for their permanent residency applications.

By comparison, it is true that temporary foreign workers benefit from being able to live with their families during their contracts. However, they are likewise disadvantaged in that they do not have an automatic pathway to permanent residence and would have to transition to another immigration program, such as the Provincial Nominee Program, if they wish to stay in Canada permanently.

It is the issue of family separation, in fact, that we see as a major reason for why Canada's temporary migration policies and global migration trends should be reversed. Of course, temporary labour migrants are well-aware that Canadian families are placed in a tough bind. The absence of a national childcare program means that Canadian families with children often have to resort to both limited and expensive day care or seek private solutions, such as hiring their own caregivers (MacDonald and Friendly 2014). In addition, the absence of a national elderly and disability care strategy compel many families with elderly parents and disabled children to resort to private models of care. The CP consequently presents these families with a solution to their caregiving needs.

Nevertheless, while the arduous situation many Canadian families face highlight the urgent necessity of establishing a national childcare and elderly care program (see, e.g., Friendly 2015; Church 2016), the

CP entrenches a system where Canadian families are continuously privileged over migrant families. The existence of programs like the CP shows how global structural imbalances facilitate the exodus of people from countries in the Global South to countries in the Global North. Countries like Canada solve their care crisis by fragmenting migrant families. As researchers and migrant activists highlight, these arrangements illustrate the hypocrisy of many Canadians in not being able to fathom living and working in the same conditions as migrant workers but who nevertheless justify these abysmal situations by arguing that migrant workers are "better off" in Canada than they are in their home countries (Pratt 2009, 7). In short, for many Canadians, though prolonged family separation is not something they would ever want to undergo, they see this as an unavoidable part of migrants' realities. As Geraldine Pratt puts it when discussing the situation of Filipina caregivers in Canada, "this recognition short-circuits discussions of ethics and civic virtue within Canada, and renders the rescue of Filipinos from the Philippines as self-evidently virtuous" (2009, 7). What is lost in the ensuing discussion is what obligations Canada has towards migrants and their families and why some families fare better than others.

Migrant activists and researchers thus seek recognition of the hardships migrant families face. Researchers consistently point to how the decision to migrate does not come easily, with migrants opting to do so for the long-term good of their families (see, for example, Bernhard et al. 2008, 16). They also underscore the negative effects of family separation on migrant workers, their partners, and their children, which not only include negative health outcomes (McGuire and Martin 2007; Ward 2010) but also include feelings of alienation, separation, and loss for parents, spouses, and children (Asis et al. 2004; Bernhard et al. 2008; De Leon 2009; Parrenas 2005; Pratt 2006). Because of gendered expectations that see caregiving as being primarily a woman's role, migrant mothers in particular are saddled with competing expectations to economically provide for their families but also to be present care providers (Vaittinen 2014). Migrant women face contradictory expectations, where they are tasked with having to economically provide for their families but are blamed for doing so, as seen in the way popular discourse in sending countries blames "absentee" migrant mothers for a range of social ills, such as their children's truancy and even in some extreme cases their spouses' infidelity (Parrenas 2005; Tungohan 2013).

That the children who migrant women leave behind experience more intense feelings of loss and rejection compared to the children who migrant men leave behind affirms the persistence of gendered expectations (Parrenas 2005). Exacerbating such feelings of abandonment is the fact that both migrant mothers and their children are aware that migrant mothers in the Caregiver Program are caring for other families. As a caregiver who was interviewed on the issue of family separation asserts, "'the hardest times are when I have to prepare for the birthdays of my employers' children. This is when I miss my children the most'" (as quoted in Cohen 2000, 80). Interestingly, some researchers found that many migrants did not anticipate feeling so bereft. As Bernhard et al. (2008) observed after interviewing Latina migrants in Toronto, "the mothers did not expect to face, did not plan for, and were not prepared emotionally or economically for the long periods of separation from their children" (16). And while it is undeniable that developments in communication technology enable cheaper, faster, and more frequent modes of contact that families to communicate more efficiently (Brown 2015; Madianou and Miller 2011; Tungohan 2013) and to show "multi-directional care" for each other (Francisco-Menchavez 2018), the physical separation migrant families undergo is still arduous for everyone involved. Put differently, maintaining ties as a family through communications technology is not a substitute for being in close physical proximity with each other.

Family reunification does not solve the problems faced by migrant families. In fact, the "staged migration" process whereby caregivers come to Canada first, followed by their families later, is a source of much family conflict (Pratt 2009b, 48). After many years of living apart, reunification presents migrant families with new challenges. Gendered expectations that see men as breadwinners and women as caregivers may continue to have an influence, particularly for the husbands of migrant women who are unused to being in a financially dependent position, at least upon first arriving in Canada (Cohen 2000; Pratt 2006). Migrant women, in turn, may have a hard time adjusting to the expectation that they are responsible for care and domestic work in their households while also still financially supporting their families. In a study of twenty-three Filipino families going through the reunification process, Geraldine Pratt and the Filipino Canadian Youth Alliance found that a quarter of former caregivers formally separated and/or divorced from their spouses when either going through the prolonged period of family separation or immediately after reuniting in Canada (Pratt 2006, 47). This places them in a vulnerable situation financially and creates undue mental and emotional hardship.

Migrant children, on the other hand, have to withstand living in a new environment with parents whom they often do not know well and may miss being with the guardians who raised them (Cohen 2000; Pratt 2006). In some cases, they also have to adjust to a lower standard of living. The migrant children in Pratt's sample, for example, went to private school in the Philippines and had access to household helpers, which meant that life in Canada led to a "disjuncture in class and life experiences" (Pratt 2006, 48). The economic realities of life in Canada mean that many migrant parents work in multiple jobs for little more than minimum wage, ensuring that less time is spent with family. Being unable to spend as much time with their parents intensifies migrant children's feelings of separation, which for some is ironic considering that they are now together (Tungohan 2013). Negative experiences in school also contribute to experiences of alienation, with some migrant children feeling unmotivated academically because they were asked to go back a few grades upon arriving in Canada (Pratt 2006). While Pratt and the Filipino Canadian Youth Alliance found that the educational attainment of children who came to Canada as teenagers was lower because of accreditation issues, they also discovered that even children who arrived at younger ages did not fare as well, with half of their sample of fourteen respondents not finishing high school (Pratt 2006, 46). Other issues, such as "being read by many Canadians as perpetual outsiders," contribute to migrant youth's settlement difficulties (Pratt 2010, 345).

The lengthy period of reunification and settlement has even led scholars such as Conely De Leon (2009) to conceptualize the term "post-reunification reconciliation" to describe the period of time adult children reconcile with their mothers after going through the traumatic experiences of living apart and then reunifying. According to De Leon, this period is "marked by a need to rebuild broken relationships" (2009). Understanding when migrant families adjust to Canada after separation and reunification consequently necessitates taking a longer-term view of settlement. Migrant activists and researchers hold that the realities of staggered migration that force migrant families to go through periods of separation, reunification, and, in some cases, post-reunification reconciliation are extremely traumatic. Thus, understanding how exactly different members of the family fare at different time periods requires an appreciation for these various transition periods.

Consequently, rather than taking policies as given, we demand that widespread policy and structural changes take place to ameliorate migrant families' experiences of trauma. That many of the most prominent migrant activists in Canada were migrant children who witnessed the hardships their parents endured and who themselves went through settlement difficulties shows that the impetus for change stems from personal experiences (De Leon 2009; Pratt 2010). Unsurprisingly, one of their major demands is for all migrant workers and their families be kept intact. For them, giving seasonal agricultural workers, temporary foreign workers, and caregivers and their families permanent residency upon arrival will ensure that migrant families are kept intact and that migrant families do not have to go through the pain of separation (and, for caregivers' families, of reunification). Because neoliberal imperatives privilege economic migrants over family-class migrants, such demands are likely to remain unheeded, at least for now.

CONCLUSION

Family immigration has long been considered an essential part of Canada's immigration policies. Yet under the Harper government and, to a lesser extent, the Trudeau government, family-class immigration was underprioritized in comparison to economic immigration. Family-class migrants who literally come to Canada as dependents of their family members (i.e., sponsors) are constructed as potential drains on Canada's welfare system and as potential fraudsters. This neoliberal perception that family-class migrants do not provide sufficient economic contributions has led the Canadian government to impose restrictions on family-class migration. Many of the policies pursued lead to the containment of diversity. These restrictions include narrower definitions of the family, provision against "fraud," and family separation for many temporary foreign workers. As a result, Canadian citizens, permanent residents, and temporary foreign workers all face their own challenges with family sponsorship and/or family separation. Contrary to the Canadian government's longstanding belief that citizens are entitled to live with their family members – which has been the basis of Canada's family immigration policies – these restrictions show that economic needs trump human rights (in this case, the right to live with one's family). Nonetheless, one of the outcomes of the COVID-19 pandemic was to make visible the importance of family supports – whether unpaid care for children, the elderly, and the sick. As one report noted: "family members – including parents and grandparents, as well as extended family members ... also needed to provide childcare and eldercare so that immigrant workers can contribute to Canada's economic recovery" (Esses et al. 2021, 29). Perhaps the harrowing experiences many Canadian families experienced during COVID-19 might create openings for a re-evaluation of family migration.

NOTES

1 It should be noted that although the Canadian government has indicated that it will continue to process family-class immigration applications during the pandemic, its policies mandating that only "essential travel" is permitted may affect the numbers of family-class immigration admissions in 2020 (Thevenot 2020).
2 Portions of this section are taken directly from Gabriel 2017.

BIBLIOGRAPHY

Abu-Laban, Yasmeen, and Christina Gabriel. *Selling Diversity: Immigration, Multiculturalism, Employment Equity and Globalization*. Peterborough, ON: Broadview Press, 2002.

Anderson, Bridget, and Vanessa Hughes. "Introduction." In *Citizenship and Its Others*, edited by Bridget Anderson and Vanessa Hughes, 1–9. New York: Palgrave Macmillan, 2015.

Angus Reid. "Immigration: Half Back Current Targets, but Colossal Misperceptions, Pushback over Refugees, Cloud Debate." October 7, 2019. https://angusreid.org/election-2019-immigration/.

Asis, Maruja, Shirlena Huang, and Brenda S.A. Yeoh. "When the Light of the Home is Abroad: Unskilled Filipino Migration and the Filipino Family." *Singapore Journal of Tropical Geography* 25, no. 2 (2004): 198–215.

Bernhard, Judith, Patricia Landolt, and Luin Goldring. "Transnationalizing Families: Canadian Immigration Policy and the Spatial Fragmentation of Caregiving among Latin American Newcomers." *International Migration* 47, no. 2 (2008): 3–31.

Bhuyan, Rupaleem, Anna C. Korteweg, and Karin Baqi. "Regulating Spousal Migration through Canada's Multiple Border Strategy: The Gendered and Racialized Effects of Structurally Embedded Borders." *Law and Policy* 40, no. 4 (2018): 346–70.

Bonjour, Saskia, and Albert Kraler. "Introduction: Family Migration as an Integration Issue? Policy Perspectives and Academic Insights." *Journal of Family Issues* 36, no. 11 (2015): 1407–32.

Brabeck, Kalina M., M. Brinton Lykes, and Rachel Hershberg. "Framing Immigration to and Deportation from the United States: Guatemalan and Salvadoran Families Make Meaning of their Experiences." *Community, Work & Family* 14, no. 3 (2011): 275–96.

Bragg, Browyn and Lloyd L. Wong. "Cancelled Dreams: Family Reunification and Shifting Immigration Policy." *Journal of Immigration and Refugee Studies* 14, no. 1 (2016): 46-65.

Brown, Rachel. "Re-examining the Transnational Nanny: Migrant Carework beyond the Chain." *International Feminist Journal of Politics* 18, no. 2 (2015): 210–29.

Canada, Parliament, House of Commons, Standing Committee on Citizenship and Immigration. *Family Reunification*. 42th Parl, 1st Sess, March 2017. (Chair Borys Wrzesnewskyj). www.ourcommons.ca/Document Viewer/en/42-1/CIMM/report-8.

Canadian Council for Refugees (CCR). "DNA Tests: A Barrier to Speedy Family Reunification." October 2011. https://ccrweb.ca/sites/ccrweb.ca/files/dnatests.pdf.

– "CCR Backgrounder – CIC Consultations on the Parent and Grandparent Program." 2012. https://ccrweb.ca/sites/ccrweb.ca/files/ccr_pgp_backgrounder_final.pdf.

– "Definition of Dependent Children. Comments on the Proposed Change to the Immigration and Refugee Protection Regulations as Published in the *Canada Gazette*." June 2013a. https://ccrweb.ca/files/family-changes-comments-age-dependency-jun-13.pdf.

– "Sponsorship of Parents and Grandparents: Comments on the Proposed Change to the Immigration and Refugee Protection Regulations as Published in the *Canadian Gazette*." June 2013b. https://ccrweb.ca/files/family-changes-comments-pgp-jun-13.pdf.

– "Conditional Permanent Residence: Failure in Policy and Practice." Media Release, October 28, 2015. http://ccrweb.ca/en/print/24140.

Canadian Press. "Government Launches Ad Campaign Aimed at Combatting Marriage Fraud." *Maclean's* (March 20, 2013). www.macleans.ca/news/government-launches-ad-campaign-aimed-at-combating-marriage-fraud/.
– "People Pay Their Way to Front of Line in Family Reunification Program." January 12, 2016. www.cbc.ca/news/canada/hamilton/headlines/people-pay-their-way-to-front-of-line-in-family-reunification-program-reports-1.3399752.
Cardoso, Tom. "'Anything Would Be Better': Critics Warn Ottawa's Family-Reunification Lottery Is Flawed, Open to Manipulation." *Globe and Mail* (June 8, 2018). www.theglobeandmail.com/canada/article-anything-would-be-better-critics-warn-ottawas-family-reunification/.
CCR. "About the CCR." 2021. https://ccrweb.ca/en/about-ccr.
Chen, Xiaobei, and Sherry Xiaohan Thorpe. "Temporary Families? The Parent and Grandparent Sponsorship Program and the Neoliberal Regime of Immigration Governance in Canada." *Migration, Mobility and Displacement* 1, no. 1 (2015): 81–98.
Church, Elizabeth. "'Elder Care Is the New Child Care,' Professor Says." *Globe and Mail* (January 3, 2016). www.theglobeandmail.com/news/national/elder-care-is-the-new-child-care-professor-says/article27989811/.
CIC Citizenship and Immigration Canada. Facts and Figures 2003. Immigration Overview. Ottawa, ON: Government of Canada, 2003.
– "Backgrounder – Applying for a Parent and Grandparent Super Visa." Ottawa, ON: Government of Canada, 2011a. www.canada.ca/en/immigration-refugees-citizenship/news/archives/backgrounders-2011/applying-parent-grandparent-super-visa.html.
– "Speaking Notes for the Honourable Jason Kenney, P.C., M.P. Minister of Citizenship, Immigration and Multiculturalism." November 4, 2011b. www.canada.ca/en/immigration-refugees-citizenship/news/archives/speeches-2011/jason-kenney-minister-2011-11-04.html.
– "Section 5: Gender-Based Analysis of the Impact of the Immigration and Refugee Protection Act." Annual Report to Parliament on Immigration. October 28, 2013. www.cic.gc.ca/english/resources/publications/annual-report-2013/section5.asp.
– "In-Canada Application for Permanent Residence (Live-in Caregivers)." Ottawa, ON: Government of Canada, 2015a. www.cic.gc.ca/english/information/applications/live-in.asp.
– "Temporary Foreign Worker Program: Hiring Foreign Workers in Occupations That Require Lower levels of Formal Training." Ottawa, ON: Government of Canada, 2015b. www.cic.gc.ca/english/resources/tools/temp/work/pilot/training.asp [Accessed 1 February 2016].
– "Work Permit Holders for Work Purposes with a Valid Permit on December 31st." Ottawa, ON: Government of Canada, 2015c. www.cic.gc.ca/english/resources/statistics/facts2013/temporary/1-1.asp.

- "What Is the Pilot Project on the Sponsorship of Undeclared Family Members?" January 30, 2020. www.cic.gc.ca/english/helpcentre/answer.asp?qnum=1493&top=14.
Cohen, Rina. "'Mom Is a Stranger': The Negative Impacts of Immigration Policies on the Family Life of Filipina Domestic Workers." *Canadian Ethnic Studies* 32, no. 3 (2000): 76–88.
Collacott, Martin. "Canadian Family Class Immigration. The Parent and Grandparent Component under Review." Vancouver, BC: The Fraser Institute, November 2013. www.fraserinstitute.org/sites/default/files/canadian-family-class-immigration.pdf.
Council of Canadians with Disabilities. "Repeal of the Excessive Demand Provisions in Canada's Immigrant and Refugee Protection Act." Brief presented to the Standing Committee on Citizenship and Immigration. Winnipeg, MB: Council of Canadians with Disabilities. www.ourcommons.ca/Content/Committee/421/CIMM/Brief/BR9256474/br-external/CouncilOfCanadiansWithDisabilities-e.pdf.
Creese, Gillian, Isabel Dyck, and Arlene Tigar McLaren. "The 'Flexible' Immigrant: Human Capital Discourse and the Family Household and Labour Market Strategies." *Journal of International Migration and Integration* 9, no. 3 (2008): 269–88.
de la Cruz, Jhong. "Caregivers Urge Canada to Fix Backlog in Permanent Residency Applications." *Inquirer* (May 1, 2018). https://usa.inquirer.net/11954/caregivers-urge-canada-fix-backlog-permanent-status-applications?utm_expid=.XqNwTug2W6nwDVUSgFJXed.1.
De Leon, Conely. "Post-reunification Reconciliation among Pinay Domestic Workers and Adult Daughters in Canada." *Canadian Women's Studies* 27, nos. 2–3 (2009): 68–72.
DeShaw, Rell. "The History of Family Reunification in Canada and Current Policy." *Canadian Issues* (Spring 2006): 9–14.
Dharssi, Alia. "Migrant Farmworkers call for Permanent Residency, Ability to Bring Families to Canada." *National Post* (January 26, 2016). https://nationalpost.com/news/migrant-farm-workers-call-for-permanent-residency-ability-to-bring-families-to-canada.
El-Assal, Kareem. "How to Improve Canada's Parents and Grandparents Immigration Program in 2020." *CIC News* (December 13, 2019). www.cicnews.com/2019/12/how-to-improve-canadas-parents-and-grandparents-sponsorship-program-in-2020-1213347.html#gs.3bat9k.
Esses, Victoria, Jean McRae, Naomi Alboim, Natalya Brown, Chris Friesen, Leah Hamilton, Aurélie Lacassagne, Audrey Macklin, and Margaret Walton-Roberts. *Supporting Canada's COVID-19 Resilience and Recovery through Robust Immigration Policy and Programs*. Ottawa, ON: Royal Society of Canada, 2021.
Francisco-Menchavez, Valerie. *Labor of Care: Filipina Migrants and Transnational Families in the Digital Age*. Chicago: University of Illinois Press, 2018.

Friendly, Martha. "Building a National Childcare Program." Ottawa, ON: The Broadbent Institute, August 27, 2015. www.broadbentinstitute.ca/canada_ready_for_child_care.

Gabriel, Christina. "Framing Families: Neo-Liberalism and the Family Class within Canadian Immigration Policy." *Atlantis* 38, no. 1 (2017): 179–94.

Gaucher, Megan. "Attack of the Marriage Fraudsters! An Examination of the Harper Government's Antimarriage Fraud Campaign." *International Journal of Canadian Studies* 50 (2014): 187–205.

– *A Family Matter: Citizenship, Conjugal Relationships and Canadian Immigration Policy*. Vancouver, BC: UBC Press, 2018.

Government of Canada. "Archived – Backgrounder – Phase I of Action Plan for Faster Family Reunification" Ottawa, ON: Author, November 11, 2011. www.canada.ca/en/immigration-refugees-citizenship/news/archives/backgrounders-2011/phase-action-plan-faster-family-reunification.html.

– "Regulations Amending the Immigration and Refugee Protection Regulations: Regulatory Impact Analysis Statement." *Canada Gazette* 147, no. 20 (May 18, 2013). www.gazette.gc.ca/rp-pr/p1/2013/2013-05-18/html/reg2-eng.html.

– "Regulations Amending the Immigration and Refugee Protection Regulations: Regulatory Impact Analysis Statement." *Canada Gazette* 150, no. 44 (October 29, 2016). www.gazette.gc.ca/rp-pr/p1/2016/2016-10-29/html/reg1-eng.html.

– "Notice – Government of Canada Eliminates Conditional Permanent Residence." Ottawa, ON: Author (April 28, 2017). www.canada.ca/en/immigration-refugees-citizenship/news/notices/elminating-conditional-pr.html.–. "Facts about Biometrics." Ottawa, ON: Author (January 24, 2020). www.canada.ca/en/immigration-refugees-citizenship/campaigns/biometrics/facts.html.

Halpert, Douglas, and Andrea Baldwin. "Who Is Family: A Look at Canadian and US Immigration Law on the Definition of Qualifying Relatives." *LawNow* 38, no. 11 (2013). www.lawnow.org/who-is-family/.

Harris, Kathleen. "Liberals Relaunch Family Reunification Lottery Despite Angry Backlash around 'Immigration Fiasco.'" CBC News (January 7, 2018). www.cbc.ca/news/politics/immigration-parents-grandparents-sponsorship-1.4442456.

Hough, Jennifer. "Canada's Live-in Caregiver Program 'Ran out of Control' and Will Be Reformed: Jason Kenney." *National Post* (June 24, 2014). https://nationalpost.com/news/politics/canadas-live-in-caregiver-program-ran-out-of-control-and-will-be-reformed-jason-kenney.

IRCC Immigration, Refugees and Citizenship Canada. "Annual Report to Parliament 2015." Ottawa, ON: Government of Canada, 2015. www.canada.ca/content/dam/ircc/migration/ircc/english/pdf/pub/annual-report-2015.pdf.

- "2018 Annual Report to Parliament on Immigration." Ottawa, ON: Government of Canada, 2018a. www.canada.ca/en/immigration-refugees-citizenship/corporate/publications-manuals/annual-report-parliament-immigration-2018/report.html.
- "Dependent Children." Ottawa, ON: Government of Canada, 2018b. www.canada.ca/en/immigration-refugees-citizenship/corporate/publications-manuals/operational-bulletins-manuals/permanent-residence/non-economic-classes/dependent-children.html.
- "Excessive Demand: Calculation of the Cost Threshold." Ottawa, ON: Government of Canada, 2018c. www.canada.ca/en/immigration-refugees-citizenship/corporate/publications-manuals/excessive-demand.html.

Joly, Yann, Shahad Salman, Ida Ngueng Feze, Palmira Granados Moreno, Michèle Stanton-Jean, Jacqueline Lacey, Micheline Labelle, et al. "DNA Testing for Family Reunification in Canada: Points to Consider." *Journal of International Migration and Integration* 18, no. 2 (2017): 391–404.

Justicia/Justice for Migrant Workers (J4MW). "The Seasonal Agricultural Workers Program." 2018. www.justicia4migrantworkers.org/bc/pdf/sawp.pdf.

Keung, Nicholas. "Foreign Caregivers Face Lengthy Wait for Permanent Status." *Toronto Star* (July 21, 2015). www.thestar.com/news/immigration/2015/07/21/foreign-caregivers-face-lengthy-wait-for-permanent-status.html.

- "Foreign Caregivers Wait Years to Call Canada Home." *Toronto Star* (January 17, 2016). www.thestar.com/news/immigration/2016/01/17/foreign-caregivers-wait-years-to-call-canada-home.html.
- "Advocates Hail End to 'Conditional' Spousal Visas." *Toronto Star* (April 28, 2017a). www.thestar.com/news/immigration/2017/04/28/advocates-hail-end-to-conditional-spousal-visas.html.
- "Disabled Son Deemed 'Medically Inadmissible' to Join Mother in Canada." *Toronto Star* (April 2, 2017b). www.thestar.com/news/immigration/2017/04/02/disabled-son-deemed-medically-inadmissible-to-join-mother-in-canada.html.

Kofman, Eleonore. "Family-Related Migration: A Critical Review of European Studies." *Journal of Ethnic and Migration Studies* 30, no. 2 (2004): 243–62.

- "Symposium on Migration, Family and Dignity." QScience Proceedings. *Family, Migration and Dignity Special Issue* (2013). http://dx.doi.org/10.5339/qpro.2013.fmd.5.

Kofman, Eleonore, and V. Meetoo. "Chapter Six – Family Migration." In *World Migration 2008: Managing Labour Mobility in the Evolving Global Economy*, 151–72. Geneva: International Organization for Migration (IOM), 2008. https://publications.iom.int/books/world-migration-report-2008-managing-labour-mobility-evolving-global-economy.

LaViolette, Nicole. "Sexual Minorities, Migration, and the Remaining Boundaries of Canadian Immigration and Refugee Law." In *Unsettled Settlers:*

Barriers to Integration, edited by Soheila Pashang, Debbie Douglas, and Avvy Go, 29–54. Toronto: DeSitter, 2012.

Liew, Jamie Chai Yun. "The Ultrahazardous Activity of Excluding Family Members in Canada's Immigration System." *Canadian Bar Review* 94, no. 2 (2016): 281–308.

Lusis, Tom, and Harald Bauder. "Immigrants in the Labour Market: Transnationalism and Segmentation." *Geography Compass* 4, no. 1 (2010): 28–44.

MacDonald, David, and Martha Friendly. "The Parent Trap: Child Care Fees in Canada's Big Cities." Ottawa, ON: Canadian Centre for Policy Alternatives, 2014. www.policyalternatives.ca/sites/default/files/uploads/publications/National%20Office/2014/11/Parent_Trap.pdf.

Madianou, Mirca, and Daniel Miller. "Mobile Phone Parenting: Reconfiguring Relationships between Filipina Migrant Mothers and their Left-Behind Children." *New Media & Society* 13, no. 3 (2011): 457–70.

Marchitelli, Rosa. "Migrant Worker Program Called 'Worse than Slavery' after Injured Participants Sent Home without Treatment." CBC News (May 16, 2016). www.cbc.ca/news/canada/jamaican-farm-worker-sent-home-in-a-casket-1.3577643.

Mas, Susana. "Foreign Caregivers Backlog Grows as Families Wait for Residency." CBC News (October 19, 2014). www.cbc.ca/news/politics/foreign-caregivers-backlog-grows-as-families-wait-for-residency-1.2778317.

McGuire, Sharon, and Kate Martin. "Fractured Migrant Families: Paradoxes of Hope and Devastation." *Family & Community Health* 30, no. 3 (2007): 178–88.

McLaughlin, Janet. "Canada's Migrant Agricultural Workers Deserve Full and Equal Rights. Here's Why." *TVO* (June 16, 2016). www.tvo.org/article/canadas-migrant-agricultural-workers-deserve-full-and-equal-rights-heres-why.

Metropolitan Action Committee on Violence Against Women and Children (METRAC). "Statement on Amendment to the Immigration and Refugee Protection Regulations: Proposed Conditional Permanent Residence Period for Sponsored Spouses." April 6, 2012. https://ccrweb.ca/files/metrac_comments.pdf.

Meurrens, Steven. "Canada Raises the Age of Dependency in Immigration." *Policy Options* (November 20, 2017). https://policyoptions.irpp.org/magazines/november-2017/canada-raises-the-age-of-dependency-in-immigration/.

Moreno, Palmira Granados, Ida Ngueng Feze, and Yann Joly. "Does the End Justify the Means? A Comparative Study of the Use of DNA Testing in the Context of Family Reunification." *Journal of Law and Biosciences* 4, no. 2 (2017): 250–81.

Nerenberg, Karl. "Prime Minister Opens Door to Citizenship for Migrant Workers." *Rabble.ca* (June 19, 2020). https://rabble.ca/news/2020/06/prime-minister-opens-door-citizenship-migrant-workers.

Organisation for Economic Cooperation and Development (OECD). "International Migration Outlook 2015." Paris: OECD Publishing, September 22, 2015. https://doi.org/10.1787/migr_outlook-2015-en.

Parrenas, Rhacel. *Children of Global Migration: Transnational Families and Gendered Woes*. Stanford, CA: Stanford University Press, 2005.

Pero, Rebecca, and Harrison Smith. "In the 'Service' of Migrants: The Temporary Resident Biometrics Project and the Economization of Migrant Labor in Canada." *Annals of the Association of American Geographers* 104, no. 2 (2014): 401–11.

Pratt, Geraldine. "Separation and Reunification among Filipino Families in Vancouver." *Canadian Issues* (Spring 2006): 46–9.

– "Circulating Sadness: Witness Filipino Mothers' Stories of Family Separation." *Gender, Place, and Culture* 16, no. 1 (2009): 3–22.

– "Listening for Spaces of Ordinariness: Filipino-Canadian Youth's Transnational Lives." *Children's Geographies* 8, no. 4 (2010): 343–52.

Preibisch, Kerry, and Evelyn Encalada. *Migrant Women Farm Workers in Canada*. Guelph, ON: Rural Women Making Change, 2008.

Preibisch, Kerry, and Luz Maria Hermoso Santamaria. "Engendering Labour Migration: The Case of Foreign Workers in Canadian Agriculture." In *Women, Migration, and Citizenship: Making Local, National, and Transnational Connections*, edited by Alexandra Dobrowolsky and Evagelia Tatsoglu, 107–30. Burlington, VT, and Hampshire, England: Ashgate Publishing, 2006.

Radwanski, Adam. "Trudeau Makes Big Play for Immigrant Voters." *Globe and Mail* (September 15, 2015). www.theglobeandmail.com/news/politics/liberals-promise-to-double-applications-for-parents-grandparents-of-new-immigrants/article26539846/.

Root, Jesse, Erika Gates-Gasse, John Shields, and Harald Bauder. "Discounting Immigrant Families: Neoliberalism and the Framing of Canadian Immigration Policy Change." *RCIS Working Paper No. 2014/7*, 2014. https://digital.library.ryerson.ca/islandora/object/RULA%3A8389.

Shachar, Ayelet. "The Race for Talent: Highly Skilled Migrants and Competitive Immigration Regimes." *New York University Law Review* 81, no. 1 (2006): 148–206.

Sorio, Connie. "From Disposable to Indispensable: Providing Foreign Migrant Workers with a Pathway to Permanent Residency." May 7, 2020. https://rabble.ca/news/2020/06/prime-minister-opens-door-citizenship-migrant-workers.

Spurr, Ben. "Trudeau Pledges to Double Family Reunification." *Toronto Star* (September 15, 2015), www.thestar.com/news/canada/2015/09/25/trudeau-pledges-sweeping-immigration-changes.html.

Thevenot, Shelby. "Canada Refines Definition of 'Essential Travel' during Coronavirus." *CIC News* (May 1, 2020). www.cicnews.com/2020/05/canada-refines-definition-of-essential-travel-during-coronavirus-0514270.html#gs.7k79yi.

Tungohan, Ethel. "Reconceptualizing Motherhood, Reconceptualizing Resistance: Migrant Domestic Workers, Transnational Hyper-maternalism, and Activism." *International Feminist Journal of Politics* 15, no. 1 (2013): 39–57.

– "April 1 Deadline Looms for Children of Temporary Foreign Workers." *Rabble.ca* (March 31, 2015). http://rabble.ca/news/2015/03/april-1-deadline-looms-children-temporary-foreign-workers.

– "Living with Compromised Legal Status: Irregular Temporary Foreign Workers in Alberta and the Importance of Imagining, Strategizing, and Inter-Provincial Legal Consciousness." *International Migration* 56, no. 6 (2018a): 207–20. https://doi.org/10.1111/imig.12506.

– "Temporary Foreign Workers in Canada: Reconstructing 'Belonging' and Remaking 'Citizenship." *Social and Legal Studies* 27, no. 2 (2018b): 236–52.

Vaittinen, Tiina. "Reading Global Care Chains as Migrant Trajectories: A Theoretical Framework for Understanding Structural Change." *Women's Studies International Forum* 47, Part B (2014): 191–202.

VanderPlaat, Madine, Howard Ramos, and Yoko Yoshida. "What Do Sponsored Parents and Grandparents Contribute?" *Canadian Ethnic Studies* 44, no. 3 (2012): 79–96.

Ward, Louise S. "Farmworkers at Risk: The Costs of Family Separation." *Journal of Immigrant and Minority Health* 12, no. 5 (2010): 672–7.

White, Autumn Melissa. "Ambivalent Homonationalisms: Transnational Queer Intimacies and Territorialized Belongings." *International Journal of Postcolonial Studies* 15, no. 1 (2013): 37–54.

Wright, Teresa. "Feds Replacing Lottery for Parent Sponsorship, More Applications to Be Accepted." *Canadian Press* (August 20, 2018). www.ctvnews.ca/politics/feds-replacing-lottery-for-parent-sponsorship-more-applications-to-be-accepted-1.4060335.

PART III

CHAPTER SEVEN

Redefining Membership and Belonging: Contestations over Citizenship and Multiculturalism

In 2015, the federal Liberals, under the leadership of Justin Trudeau, were swept rather unexpectedly to power in Canada. In his televised victory speech, Trudeau was met with thunderous applause when he extolled the party faithful to: "Have faith in your fellow citizens, my friends. They are kind and generous. They are open-minded and optimistic. And they know in their heart of hearts that a Canadian is a Canadian is a Canadian" (Trudeau 2015). The refrain of "a Canadian is a Canadian is a Canadian" also acquired an ongoing presence in communications from members of Trudeau's government, in the media, and in Canadian political culture more broadly even after the election. The repetitive refrain signalled the idea that there should be no legal or hierarchical distinctions between Canadian citizens in law, in treatment, or in membership and belonging to the political community. As we will show in this chapter, however, over the course of the 2000s multiculturalism as well as naturalization were impacted by neoliberalism and criminalization. While these impacts remain contested, we argue the trend towards "containing diversity" has now extended into policies that are also popularly associated with enabling and celebrating diversity.

In a world of nation-states, membership in a political community has come to be defined by citizenship. In the particular case of Canada, a settler colony with an Indigenous population, immigration has been key to the building of a settler society. This nation-building project relies on settlers coming to see themselves as members or citizens of a new polity (see also Battell, Lowman, and Barker 2015). Most Canadians acquire citizenship at birth; however, the 2016 census showed that more than one in five Canadians, or 21.9 per cent of the population, are foreign born (Statistics Canada 2017). As such, many Canadians have acquired citizenship by naturalization. Long considered unproblematic, naturalization in Canada is today more accurately characterized as a contested policy field. This was perhaps most evident in 2014, when the Conservative government of Stephen Harper introduced sweeping changes to the Citizenship Act, as we outline below.

Multiculturalism has also been an area of contestation in Canada. Since its inception over fifty years ago as a national policy in 1971, multiculturalism has enjoyed the formal support of successive federal governments, including most recently the Conservative government of Prime Minister Stephen Harper (2006–15) and the Liberal government of Prime Minister Justin Trudeau (2015–). It is also constitutionally entrenched in Section 27 of the Canadian Charter of Rights and Freedoms. However, while multiculturalism was formulated with "national unity" as a central plank, its place in supporting the inclusion of all Canadians has long been fraught. For instance, Indigenous peoples and French speakers in and outside the province of Quebec have utilized distinct constitutional and legal provisions for making claims on the state, rendering the policy of little direct appeal. It was only in the 1980s, with pressure from racialized minorities, that the policy took up anti-racism, but the extent of this has varied by the government of the day (Abu-Laban 2014a). By the late 1980s, a more visible backlash against the policy and minorities was also evident, which took on new dimensions after September 11, 2001.

As this chapter will detail, the role of naturalization and multiculturalism in supporting the inclusion of diverse immigrants and citizens and a particular type of nation-building project has been impacted by neoliberalism and criminalization. When it comes to naturalization, for example, the Harper Conservatives' policy changes emphasized that citizenship is both valuable and a privilege that needs to be protected from "abuse," "fraud," and "terrorism." Although the Trudeau Liberals went on to introduce their own changes to repeal some elements of the Harper-era citizenship changes, a concern with fraud remained intact. While federal multiculturalism policy has not been subject to the same substantive policy changes seen in citizenship, as we trace, over the course of the 2000s, symbolic shifts have impacted its language and focus. In this chapter, we examine the evolution of naturalization and multiculturalism in the post–September 11 period. Our findings show how membership and belonging during this period have been subject to redefinition in both national and subnational (provincial) policy debates. As such, new questions concerning values, the place of religious minorities, or the extension (or revocation) of citizenship are deeply revealing of the instability of multicultural citizenship in Canada, and reflective of broader international trends.

As we have traced to this point in the book, the rationales that frame immigration policy in countries in the Global North, and in Canada specifically, have been overwhelmingly advanced in relation to the imperatives of neoliberal globalization: the need to attract the "best and brightest" – generally the high skilled – in a global competition for talent. Citizenship policy, in contrast, remains squarely within the realm of the national. This said, however, the recent popularity of both citizenship education tests and civics is intimately related to attempts to generate social solidarity in the context of globalized societies (Gifford 2004, 147). To do so, national states have mobilized a "landscape of national citizenship [that has] reproduced a mode of citizenship as a singular identity awarded and controlled within and by the state" (Desforges et al. 2005, 440–1). Despite the fact that Canada has emerged as a model in cross-national research not only of successful integration and immigration but also multiculturalism, the case of Canada reflects some striking similarities to themes evident in other Western states when it comes to more punitive citizenship education, testing, and laws, as well as when it comes to multicultural backlash (Lentin and Titley 2011) and citizenship revocation (Winter and Previsic 2019).

To illustrate our argument about how containing diversity has extended to citizenship and multiculturalism, we proceed in four parts. First, we situate Canada's historical approach to naturalization and multiculturalism in a comparative context. Second, we address symbolic changes in multiculturalism policy in the post-9/11 period. Third, we examine substantive policy changes in citizenship policy and testing in the same period. Finally, we consider the combined implications of Canada's shifting naturalization and multicultural polices.

Our analysis examines the ongoing relevance of social inequality and racism from 9/11 to COVID-19, as well as the challenges posed by xenophobic populism. Overall, we suggest that the complex interplay between race, gender, citizenship status, and other forms of difference calls for anti-racist responses to "containing diversity" attuned to intersectionality.

NATURALIZATION AND MULTICULTURALISM: CANADA IN COMPARISON

Canada stands out in relation to both naturalization and multiculturalism from an international comparative perspective. In this section, we situate Canada in a comparative perspective to show how key practices and alternatives may or may not be desirable from the vantage point of the inclusion of newcomers and minorities. Although there are ways in which naturalization and multiculturalism may overlap, for ease in the discussion, consideration of naturalization will be followed by multiculturalism.

Naturalization

Canada has one of the highest naturalization rates in the world (Alboim and Cohl 2012, 41). Reflecting on this, Will Kymlicka argued back in 2003 that the Canadian model of naturalization has proved relatively uncontroversial for at least four key reasons. First, the process of acquiring citizenship is not onerous (2003, 197). Second, acquiring Canadian citizenship is not perceived as assimilation or a negation of previous national identity and loyalty (2003, 197). Here he highlights the policy of multiculturalism and the public acceptance of dual citizenship. Third, the promotion of citizenship and public funding of language training encourage migrants to take up Canadian citizenship (2003, 197). Lastly, the distinction between citizens and status of non-citizens is not marked by exclusion or legal precariousness (Kymlicka 2003, 198).

While Kymlicka highlighted these reasons in 2003, as we have illustrated thus far, the path to permanent residency and citizenship has arguably been less generous in more recent years. This is evident in the growing rates of temporary migration that we have discussed previously. As we will detail further in this chapter, however, policy changes in Canadian citizenship over the 2010s further demonstrate this shift. To answer the question of what accounts for this shift towards a less generous path to permanent residency, it is helpful to think of migration and citizenship together and to consider Canada in comparative context.

In a useful 2007 article, legal scholar Catherine Dauvergne explores the relationship between migration law on the one hand and citizenship law on the other. She points out how together they have worked "in tandem to create the borders of the nation" (2007, 490). Historically, migration policy and law has done the "dirty work" of excluding people by policing the borders and surveilling for things like criminality, disease, or qualifications (Dauvergne 2007, 495). In contrast, citizenship policy and law focus more squarely on loyalty and national values; however, its exclusionary impulses tend to be less obvious because it typically also invokes inclusionary language (2007, 494–5). In settler colonies such as Australia, Canada, and the United States, designed as white settler societies of Britain, migration law has served as the main barrier to formal membership. As Dauvergne describes: "once newcomers are accepted as migrants, the hurdle for full membership in the form of citizenship is a low one" (2007, 493). In other words, applying for citizenship is quicker and easier with a greater chance of success than applying for permanent residency in the first place.

Nevertheless, she points out, citizenship's "bite" is felt in the exclusions of those applicants with criminal convictions and the scrutiny attached to the citizenship application itself (Dauvergne 2007, 495–6). That said, Dauvergne argues that any shifts within the dichotomy of citizenship law/migration law are related to states' attempts to safeguard sovereignty. The outcome she observes is that for some "privileged subjects of globalization" citizenship is more flexible. But "for those already disadvantaged and excluded, however, citizenship law is becoming increasingly exclusionary" (2007, 498).

The process of drawing lines in the population between citizens, residents, and those without legal status rests on a complex legal system embedded in national norms and histories that vary from state to state. In general, four elements combine to make up nationality law and are generally acknowledged as significant to accessing citizenship. In the scheme helpfully articulated by Weil (2001), these elements are:

- Birthplace, or *jus soli*: the fact of being born in a territory over which the state maintains, has maintained, or wishes to extend its sovereignty;
- Bloodline, or *jus sanguinis*: citizenship as a result of nationality of one parent or other more distant ancestors;
- Marital status, such as marriage to a citizen of another country, which can lead to the acquisition of the spouse's citizenship;
- Past, present, or future residence within the country's past, future, or intended borders (including colonial borders). (17)

Dauvergne identifies two developments that impact citizenship and migration law. First, birthright citizenship, as embodied by the *jus solis* principle, is being eroded. This erosion has been motivated, she argues, by the sentiment that children of "undesirable migrants" should not be given citizenship as a result of the accident of birth (2007, 497). She highlights cases in Australia and Ireland and argues these cases uphold the dichotomy: "citizenship law may be about formal equality but it is predicated on migration law functioning as an effective pre-screening of potential members" (2007, 498). Second, states have moved to make citizenship more *meaningful* in ways that directly challenge the dichotomy of citizenship law/migration law. Dauvergne highlights issues like calls for a "national language" in the United States, Australian proposals focusing on longer residency requirements and stricter language and knowledge tests, and Canada's proposals to limit citizenship by descent to the first generation of children born outside Canada to a Canadian parent (2007, 498). In Canada this proposal was passed into law in 2009 (IRCC 2020) and carries implications for Canadians working or stationed abroad, and especially Canadians born abroad if their children are also born abroad. In other cases, like India and Italy, states have also been engaged in a project of making citizenship more meaningful, but are directing their efforts at their diaspora populations (Dauvergne 2007, 498–502). In Dauvergne's estimation, all these changes share a similar aim, which is "making citizenship a more valuable prize," and additionally such changes are "cast in the lofty language of inclusion" (2007, 505).

Dauvergne's analysis rests on thinking about citizenship as a status. Yet, in drawing attention to the increasing emphasis on the value of citizenship and by extension to shifts in citizenship law, we wish to build on her analysis by considering the actual practices that are implicated in these shifts. Returning to the case of Canada is instructive to highlight such features as citizenship education and testing for newcomers that underwent important changes after 2006. As backdrop it could be noted that the Canadian Citizenship Act (1947) established a formal definition of a Canadian citizen and enshrined the terms of naturalization. Prior to this, both Canadian-born and naturalized citizens were British subjects (Martin 1993, 72). In 1977, the major changes to the Citizenship Act came into force. Under its terms, citizenship became more widely available (Dolin and Young 2002).

Between 2006 and 2012, the Conservative administration introduced a set of regulatory reforms that marked a major departure from the efforts of the late 1970s to make Canada's naturalization process more inclusionary. Specifically, there were changes to the citizenship guide, test, and ceremony, which were also connected with multiculturalism, as we discuss later. These changes were promoted as enhancing the value and meaning of Canadian citizenship. But other measures criminalized aspects of the naturalization process and rendered newcomers themselves suspect – what we have referred to earlier, following Dauvergne, as citizenship's bite. This included, for example, "greater scrutiny when verifying applicants' eligibility for citizenship, as well as ensuring adequate language proficiency of newcomers" (CIC 2013, 30). It is here that a discourse of abuse and fraud, as well as themes relating to terrorism, came to the fore. The latter, in the post-9/11 environment, involved a process in which Canadians who were, or who were perceived to be, Arab and/or Muslim were experiencing new forms of discrimination and surveillance (Abu-Laban 2013). Indeed, as Winter and Previsic (2019) show, the imagined targets for citizenship revocation were fixated on Muslims in political commentary in the House of Commons, in English- and French-language newspapers, and in online public comments of news articles. According to then Minister of Immigration Jason Kenney in a 2013 statement on preventing fraud: "Canada's doors are open to a vast majority of newcomers who are hardworking and follow the rules, but Canadians have no tolerance for anyone who tries to jump the immigration line to gain entry to Canada or acquire permanent residency or citizenship through fraudulent means" (Canadian Press 2013). This emphasis on fraud was central to treating immigrants as potential criminals and a threat to law and order, but it went further to also treat immigrants as potential terrorists, and a threat to security and the loyalty expected of good citizens. Specifically, beginning in 2013, the Harper Conservatives also sought to pass legislation revoking citizenship – that is, taking away citizenship – from Canadians convicted of terrorist charges. As Minister Kenney articulated it: "anyone who commits a terrorist act has clearly rejected *Canadian values* and the *loyalty* to our country that citizenship requires" (Kenney 2013a; emphasis added).

Months later, in February 2014, the federal government introduced sweeping changes to the Citizenship Act. In announcing Bill C-24, The *Strengthening Canadian Citizenship Act*, it was clear that it embraced the twin impulses of the value of citizenship and the need to protect it from fraud and disloyalty. Former Conservative Minister of Immigration Chris Alexander introduced the Act by stating: "These significant and long-needed reforms fulfill the Government's commitment in four specific ways: they reinforce the *value* of citizenship; they strengthen the integrity of the system and counter *fraudulent* attempts to gain citizenship; they improve the efficiency of the citizenship program by streamlining application processing and helping qualified applicants acquire citizenship faster; and not least importantly, they *honour* those who have served, and who currently serve, Canada" (Alexander 2014; emphasis added). In Alexander's words, on the occasion of the largest changes to Canadian citizenship since 1977, Canadian citizenship was also presented as an honour: "As we reform the immigration system, it's also critical to ensure that we protect and strengthen the great value of Canadian citizenship and *remind individuals that citizenship is not a right ... it's a privilege*" (Alexander 2014; emphasis added). This significant turn of phrase, presenting the membership associated with citizenship as a privilege served to underscore the idea that citizenship was conditional, rather than an irrevocable entitlement.

By the summer of 2015, the new citizenship legislation introduced by the Harper Conservative government went into effect reflecting on the idea that citizenship was a privilege. Among other things, this legislation allowed for the revocation of citizenship from dual nationals on grounds of security and introduced new financial and linguistic barriers to acquiring citizenship. As with the provisions associated with the bill, the Act was buttressed by language drawing on ideas relating to fraud and security, and implicated all immigrants, new citizens, and dual citizens alike. For example, federal officials could revoke citizenship if it was decided that a naturalized citizen did not intend to live in Canada, committed a crime or fraud, or acted against Canada's national interest, and such a decision could not be appealed in federal court (Abu-Laban 2016). The sweeping categories for revoking citizenship triggered concerns for many non-governmental organizations (NGOs). The Canadian Arab Institute, for instance, issued a policy brief raising concerns that the changes, in light of post-9/11 stereotypes around terrorism, would disproportionately and unfairly effect Canadians of Arab origin (Thompson 2014).

Some but not all of the Harper government's changes to the Citizenship Act were subsequently overturned by the Trudeau Liberals and the *status quo ante* restored in many areas. Following through on the election mantra of "a Canadian is a Canadian" in June 2017, the Trudeau government passed Bill C-6. Importantly, this bill repealed provisions enabling the revocation of citizenship from dual citizens convicted of spying, treason, and terrorism offences, and also allowed for the possibility that minors could apply for citizenship without a parent. In addition, the Liberals made citizenship relatively easier to acquire. This included a host of changes to language and citizenship test requirements, physical presence requirements, and income tax filing as follows:

- *official language knowledge and passing the citizenship test* will only be required of those between aged 18–54 [as opposed to aged 14–64 with the Harper provisions];
- *days spent in Canada before acquiring permanent residency* will partially count towards the physical presence requirement for citizenship [as opposed to not at all under the Harper provisions];
- *applicants have to be physically present for 3 out of 5 years with no minimum number of days* [as opposed to 4 out of 6 years, with a minimum of 183 days as with the Harper provisions, though prior to 2015 residency was not expressly defined as physical presence];
- an *income tax filing* will have to be done for 3 out of 5 years [as opposed to 4 out of 6 years as with the Harper provisions].

Overall, the Liberal government's legislation made it easier to get citizenship and harder to lose it compared to the Harper Conservatives. The legislative changes were presented by the Liberals as part and parcel of easing integration: "a Canadian is a Canadian." In introducing the changes, Ahmed Hussen, then Liberal minister for the federal department of Immigration, Refugees and Citizenship Canada (IRCC) framed citizenship as an invitation into a new family. In his words, "One of the strongest pillars for successful integration into Canadian life is achieving Canadian citizenship and becoming part of the Canadian family. The Government encourages all immigrants to take the path towards citizenship and take advantage of everything that being a Canadian has to offer" (IRCC 2017).

However, not all the Harper-era changes were rejected. Our analysis also shows how the Liberal government retained key restrictions on citizenship and naturalization introduced by the Harper Conservatives. For example, the Liberals retained provisions limiting citizenship by descent to one generation born abroad (Meurrens 2016, 3). Significantly, dual nationals can still potentially lose their Canadian citizenship if they are found guilty of fraud at the time of application (Government of Canada 2017). The power given to immigration bureaucrats for making that determination combined with the limited avenues for recourse have raised questions regarding the compatibility of this provision with the Canadian Charter of Rights and Freedoms (Meurrens 2016, 3). Notably, under the Trudeau Liberals, there has been a dramatic increase in the number of people whose citizenship has been revoked for reasons of fraud (Smith 2017). The theme of fraud thus has some traction among Liberals and Conservatives alike. As a result, naturalization has not only become more contested over the period between 2001 and 2021, but has overall moved in a more exclusionary direction, in keeping with many other states. This also suggests how containing diversity has impacted membership in the political community.

Multiculturalism

From an international comparative perspective, Canada stands out for three reasons when it comes to multiculturalism. First, the very term "multiculturalism" was coined in Canada. Its emergence stemmed from criticisms of non-British, non-French, and non-Aboriginal minorities – especially second generation Ukrainian-Canadians in the western provinces – to the idea of Canada consisting of two cultures. These criticisms were strongly articulated when in 1963 the federal Liberals launched the Royal Commission on Bilingualism and Biculturalism, a commission designed to deal with growing assertions by francophones in and outside Quebec for recognition and equality (Breton 1986). The demand by minorities for what came to be called "multiculturalism" was a challenge to Canada's longstanding goal of Anglo-conformity, whereby minorities were supposed to conform to the dominant British-origin group culturally and linguistically. It was also a plea for recognition and inclusion in public institutions, symbols, and discourse (Abu-Laban 2014a; Abu-Laban and Stasiulis 1992; Breton 1984, 44).

The second reason Canada stands out from an international comparative perspective is that it was the first Western country to pass an official policy of multiculturalism in 1971. The policy of multiculturalism, or more specifically multiculturalism within a framework of English and French bilingualism, emerged by way of Liberal Prime Minister Pierre Elliot Trudeau's response to the findings and recommendations of the Royal Commission on Bilingualism and Biculturalism. Speaking in the House of Commons to make the announcement, Prime Minister Trudeau asserted that "although there are two official languages, there is no official culture, nor does any ethnic group take precedence over any other" (Canada, House of Commons 1971). Of course this formulation could be read as a symbolic challenge to Anglo-conformity, as well as a symbolic challenge to constitutional and other claims of francophone Quebecers based on being a "founding people." In 1988 the Canadian Multiculturalism Act was passed which seeks to preserve and enhance multicultural diversity, reduce discrimination, promote the access and participation of all Canadians, and ensure cultural sensitivity in federal institutions (Brosseau and Dewing 2018). This Act served to give a firmer legal base for multiculturalism than the policy alone.

The third reason Canada stands out in relation to multiculturalism is that the relatively higher degree of integration experienced by immigrants – including political, social, and economic integration – has been attributed in part to the presence of multiculturalism policy in cross-national comparative research. For example, Bloemraad (2006) studied the experiences of immigrants from Portugal and refugees from Vietnam in Canada compared to the same immigration groups in the United States. She found that immigrant groups achieved greater degrees of incorporation in Canada on a range of indicators. In particular, they were more likely to become citizens, be involved in community organizing, and get elected to political office in Canada. Bloemraad attributed these differences to the Canadian government's support for settlement services as well as official multiculturalism.

More broadly, comparative studies looking at countries of both Europe and North America suggest Canada is among the best of world states when it comes to integrating immigrants. This assessment was made all the more notable by the fact that at the time of the study some 20 per cent of the Canadian population were immigrants, as compared to 6 per cent in the only two countries that scored ahead of Canada, specifically Sweden and Portugal (Friesen 2011). Perhaps reflecting the longstanding emphasis on multiculturalism, the Canadian government has explicitly defined integration through the metaphor of a "two-way street," suggesting that immigrants not only adapt and evolve, but so too does the receiving country. While in practice the emphasis may be more on immigrants doing the adaptation (Li 2002, 52), Canada's programs supporting newcomers have notably been voluntary, rather than coercive or punitive (Banting and Kymlicka 2013).

Until recently, Canada was among only a few countries to have developed an "official" policy of multiculturalism. Indeed, multiculturalism achieved constitutional recognition in the 1982 Canadian Charter of Rights and Freedoms. Section 27 holds that the Charter "will be interpreted in a manner consistent with the preservation and enhancement of the multicultural character of Canadians." Yet, interestingly, over the course of the 2000s, it is politicians in Europe and other Western countries who have been among the most vociferous in rejecting multiculturalism globally and who have generated much international media coverage. Hence, for example, in 2010, then Christian Democratic German Chancellor Angela Merkel proclaimed that multiculturalism had "failed, utterly failed" and that the onus was on immigrants to do more to integrate culturally and linguistically in Germany since people of different backgrounds could not live happily "side by side" (Weaver 2010). Likewise, in 2011, former British Conservative Prime Minister David Cameron declared "state multiculturalism" a failure. In a speech that garnered congratulations from the leader of the far-right now National Rally in France, Marine Le Pen, Cameron singled out British Muslims and blamed multiculturalism for "homegrown terrorism" (Batty 2011). In Cameron's words, "under the doctrine of state multiculturalism we have encouraged different cultures to live separate lives, apart from each other and the mainstream" (Cameron 2011).

More recently, in the words of one analyst, British Conservative Prime Minister Theresa May, in power from 2016 to 2019 gave "multiculturalism a very public burial, a shift that seems entirely in tune with the defensive impulses that lead a small majority of voters to opt for Brexit" (de Bellaigue 2018). In the United States, the xenophobic populist and anti-immigration rhetoric of US President Donald Trump has also been viewed as an attack on multiculturalism, and more broadly on progressive and democratic politics (Sandel 2018). In Australia, Pauline Hanson, founder of the One Nation political party, has repeatedly criticized multiculturalism and immigration. As a federal MP in 1996, she claimed: "we are in danger of being swamped by Asians," and in her maiden speech in the Australian Senate in 2016 that "now we are in danger of being swamped by Muslims" (Murphy 2016). Indeed, in 2016 she added: "If you are not prepared to become Australian and give this country this undivided loyalty, obey our laws and respect our country and our way of life, then I suggest you go back to where you came from" (quoted in Murphy 2016). It should be noted that the One Nation party won an all-time high of four seats in 2016 in the national Senate and has achieved greater success at the regional/state levels.

These varied criticisms raise the question of what is meant by "multiculturalism," a question that grows in relevance when moving beyond the Canadian context where multiculturalism is explicitly embraced as policy and constitutionally entrenched. In an effort to foster better comparative research, Banting and Kymlicka (2013) developed a "multiculturalism index." This index alerts researchers to a plethora of different kinds of policies that might be seen to support racialized or immigrant minorities, even in the absence of an explicit multiculturalism policy. These policies include:

(1) constitutional, legislative or parliamentary affirmation of multiculturalism, at the central and/or regional and municipal levels;
(2) the adoption of multiculturalism in school curriculum;
(3) the inclusion of ethnic representation/sensitivity in the mandate of public media or media licensing;
(4) exemptions from dress-codes, either by statute or by court cases;
(5) allowing of dual citizenship;
(6) the funding of ethnic group organizations to support cultural activities;
(7) the funding of bilingual education or mother-tongue instruction;
(8) affirmative action for disadvantaged immigrant groups. (Banting and Kymlicka 2013, 8)

Interestingly, using this set of eight policies led Banting and Kymlicka to find that in comparison with the year 2000, a number of European countries actually had developed *stronger* policies by the year 2010. This despite the more vocal criticisms that emerged over the course of the 2000s, and that clearly linked to the turn towards addressing themes of security and terrorism following September 11, 2001. These countries include Austria, Belgium, Finland, Germany, Greece, Ireland, Norway, Portugal, Spain, and Sweden. Only a handful of European countries – France, Switzerland, and the United Kingdom – had *stable* policies between 2000 and 2010. Despite all the criticisms, only a few European countries had *weaker* multiculturalism policies in 2010 as compared to 2000: Denmark, Italy, and the Netherlands (Banting and Kymlicka 2013, 23). Canada was also stable in relation to multicultural index policies between 2000 and 2010 (Banting and Kymlicka 2013, 25).

When it came to the degree to which multicultural index policies were *embraced*, however, Canada along with Australia led the way among OECD countries for the strongest support of all eight policies identified (Banting and Kymlicka 2013, 25). Banting and Kymlicka (2013) also noted that many countries have adopted policies that are not accounted for in the multiculturalism index in recent years. These include clearly anti-multicultural policies (e.g., following a referendum in 2009 Switzerland banned architectural features like minarets, used commonly in mosques); some countries have adopted measures which are coercive in relation to integration and social services (e.g., proving language competency before being able to access social assistance); and some refuse naturalization on grounds of a presumed excessive attachment to religion and/or country of origin (e.g., France and Germany) (Banting and Kymlicka 2013). There is, more to the point, a general retreat from using the word "multiculturalism," particularly in many European countries, even if there appears to be a pattern of stable if not growing support for certain policies which might been seen to support minorities and immigrants (Banting and Kymlicka 2013). It is precisely this retreat that raises questions about how forms of racialized inequality are to be countered, and indeed whether the retreat from multiculturalism itself reflects and functions to legitimate today's expressions of racism and racialized inequality (Lentin and Titley 2011).

In sum, it is true that there are a range of policies that may be seen to support immigrant and racialized minorities that states may adopt or have adopted. However, it is significant that European public discourse is exhibiting a pattern of retreat from using the very word "multiculturalism," at the same time that in some locales coercive policies of integration, or even anti-multiculturalism initiatives are being more readily entertained. What this suggests to us is the need to be attentive to complexity, nuance, and contradictions. In what follows, we offer such an analysis by turning to the case of contemporary Canada and looking at discourse and policy shifts, public opinion and debates, and new public symbolism. We show how, despite growing socio-economic inequalities between identifiable groups, contemporary multicultural discourse and policy suggests a more piercing focus on values that bear striking resemblance to discussions in Europe, even though neither the word "multiculturalism," nor the 1971 policy, are disappearing from the Canadian context.

THE WORD "MULTICULTURALISM," NEOLIBERALISM, AND ADVOCACY

Multiculturalism was first advanced in the 1970s, during the consolidation of the Canadian welfare state. In Canada this took the form of providing support for unemployment insurance, health care, and old age security. Welfare state consolidation also included support for disadvantaged groups to make claims on the state in the name of Canadian citizenship, including support for women, Indigenous peoples, and minorities (Abu-Laban and Gabriel 2002). The policy of multiculturalism and its entrenchment in the 1982 Charter were the outcome of efforts by minority collectives, such as non-British, non-French, non-Aboriginal groups (Abu-Laban and Stasiulis 1992). Likewise, in the 1980s, the policy's expansion to incorporate issues of anti-racism was a reflection of the demands of growing numbers of racialized minorities – or to use the increasingly out-of-vogue parlance of the Canadian state, "visible minorities" – who immigrated to Canada in larger numbers after 1967, once Canadian immigration policy become formally non-discriminatory regarding race/ethnicity.

The continued embrace of the term multiculturalism in the Canadian context stems in part from the institutional support it has received as a policy. But multiculturalism is also part of the enduring language of the 1982 Charter as well as a law contained in the 1988 *Canadian Multiculturalism Act*. Beyond law and policy, the term multiculturalism has become an expression of Canadian national identity. The term enjoys support among the Canadian public, including in Quebec where the federal policy itself has been conversely viewed with scepticism because it bypassed the longstanding demands for constitutional recognition based on being a "founding people" at Confederation (Abu-Laban 2014a). Despite this scepticism around the policy, a 2010 poll found that just the word "multiculturalism" generated very positive or positive responses from 73 per cent of respondents across Canada, including 71 per cent of those from Quebec (Association for Canadian Studies 2010).

More recently, in 2018, a poll conducted by the Canadian Race Relations Foundation and Environics found that without any prompting, 43 per cent of respondents defined Canada by multiculturalism; the next three largest responses were as follows: land/geography (17 per cent), freedom/free country/geography (14 per cent), and friendly/humble/nice people (11 per cent) (Ma 2018). Still, although multiculturalism might generate more "Canadiana" resonance than land or niceness, it is also important to note that surveys can vary depending on the timing, as well as the question asked. For example, on the exact same 2018 survey, a majority of respondents (51 per cent) agreed that "some immigrants are not adopting Canadian values" (Ma 2018).

This might suggest that attacking immigrants and new Canadians for their values and loyalty may resonate for some sections of the public.

The province of Quebec, the recipient of many immigrants particularly in Montreal, had by the 1990s adopted its own policy of "interculturalism," which emphasizes the primacy of the French language/culture within a context of cultural pluralism. While Quebec's lexicon for the policy is different, many analysts suggest that in practice there are not significant differences between "multiculturalism" and "interculturalism" (Juteau et al. 1998). However, some Quebec intellectuals, such as Gérard Bouchard, have advocated the usage of interculturalism to deal with the complex situation of francophones as a majority in Quebec but a minority in Canada/North America (Canadian Press 2011). In Bouchard's words, "any model that seeks to manage Quebec's ethno-cultural diversity effectively must take into account the existence of an ethno-cultural majority and the uncertainty that is associated with its future" (Canadian Press 2011; see also Blad and Couton 2009, and Bouchard 2011). The growing criticisms of multiculturalism in European countries have also provided some advocates of interculturalism with a new take on it being an international alternative to multiculturalism (Canadian Press 2011; Meer et al. 2016, 2915; see also Lentin and Titley 2011, 209–10 on rebranding multiculturalism as interculturalism in Ireland).

Still, even in the second decade of the 2000s, public opinion polls suggested the majority of Canadians viewed multiculturalism policy itself with favour. For example, a 2012 poll conducted by the Association for Canadian Studies found 58 per cent of Canadians had a very positive or somewhat positive attitude towards multiculturalism policy, in contrast with 35 per cent who had a somewhat negative or negative attitude towards the policy. Support for multiculturalism was also strongest with younger Canadians: 74 per cent of Canadians aged eighteen to twenty-four held positive views of the policy (Association for Canadian Studies 2012). Given this show of support among younger adults, it would be premature to talk about the "death" of multiculturalism in Canada, as has been the case in much media commentary in Europe in the 2000s (Lentin and Titley 2011; Torres 2013).

Of course, the continued resilience of the term in Canada does not mean that the policy has not experienced forms of backlash, or what Phil Ryan (2010) has called in the Canadian context "multicultiphobia."

One very evident period in which the policy came to be more openly attacked was in the late 1980s and early 1990s in the context of constitutional debates. This came on the heels of two major failed attempts to secure Quebec's signature on the 1982 changes, which the province still has not formally agreed to even though the Charter applies in Quebec (Abu-Laban and Stasiulis 1992). In this period, the western-Canadian based Reform Party criticized the policy and advocated the abolition of both a separate Department of Multiculturalism in the federal bureaucracy as well as the concept of multiculturalism itself. Party leaders also advocated for greater state responsibility for promoting and preserving a national culture (Abu-Laban 2014a).

The Reform Party (1987–2000) eventually became the Canadian Alliance Party (2000–3), and then subsequently the Canadian Alliance merged with the Progressive Conservative Party to become the Conservative Party headed by former prime minister Stephen Harper. Harper was first elected as a Reform member of Parliament, but the policy of multiculturalism was undergoing changes well before he became Conservative prime minister in 2006, in part related to the critiques of the Reform Party.

Between 1993 and 2003, a series of changes disbanded the separate Department of Multiculturalism. Beginning initially with the short-lived Progressive Conservative government headed by Prime Minister Kim Campbell in 1993, and continuing with the Liberal governments of Prime Ministers Jean Chrétien and Paul Martin, the area of multiculturalism was moved from its own separate department into the Department of Canadian Heritage. In this period, there was a stress on multiculturalism fostering attachment to Canada among all people.

Perhaps one of the most evident changes through the late 1990s and 2000s was when the Liberal government of Prime Minister Jean Chrétien, in power from November 1993 to 2003, embraced the tenets of neoliberalism. Neoliberalism, which places stress on limiting social spending, individual self-sufficiency, and the fairness of the market, introduced dramatic changes to both the rationale of multiculturalism and the operation of the state in relation to minorities. As we have argued elsewhere (Abu-Laban and Gabriel 2002), the rationale for multiculturalism shifted from its initial focus on equity to instead supporting Canada's global competitiveness and trade links internationally. Correspondingly, cuts to funding, along with the removal of core funding, provided a markedly different atmosphere for community groups to organize, to advocate, and to engage the policy process nationally. As a result, this compromised a strong civil society voice for an anti-racist equity agenda (Abu-Laban 2014a).

By the time Stephen Harper came to power, first with minority governments in 2006 and 2008, and then as a majority government between 2011 and 2015, there was no direct attack on multiculturalism made by the Conservatives. Nor was there any attempt to seek the elimination of multiculturalism as either a policy or a discourse. However, this period was characterized by clear efforts to reposition the area of multiculturalism by moving it from the Department of Canadian Heritage into the Department of Citizenship and Immigration Canada. We read this move as symbolically linking multiculturalism with incoming immigrants, and also marginalizing multiculturalism from the relative status and resources accorded to official languages, still housed in the Department of Canadian Heritage.

As we discus below, under the Harper Conservatives, there were also clear efforts to give a more explicit and traditional content to Canadian identity and history. This was combined with shifting forms of political engagement (and non-engagement) with civil society groups on the issue of racism, alongside the changes to Canadian citizenship legislation discussed earlier. We situate these efforts to reshape Canadian identity and political engagement in the post-9/11 context, which was characterized by heightened forms of state surveillance and discourses of national security impacting Arabs and/or Muslims, and/or those who were perceived to be Arab or Muslim. The period also saw new public debates about the place of religion, and religious minorities, in Canada.

For example, the 2005 debate in the province of Ontario over Shari'a law in the context of arbitration in family law generated intense Canadian and international coverage. Likewise, new public debates about the place of religious minorities sparked "reasonable accommodation" debates in Quebec in 2007. Reasonable accommodation focused on religious minorities, primarily Muslims. A provincial commission in Quebec on reasonable accommodation, for example, emphasized secularism as a Quebec value. In October 2017 the Quebec Liberal government of Premier Philippe Couillard attempted to advance "religious neutrality" legislation that implicitly targeted the tiny minority of Muslim women who wear the *niqab* (a head and face cover) by requiring its removal in civil servants' giving of public service, or in the receiving of public services as a citizen. This legislation, known as Bill 62, was suspended by the ruling of a Quebec superior court judge pending the Quebec government producing clearer guidelines (Abu-Laban 2013; 2017). The issue came alive again after the 2018 election of a majority win for the Coalition Avenir Québec led by Premier François Legault. In June 2019 the Legault government passed Bill 21, aimed at eradicating religious symbols in the public sector, including banning the wearing of religious symbols by public professionals like teachers, police officers, and judges (Abu-Laban and Nath 2021, 520). Given the propensity to target racialized religious minorities, it is not surprising that this legislation faces legal challenge by the National Council of Canadian Muslims and the Canadian Civil Liberties Association.

Turgeon et al. (2019) use survey data to suggest that policy preferences in Quebec when it comes to minority religious symbols reflect on a distinct understanding of liberalism in relation to the role of the state in promoting freedom, that differs from how liberalism is understood in the rest of Canada. In other words, those with liberal attitudes in Quebec tend to support restrictions, whereas those with liberal attitudes outside of Quebec tend not to (Turgeon et al. 2019). These insights are important for understanding both the complexity of liberalism as well as the distinct contexts in and outside Quebec.

At the same time, anti-Muslim racism, sometimes called Islamophobia, has also been identified in the hostility towards Arabs and Muslims evident in national public policy and public discourse since 9/11 (Abu-Laban 2013; Razack 2008). Today, anti-Muslim racism is frequently advanced through stereotypes about Muslims and Arabs that posit them as irrational, barbaric/violent, and collectively presenting a cultural threat to Western security, democratic citizenship, and gender equality. These culturally based tropes also found expression in the 2015 federal election. Some noteworthy examples included the Conservative government's emphasis on security and lukewarm response to accepting the growing number of Syrian refugees (discussed in chapter two); the Conservatives' reticence to accept the successful legal challenge launched by a permanent resident wearing a niqab to be able to take the oath of citizenship with her face covered;

and the former Conservative minister of immigration, Chris Alexander, floating the prospect of creating a "barbaric cultural practices hotline." The proposed telephone tip line would have allowed concerned Canadians to report on co-citizens whom they suspected of engaging in cultural practices deemed harmful to women. The terminology of barbaric cultural practices echoed the 2015 *Zero Tolerance for Barbaric Cultural Practices Act,* which sought to bar immigrants and refugees who practised polygamy, to reiterate that the minimum age for marital consent is sixteen years, and to criminalize forcing a child under age sixteen to marry. In light of this litany of stereotypes frequently associated with racialized immigrants, and particularly Muslims, Trudeau's subsequent election victory speech was quite pointed when he prefaced his "a Canadian is a Canadian" statement by recounting the campaign stop where he met a young mother wearing a *hijab* who wanted her infant Canadian daughter to also have that option in future (Trudeau 2015).

In what follows, the debates surrounding the content of Canadian identity and history are considered from the vantage point of the citizenship guide and test. Our focus underscores how the new politics of membership and belonging involve both naturalization and multiculturalism. We consider shifts in Canadian citizenship legislation itself along with the government's responses to anti-racism advocacy. Our analysis illuminates key differences and similarities between the Harper Conservatives and Trudeau Liberals.

THE NEW POLITICS OF MEMBERSHIP AND BELONGING: THE CITIZENSHIP GUIDE

The question of citizenship acquisition and citizenship tests need to be placed within broader debates concerning migration. In particular, there has been an evident international policy convergence in Western liberal democracies around strengthening citizenship tests as part of a more generalized effort to control and manage the immigration, refugee, and citizenship systems (Paquet 2012, 243–9). It is in this context that we situate our discussion of the 2009 changes to the Canadian citizenship test and guide. The revamped test upped the requirements for official language knowledge as well as the number of correct answers required to pass. As well, a newly designed citizenship guide was introduced to help would-be citizens study for the test.

Aimed at helping new immigrants selected for permanent residence prepare for the citizenship test, the Harper Conservative's citizenship guide, entitled *Discover Canada: The Rights and Responsibilities of Citizenship*, makes heavy use of a particular rendition of military history. As a consequence, Ian McKay and Jaime Swift (2012) have suggested Canada was being rebranded as a "Warrior Nation." As McKay and Swift noted about the visual impact of the Citizenship Guide, "Warriors are *the* significant Canadians – no one else is in the running. For example, in thirty images on 'Canada's History' twenty depict plainly military events or figures," in contrast to none that appeared in the Liberal guide of 2005 (McKay and Swift 2012, 55). Moreover, war is sanitized and made to look like a romantic adventure, since "No blood, refugees or bombed out cities are in sight ... Even better we have acquired a whole new cast of Canadian heroes, fighting for the Empire long before Canada took shape in 1867" (McKay and Swift 2012, 15).

The 2009 citizenship guide produced a singular history aimed not only at would-be citizens but at all Canadians (Abu-Laban 2014a). Importantly, the guide was connected to the Conservative government's operation of multiculturalism since it was singled out for special highlight in conjunction with the annual requirement to report on the Multiculturalism Act. To quote former Minister of Citizenship, Immigration and Multiculturalism Jason Kenney, "I believe that *Discover Canada*, by placing increased emphasis on Canada's values, history and symbols, will promote civic memory and pride among newcomers and citizens alike (Kenney 2011, 5). In effect, however, the guide sidelined social history – that is, the histories of diverse collectives like Indigenous peoples, Francophones, women, workers, and minorities (Abu-Laban 2014b). This was significant because a key component of the initial impetus for multiculturalism came from the desire of minorities to see themselves reflected in public institutions, symbols, and history. Indeed, the very title of Book IV of the 1970 Royal Commission on Bilingualism and Biculturalism was *The Cultural Contribution of Other Ethnic Groups* (Government of Canada).

The Conservative government's emphasis on military history in *Discover Canada* was also evident in other areas of policy and spending.

In 2012 the government committed $28 million to commemorating the War of 1812; likewise, the new Canadian twenty-dollar bill released in 2012 featured an image commemorating the First World War battle of Vimy Ridge (Abu-Laban 2014b). The explicit linking of multiculturalism, citizenship, and the military was also seen in a 2012 operational bulletin announcing that a member of the Canadian Forces, preferably an Afghanistan veteran, should play a prominent role in all citizenship ceremonies (Friesen 2012). Given Canada's complex history as a settler colony, this emphasis on a singular, militarized history was alienating to different groups, including many francophones in and outside Quebec, Indigenous peoples, and other minorities (see Ladner and McCrossan 2014; Noël 2014). Indeed, a group of leading Canadian historians sought to have Canadians discuss "Why do symbols of militarism and royalty – Mounties, soldiers and Queen's – appear in many recent representations of the Canadian nation?" precisely because the citizenship guide so heavily stressed Canada's historic ties with the British Empire and the role of the monarchy (Jones and Perry 2012, 73–4).

The new guide also picked up on post-9/11 debates and negative stereotypes concerning Muslims in an implicitly Islamophobic statement about "barbaric cultural practices." As feminist scholars have noted, since September 11, gender equality has been appropriated into a clash of civilizations discourse which constructs Muslim men as barbaric and dangerous and Muslim women and girls as oppressed and in need of rescue by Western law (Razack 2008). Exemplifying this trend, the 2009 *Discover Canada* guide contains the following statement: "In Canada, men and women are equal under the law. Canada's openness and generosity do not extend to barbaric cultural practices that tolerate spousal abuse, 'honour killings', female genital mutilation and gender-based violence. Those guilty of these crimes are severely punished under Canada's criminal laws" (Government of Canada 2012, 10). This statement draws on stereotypes that have been problematically associated with Islam, like spousal abuse, honour killings, and female genital mutilation, and presents them as the distinct problem of a "barbaric other" in contrast to us, the us being "civilized Canadians." Overall, the guide begins to articulate a new politics of membership and belonging, where issues of Canada's commitment to democracy and gender equality are trumpeted as absolute.

What is notable is that the "barbaric cultural practices" statement is really not *qualitatively* all that different from what the tiny town of Herouxville, Quebec, did in 2007 when it made national and international headlines for issuing its controversial code of conduct. This code also drew on stereotypes designed to purportedly instruct newcomers that in Canada women do not cover their faces (except at Halloween), that boys and girls can swim together, and that women could not legally be stoned to death (Abu-Laban 2013). However, in the case of the Conservative Government's *Discover Canada* guide, it was a national government of a country where one-fifth of the population are immigrants, as opposed to a tiny hamlet where there were next to no incoming immigrants.

This new politics of membership and belonging was also on display in December 2011, when then Minister Jason Kenney announced that anyone covering their face cannot get Canadian citizenship unless they remove it at the citizenship ceremony. This ruling was implicitly aimed at the minority of Muslim women who wear the niqab. In his statement, Kenney specifically drew on a discourse of gender equality to justify the ruling. The rather sudden decision to ban the extension of citizenship to women wearing the niqab paralleled repeated attempts by the Quebec government to ban government services or government employment to women wearing the niqab. In fact, in recent years Quebec has been the most proactive of provincial governments in challenging religious symbols (Stasiulis 2013). As noted earlier, the most recent example of this was Bill 21, passed in Quebec in 2019 and which banned religious symbols in the public sector. The paralleling of national and local restrictions concerning implicit or direct references to Muslims is in line with recent developments in many European and other Western countries. As scholars have argued, "the crisis of multiculturalism and apparent Muslim excess have become, to a large extent, reciprocally determining" even if the policies, context, and immigration patterns are nationally distinctive (Lentin and Titley 2011, 30).

The implications of *Discover Canada* extend beyond symbols of national belonging, to touch on access to citizenship itself. The accompanying citizenship test that went with the 2009 guide made it more difficult to acquire Canadian citizenship, particularly for some immigrant groups. In other words, changes to the citizenship test were not neutral. Indeed, former Conservative Minister Kenney contended that the test was sufficiently basic, and more to the point and reflecting on the new politics of membership and belonging he stressed, "we had devalued Canadian citizenship with the former guide and test ... [because] there was virtually nothing on Canadian history; there wasn't a single line on military history" (quoted in Mills 2012). Specifically, after 2009 the number of correct answers needed to pass went up, and there was a greater onus placed on being able to speak English or French.

Both the guide and the test questions have proven to be particularly challenging for groups coming from non-English-speaking countries, including the test's use of technical language. As a consequence, more people began to fail the new test once introduced (Mills 2012). For example, nearly half of all immigrants from Afghanistan failed the test in 2011, compared to only 21 per cent in 2009, before the changes. Similarly, over 41 per cent of immigrants from Vietnam failed the test in 2011 compared to less than 15 per cent before the changes (Mills 2012). By way of contrast, 98 per cent of immigrants from the United States, Australia, and the United Kingdom passed the test in 2011 (Mills 2012).

In June 2013 the Conservative government announced that those who had failed the written test would be able to take it again (Cohen 2013). Prior to this, those who had failed the written test could only appeal to a citizenship judge. Because of the increasing number of failures, as well as the fact that it was taking some applicants as long as twenty-nine months to actually see a judge, the new ruling was applied retroactively to those waiting to see a judge and was expected to make a difference (Cohen 2013). If an applicant failed the written test a second time, they could also appeal to a judge.

Although these changes were welcomed by immigrant advocacy groups and lawyers, it should be noted that the content of the test remained the same. Despite Kenney's claims that the test was sufficiently basic, in point of fact the changes introduced resulted in a dramatic decline in naturalization rates, especially for recent immigrants. A 2019 study published by Statistics Canada found that the citizenship rate for recent immigrants in Canada from five to nine years has steadily fallen from its high point of 75.4 per cent in 1996 to its low point of 60.4 per cent in 2016 (Hou and Picot 2019, 2). Among recent immigrants, those who saw deep declines included immigrants who did not speak French or English as a mother tongue, had low income, and had high school or less education levels, as did those coming from countries in Central America, the Caribbean, Eastern Europe, Africa, Southeast Asia, East Asia, and West Asia (Hou and Pigot 2019, 3).

Importantly, Canadian citizens themselves also do not do well on the test. A 2019 survey of over 1,600 Canadian citizens replicated ten typical questions found on the citizenship test. Only 12 per cent of respondents got eight or more answers correct, the standard considered a pass; the average score was five out of ten (CTV News 2019). Even among respondents with a postgraduate degree, only 21 per cent scored high enough to pass. Given these kind of results among extant Canadian citizens, including those with higher education, we would ask why the knowledge demanded for the test is relevant for being a citizen?

When the Trudeau Liberals came to power in 2015, they soon announced plans to revamp the 2009 citizenship guide. As of June 2022 this plan, nearly eight years later, was still in the works. Notably, the Liberals were also elected in the wake of the 2015 Calls to Action of the Truth and Reconciliation Commission of Canada (TRC). The TRC report posits reconciliation as an ongoing process to establish and maintain "respectful relationships" between Aboriginal and non-Aboriginal Canadians. Moreover, "A critical part of this process involves repairing damaged trust by making apologies, providing individual and collective reparations, and following through with concrete actions that demonstrate real societal change" (TRC 2015, 17–18). The Liberal government has a stated commitment to the process of reconciliation, and the TRC calls are wide ranging and touch on a number of levels of government and different societal institutions. This includes around issues relating to citizenship. For example, Call 93 seeks revisions to the citizenship guide to include overviewing treaties and the history of residential schools. Call 94 likewise seeks to replace the oath of citizenship to incorporate recognition of treaties. These are worded as follows:

93. We call upon the federal government, in collaboration with the national Aboriginal organizations, to revise the information kit for newcomers to Canada and its citizenship test to reflect a more

inclusive history of the diverse Aboriginal peoples of Canada, including information about the Treaties and the history of residential schools.

94. We call upon the Government of Canada to replace the Oath of Citizenship with the following:

> I swear (or affirm) that I will be faithful and bear true allegiance to Her Majesty Queen Elizabeth II, Queen of Canada, Her Heirs and Successors, and that I will faithfully observe the laws of Canada including Treaties with Indigenous Peoples, and fulfill my duties as a Canadian citizen. (TRC 2015, 10–11)

Because of civil society input from First Nations, Inuit, and Métis organizations, among others, a new guide promises to scrap reference to barbaric cultural acts, utilize a more complex and multifaceted narrative reflecting social history as opposed to military history, and pay greater attention to Canada's diversity (Levitz 2017).

That the promised guide did not materialize by the 2021 election is striking. Still, the very possibility that reference to barbaric cultural practices might be removed from a new citizenship guide led Calgary Conservative MP Michelle Rempel to sponsor a petition demanding that explicit condemnation of female genital mutilation (FGM) be in the guide (Maloney 2017). That the largest number of signatories were from Alberta might suggest this is an issue that plays well where the Harper Conservatives had a regional base, but in any case, it is not clear how the Liberals will respond. Hence, while there are discussions of rescinding Harper-era legislation referencing barbaric cultural practices, there has also been equivocation by the Liberals when it comes to calling FGM barbaric, as well as speculation over what will be in the guide (Maloney 2017). It also remains to be seen whether a guide that is responsive to the complexities of Canada's history and diversity – including potentially in relation to Indigenous peoples and residential schools – can also be done simply and in a way that boosts success rates for the citizenship test.

As it stands, the citizenship test has become a paradigmatic feature of containing diversity and therefore raises issues about racialized exclusion, as it has elsewhere. This situation should compel us to question to what extent can a citizenship test measure or imbue loyalty or citizenship (Greenwood and Robins 2002, 520)? Not surprisingly, the premises behind recent reforms are widely debated. For example, Shelly Wilcox challenges the prevailing orthodoxy that accompanies existing naturalization provisions on a number of grounds. She argues that a formal process "no matter how substantive and symbolic" cannot produce deep social solidarity (2004, 573). Wilcox also queries whether history and civic examinations are effective measures for the competencies required of citizenship. And even if they were, for us, her last point is the most compelling: "conditioning naturalized citizenship upon citizenship competencies would demand more of naturalized citizens than of birthright citizens" (2004, 580).

(DIS)ENGAGING CIVIL SOCIETY AND THE POLITICS OF ANTI-RACISM

Canada in the twenty-first century is not free of racialized forms of inequality, just as it was not historically in its development as a settler colony nor in the contemporary interface between the state and Indigenous peoples. Three major contemporary trends speak to the way in which racial inequality manifests itself in relation to immigrants and minorities.

First, the political climate in the years following September 11, 2001, has led to renewed policy justifications for security, surveillance, and even torture. These justifications have been especially felt by those Canadians who are (or who are perceived as) Muslim and/or Arab. The political climate has dramatically exposed the fault lines of Canadian multiculturalism (Abu-Laban 2013). It has also made Arab and/ or Muslim men and women "visible" in particular ways: women, for example, become hyper visible in debates about the hijab or niqab (Dobrowolsky 2008).

Second, there is evidence of a more generalized and growing trend of racialized and gendered forms of inequality among immigrants and Canadian-born racialized minorities (Galalbuzi 2012; Sharma 2012). For example, incoming immigrants have not had the same success in the labour market since the 1990s as they once had in the 1970s and 1980s, including those selected for their high skills (Hiebert 2006). Many immigrant women have been relegated to care work that is both demanding and poorly paid, such as nannies. These workers face a less generous welfare state in the current era which, outside of responses to support workers and students during the COVID-19 pandemic, has been characterized by neoliberal restraint; at the same time, their lived socio-economic reality is not as visible to the public or evident in public debates (Dobrowolsky 2008). Not least, studies continue to show that Canadian-born racialized minorities face racism and socio-economic disadvantages, including in employment (Block and Galabuzi 2011). The COVID-19 pandemic has further exacerbated racism, particularly for Chinese and Asian Canadians, as well as amplifying racialized and gendered inequities in earnings and job loss as well as health and death rates from COVID-19 (Abu-Laban 2021).

This deepening racialization of inequality has been further aggravated by a third major trend, which we identified in chapter five. The increasing use of temporary migrant workers who are denied Canadian citizenship has grown steadily since the mid-1980s. But it was in 2006 that the number of all temporary residents admitted annually to Canada, including workers, students, and others, exceeded the number of those selected for permanent residence (Rajkumar et al. 2012, 484). The array of programs to facilitate temporary entry has led to a plethora of rules and practices governing issues relating to employment, employment for spouses, as well as social services like settlement services. This plethora of rules and practices has together deepened inequalities among non-citizens, as well as between non-citizens and citizens (Rajkumar et al. 2012).

In light of these trends, it is perhaps especially salient that issues relating to racism and anti-racism increasingly disappeared from the federal multiculturalism agenda under the Harper Conservatives. As noted previously, in the 1980s racialized ("visible") minorities pushed to have issues of racism taken up under the rubric of multiculturalism, and their success in doing so was symbolized in the creation of a "race relations" unit in the federal multiculturalism directorate, as well as providing impetus for the passage of employment equity legislation in the mid-1980s (Stasiulis 1988, 90–2). In the 1990s, anti-racism in Canada continued to be a theme under the federal Liberals of Jean Chrétien and Paul Martin, although as noted, the neoliberal turn made it more difficult for groups to organize, to receive state funding, and to band together in the name of equity and fighting racism (Abu-Laban

2013; Kobayashi 2008). Under the Harper Conservatives, anti-racism was far less on display in relation to funded projects or ongoing discourse. In fact, under Minister Jason Kenney, political discourse was more focused on what was termed "bridge building." For example, funded projects aimed at providing mentorship and employment training for second-generation youth, as exemplified by a program linking Somali-Canadian youth with Jewish-owned businesses and professions. Notably, while Kenney held up the Somali-Jewish Canadian Mentorship Project as a model for other "cross-cultural projects" (2010, iii), in fact, at the best it was about fostering conditions for individual success, rather than acknowledging or attempting to eliminate structural barriers that might produce inequalities (Abu-Laban 2014a).

Minister Kenney's statement in relation to the United Nations–sponsored International Day for the Elimination of Racial Discrimination likewise showed the Conservative government's efforts to bypass discussions relating to racism in Canada. In his 2013 statement, Kenney deflects attention from racism in Canada by treating it as a problem that exists in other countries, referencing Canada's "successful pluralism" as evidence of this:

> The International Day for the Elimination of Racial Discrimination is an opportunity for Canadians to join with other freedom-loving people around the world in reaffirming our commitment to reject and eliminate all forms of racial discrimination.
>
> While we can be proud of our own country's successful pluralism, we need to ensure that all Canadian citizens reject extremism, do not import ancient enmities, and continue to embrace Canada's tradition of ordered liberty, which guarantees the equality of all citizens under the law.
>
> Through initiatives such as the Office of Religious Freedom, our Government will also continue to condemn acts of racial hatred around the world. These acts often accompany the targeting of religious communities.
>
> As Minister of Citizenship, Immigration and Multiculturalism, I encourage all Canadians to continue to uphold the fundamental values of our free, democratic and peacefully pluralist society and to reject all forms of unjust discrimination. (2013b)

By positioning Canada as a country of successful pluralism, Kenney justified immigration restrictions, or what he described as the need to not "import ancient enmities" since they would only be in Canada from abroad. He then used this justification to bolster support for the Office of Religious Freedom designed to deal with racism abroad, in the process reflecting on a slippage between religion and race.

Unlike any other previous federal government since multiculturalism was introduced in 1971, the Harper Conservatives did show a high degree of willingness to redress very select points of *historic* discrimination experienced in Canada by select groups. By way of contrast to actions taken by the Harper government that we discuss below, the 1988 redress for the internment of Japanese Canadians during the Second World War was a hard-fought battle for recognition by minority Canadians (Kobayashi 2008). Moreover, when Progressive Conservative Prime Minister Brian Mulroney eventually apologized, extended a modicum of individual compensation, and funded what would become the Canadian Race Relations Foundation, this was done on the grounds that it would be the last redress request the federal government would consider (Mackenzie 2010, 48). Through the 1990s, and reiterating Prime Minister Pierre Elliott Trudeau's classic refusal, successive Liberal governments also rejected the requests of groups seeking redress and compensation for past injustices (Mackenzie 2010, 48). This included refusing to entertain claims regarding the head tax used on Chinese Canadians, a policy measure which worked to discourage the settlement of female spouses and children of this collectivity historically. In marked distinction, during the 2006 election campaign Stephen Harper pledged that his government would deal with redress for the head tax previously rejected by the Liberals (Edwards and Calhoun 2011, 78).

Moreover, on June 22, 2006, Harper made good on this promise and gave a formal apology to all Chinese Canadians, as well as compensation of $20,000 per individual to those who paid the head tax or to their surviving spouse. This apology was called an "exemplar of collective apology" (Edwards and Calhoun 2011, 86). This assessment is relevant since issues of redress have become more prominent on the international agenda in the twenty-first century, but not all apologies are equally meaningful (James 2008).

Indicating the significance of redress politics in relation to multiculturalism, on the same day as the apology for the head tax was given, it was also announced that Canada would give $24 million to a "Community Historical Recognition Programme" (Heritage Canada 2008). This program sought to "help commemorate and educate Canadians about the historical experiences and contributions of communities affected by wartime measures and immigration restrictions" (CIC 2011, 17), further indicating the prominence of issues of historic redress under the Harper government. Projects funded through this initiative included a memorial wall, a time capsule, and a booklet on Italian-Canadian internment during the Second World War; and, as noted in chapter two, the monument at Halifax's Pier 21 of the ship M.S. *St. Louis* and the Jewish refugees fleeing Nazi persecution in 1930 who were denied entry to Canada and turned back to their deaths (CIC 2011, 17).

The funding of such commemorative and educational activities about important historical events that have shaped the experience of groups, and Canada's history, is arguably positive. Even so, this should not preclude critical attention to the limitations and implications of that particular program. The program restricted consideration to wartime measures and immigration restrictions, when in fact collective injustices may happen outside of a war or immigration context. The main groups to have participated in this program were from the Canadian Chinese, Ukrainian, Italian, Jewish, and South Asian communities (James 2013). James has argued that the overall approach could be critiqued as one of "neoliberal heritage redress" (2013). In essence, neoliberal heritage redress mirrors neoliberal multiculturalism by placing limitations on both the possibility and use of state funding, allowing the government to pick select groups that will be rewarded, as well as working to make contemporary claims for social justice, equity, and anti-racism disappear (James 2013). Therefore, in the context of growing forms of racialized inequality experienced by both incoming immigrants and minorities in Canada, under the Harper Conservatives multicultural discourse and funding increasingly retreated from a focus on racism and anti-racism. Perhaps paradoxically, the linkage between multiculturalism policy and claims for historic redress by specific groups was effective in sidelining contemporary forms of racism and anti-racist initiatives.

In a marked contrast to the Harper Conservatives, the Trudeau Liberals appointed one of the most diverse cabinets in terms of gender, ethnicity, and religion that the country had ever seen in its first mandate (2015–19). Moreover, the Liberal government's accompanying mantra "diversity is our strength" has been backed by important policy shifts when it comes to immigration, multiculturalism, and anti-racism. In particular, the Trudeau government immediately withdrew any appeal to what informally became known as the "niqab ban" from citizenship ceremonies. As noted in chapter three, the government also admitted 25,000 Syrian refugees in its early days in office in 2015–16. The Liberals also moved multiculturalism back to the Department of Canadian Heritage and refocused multiculturalism policy on combating racism (Abu-Laban 2017b). In fact, Prime Minister Trudeau's February 2018 budget announcement included an infusion of an additional $23 million over two years for multiculturalism and the formation of a new national anti-racism plan, further solidifying this shift in anti-racism policy (Levitz 2018). In 2019 a new federal secretariat of anti-racism was established that takes a "whole-of-government" approach across federal agencies to address the impacts of policies, services, and programs (Canadian Heritage 2021, 13).

Still, at the start of 2017, a tragic shooting occurred in a mosque in Ste. Foy, Quebec. Six worshippers were killed and nineteen were injured. The killer who, among other things, was described as "pro-Trump and pro-Le Pen" (Perkel 2017), symbolized the antipathy towards those who are different – especially Muslims, immigrants, and refugees – widely in evidence globally (Mahrouse 2018). Indeed, as noted, mere months after this incident, the Liberal government of Quebec Premier Philippe Couillard implicitly targeted Muslim women who wear the niqab by passing legislation requiring its removal in giving or receiving public services. The courts subsequently prevented the legislation's enactment. However, in 2019, Bill 21 did pass into law by the Legault government. And Muslim Canadians have continued to be targets for violence, as seen tragically in London, Ontario, in 2021 when a family of four were seemingly deliberately killed by a man driving a truck.

At the same time that there has been a denial of racism (Mahrouse 2018), the expressions of racism in Canada in recent years have also witnessed new technologies of communication that can be used to sow seeds of hatred, along with a global rise in xenophobic populism and a powerful anti-immigration discourse mobilized in recent elections from Brexit to Trump. In Canada, the anti-immigration and anti-multiculturalism rhetoric of the People's Party of Canada, formed in 2018, made its way into the 2019 federal election. The failure of the People's Party of Canada to garner any seats in the 2019 election – not to mention that its leader, Maxime Bernier, a seasoned politician, lost his own seat – did not prevent its re-emergence in the 2021 election.

But Canadians are not immune to racism. Indeed, racist taunts, and in some cases brutal acts of violence directed at minorities, especially Asian Canadians, occurred in all regions of Canada in the lead-up to and wake of the COVID-19 pandemic (Brend 2020; Lau 2020; Rowe 2020; Taschner 2020; Ziafati 2020). Moreover, pandemic policy responses in relation to health, health inequities, and the social and economic fallout from isolation intersect in complex ways with gender, race, class, and citizenship status (Timothy 2020). This was further reinforced by Canadians' responses in support of Black Lives Matter following the murder of an unarmed African American man, George Floyd, by Minneapolis police in May 2020. There are some signs that both in policy circles and in civil society there is growing awareness of racism and a quest for change (Abu-Laban 2021). Given all that the COVID-19 pandemic and its aftermath have ushered in, the time is especially ripe for considering the complex interplay between race, gender, citizenship status, and other forms of difference, and the need for anti-racist responses to be attuned to intersectional analysis.

CONCLUSION

Canada is a remarkably lively as well as pertinent place to consider contemporary debates over multiculturalism. It is the country that gave birth to the term multiculturalism and has maintained its 1971 policy for over forty years. While in some places politicians may harness language to talk about multiculturalism in relation to failure, or to even proclaim its death, the policy's longevity in Canada suggests otherwise. Moreover, the fact that successive Quebec governments, while rejecting the term "multiculturalism," have nevertheless pursued their own policies of "interculturalism" suggests that the ideal of cultural pluralism still finds political and popular support in Canada. In short, the word "multiculturalism" is not about to disappear from the national lexicon.

As this chapter has indicated, however, Canadian multiculturalism policy has not been static. In the twenty-first century, in fact, its role in supporting the inclusion of diverse incoming immigrants and citizens has faced new challenges. The turn to neoliberalism has had implications for the ability of minority groups to organize, on a national basis, since they lack the state funding they once had. Moreover, the redefining of membership and belonging pursued by the Harper government lingers in discourses that can be mobilized in relation to "Canadian" values, loyalty, and history in ways that produce points of exclusion for many Canadians, including francophones, Indigenous peoples, and other minorities. As we have outlined, the introduction of policies which made citizenship more difficult to obtain, and offered new grounds for revoking citizenship, likewise find parallels in other countries, and elements of these policies still linger with the Trudeau government. In particular, discourses that explicitly or implicitly focus on Muslims as a problem that multiculturalism must overcome remain apparent in contemporary race politics.

Although these developments may have parallels in other locales, a distinct feature of the Canadian context is that multiculturalism still finds support as an idea, and to a lesser extent as a policy. This is true not only among politicians but also among the general public. However, in comparison with the past, anti-racism has been inconsistently featured in recent multicultural discourse and policy. Given that racialized inequality and racism still find expression in contemporary Canada, it is an open question as to whether and how the Canadian state and civil society groups will or will not be able to respond. The refrain that "a Canadian is a Canadian is a Canadian" is an important symbolic feature of the Trudeau Liberal government's approach to Canadian citizenship. However, as this chapter has suggested, this belies some fundamental consistencies which speak to the way in which Canadian citizenship is still deeply racialized and exclusionary, reflecting and feeding the process that we have termed "containing diversity."

BIBLIOGRAPHY

Abu-Laban, Yasmeen. "On the Borderlines of Human and Citizen: The Liminal State of Arab Canadians." In *Targeted Transnationals: Policies and Discourses Take Aim at Arab Canadians*, edited by Bessma Momani and Jenna Hennebry, 68–85. Vancouver: UBC Press, 2013.

– "Reform by Stealth: The Harper Conservatives and Canadian Multiculturalism." In *Debating Multiculturalism in Canada*, edited by Jack Jedwab, 149–72. Queen's School of Policy Studies. Montreal: McGill-Queen's University Press, 2014a.

– "The Politics of History Under Harper." *Labour/Le Travail* 73 (Spring 2014b): 215–17.

– "The Political Economy of International Migration and the Canadian Example." In *International Political Economy*, edited by Greg Anderson and Christopher J. Kukucha, 476–91. Toronto: Oxford University Press, 2016.

– "Building a New Citizenship Regime? Immigration and Multiculturalism in Canada." In *Citizenship in Transnational Perspective: Australia, Canada and New Zealand*, edited by Jatinder Mann, 263–83. London: Palgrave Macmillan, 2017.

– "Multiculturalism: Past, Present and Future." *Diversity/Diversités* (October 2021).

Abu-Laban, Yasmeen, and Christina Gabriel. *Selling Diversity: Immigration, Multiculturalism, Employment Equity and Globalization*. Peterborough: Broadview Press, 2002.

Abu-Laban, Yasmeen, and Nisha Nath. "Citizenship, Multiculturalism and Immigration: Mapping the Complexities of Inclusion and Exclusion through Intersectionality." In *The Palgrave Handbooks of Gender, Sexuality, and Canadian Politics*, edited by Manon Tremblay and Joanna Everitt, 507–27. London: Palgrave Macmillan, 2020.

Abu-Laban, Yasmeen, and Daiva Stasiulis. "Ethnic Pluralism under Siege: Popular and Partisan Opposition to Multiculturalism." *Canadian Public Policy* 18, no. 4 (1992): 365–86.

Alboim, Naomi, and Karen Cohl. *Shaping the Future: Canada's Rapidly Changing Immigration Policies*. Toronto: Maytree Foundation, 2012. https://maytree.com/wp-content/uploads/shaping-the-future.pdf.

Alexander, Chris. "Speaking Notes for Chris Alexander, Canada's Citizenship and Immigration Minister at a News Conference to Announce the Tabling of Bill C-24: The Strengthening Canadian Citizenship Act." Speech from February 6, 2014. www.canada.ca/en/news/archive/2014/02/speaking-notes-chris-alexander-canada-citizenship-immigration-minister-news-conference-announce-tabling-bill-c-24-strengthening-canadian-citizenship-act.html.

Association for Canadian Studies. "Younger Canadians Believe Multiculturalism Works; Older Canadians, Not so Sure." April 24, 2012.

Banting, Keith, and Will Kymlicka. "Is There Really a Retreat from Multiculturalism Policies? New Evidence from the Multiculturalism Policy Index." *Comparative European Politics* 11, no. 5 (2013): 577–98.

Battell Lowman, Emma, and Adam J. Barker. *Settler Identity and Colonialism in 21st Century Canada*. Halifax: Fernwood Publishing, 2015.

Batty, David. "Marine Le Pen Praises Cameron Stance on Multiculturalism." *The Guardian* (February 10. 2011). www.guardian.co.uk/world/2011/feb/10/marine-le-pen-cameron-multiculturalism.

Black, Debra. "Immigration Experts Say Bill C-24 Discriminatory and Weakens Citizenship." *The Toronto Star* (June 27, 2014). www.thestar.com/news/immigration/2014/06/27/immigration_experts_say_bill_c24_discriminatory_and_weakens_citizenship.html.

Blad, Cory, and Philippe Couton. "The Rise of an Intercultural Nation: Immigration, Diversity and Nationhood in Quebec." *Journal of Ethnic and Migration Studies* 35, no. 4 (2009): 645–67.

Block, Sheila, and Grace-Edward Galabuzi. *Canada's Colour Coded Labour Market: The Gap for Racialized Workers*. Ottawa: Canadian Centre for Policy Alternatives, March 2011. www.wellesleyinstitute.com/wp-content/uploads/2011/03/Colour_Coded_Labour_MarketFINAL.pdf.

Bloemraad, Irene. *Becoming a Citizen: Incorporating Immigrants and Refugees in the United States and Canada*. Berkeley: University of California Press, 2006.

Brend, Yvette. "'Go Back to China' Comment Prompts VPD Investigation." CBC News (March 7, 2020). www.cbc.ca/news/canada/british-columbia/racist-attack-no-frills-covid-19-coronavirus-mask-slur-1.5488923.

Breton, Raymond. "The Production and Allocation of Symbolic Resources: An Analysis of the Linguistic and Ethnocultural Fields in Canada." *Canadian Review of Sociology and Anthropology* 21, no. 2 (1984): 123–44.

– "Multiculturalism and Canadian Nation Building." In *The Politics of Gender, Ethnicity and Language in Canada*, edited by Alan Cairns and Cynthia Williams in cooperation with the Royal Commission on the Economic Union and Development Prospects for Canada, 27–66. Toronto: University of Toronto Press, 1986.

Brosseau, Laurence, and Michael Dewing. *Canadian Multiculturalism*. Background Report, Library of Parliament. Publication No. 2009–20-E (Revised January 3, 2018).

Cameron, David. "Speech on Radicalisation and Islamic Extremism." Full transcript. *NewStatesman* (February 5, 2011). www.newstatesman.com/blogs/the-staggers/2011/02/terrorism-islam-ideology.

Canadian Heritage. *Annual Report on the Operation of the Canadian Multiculturalism Act* 2006–2007. Ottawa: Government of Canada, 2008.

– *Annual Report on the Operation of the Canadian Multiculturalism Act 2009–2010*. Ottawa: Government of Canada, 2011.

- *Annual Report on the Operation of the Canadian Multiculturalism Act 2019–2020 (Building a Better Canada through Diversity)*. Her Majesty the Queen in Right of Canada, 2021.
Canadian Press. "Quebec Intellectuals Promote Wave of 'Interculturalism.'" *CTV News* (March 6, 2011). www.ctvnews.ca/quebec-intellectuals-promote-wave-of-interculturalism-1.615194.
- "'Sometimes Marriage Is a Scam': Ottawa Launches Fresh Ad Campaign Targeting Immigration Fraud." *The National Post* (March 20, 2013). https://nationalpost.com/news/politics/sometimes-marriage-is-a-scam-ottawa-launches-fresh-ad-campaign-targeting-immigration-fraud.
Citizenship and Immigration Canada (CIC). *Discover Canada: The Rights and Responsibilities of Citizenship*. Ottawa: Government of Canada, 2012. www.canada.ca/content/dam/ircc/migration/ircc/english/pdf/pub/discover.pdf.
- *Annual Report to Parliament on Immigration*. Ottawa: Government of Canada, 2013. www.canada.ca/en/immigration-refugees-citizenship/corporate/publications-manuals/annual-report-parliament-immigration-2013.html.
Cohen, Tobi. "Failed Your Citizenship Exam? The Federal Government to Offer a Second Chance." *The Vancouver Sun* (June 2, 2013). www.vancouversun.com/news/national/Failed+your+citizenship+exam+Federal+government+offer/8468251/story.html.
CTV News Staff. "Nearly 9 in 10 Canadians Would Fail the Citizenship Test." *CTV News* (July 1, 2019). www.ctvnews.ca/canada/nearly-9-in-10-canadians-would-fail-the-citizenship-test-poll-1.4489704.
Dauvergne, Catherine. "Citizenship with a Vengeance." *Theoretical Inquiry in Law* 8, no. 2 (2007): 489–507.
de Bellaigue, Christopher. "The New Europeans." *The New York Review of Books* (June 7, 2018). www.nybooks.com/articles/2018/06/07/the-new-europeans-muslims/.
Desforges, Luke, Rhys Jones, and Mike Woods. "New Geographies of Citizenship." *Citizenship Studies* 9, no. 5 (2005): 439–51.
Dobrowolsky, Alexandra. "Interrogating 'Invisibilization' and 'Instrumentalization': Women and Current Citizenship Trends in Canada." *Citizenship Studies* 12, no. 5 (2008): 465–79.
Edwards, Jason A., and Lindsey R. Calhoun. "Redress for Old Wounds: Canadian Prime Minster Stephen Harper's Apology for the Chinese Head Tax." *Chinese Journal of Communication* 4, no. 1 (2011): 73–89.
Friesen, Joe. "Canada Near Top at Integrating Immigrants, Survey Says." *The Globe and Mail* (February 28, 2011). www.theglobeandmail.com/news/politics/canada-near-top-in-integrating-immigrants-survey-says/article568517/.
- "Ottawa Pumps up Military Role in Citizenship Ceremonies." *The Globe and Mail* (August 24, 2012). http://m.theglobeandmail.com/news

/politics/ottawa-pumps-up-military-role-in-citizenship-ceremonies
/article2083103/?service=mobile.
Galabuzi, Grace-Edward. "Hegemonies, Continuities, and Discontinuities of Multiculturalism and the Anglo-Franco Conformity Order." In *Home and Native Land: Unsettling Multiculturalism in Canada*, edited by May Chazan, Lisa Helps, Anna Stanley, and Sonali Thakkar, 58–82. Toronto: Between the Lines, 2011.
Gifford, Christopher. "National and Post-National Dimensions of Citizenship Education in the UK." *Citizenship Studies* 8, no. 2 (2004): 145–58.
Government of Canada. "Applying for Citizenship? Here Are the Changes You Need to Know." 2017. https://publications.gc.ca/collections/collection_2017/ircc/Ci4-172-2017-eng.pdf.
Government of Canada, House of Commons. *Debates*. 28th Parliament, 3rd Session. October 8, 1971: 8545–8548.
Greenwood, John, and Lynton Robins. "Citizenship Tests and Education: Embedding a Concept." *Parliamentary Affairs* 55, no. 3 (2002): 505–22.
Hiebert, Daniel. "Winning, Losing and Still Playing the Game: The Political Economy of Immigration in Canada." *Tijdschrift voor Economische en Sociale Geografie* 97, no. 1 (2006): 38–48.
Hou, Feng, and Garnett Picot. "Trends in the Citizenship Rate among New Immigrants to Canada." *Statistics Canada*, Economic Insights Series (November 2019). Catalogue no. 11–626-X.
Immigration, Refugees and Citizenship Canada (IRCC). "Government of Canada Implements New Legislative Changes to the Citizenship Act." Press release, October 4, 2017. www.canada.ca/en/immigration-refugees-citizenship/news/2017/10/government_of_canadaimplementsnewlegislativechangestothecitizens.html.
– "Changes to Citizenship Rules 2009–2015." 2020. www.canada.ca/en/immigration-refugees-citizenship/services/canadian-citizenship/act-changes/rules-2009-2015.html.
James, Matt. "Wrestling with the Past: Apologies, Quasi-Apologies, and Non-Apologies in Canada." In *The Age of Apology: Facing Up to the Past*, edited by Mark Gibney, Rhoda E. Howard Hassmann, Jean-Marc Coicaud, and Niklaus Steiner, 137–53. Philadelphia: University of Pennsylvania Press, 2008.
– "Neoliberal Heritage Redress." In *Reconciling Canada: Critical Perspectives on the Culture of Redress*, edited by Jennifer Henderson and Pauline Wakeham, 31–46. Toronto: University of Toronto Press, 2013.
Jones, Esyllt, and Adele Perry. *People's Citizenship Guide: A Response to Conservative Canada*. Winnipeg: Arbiter Publishing, 2012.
Juteau, Danielle, Marie McAndrew, and Linda Pietrantonio. "Multiculturalism à la Canadian and Intégration à la Québécoise: Transcending Their Limits." In *Blurred Boundaries: Migration, Ethnicity, Citizenship*, edited by Rainer Bauböck and John Rundell, 95–110. Aldershot: Ashgate, 1998.

Kenney, Jason. "Foreword by the Minister." In *Annual Report on the Operation of the Canadian Multiculturalism Act 2008–2009*, by Citizenship and Immigration Canada (CIC), iii–iv. Ottawa: Government of Canada, 2010.

– "Foreword: Minister of Citizenship, Immigration and Multiculturalism." In *Annual Report on the Operation of the Canadian Multiculturalism Act, 2009–2010*, by Citizenship and Immigration Canada (CIC), 5. Ottawa: Government of Canada, 2011.

– "NDP Defends Citizenship for Convicted Terrorists." Email Communique from jason.kenney@parl.gc.ca. June 13, 2013a.

– "Statement—Minister Kenney Issues Statement on the International Day for the Elimination of Racial Discrimination." March 21, 2013b. www.canada.ca/en/news/archive/2009/03/minister-kenney-issues-statement-international-day-elimination-racial-discrimination.html.

Kobayashi, Audrey. "Ethnocultural Political Mobilization, Multiculturalism and Human Rights in Canada." In *Group Politics and Social Movements in Canada*, edited by Miriam Smith, 131–57. Peterborough, ON: Broadview Press, 2008.

Kymlicka, Will. "Immigration, Citizenship, Multiculturalism: Exploring the Links." *The Political Quarterly* 74, no. 1 (2003): 195–208.

Ladner, Kiera L., and Michael McCrossan. "Whose Shared History?" *Labour /Le Travail* 73 (Spring 2014): 200–2.

Lau, Rachel. "Selective Xenophobia: What COVID-19 Is Teaching Us about Who We Target When It Comes to Racism." *CTV News* (March 11, 2020). https://montreal.ctvnews.ca/selective-xenophobia-what-covid-19-is-teaching-us-about-who-we-target-when-it-comes-to-racism-1.4848134.

Lentin, Alana, and Gavan Titley. *The Crises of Multiculturalism: Racism in a Neoliberal Age*. London: Zed Books, 2011.

Levitz, Stephanie. "New Citizenship Study Guide Highlights Indigenous Peoples, Canadian Responsibilities." *The Toronto Star* (July 23, 2017). www.thestar.com/news/canada/2017/07/23/new-citizenship-study-guide-highlights-indigenous-peoples-canadian-responsibilities.html.

– "Liberals' Budget Includes $23M for Multiculturalism and Anti-racism Strategy." *CTV News* (February 28, 2018). www.ctvnews.ca/politics/liberals-budget-includes-23m-for-multiculturalism-anti-racism-strategy-1.3823101.

Li, Peter S. *Destination Canada: Immigration Debates and Issues*. Toronto: Oxford University Press, 2002.

Ma, Lillian. "Immigration and Citizenship in Canada: Public Opinion and Social Trends." *Conference Presentation for the Canadian Race Relations Foundation*. Annual Metropolis Meetings, Calgary, March 22, 2018. https://crrf-fcrr.app.box.com/s/vig9r3w8l456hpzk5s2vjvrm3fqxf78n.

Mackenzie, Hector. "Does History Mean Having to Say You're Sorry?" *Canadian Issues Newsletter* (2010). Association of Canadian Studies, 47–50.

Mahrouse, Gada. "Minimizing and Denying Racial Violence: Insights from the Quebec Mosque Shooting." *Canadian Journal of Women and the Law* 30, no. 3 (2018): 471–93.

Maloney, Ryan. "Tories Push Liberals to Keep FGM Warning in Citizenship Guide." *The Huffington Post* (November 29, 2017). www.huffingtonpost.ca/2017/11/29/tories-push-trudeau-to-keep-fgm-warning-in-citizenship-guide_a_23292216/.

Martin, Paul Sr. "Citizenship and the People's World." In *Belonging: The Meaning and Future of Canadian Citizenship*, edited by William Kaplan, 64–78. Montreal and Kingston: McGill-Queen's University Press, 2003.

McKay, Ian, and Jamie Swift. *Warrior Nation: Rebranding Canada in an Age of Anxiety*. Toronto: Between the Lines, 2012.

Meer, Nasar, Tariq Modood, and Ricard Zapata-Barrero, eds. *Multiculturalism and Interculturalism: Debating the Dividing Lines*. Edinburgh: Edinburgh University Press, 2016.

Meurrens, Steven. "Analyzing the Liberal Changes to Canada's Citizenship Act." *Policy Options* (February 29, 2016). https://policyoptions.irpp.org/2016/02/29/analyzing-the-liberal-changes-to-canadas-citizenship-act/.

Mills, Carys. "How Applicants Are Stumbling on the Final Step to Becoming Canadians." *The Globe and Mail* (June 29, 2012). www.theglobeandmail.com/news/national/how-applicants-are-stumbling-on-the-final-step-to-becoming-canadians/article4382633/.

Murphy, Katharine. "Pauline Hanson Calls for Immigration Ban: 'Go Back to Where You Came From.'" *The Guardian* (September 14, 2016). www.theguardian.com/australia-news/2016/sep/14/pauline-hanson-first-speech-senate-calls-for-immigration-ban.

Noël, Alain. "History under Harper: Leaving Québec, and Much Else, Outside Canada." *Labour/Le Travail* 73 (Spring 2014): 210–12.

Paquet, Mireille. "Beyond Appearances: Citizenship Tests in Canada and the UK." *Journal of International Migration and Integration* 13, no. 2 (2012): 243–60.

Perkel, Colin. "The Political Leanings of Suspected Mosque Shooter Alexandre Bissonnette. *Macleans* (January 31, 2018). www.macleans.ca/news/canada/the-political-leanings-of-suspected-mosque-shooter-alexandre-bissonnette/.

Rajkumar, Deepa, Laurel Berkowitize, Leah F. Vosko, Valerie Preston, and Robert Latham. "At the Temporary-Permanent Divide: How Canada Produces Temporariness and Makes Citizens through Its Security, Work and Settlement Policies." *Citizenship Studies* 16, nos. 3–4 (2012): 483–510.

Razack, Sherene. *Casting Out: The Eviction of Muslims from Western Law and Politics*. Toronto: University of Toronto Press, 2008.

Rowe, Daniel J. "COVID-19: Korean Consulate Issues Warnings after Violent Attack in Montreal." *CTV News* (March 18, 2020). https://montreal.ctvnews.ca/covid-19-korean-consulate-issues-warning-after-violent-attack-in-montreal-1.4856453.

Royal Commission on Bilingualism and Biculturalism. *Book IV: The Cultural Contribution of the Other Ethnic Groups*. Ottawa: Government of Canada, 1970.

Ryan, Phil. *Multicultiphobia*. Toronto: University of Toronto Press, 2010.

Sandel, Michael. "Right-wing Populism Is Rising as Progressive Politics Fails – Is It Too Late to Save Democracy?" *NewStatesman* (May 21, 2018). www.newstatesman.com/2018/05/right-wing-populism-rising-progressive-politics-fails-it-too-late-save-democracy.

Sharma, Nandita. "Canadian Multiculturalism and Its Nationalisms." In *Home and Native Land: Unsettling Multiculturalism in Canada*, edited by May Chazan, Lisa Helps, Anna Stanley, and Sonali Thakkar, 84–101. Toronto: Between the Lines, 2011.

Smith, Marie-Danielle. "Dramatic Increase in People Having Citizenship Revoked since Trudeau Elected." *The National Post* (February 10, 2017). http://nationalpost.com/news/politics/dramatic-increase-in-people-having-canadian-citizenship-revoked-since-trudeau-elected.

Stasiulis, Daiva K. "The Symbolic Mosaic Reaffirmed: Multiculturalism Policy." In *How Ottawa Spends: 1988–89*, edited by Katherine A. Graham, 81–112. Ottawa: Carleton University Press, 1988.

– "Worrier Nation: Quebec's Value Code for Immigrants." *Politikon* 40, no. 1 (2013): 183–209.

Statistics Canada. "Immigration and Ethnocultural Diversity: Key Results from the 2016 Census." *The Daily* (October 25, 2017). www150.statcan.gc.ca/n1/daily-quotidien/171025/dq171025b-eng.htm.

Taschner, Eric. "Canadian Actor Subjected to COVID-19 Racism in North Bay." *CTV News* (March 27, 2020). https://northernontario.ctvnews.ca/canadian-actor-subjected-to-covid-19-racism-in-north-bay-1.4871499.

Thompson, Andrew S. "The Need to Protect Rule of Law: A Response to Bill C-24." Policy brief, Canadian Arab Institute, May 2014. https://new.canadianarabinstitute.org/publications/policy-briefs/response-bill-c-24/.

Timothy, Roberta K. "Coronavirus Is Not the 'Great Equalizer' – Race Matters: UofT Expert." *UofT News* (April 8, 2020). www.utoronto.ca/news/coronavirus-not-great-equalizer-race-matters-u-t-expert.

Torres, Carlos Alberto. "Is Multiculturalism Dead?" *The Huffington Post* (February 28, 2013). www.huffingtonpost.com/carlos-alberto-torres/is-multiculturalism-dead_b_2641808.html.

Trudeau, Justin. "Justin Trudeau, for the Record: 'We Beat Fear with Hope." Speech transcript, *Maclean's* (October 20, 2015). www.macleans.ca/politics/ottawa/justin-trudeau-for-the-record-we-beat-fear-with-hope/.

Truth and Reconciliation Commission of Canada (TRC). "Honouring the Truth, Reconciling for the Future: Summary of the Final Report of the Truth and Reconciliation Commission of Canada." Winnipeg: Truth and Reconciliation Commission of Canada, 2015a. www.trc.ca/assets/pdf/Honouring_the_Truth_Reconciling_for_the_Future_July_23_2015.pdf.

- "Truth and Reconciliation Commission of Canada: Calls to Action." Winnipeg: Truth and Reconciliation Commission of Canada, 2015b. http://trc.ca/assets/pdf/Calls_to_Action_English2.pdf.
Turgeon, Luc, Antoine Bilodeau, Stephen E. White, and Alisa Henderson. "A Tale of Two Liberalisms? Attitudes toward Minority Religious Symbols in Quebec and Canada." *Canadian Journal of Political Science* 52, no. 2 (June 2019): 247–65.
Weaver, Matthew. "Angela Merkel: German Multiculturalism Has 'Utterly Failed.'" *The Guardian* (October 17, 2010). www.guardian.co.uk/world/2010/oct/17/angela-merkel-german-multiculturalism-failed.
Weil, Patrick. "Access to Citizenship: A Comparison of Twenty-Five Nationality Laws." In *Citizenship Today: Global Perspectives and Practices*, edited by T. Alexander Aleinkoff and Douglas Klusmeyer, 17–35. Washington: Carnegie Institute, 2001.
Wilcox, Shelley. "Culture, National Identity, and Admission to Citizenship." *Social Theory and Practice* 30, no. 4 (2004): 559–82.
Winter, Elke, and Ivana Previsic. "The Politics of Un-belonging: Lessons from Canada's Experiment with Citizenship Revocation." *Citizenship Studies* 23, no. 4 (2019): 338–55.
Ziafati, Noushin. "'I'm Profoundly Tired by It': Members of Halifax Community Speak Out about Racism during Pandemic." *The Chronicle Herald* (April 8, 2020). www.thechronicleherald.ca/news/local/im-profoundly-tired-by-it-members-of-halifax-community-speak-out-about-racism-during-pandemic-434662/.

CHAPTER EIGHT

Towards a Politics of Global and Social Justice

The realities of the global COVID-19 pandemic showed the extent to which existing immigration and integration policies have created hierarchies of belonging. The pandemic, in fact, served to make clear that, contrary to hopeful invocations that "we are all in this together," some communities fared worse than others during COVID-19, be they migrant workers who find themselves at higher risk of contagion because of substandard employment and housing, asylum seekers whose applications for refugee status have stalled because of border closures, family-class migrants who find that they are indefinitely separated from their family members, and many others. Studies highlight how Black, Indigenous, and racialized people faced higher rates of COVID-19-infection and COVID-19-related deaths because they were more likely to work in front-line, public-facing jobs (Kobayashi 2020, 53; Lightman 2021; Wilson 2021) and lived in neighbourhoods where there is higher COVID-19 spread (Carman 2020). In addition, such research also suggests that women, racialized minorities, and immigrants in Canada were experiencing disproportionately higher rates of job loss, financial distress, and heightened levels of anxiety associated with the pandemic (CERC 2020; Grant et al. 2020; Wherry 2020). Thus, it is clear that the pandemic has *magnified* existing social and economic injustices.

Some see the pandemic as bringing us to a crossroads: should we continue with the status quo, or should we create new norms of being and doing? To be sure, efforts to control entry, limit membership, and devalue caring labour and social reproduction rest uneasily with ideals of equality. These also bring up questions of care ethics: would border restrictions actually ensure a higher quality of care because the demands on the social welfare state are lessened? Or would border restrictions make it harder for humans to meet their care responsibilities.

In this chapter, we take up the challenge of reflecting on various normative visions of what could be. This undertaking compels us to revisit other existing political theories, which more explicitly consider political membership and borders in order to understand whether and how the current emphasis on containing diversity fits within theorists' normative visions of what justice looks like. In what follows, we consider how political theorists have reflected on the legitimacy of national borders. What are their main points of disagreement? What are their solutions to these issues and how might that further inform our collective conversation and understanding? Given that the pandemic led countries and even regions within countries (e.g., prohibitions against inter-provincial travelling in Canada) to close their borders, with highly contentious policies regarding mandatory masking and proofs of vaccination now being imposed for travelers entering Canada (Government of Canada 2021) and being debated within spaces such as universities (Cyr and Xu 2021), restaurants (Lazaruk 2021), and even concert halls (Friend 2021), the "border" debates have never been more relevant. Discussions on whether to close, open, or abolish borders become especially timely today.

We argue for greater attention to competing normative visions on the question of borders as a prelude to considering social and global justice in new ways by attending to care and relationality, solidarity, and Indigenous rights. Such scholarly attention can not only advance the conversation and political imagination concerning migration, but it can also offer alternatives to containing diversity. As we detail further, what we contribute is a critique of unjust structures that takes seriously considerations of care and relationality. We see solidarity across difference and borders as challenging unjust structures and processes (see also Robinson 2015, 305). Indeed, issues relating to care, relationality, and migration have actually been made more evident in the wake of COVID-19, perhaps ironically in light of border closures. As a result, we are in a unique moment to reflect in creative ways about new possibilities that may embrace diversity on a path to social and global justice.

DEFENDING AND CHALLENGING A WORLD OF STATES AND NATIONAL CITIZENS: NORMATIVE PERSPECTIVES

Political theorists are divided on the question of borders. They debate whether it is just or fair for countries to have the discretion to decide who should enter and settle inside their territories. These debates hinge on whether theorists prioritize national sovereignty, self-determination, and care for the community *first*, as seen through concerns that opening immigration will lead to compromising the national welfare state or the pursuit of individual freedom and global justice. Prioritizing the former leads theorists to endorse closing or restricting borders, whereas prioritizing the latter lead theorists to advocate for opening borders, if not eradicating them all together.

In what follows, we critically assess each of these perspectives. We recognize the diversity of approaches within each perspective. Nevertheless, for the sake of brevity, we focus the bulk of our analysis on political thinkers whose ideas were formative in developing each approach. Namely, we focus on Michael Walzer's work on communitarianism, Joseph Carens's work on liberalism, Seyla Benhabib's work on cosmopolitanism, and Harsha Walia's work on "no borders" politics. We analyse the rationale behind each approach, its main arguments, and the responses of other scholars to these works.

Communitarian "Closed Border" Perspectives

Communitarian perspectives on immigration can be traced to Walzer's theories of distributive justice. Walzer's ideas are based on the conception of "a group of people committed to dividing, exchanging, and sharing social goods" while living within the "bounded world" of a single "political community" (1983, 31). Membership is the first social good that must be distributed, after which other goods can be distributed. Not being a part of such a community – that is, being stateless – is "a condition of infinite danger" (1983, 32). A world where people do not live within communities is an alienating and undesirable place. At the heart of the Communitarian approach is a disavowal of how liberal theory assumes that individual liberty is the highest good, which Walzer argues is too individualistic and "radically misrepresent real life" (1990, 9). Rather than seeing liberty as the pathway to happiness, communitarians see such mobility as forcibly untethering individuals from their communities and draw attention to the "underside of sadness and discontent" wrought by these arrangements (1990, 13). Although Walzer concedes that human beings should have the mobility to move to different countries, he believes that, if given a choice, most would prefer not to move because doing so entails leaving behind their communities (1983, 38).

Walzer therefore affirms the conventional practice of closed borders in a world of nation-states. He reasons that, "we who are already members do the choosing, in accordance with our own understanding of what membership means in our community and what sort of a community we want to have" (1983, 32). Although Walzer condemns policies that manipulate the composition of the population of a given country, such as "ethnic," "class," or "intelligence" quotas for giving birth because these enable the "dominance of political power over kinship and love," he nevertheless believes that communities can justifiably determine the size of their populations by collectively deciding the number of people who can become members and the "sorts of people" who can do so (1983, 35). After all, for him, a community's ability to include and exclude people is the "core of communal independence [and] ... suggest the deepest meaning of self-determination. Without them, there could not be *communities of character*, which are historically stable, ongoing associations of men and women with some special commitment to one another and some special sense of their common life" (1983, 62; emphasis in original). As David Ingram (2002) puts it: "Bounded associations in which persons care deeply about one another because of a sense of shared history or shared identity (however this is understood) are necessary for sustaining relationships of full reciprocity. A world without such associations, in which we all related to one another simply as individuals without regard to contingent histories of association, would be cold and uncaring if not morally unthinkable. We cannot extend our care for others without diluting it, and so some closure must exist" (408). Excluding people from membership is imbued with a moral purpose, which is to retain the integrity and longevity of communal arrangements. As Walzer further argues, "the restraint of entry serves to defend the liberty and welfare, the politics and culture of a group of people committed to one another and their common life" (1983, 39). Recognizing the distinction between "members" and "strangers" is important to maintain community (Walzer 1983, 34). Closed borders therefore strengthen not just cultural ties but also political identities.

That there are people who wish to leave their communities and enter others because of the need to secure their economic livelihoods and/or because their lives are under threat provides important exceptions to Walzer's theory of limited membership. When assessing the rights of guest workers who move into a given country to work in jobs that the state's citizens do not want to do, Walzer believes they have the right to be members within the community. He insists that "the processes of self-determination through which a democratic state shapes its internal life must be open and equally open to all those men and women who live within its territory, work in the local economy, and are subject to local law" (1983, 60). As such, states that claim to be democratic but do not confer on all of its residents, including guest workers, the rights of membership are being tyrannical. If these states opt not to give guest workers the full rights of membership, then they should find other ways to meet their economic needs. While states can determine who enters, people who do enter should be treated like other citizens. All residents of a territory should "hold a single political status" (1983, 62).

Similarly, Walzer argues that states are obligated to allow the entry of refugees fleeing persecution. (Note that he only considers the case of people seeking asylum and does not consider, say, the case of climate refugees.). He invokes the principles of "mutual aid" when justifying the entry of refugees, asserting that barring their entry would require the unnecessary use of force against persecuted groups (1983, 51). Again, though, he issues an important addendum to his theory. He believes that countries' primary obligation should be towards refugees whose policies led to their displacement, such as refugees going to the United States to flee the war in Vietnam. Those who were "persecuted or oppressed by someone else" can be accepted as refugees depending on the country's cultural and ideological attributes; those "who are persecuted because they are like us" receive priority (1983, 49). When too many refugees seek entry and "we are forced to choose among the victims, we will look, *rightfully*, for some more direct connection with our own way of life" (1983, 49; emphasis added). Higher numbers of outsiders entering the state, after all, dilutes community bonds and arguably makes it difficult to distribute social goods within the community.

Walzer's arguments also apply to the question of economic immigrants seeking to naturalize. While he recognizes the impulse human beings have to leave their communities, providing an *unrestricted* right to enter and exit states negatively affects the ability of states to meet the needs of their members whose interests states should prioritize over outsiders. Walzer asks, "how much of their wealth do they have to share?" answering in response that countries have to impose limits or else "communal wealth would be subject to indefinite drainage" (1983, 48). Walzer's stance towards countries' responsibility towards accepting the entry of migrants, whether they are refugees or economic migrants, can be seen most clearly in his response to the "Good Samaritan" story, which teaches the significance of helping strangers. Walzer acknowledges that communities have an obligation to help but also emphasizes the following: "I need not take the injured stranger in my home, except briefly, and I certainly need not care for him or associate with him for the rest of my life" (1983, 33).

Interestingly, when evaluating the larger problem of power imbalances between states that compel individuals from poor states to move to more affluent states, as in his example of poor Southeast Asian migrants entering Australia, Walzer widens the scope of his analysis. He believes that modes of redistribution should be considered, either in terms of ceding territory or restructuring balances of power (1983, 47). He does not develop this idea further, however, nor does he discuss whether and how this can be done. Moreover, Walzer remains silent on the issue of family reunification, and states' obligations to accept the family members of those who have already settled within their territories.

While there are conservative theorists who see in Walzer's analysis an endorsement of immigration control (see Meilandar 2001), assessing his arguments in light of COVID-19 shows the logic behind his claims more clearly. A communitarian approach that centres community first is what countries have endorsed. Borders mostly closed during COVID-19 to preserve the larger community's health and safety, with rare exceptions made for migrant workers to ensure the integrity of countries' supply chains. The need to limit contagion and restrict travel – even within countries – is logical, given COVID-19's easy spread. In fact, quickly opening borders, and, by extension, provinces, cities, towns, and even schools and work sites is now seen as showing a *lack* of care because these actions appear to prioritize economic growth.

Yet closing borders to ensure greater care for the larger community during COVID-19 may also mean that it becomes harder for some people within borders to give and receive care. When nation-states, provinces, towns, and spaces such as hospitals and long-term-care homes effectively close their borders and bar the entry of outsiders, families living in different sites find that their caring needs are compromised. Families with sick and terminally ill members had to scramble to find care if they were unable to qualify for border-crossing exceptions that some countries provided. Traditional mourning rituals could not take place because of prohibitions on gatherings.

In addition, even as borders remain closed and most workplaces are shut, they nevertheless remain selectively open for essential workers. That many of these essential workers are racialized immigrants illustrate how certain bodies become the givers – and are never the receivers – of care. For the community to remain safe and intact, certain individuals have to compromise their safety.

Hence, we wonder whether the underlying logic of communitarianism during COVID-19 – that borders need to close to ensure care for one's community – applies to everyone equally. Does a communitarian approach invariably create hierarchies of care? Does it prioritize the caring needs of some over others?

Liberal Open Borders and Cosmopolitan Porous Borders Perspectives

LIBERAL PERSPECTIVES

Liberals disagree with communitarian conceptualizations of membership. They believe in the "equal moral worth of individuals" and "treat the individual as prior to the community" (Carens 1987,

252). Individuals are free moral agents who should be free to decide how they want to live their lives and their own values. Thus, liberal theorists see the preservation of individual liberty as being key to justice.

An important feature of liberty concerns the idea of voluntary association, whereby individuals are free to join communities and groups that fit with their beliefs. Carens's espousal of open borders is an extension of this idea. He argues that "open borders contribute to human freedom" (2013, 236). Locking people into their communities of birth is an egregious injustice. Indeed, Carens (1987) argues that today's immigration system is similar to feudalism in that those who were fortunate enough to be born in affluent and stable countries receive more advantages than those who are born in poor countries. Oppressive social institutions that existed historically, such as feudalism and slavery, were so deeply entrenched in society's practices that the fundamental injustices they wrought were masked and it seemed they would never end. Similarly, Carens holds that people "wind up legitimating what should only be endured" when it comes to immigration (2000, 636). Much like people who once took for granted the validity of feudalism and slavery, Carens "calls into question the complacent certitude that there is nothing fundamentally wrong with the way we have constructed our collective lives and with our decision to exclude others from the social resources we enjoy" (2000, 640). A crucial way to eradicate unfair advantages wrought by place of birth, would be through an open-borders policy.

Although other political theorists have written about open borders (see Lenard 2010; Sandelind 2013), Carens's ideas concerning open borders are the basis for many of these theories. Carens emphasizes that his vision of open borders still recognizes that sovereign states are free to make their own policies. He stresses, though, that recognizing sovereign states' ability to form policies does not then mean that all of their policies are moral. Restrictions to immigration, which states are allowed to enforce, are in many circumstances immoral. More significantly, Carens also emphasizes that his normative vision of open borders may in practice be better realized when there is a commitment to reducing international economic inequality (2013, 252).

To justify open borders, Carens employs numerous analytical approaches, the most effective of which involves taking a "cantilever" approach, whereby he justifies the exercise of a given right by showing it is similar to another right. Specifically, he questions why internal movement within a given country as in Canada, the United States, and in other Western states is seen as a fundamental human right, whereas movement between countries is not. The same reasons for moving from one state or province to another, after all, are similar to the reasons people move countries (2013, 239). Creating a "radical disjuncture" between the right to free movement within states and prohibitions against the same right when practised between states has no moral justification for Carens, particularly when one accepts freedom of movement as a human right (2013, 240).

Carens's espousal of individual freedom is also witnessed in his repudiation of communitarian claims. He argues that a world with open borders does not mean that political communities are abandoned and that human beings will move from one place to another without forming lasting ties (2013, 287). He even agrees with Walzer by stating that "most people would find it more attractive to stay in their communities of origin" (2013, 287). With this in mind, giving people the right to free movement does not mean communities will be destroyed because most people would prefer to remain tied to their communities. As an example, Carens looks at the European Union and shows that cultural and political communities are still left intact. It is therefore not untenable to see the same strengths emerging from a global arrangement. The "universal" right to free movement does not lead to the sacrifice of particular forms of membership.

Of course, Carens emphasizes that his espousal for open borders is not meant to rectify all "underlying injustices that make people want to move," but rather serves to draw attention to how Western complicity – namely, "our responsibility for poverty and oppression elsewhere" – push people to move (2000, 637). He refutes arguments on how open borders nullify countries' ability to self-determine membership by insisting on the primacy of seeing individuals as having "equal moral worth," which means that states that identify as being liberal have to reconsider whether their immigration policies uphold these values (1999, 1088).

That an open-borders approach may lead to the weakening of community ties and comes at the expense of those who are already members of the state is an issue that Carens considers. He states that "the homeless in rich societies today are not homeless because of the presence of immigrants but because of the unwillingness of the better off to address their plight" (2000, 642). These scenarios for him are false dilemmas.

Ultimately, Carens argues that in a world of open borders, as in the world of closed borders, "states would be morally obliged to ensure appropriate access to citizenship for immigrants and their children, to secure the legal right of residents and temporary foreign workers, and to create a political culture of respect and inclusion for migrants" (2013, 288). The key difference, however, is that open borders enshrine the freedom of mobility to all individuals, regardless of where they were born. In this respect, they are no longer tied to the circumstances of their birth. By upholding individual liberty as a primary requirement for justice, open borders advocates believe that ensuring the free movement of people is necessary for freedom.

COSMOPOLITAN PERSPECTIVES

Theorists of cosmopolitanism, like liberal theorists, underscore the primacy of the individual when making moral claims. However, cosmopolitan scholars' starting points are different from liberals. Whereas liberal thinkers begin from the perspective of the individual, whose freedom they see as being sacrosanct, cosmopolitan thinkers start from the perspective of the "cosmos" or the world and see all individuals as *kosmopolites* or "citizens of the world" who, "regardless of state or community affiliation, belong to the same community of people" (Wonicki 2009, 272). Distinctions on the basis of social locations such as race, class, gender, etc. and on the basis of nationality and citizenship are irrelevant when considering claims to justice. In subscribing to the perspective that "cosmopolitan justice is justice without borders" (Tan 2004, 1), cosmopolitans see the importance of creating a theory of justice that has as its basis the universality of human worth. They therefore argue that individuals have a "moral obligation not only towards their fellow citizens but also their fellow non-citizens" (Wonicki 2008, 272).

Theorists are divided on how these moral obligations are best met. On the one hand, there are those who believe that cosmopolitanism logically leads to forms of "global government" or "world citizenship" whereby all individuals have an equal say in governance (Linklater 1998, 37). Such understandings inevitably lead some theorists such as Raffaele Marchetti (2008) to endorse a "world migratory regime" based on "an interpretation of cosmopolitan citizenship in terms of freedom of movement" (472). Much like Carens, Marchetti argues that unrestricted movement across borders ensures that human beings can "maximize" their life choices (2008, 473). Unlike Carens, however, Marchetti is also committed to the creation of a political system that enshrines individuals' political capacity. His normative vision involves the creation of institutional arrangements that guarantee that all human beings have an equal say in determining policies, particularly as they pertain to immigration. Specifically, Marchetti's world migratory regime entails the creation of an international convention, which establishes codes of conduct and rules of governance, and an international agency, where "conflicting claims about the global issue of migration can be publicly discussed and weighed by all stakeholders on an equal standing" (2008, 486). States no longer have the sole authority to determine migration decisions, that is, "they would lose their absolute privilege of admission" (Marchetti 2008, 473) and would instead become obligated to follow global policies on immigration that are established by consensus.

On the other hand, there are cosmopolitan thinkers who see such arrangements as being "remote, bureaucratic, oppressive, and culturally bland" (Parekh 2002, 12). Instead, theorists such as Seyla Benhabib (2004) believe that cosmopolitan claims to universal justice can be respected while also recognizing the importance of community ties and state sovereignty. A way to reconcile both visions is through "porous borders" that Benhabib distinguishes from an open-borders framework by stressing that states should retain the capacity to regulate who enters their territories but that this right to control borders is limited by their humanitarian obligations and by cosmopolitan norms on human equality (2004, 221). Benhabib's concept of "porous borders" is an attempt to reconcile competing claims for state sovereignty and for universal human rights. For example, she argues that asylum seekers and refugees should have the right to "first admittance" within states but that states should be left to decide how to "regulate the transition from first admission to full membership" (2004, 3, 221). She also argues, to use another example, that while states that prevent people from being citizens on the basis of "sex, race, skin color ... disrespects their moral agency" and "contradicts the moral agency we owe each human being," (2007, 452), states should nevertheless be able to "determine *certain* conditions of entry as well as membership" (2007, 453). This means that asking prospective migrants to "show certain qualifications, skills, and resources" before allowing them into the country as citizens are justified because these criteria are attributes that would-be migrants have control over (2004, 139). Screening migrants in this way can help states meet their economic needs (2007, 453). To cite yet another example of Benhabib's attempts to establish a middle ground between state sovereignty and universal human rights, she holds that states have the right to determine naturalization policies but that these polices should not violate human rights norms (2004, 221).

Ultimately, Benhabib argues that while the competing imperatives to respect universal human rights and state sovereignty are constantly at odds, "the new politics of cosmopolitan membership is about negotiating this complex relationship between rights of full membership, democratic voice and territorial residence" (2007, 449).

While both liberal and cosmopolitan visions of open borders may appear to be completely untenable because of COVID-19, which led to all states closing their borders, open-border theorists argue that the COVID-19 moment actually *supports* their claims. David Owen (2021), for instance, points to how the current pandemic spread easily *in spite of* the existence of "highly regulated borders" (153). As he argues, "we have little reason to think that actually having open borders would make a significant difference to our exposure to the pandemic" (153). Owens claims that the concept of open borders, with its emphasis on looking broadly at inequalities between people and between states, can even draw attention to persisting global inequalities "in a world of globalized interdependency" and, in line with cosmopolitan visions outlined above, begin the process of building a "global basic structure" that addresses these inequities (157).

NO-BORDERS PERSPECTIVES

The no-borders approach departs from communitarian and liberal variants of "open borders." According to proponents of this approach, such as Nandita Sharma, the very existence of borders is problematic. She argues that borders reinforce inequalities. For instance, there are huge variations in the ways different groups experience borders, with affluent expatriates and international tourists facing no problems with crossing borders compared to migrant workers (2006, 4).

An open-borders approach thus does not rectify the vast inequities experienced by different groups of migrants, nor does it resolve issues of power inequality between states. Citing poet Minnie Bruce Pratt, Sharma (2006) asks, "why are we in thrall with the institutions that oppress us?" (139). She encourages the dismantling of an unequal and unjust "global system of nationalized apartheid" (141).

To understand the no-borders approach requires analysing its proponents' starting points. Communitarians value community and the importance of maintaining boundaries around it in order to better distribute key goods, such as membership, whereas Liberals see freedom – including the freedom not to be locked into the circumstances of one's birth – as the most fundamental human good. No-borders advocates, in contrast, take a larger, more macro-level perspective whereby the "relationship between capitalism and the equally global system of nation-states" is the focus (Sharma and Wright 2009, 117). Rather than taking as given the existence of nation-states, no-borders advocates interrogate *how* nation-states were first configured, arguing that the imperatives of capitalist expansion led to the subsequent establishment of modes of national governance that in turn led to the creation of national identities (Sharma and Wright 2009, 117).

This interrogation of how nation-states were formed meant that even nationalist liberation projects in former colonies were to the benefit of the bourgeois. Though nationalist liberation projects emerged because of the desire for autonomy and freedom from colonial rule, they have "failed to deliver liberation [and] have also successfully inserted new national states (and the people ruled by them) into the global order of capitalism with its reliance on national states to guarantee profits" (Sharma and Wright 2008, 118). Rather than becoming free from oppressive rule, these nationalist movements instead entrench the rule of a new set of elites "who are or come to be structurally embedded within the same global system of capitalist colonization as the previous sets of elites" and who dominate human beings (Sharma and

Wright 2008, 118). By using nationalist rhetoric, elites within nation-states – including previous colonies – eschew decolonization, deny the benefits they receive from being part of the global capitalist system, and justify "protect[ing] the nation from outside incursions against its sovereignty" (Sharma 2006, 43). Doing so invariably means fortifying borders against those deemed as threats, which may mean restricting the entry of migrants into the state or curtailing the rights of migrants who already live and work inside the state. In short, threats are both internal and external.

Reflecting on the emergence of xenophobic, far-right governments in the latter half of the 2010s, Walia (2021) notes further that borders are selectively extended, with far-right neoliberal governments using the current moment of the global pandemic as a "pretext" to extend the border (11). Rather than only being a *physical* boundary, nation-states deploy various "border governance strategies" to contain migrants and refugees: exclusion through the use of "walls, detention centres, and deportations" (79); "territorial diffusion" through the "internalization" of border regimes that lead to the apprehension of migrants inside the territory (e.g., immigration raids, policies restricting access to social welfare programs only to migrants with status) (84); "commodified inclusion" through practices that diminish migrant workers' labour rights and render them perpetually at risk of deportation (85); discursive practices that portray migrants and refugees as outsiders, with only some groups deserving of inclusion; and finally, the externalization of border practices that extend the reach of the state *beyond* the border (e.g., policies that allow for the apprehension of potential border crossers outside state territories) (87). The combined effect of these governance strategies is to entrench migrants' and refugees' exclusion into the everyday workings of the nation-state, making it difficult to ever get a reprieve from border violence; from a structural perspective, these border governance strategies ensure the continued dominance of richer nation-states in shaping immigration and trade policies through what Walia describes as "border imperialism" (87). Borders are therefore simultaneously extended to expand the reach of capital and strengthened to restrict the entry of human beings who have been displaced by such capitalist and colonial encroachments. Although borders are selectively opened to allow some migrants entry, Walia, citing David McNally, holds that migrants are accepted but "only on [nation-states'] own terms: frightened, oppressed, vulnerable" (2013, 70).

For no-borders advocates, then, having separate nation-states, within which human beings acquire citizenship shows the existence of a "global apartheid" regime. In contrast to liberals' belief that widening access to citizenship enables the enjoyment of equal rights, Sharma believes that instead, "citizenship has acted as a difference-making device ... [and] has constructed complex and layered levels of inequality" (2006, 142). For Sharma and Walia, the solution does not lie in widening access to citizenship, such as through Carens's approach, but rather to "reject global apartheid" (Sharma 2006) by creating a world without borders. For Sharma, having no borders means, first, that "people must have the power to stay; that is, people must have the power to prevent their displacement" (Sharma 2006, 165). This also means that "people must have the self-determinacy of movement" and are not made to stay in "holding pens" where they are "denied the option of leaving" and are not discriminated against in the places where they move (Sharma 2006, 165). Sharma (2006) urges a rethinking of existing arrangements by, for example, looking at how our investments in national territorial sovereignty and in nationalism encourage exploitation and reify divisions between communities (2020). Walia, too, sees in nationalism a "reactionary" response that dismantles possible forms of "internationalist solidarity" and that entrenches global apartheid (2021, 211). Only by opening one's mind to other possibilities can the "democratic potential" of the "multitude" against "the homogenizing dimensions of the national state's transcendent 'sovereign' power" be realized (2006, 167). During COVID-19, the structural inequities between states and the harms that exist from bordering regimes becomes even clearer: border closures mean refugees are rejected, migrant workers are compelled to labour in harmful work sites and placed into immigration detention, and police audits are conducted to supposedly check compliance with public health measures but actually function as a way to enforce immigration control (Walia 2021, 11–12). No-borders perspectives provide a critique of persisting structural inequities, encouraging consideration of more just arrangements. In the time of the pandemic, a no-borders approach makes clear that "flattening the curve requires flattening all inequality" (Walia 2021, 13).

INDIGENOUS CRITICISMS OF OPEN BORDERS/NO BORDERS

The inability of open- and no-borders perspectives to sufficiently account for the persisting effects of settler colonialism on the lives of Indigenous peoples nevertheless makes such structural critiques appear incomplete. Indigenous criticisms of the open-borders/no-borders positions are especially pertinent in light of the 2007 passage of the Universal Declaration on the Rights of Indigenous Peoples (UNDRIP) as well as the 2015 calls to action of the Truth and Reconciliation Commission of Canada that was tasked with understanding the practices and legacies of the Indian residential school system. The no-borders approach has been extensively criticized by those who see such approaches as diluting Indigenous claims for sovereignty and as ignoring migrant complicity in bolstering colonialist institutions established by White European settlers in settler colonies like Australia, the United States, and Canada. As Dean Itsuji Saranillio argues, "while migration in and of itself does not equate to colonialism, migration to a settler colonial space, where Native lands and resources are under political, ecological, and spiritual contestation, means the political agency of immigrant communities can bolster a colonial system initiated by White settlers. This is particularly so since the avenues laid out for success and empowerment are paved over Native lands and sovereignty" (2013, 286). To be clear, Saranillio recognizes that multiple pathways compel different migrants to leave their countries, with many, such as his own family, coming to countries like the United States forcibly because of war and economic necessity. Relatedly, Jodi Byrd recognizes the realities of forced migration by calling migrants "forced into the Americas through the violence of European and Anglo-American Colonialism and Imperialism around the globe" (2011, xix).

These observations resonate with Ena Dua and Bonita Lawrence's trenchant observation that anti-racist scholars, including anti-racist and postcolonial migration theorists and activists, have often failed to see their participation in Indigenous dispossession. The default assumption most anti-racist theorists make at the time, in fact, is that Indigenous struggles are much like those of other racialized groups, thereby ignoring how Indigenous communities' challenges are rooted in historical and ongoing colonization. As Dua and Lawrence argued:

"People of color are settlers. Broad differences exist between those brought as slaves, currently work as migrant laborers, are refugees without legal documentation or are emigres who have obtained citizenship. Yet people of color live on land that is appropriated and contested, where Aboriginal peoples are denied nationhood and access to their own lands" (2005, 134). Hence, terms such as "settlers of colour" are used to expose migrant complicity in ongoing Indigenous oppression.

From this vantage point, no-borders approaches may inadvertently ignore the specific struggles of Indigenous communities. Free movement in a borderless world, after all, ignores Indigenous ties to the land and risks minimizing how Indigenous nations are still enmeshed in an ongoing colonial relationship with settler states. Dua and Lawrence state that:

> Canada's immigration goals, then, can be used to restrict Aboriginal rights. Antiracist activists need to think through how their campaigns can preempt the ability of Aboriginal communities to establish title to their traditional lands. Recent tendencies to advocate for open borders make this particularly important. Borders in the Americas are European fictions, restricting Native people's passage and that of peoples of color. However, to speak of opening borders without addressing Indigenous land loss and ongoing struggles to reclaim territories is to divide communities that are already marginalized from one another. The question that must be asked is how opening borders would affect Indigenous struggles at reclaiming land and nationhood. (2005, 136)

Rather than advocating for no borders, the aforementioned theorists, as well as Corey Snelgrove, Rita Dhamoon, and Jeff Corntassel (2014) advocate having settlers and Indigenous people hold that white supremacy may affect these groups differently but "comes at the expense of all of us" (Saranillio 2013, 291). Seeing how the logics of capitalism and colonialism compel migrants' departure from their countries *and* have led to ongoing Indigenous dispossession make clear that the logics of white supremacist settler colonialism are imbued in both processes. Soma Chatterjee (2019) supports examining settler colonialism by seeing how "labour-capital-nation" affects Indigenous and immigrant communities, seeing poignant commonalities in how both communities have histories of displacement and marginalization.

Indigenous critiques of both approaches also point to how border debates tend to conceive of borders exclusively as human made. None of these approaches considers how "white supremacy, capitalism, and heteropatriarchy have targeted and continue to murder, disappear, attack, criminalize and devalue [Indigenous] bodies, minds, and spirits" and how "several of the plant and animal nations we share territory with have been exterminated" (L. Simpson 2016, 21). Seen in this light, even the notions of justice proposed by open-borders and no-borders advocates is a Western concept that is at odds with Indigenous notions of justice, which involves "the return of land, the regeneration of Indigenous political, educational, and knowledge systems, the rehabilitation of the natural world, and the destruction of white supremacy, capitalism, and heteropatriarchy" (L. Simpson 2016, 21).

A potential way forward is to create movements centred on Indigenous resurgence. Doing so entails going beyond the open-borders or no-borders debates, which reify white settlers' claims to sovereignty by leaving unchallenged nation-states (open-borders approaches) and potentially ignoring Indigenous ties to the land, to communities, and to the natural world (open-border and no-border approaches), though we emphasize that proponents of both approaches have clarified previous theories to make clear their ongoing solidarity with Indigenous movements (see, e.g., Sharma 2021; Walia and Dilts 2019, 18).

Indigenous resurgence uses Indigenous "institutions, values, and ethics" to "re-center and reinvigorate Indigenous nationhood" while also paving the way for the eradication of other power structures, such as "capitalism and "colonial gender systems" (Snelgrove et al. 2014, 18). Through Indigenous resurgence, "building new worlds" and creating "constellations of co-resistance" with other movements (L. Simpson 2016, 31) – including with migrant movements – becomes possible.

Taking these visions into account, in the next section we offer a critical reflection that bridges open-borders/no-borders and Indigenous resurgence perspectives. Importantly, we bring critical attention to a feminist care ethics approach, illustrating what such an approach brings when building solidarities and considering new possibilities.

We offer this reflection as an analytical alternative to the Canadian state's current practices of containing diversity.

COUNTERING CONTAINING DIVERSITY: TOWARDS A POLITICS OF SOCIAL AND GLOBAL JUSTICE

The normative theoretical perspectives on migration and borders that we have discussed stem from the communitarian, liberal/cosmopolitan, and critical traditions. They may well be understood as competing moral visions based on what different theories prioritize. Reflecting on these also allows for better differentiating what is at stake in each of these accounts. We do this with an eye to considering how the open-borders and no-borders perspectives might be bridged and built upon.

Communitarians uphold the sanctity and boundedness of communities. There may be instances in which this perspective is especially compelling. For example, it may be seen to offer a roadmap for protecting a way of life and for encouraging a sense of belonging. Also, it is a perspective that is easily understood and applied in our world of nation-states. However, when it comes to global migration, the communitarian perspective effectively propels a justification of the status quo world of nation-states, and relatedly, a range of biases, exclusions, and forms of violence at the border. Given the concerns we have highlighted both with respect to global migration and with respect to Canada's turn towards containing diversity, we do not find this a vision that is either compelling or offering much by way of remedy for the inequities we see in the field of migration.

In contrast with communitarian theories, the arguments and debates concerning variants of open borders and no borders share a commonality in challenging how things stand, although they do so in different, and even contradictory, ways as concerns the future of the nation-state. Liberals believe that freedom – and thus individuals' rights to free movement through open borders – should be upheld, and cosmopolitans see the universality of human rights and the connection of all human beings to a global cosmos as necessitating policies such as world migratory regimes or porous borders. Conversely, no-borders theorists indict the perpetuation of capitalist and colonialist practices and see the abolition of borders as being the only way forward to rectify endemic global inequality.

Indigenous criticisms of such approaches sharply point to how the opening and removal of borders can significantly dilute Indigenous claims. Both open-borders and no-borders approaches tend to accept the primacy of Westphalian sovereignty, which holds that sovereignty is "territorial, hierarchical and exclusive" and neglects how such conceptions are incompatible with Indigenous notions of sovereignty (Ellerman and O'Heran 2021, 26; see also Bauder and Mueller 2021). Although open-borders and no-borders approaches trenchantly critique how the state uses "force, violence, and exclusionary practices" to maintain its boundaries (A. Simpson 2020, 686), its adherents risk framing the "problem" as one that can be solved through opening *or* abolishing borders while leaving intact legal orders that leave intact the Westphalian state. Seeing the open-borders/no-borders debate so starkly also affects the types of questions we ask and indeed limits how we think of what a radical, transformative future could look like.

As such, at this juncture we find it useful to draw from the work of Harald Bauder (2016), who suggests the open-borders and no-borders positions should be approached dialectically. Doing so entails recognizing that while the two positions are contradictory, they are not necessarily antagonistic (Bauder 2016, 68). In his estimation, the two positions are not antagonistic, as they share being "critiques of existing border regulations and of bordering practices that distinguish between people based on their place of birth, citizenship, ancestry, race or wealth" (Bauder 2016, 57). The purpose that a critical and dialectical approach to open borders/no borders serves is twofold. First, it raises our awareness concerning a contingent possibility in our world of nation-states for open borders (2016, 60). Second, it raises our awareness of the utopian idea of no borders as a "possibilia," a term he draws from the work of German theorist Ernst Block. For Bauder, "possibilia is based on conditions and practices that do not yet exist and that we cannot yet imagine with today's concepts and ways of making sense of the world" (2016, 60).

We suggest that the act of considering open borders as well as no borders presents an important path into a new kind of conversation on migration by opening the political imagination. At the same time, however, we note some words of caution about such a conversation.

Will Kymlicka observes that a fundamental dividing line in contemporary political philosophy exists between theorists (like Bauder) who advocate for "mobility based" interests and rights and those who advocate for "place-based" interests and rights (Kymlicka 2018, 172). We therefore take seriously Kymlicka's concern that international instruments supporting minority and particularly Indigenous rights may be jeopardized in the absence of consideration of interests connected to a specific territory and being able to control entry into territory (Kymlicka 2018, 172). Indeed, as he points out in considering the invasion of the Americas in the first place, "the interests that Europeans had in gaining access to indigenous peoples' territory were granted weight by theories of terrestrial cosmopolitanism, exacerbated by prejudice about the value of the Indigenous ways of life that were radically disrupted by European settlement" (Kymlicka 2018, 172).

We end by considering three key issues that might be considered along the path of a new conversation which may work to provide guideposts for imagining, if not building, a better world. These issues relate to care, to solidarity, and to the rights of Indigenous peoples.

Care and Relationality, Solidarity, and Indigeneity

As we have elaborated in this book, relationships of care as well as care work are highly devalued in immigration processes. For instance, care work is often not considered part of "high skilled" immigration. The family is also a site of migration restriction. As part of a new kind of conversation on migration, a critical ethics of care perspective, we argue, considers issues largely unaddressed by the extant normative debate on borders and may perhaps even present a new way of conceptualizing migration altogether (Abu-Laban 2012).

Rather than viewing human beings as atomized individuals, we see value in care ethicists' vision of human beings as interdependent and embedded in relationships with other people (Held 1993, 2006; Kittay 1999). Indeed, human beings' life choices are typically constructed on the basis of their "roles, obligations, and senses of attachment to others" (Tronto 2001, 72; see also Munawar 2019). Conceptualizing migrants' decision to leave their home countries to seek greener economic pastures abroad, or to traverse dangerous routes to find refuge away from persecution, can in most cases be best understood not as an individual decision but as a decision to ensure the well-being of their families (Francisco-Menchavez 2018).

By highlighting the attachments human beings have to each other and, especially for Indigenous theorists, the relationships we have with the environment in which we live (Thomas 2015), a relational perspective shows the shortcomings of liberal approaches that are too individualist and that uncritically endorse without nuance values like "freedom, autonomy, and toleration" (Robinson 2010, 132; see also Kittay 2001, 523). Care ethics also raise questions about liberal approaches for presenting a flawed, bifurcated mapping of relationships that do not fully capture existing realities, such as by contrasting "autonomy and dependence, sovereignty and intervention, and self-determination and imperialism" (Robinson 2010, 134).

In addition, by emphasizing the interdependence characterizing human beings' and states' relationships with each other, care ethicists also stress the responsibility to alleviate human suffering. This might happen through, for example, generous refugee policies, and stem not from notions of "cosmopolitan justice" but from a recognition of a "common history and an interdependent future" (Robinson 2010, 139). Care ethicists also illustrate the shortcomings to communitarian approaches that take as given inequalities that emerge within the community, such as relationships of care that lead women to be unequal to men, and that negate consideration of policies that are needed to redress such inequality (Kittay 2001).

The COVID-19 moment highlighted strains on health care systems globally. In various jurisdictions it led to closing schools as well as physical distancing and isolation in homes. These developments have made clear to many the essential nature of care work in and outside the home. Such care work includes the work involved in food supply chains and grocery stores as well as the childcare required for those working in areas deemed essential. In the words of Nancy Fraser, responses to the pandemic "lights up a whole understanding" about what she calls "the unpaid bill for social reproduction" under conditions of neoliberal capitalism (cited in Chang 2020). Just as Fraser queries "why would we have non-essential work at all, why wouldn't we just have leisure?" we likewise query why immigration policy would continue to devalue care work through an invidious discourse of "skills," as if unpaid or paid care work matters less.

Critical feminist ethics of care perspectives point to how relationships of power and interdependency define human relationships and states' relationships with each other. These perspectives pave the way for a more nuanced understanding of citizenship and migration. By showing how interdependency and power characterize relationships at the micro, meso, and macro levels, care ethicists suggest that it is important to analyse migration policies within the context of these networks (Williams 2011), allowing for a better appreciation for how "the nature and extent of dependence and interdependence in social, political, and economic life is constantly shifting and evolving, with different kinds of costs and benefits for different actors" (Robinson 2010, 141). Seen in this light, debates take on a different dimension and, as a result, produce a different set of answers concerning the range of issues raised in this volume. This includes, for example, debates about whether and how many refugees to accept, the abolition or the reform of migrant domestic worker programs, the trade-off on how many family-class versus economic-class migrants to accept, what discourses of citizenship and membership are being promoted by the state, and whether borders should be open or not.

Care ethics encourages a way out of such oppositional frameworks. Such an approach looks first at how different communities experience and resist the border in order to see the values these communities uphold. An examination of the values that communities uphold reveals the salience of *relationality*. Specifically, a critical ethics of care approach shows how cross-border solidarity networks build relations of care despite the presence of border controls and restrictive immigration policies, showing the potency of care within, across, and between borders.

In the Canadian context, perhaps one of the most salient instances of such cross-border solidarity and a relational concern for care concerns the work of refugee support groups on both sides of the US–Canada border. These groups have been trying to ensure that refugees crossing from the United States to Canada are able to safely make a claim in Canada. For instance, on the US side in Plattsburgh, New York, the coalition of faith, service, and activist groups "Plattsburgh Cares" has worked to ensure that asylum seekers crossing from the United States to Canada have gloves and mittens along with information (Dickson 2020; Plattsburgh Cares n.d.). Information for refugees seeking asylum in Canada includes advice on what to expect when crossing from the United States to Canada at a regular crossing, as well as what to expect when crossing from the United States to Canada at the irregular crossing of Roxham Road (Plattsburgh Cares n.d.). On the Canadian side, Canada's March 2020 announcement in response to the COVID-19 pandemic that refugee claimants arriving from the United States would be returned resulted in a coalition forming. This coalition involved the Canadian Council for Refugees, Amnesty International Canada, the Canadian Association of Refugee Lawyers, and the British Columbia Civil Liberties Union issuing a joint call for the Canadian government to re-open the border to asylum claims (Dickson 2020).

Along with defending refugees, combating racism is another site of cross-border solidarity and relational care. As noted in this book, Canadian government efforts to combat racism have at best been uneven, and also it can be further observed that they have been accorded relatively limited funding by the Canadian state. These realities help sustain the argument that Canada is a place where racism goes generally unacknowledged as a major social problem (Smith 2003; Thompson 2020, 245). In contrast, another instance of cross-border organizing and solidarity can be seen in the struggle against racism and the intersectional organizing evidenced in responses to Black Lives Matter. From its origins in the wake of a US verdict exonerating George Zimmerman for the murder of Trayvon Martin, a seventeen-year-old Black boy, Black Lives Matter emerged into a now global movement, working particularly in the United States, United Kingdom, and Canada in an effort to combat racism. Notably, it has been especially effective in drawing attention to police brutality, incarceration, and racial inequality, themes which Debra Thompson notes have had resonance in such diverse locales as London, Paris, Palestine, Sydney, as well as Toronto (Thompson 2020, 241). Speaking to the Canadian context, Thompson argues that in its creation by queer Black women, and in its use of intersectional understandings of identity, Black Lives Matter has worked at grassroots levels to advocate for all peoples of African descent, including women, immigrants, and the undocumented (Thompson 2020, 241). The resonance of this movement across lines of social divide in Canada and around the world was also evident in the global mass protests that took place – in spite of conditions of COVID-19 health restrictions – to decry the murder of an unarmed

African American man, George Floyd, by Minneapolis police. Video images of a police officer pressing his knee on his neck even as Floyd pleaded for air were reflected in the common slogan and chant heard at the protests: "I can't breathe" (Rycroft and Jordans 2020). From this brutal act of police violence came global expressions of relationality and care.

Not least, No One Is Illegal, which began in Germany in 1997, has emerged as an international network of loosely affiliated anti-racist and religious groups focused on the rights of asylum and non-resident immigrants to stay. In the Canadian context, by the 2000s, No One Is Illegal operated in several cities, including Vancouver, Toronto, Ottawa, and Montreal, and overtly questions the legitimacy of borders and their implications for migrants and refugees as well as for Indigenous peoples. As such, as observed by Craig Fortier, the network of No One Is Illegal groups in Canada serve to challenge traditional understandings of citizenship rights and the state being benevolent and also have worked to nuance a no-border stance by reframing justice for migrants in relation to Indigenous sovereignty (Fortier 2013, 275). In shaping new framings of migrant justice and challenging borders, No One Is Illegal groups have impacted political discourse by "challenging the legitimacy of the colonial Canada state's right to determine immigration by supporting calls for indigenous sovereignty" (Fortier 2013, 289).

By focusing on how the colonial state harms both Indigenous and migrant groups, it becomes possible to identify the ways Indigenous and migrant struggles are interlinked. The colonial state and settler colonial state harm both: the same violence inflicted by the settler-colonial state that led to the dispossession of Indigenous Peoples is the same violence that colonial states inflicted on their colonies. Such violence placed former colonies in relationships of dependency to affluent countries and ultimately pushed refugees and asylum seekers to flee their homes and compelled immigrants to seek economic opportunities abroad. Rather than accepting, as many immigration researchers do, the validity of the present-day state system, when we question the very legitimacy of how colonial and settler-colonial states "came to be" (Volpp 2015, 296), we can then understand how Indigenous peoples and migrant communities constitute a "community of shared fate" (Williams 2010, 41). Under these conditions it might be possible to envisage that the colonial *and* settler-colonial state become the target of Indigenous and migrant communities' activism. As Harsha Walia (2012) notes, for example, it is not possible to "supplant the colonial logic of the state itself" without efforts made to challenge its dominance through the creation of new frameworks, new imaginings, and new ways of being. Such new frameworks may even be ushered in not through legal text or statistical findings, but through creative outputs, such as poetry, which, as Anne McNevin (2020) describes, "are forms of knowledge and witnessing that cut through the obfuscations of bureaucratic, scientific and legal language."

Examining such networks of solidarity that are borne out of these new framings opens the possibility of considering the questions, tensions, and possible negotiations that might emerge in the open-/no-borders calls and their interface with Indigenous rights, as well as Indigenous resurgence (Snelgrove et al. 2014). For instance, Edmonton's Brown, Black and Fierce! Collective – whose membership includes "Indigenous People, Black People and People of Colour" – is one such attempt to challenge colonial logics. They do this through their use of "ethical relationality," which Cree Scholar Dwayne Donald argues "seeks to more deeply understand how our different histories and experiences position us in relation to each other" (as quoted in Todd 2015). For the Brown, Black and Fierce! Collective, being in solidarity with each other additionally entails forming linkages across time by looking at the histories of the relationships between Indigenous People and People of Color, including histories of these communities "teaming up" (Roberts as quoted in Todd 2015).

Canada has relied on immigration precisely because it is a settler colony, and as a particular form of state formation, settler colonies need to also be centred in international migration research more than they have been (Abu-Laban 2019). In the final analysis, we would be remiss to discuss any form of new conversation concerning migration and the political imagination in the absence of stressing the central place issues of Indigeneity ought to hold in such a discussion. A focus on solidarity may provide new avenues into considering relational realities where border resistance is central to caring relations and social change. We take it as significant, for example, that in 2015 as awareness of Syrian refugees mounted, Mi'kmaq leader Stephen Augustine sought acknowledgement of the model Mi'kmaq set in place historically to welcome immigrants and those fleeing for safety arguing that refugees "need to come to North America and we need to welcome them in the way Aboriginal People welcomed people to eastern Canada and Canada in general" (cited in Todd 2015). Likewise, it is significant that in 2006 the Sandy Bay Anishinaabe First Nation sought to adopt a Nigerian refugee claimant through traditional practices, but the Canadian Federal Court overruled the adoption and deported her anyway (Ritskes 2015). Such examples show the points of common interest that may provide guideposts out of contested theoretical debates through relationality, care, and practice.

Such practices of solidarity may be set to grow. Within Canada, the calls to action of the 2015 Truth and Reconciliation Commission (TRC) drew attention to the relationship of newcomers and Indigenous peoples and have served to raise public awareness not only of residential schools but to ongoing issues of colonial control pertaining to land, power and sovereignty. A big part of the TRC involves centering Indigenous knowledges, especially in educational institutions. Part of this means being cognizant of Indigenous ways of knowing that are relational and that involve relationships with more-than-human kin. On the ground, there are grassroots sites of encounter that have newly emerged in the wake of the TRC calls involving cities and civil society groups. For example, in Edmonton these have included refugees being welcomed at airports by First Nations groups, or in the face of the restrictions of COVID-19, efforts in 2020 to jointly commemorate the national Indigenous Peoples Day in Canada alongside World Refugee Day through online programming (Roots of Resilience, 2020).

Encouraging "co-resistance" (L. Simpson 2016) between migrants and Indigenous peoples also enables more respect for the environment and to the land. Indigenous understandings of relationality, which emphasize "the *process* of connection," hold value in "*responsibility* and *reciprocity* towards human and more-than-human kin" (Dudgeon and Bray 2019, 3; emphasis in original). Both racialized migrant communities and Indigenous communities are disproportionately impacted, for instance, by climate change. On the one hand, many Indigenous communities are located in areas that are "particularly exposed to climate change and environmental degradation" and are pushed out by forest fires and rising sea levels (Chazallnoel 2018). On the other hand, working-class racialized migrant communities tend to be concentrated in areas that have close proximity to toxic waste and with poor air quality (Lammy and Bapna 2019). Consequently, "environmental racism has long blighted Indigenous people and people of color" (Lammy and Bapna 2019).

Thus, Indigenous and migrant activist efforts calling for actions against climate change *and* deeper respect for the land and for more-than-human kin are illustrative of the shared fate of both. Such initiatives are suggestive of the way forms of solidarity may continually emerge. In doing so, path can be found that involves greater care for migrants, Indigenous peoples, and the planet. Undoing colonial and settler-colonial ways of doing, being, and knowing by seeking sites of solidarity is a crucial way forward.

BIBLIOGRAPHY

Abu-Laban, Yasmeen. "A World of Strangers or a World of Relationships? The Value of Care Ethics in Migration Research and Policy." In *Rooted Cosmopolitanism: Canada and the World*, edited by Will Kymlicka and Kathryn Walker, 156–77. Vancouver, BC: UBC Press, 2012.

– "Immigration and Settler-Colonies Post-UNDRIP: Research and Policy Implications." *International Migration* (December 30, 2019, Early View): 1–17.

Abu-Laban, Yasmeen, Radha Jhappan, and François Rocher. *Politics in North America: Redefining Continental Relations*. Peterborough, ON: Broadview Press, 2008.

Bader, Veit. "Citizenship and Exclusion: Radical Democracy, Community, and Justice. Or What Is Wrong with Communitarianism?" *Political Theory* 23, no. 2 (1995): 211–46.

Bauder, Harald. *Migration Borders Freedom*. London and New York: Routledge, 2016.

Bauder. Harald, and Rebecca Mueller. "Westphalian v. Indigenous Sovereignty: Challenging Colonial Territorial Governance." *Geopolitics* (2021). https://doi.org/10.1080/14650045.2021.1920577.

Benhabib, Seyla. *The Rights of Others: Aliens, Residents, and Citizens*. New York: Cambridge University Press, 2004.

– "Democratic Exclusions and Democratic Iterations: Dilemmas of 'Just Membership' and Prospects of Cosmopolitan Federalism." *European Journal of Political Theory* 6, no. 4 (2007): 445–62.

– "Claiming Rights across Borders: International Human Rights and Democratic Sovereignty." *American Political Science Review* 103, no. 4 (2009): 691–704.

Byrd, Jodi. *The Transit of Empire: Indigenous Critiques of Colonialism*. Minneapolis: University of Minnesota Press, 2011.
Carens, Joseph. "Aliens and Citizens: The Case for Open Borders." *Review of Politics* 49, no. 2 (1987): 251–73.
– "Open Borders and Liberal Limits: A Response to Isbister." *International Migration Review* 34, no. 2 (2000): 636–43.
– *The Ethics of Immigration*. Oxford: Oxford University Press, 2014.
Carman, Tara. "COVID-19 Mortality Rate Higher in Neighbourhoods with More Visible Minorities: Stats Can." *CBC News* (November 17, 2014). www.cbc.ca/news/canada/british-columbia/covid19-minorities-health-bc-canada-1.5801777.
CERC, The Canada Excellence Research Chair in Migration and Integration. "Interactive Dashboard Helps Assess COVID-19 Impact on Immigrant Workers." June 12, 2020. www.ryerson.ca/cerc-migration/news/2020/06/Interactive-Dashboard-Canadian-Perspective-Survey/.
Chang, Clio. "Taking Care of Each Other Is Essential Work: As Coronavirus Shows Us the Value of Care, Theorist Nancy Fraser Asks Us to Imagine a More Socialist Feminist Future." *Vice* (April 7, 2020). www.vice.com/en_ca/article/jge39g/taking-care-of-each-other-is-essential-work.
Chatterjee, Soma. "Immigration, Anti-racism, and Indigenous Self-determination: Towards a Comprehensive Analysis of the Contemporary Settler Colonial." *Social Identities* 25, no. 5 (2019): 644–61.
Chazalnoel, Mariam Traore. "Environmental Migration and Indigenous Peoples: What Is at Stake?" IOM-UN Migration (September 11, 2018). https://medium.com/@UNmigration/environmental-migration-and-indigenous-peoples-what-is-at-stake-edb077c028b7.
Cho, Sumi, Kimberlé Williams Crenshaw, and Leslie McCall. "Toward a Field of Intersectionality Studies: Theory, Applications and Praxis." *Signs: Journal of Women in Culture and Society* 38, no. 4 (2013): 785–810.
Clarkson, Stephen. *Uncle Sam and Us: Globalization, Neoconservatism and the Canadian State*. Toronto: University of Toronto Press, 2002.
Cyr, Alex, and Xiao Xu. "Canadian Universities Are Largely Rejecting Mandatory Vaccination Measures Despite Growing Concerns among Students, Professors." *Globe and Mail* (August 11, 2021). www.theglobeandmail.com/canada/article-university-of-ottawa-makes-covid-19-vaccination-mandatory-for-in-class/.
Dickson, Janice. "Four Asylum Seekers Turned Away at Canada-US Border." *Globe and Mail* (April 3, 2020). www.theglobeandmail.com/politics/article-six-asylum-seekers-turned-away-at-canada-us-border/.
Ellerman, Antje, and Ben O'Heran. "Unsettling Migration Studies: Indigeneity and Immigration in Settler Colonial States." In *Research Handbook on the Law and Politics of Migration*, edited by Catherine Dauverge, 21–34. Northampton, MA: Elgar, 2021.
Engster, Daniel. *The Heart of Justice*. Oxford: Oxford University Press, 2007.

Eze, Michael. "What Is African Communitarianism? Against Consensus as a Regulative Ideal." *South African Journal of Philosophy* 27, no. 4 (2008): 386–99.

Fortier, Craig. "No One Is Illegal Movements in Canada and the Negotiation of Counter-National and Anti-colonial Struggles from within the Nation-State." In *Producing and Negotiating Non-Citizenship: Precarious Legal Status in Canada*, edited by Luin Goldring and Patricia Landolt, 274–90. Toronto: University of Toronto Press, 2013.

– "No One Is Illegal, Canada Is Illegal! Negotiating the Relationships between Settler Colonialism and Border Imperialism through Political Slogans." *Decolonization: Indigeneity, Education & Society* (September 21, 2015). https://decolonization.wordpress.com/2015/09/21/no-one-is-illegal-canada-is-illegal-negotiating-the-relationships-between-settler-colonialism-and-border-imperialism-through-political-slogans/.

Francisco-Menchavez, Valerie. *The Labor of Care: Filipina Migrants and International Families in the Digital Age*. Urbana-Champaign: University of Illinois Press, 2018.

Friend, David. "Live Nation Canada to Require Vaccination Proof or Negative Test at Concerts." *Global News* (August 18, 2021). https://globalnews.ca/news/8121736/live-nation-canada-to-require-vaccination-proof-or-negative-test-at-concerts/.

Goodyear-Grant, Elisabeth, Allison Harell, and Laura Stephenson. "Concern about Pandemic Differs across Gender and Race Lines: Women and Racialized Canadians Worry More about COVID-19 Largely because They Are More at Risk. This May Have Future Mental Health Implications." *Policy Options* (May 21, 2020). https://policyoptions.irpp.org/magazines/may-2020/concern-about-pandemic-differs-across-gender-and-race-lines/.

Government of Canada. *COVID-19: Travel, Testing, Quarantine, and Borders*. 2021. https://travel.gc.ca/travel-covid/travel-restrictions/wizard-start.

Held, Virginia. *Feminist Morality: Transforming Culture, Society, and Politics*. Chicago: University of Chicago Press, 1993.

– *The Ethics of Care*. New York: Oxford University Press, 2006.

Ingram, David. "Immigration and Social Justice." *Peace Review* 14, no. 4 (2002): 403–13.

James, Matt. "Neoliberal Heritage Redress." In *Reconciling Canada: Critical Perspectives on the Culture of Redress*, edited by Jennifer Henderson and Pauline Wakeham, 31–46. Toronto: University of Toronto Press, 2013.

Kittay, Eva Feder. *Love's Labour: Essays on Women, Equality, and Dependency*. New York: Routledge, 1999.

– "A Feminist Public Ethic of Care Meets the New Communitarian Family Policy." *Ethics* 111, no. 3 (2001): 523–47.

Kobayashi, Audrey. "Colonialism as a Precondition of Uneven COVID-19 Experiences." In *Impacts of COVID-19 in Racialized Communities*, 52–5. Ottawa, ON: Royal Society of Canada, 2020.

Koopmans, Ruud, and Michael Zern. "Cosmopolitanism and Communitarianism: How Globalization Is Reshaping Politics in the Twenty-First Century." In *The Struggle over Borders: Cosmopolitanism and Communitarianism*, edited by Pieter De Wilde, Ruud Koopmans, and Wolfgang Merkel, 1–34. Cambridge: Cambridge University Press, 2019.

Kymlicka, Will. "Immigration, Citizenship, Multiculturalism: Exploring the Links." *The Political Quarterly* 74, no. S1 (2003): 195–208.

– "Minority Rights." In *The Oxford Handbook of International Political Theory*, edited by Chris Brown and Robyn Eckersley, 166–78. Oxford: Oxford University Press, 2018.

Lamy, David, and Manish Bapna. "There Is No Climate Justice without Racial Justice." *Time Magazine* (May 3, 2021). https://time.com/6017907/climate-emergency-racial-justice/.

Lawrence, Bonita, and Enakshi Dua. "Decolonizing Antiracism." *Social Justice* 32, no. 4 (2005): 120–43.

Lazaruck, Suzanne. "Covid-19: Are We Ready? BC's Indoor Mask Policy Relaxed for Canada Day." *Vancouver Sun* (June 21, 2021). https://vancouversun.com/news/local-news/are-we-ready-covid-indoor-mask-policy-relaxed-for-canada-day.

Lenard, Patti. "Culture, Free Movement and Open Borders." *The Review of Politics* 72, no. 4 (2010): 627–52.

Lightman, Naomi. "Caring during the COVID-19 Crisis: Intersectional Exclusion of Immigrant Women Health Care Aides in Canadian Long-Term Care." *Health and Social Care* (2021). https://doi.org/10.1111/hsc.13541.

Linklater, Andrew. "Cosmopolitan Citizenship." *Citizenship Studies* 2, no. 1 (1998): 23–41.

Marchetti, Raffaele. "Toward a World Migratory Regime." *Indiana Journal of Global Legal Studies* 15, no. 2 (2008): 471–87.

McNevin, Anne. "Borders, Migration, and the Urgency of Imagination." *Vacarme* (February 16, 2020). https://vacarme.org/article3308.html.

Meilaender, Peter. *Toward a Theory of Immigration*. New York: Palgrave-Macmillan, 2001.

Munawar, Sarah. *In Hajar's Footsteps: A De-colonial and Islamic Ethic of Care*. PhD diss., University of British Columbia. https://open.library.ubc.ca/soa/cIRcle/collections/ubctheses/24/items/1.0387144.

Owen, David. "Open Borders and the COVID-19 Pandemic." *Democratic Theory* 7, no. 2 (2021): 152–9.

Parekh, Bhikhu. "Cosmopolitanism and Global Citizenship." *Review of International Studies* 29, no. 1 (2003): 3–17.

Pevnik, Ryan. *Immigration and the Constraints of Justice: Between Open Borders and Absolute Sovereignty*. Cambridge: Cambridge University Press, 2011.

Plattsburgh Cares. "For Asylum Seekers Crossing into Canada." N.d. https://plattsburghcares.org/wp-content/uploads/2019/01/newEnglish_FINAL_5-15-18.pdf.

Ritskes, Eric. "Against the Death Maps of Empire: Contesting Colonial Borders through Indigenous Sovereignty." *Decolonization: Indigeneity, Education & Society* (October 14, 2015). https://decolonization.wordpress.com/2015/10/14/against-the-death-maps-of-empire-contesting-colonial-borders-through-indigenous-sovereignty/.

Robertson, Roland. *Globalization: Social Theory and Global Culture*. London: Sage Publications, 1992.

Robinson, Fiona. "After Liberalism in World Politics? Towards an International Political Theory of Care." *Ethics & Social Welfare* 4, no. 2 (2010): 130–44.

– "Care Ethics, Political Theory and the Future of Feminism." In *Care Ethics and Political Theory*, edited by Daniel Engster and Maurice Hamington, 293–311. Oxford: Oxford University Press, 2015.

Roots of Resilience. "The Meaning of Welcoming: A Conversation and Celebration." 2020. www.rootsresilience.ca.

Rycroft, Rick, and Frank Jordans. "Thousands Protest across 3 Continents to Honor George Floyd and Support the Black Lives Matter Movement." *Time* (June 6, 2020). https://time.com/5849493/black-lives-matter-george-floyd-protest-worldwide/.

Sandelind, Clara. "Territorial Rights and Open Borders." *Critical Review of International Social and Political Philosophy* 18, no. 5 (2015): 487–507.

Saranillio, Dean Itsuji. "Why Asian Settler Colonialism Matters: A Thought Piece on Critiques, Debates, and Indigenous Difference." *Settler Colonial Studies* 3, nos. 3–4 (2013): 280–94.

Schain, Martin A. *Shifting Tides: Radical-Right Populism and Immigration Policy in Europe and the United States*. Washington, DC: Migration Policy Institute, 2018. www.migrationpolicy.org/research/radical-right-immigration-europe-united-states.

Sharma, Nandita. *Home Economics: Nationalism and the Making of 'Migrant Workers' in Canada*. Toronto: University of Toronto Press, 2006.

– *Home Rule: National Sovereignty and the Separation of Natives and Migrants*. Durham, NC: Duke University Press, 2020.

– "Against All Nationalism." *Briarpatch Magazine* (March 26, 2021). https://briarpatchmagazine.com/articles/view/against-all-nationalisms.

Sharma, Nandita, and Cynthia Wright. "Decolonizing Resistance, Challenging Colonial States." *Social Justice* 35, no. 3 (2009): 120–38.

Simpson, Audra. "The Sovereignty of Critique." *South Atlantic Quarterly* 119, no. 4 (2020): 685–99.

Simpson, Leanne Betasamosake. "Indigenous Resurgence and Co-Resistance." *Critical Ethnic Studies* 2, no. 2 (2016): 19–34.

Smith, Andrea. "Indigeneity, Settler Colonialism, White Supremacy." In *Racist Formation in the Twenty-First Century*, edited by Daniel Martinez HoSang, Oneka LaBennet, and Laura Pulido, 66–90. Berkeley: University of California Press, 2012.

Smith, Malinda. "Race Matters and Race Manners." In *Reinventing Canada: Politics of the 21st Century*, edited by Janine Brodie and Linda Trimble, 108–30. Toronto: Prentice Hall, 2003.

Snelgrove, Corey, Rita Dhamoon, and Jeff Corntassel. "Unsettling Settler Colonialism: The Discourse and Politics of Settlers and Solidarity with Indigenous Nations." *Decolonization: Indigeneity, Education & Society* 3, no. 2 (2014): 1–32.

Tan, Kor-Chor. *Justice without Borders: Cosmopolitanism, Nationalism, and Patriotism*. New York: Cambridge University Press, 2004.

Thomas, Amanda C. "Indigenous More-Than-Humanisms: Relational Ethics with the Hurunui River in Aotearoa New Zealand." *Social & Cultural Geography* 16, no. 8 (2015): 974–90.

Thompson, Debra. "The Intersectional Politics of Black Lives Matter." In *Turbulent Times, Transformational Possibilities? Gender Politics Today and Tomorrow*, edited by Alexandra Dobrowolsky and Fiona MacDonald, 240–57. Toronto: University of Toronto Press, 2020.

Todd, Zoe S. "Enacting Solidarity between Displaced and Dispossessed Peoples: Resistance-through-Art-in-the-Prairies." *Decolonization: Indigeneity, Education & Society* (October 13, 2015). https://decolonization.wordpress.com/2015/10/13/enacting-solidarity-between-displaced-and-dispossessed-peoples-resistance-through-art-in-the-prairies/.

Tronto, Joan. "Who Cares? Public and Private Caring and the Rethinking of Citizenship." In *Women and Welfare: Theory and Practice in the United States*, edited by Nancy J. Hirschmann and Ulrike Liebert, 65–83. New Brunswick, NJ: Rutgers University Press, 2001.

Volpp, Leti. "The Indigenous as Alien." *UC Irvine Law Review* 5 (2015): 289–326.

Walia, Harsha. "Decolonizing Together: Moving beyond a Politics of Solidarity toward a Practice of Decolonization." *Briarpatch Magazine* (January 1, 2012). https://briarpatchmagazine.com/articles/view/decolonizing-together.

– *Undoing Border Imperialism*. Oakland, CA: AK Press, 2013.

– *Border and Rule: Global Migration, Capitalism, and the Rise of Racist Nationalism*. Winnipeg, MB: Fernwood, 2021.

Walia, Harsha, and Andrew Dilts. "Dismantle and Transform: On Abolition, Decolonization, and Insurgent Politics." *Abolition Journal* 1 (2018): 12–21.

Walzer, Michael. *Spheres of Justice: A Defense of Pluralism and Equality*. New York: Basic Books, 1983.

– "Response to Veit Bader." *Political Theory* 23, no. 2 (1995): 247–9.

Wherry, Aaron. "One Country, Two Pandemics: What COVID-19 Reveals about Inequality in Canada." *CBC News* (June 13, 2020). www.cbc.ca/news/politics/pandemic-covid-coronavirus-cerb-unemployment-1.5610404.

Williams, Fiona. "Towards a Transnational Analysis of the Political Economy of Care." In *Feminist Ethics and Social Policy: Towards a New Global Political*

Economy of Care, edited by Rianne Mahon and Fiona Robinson, 127–44. Vancouver, BC: UBC Press, 2011.

Williams, Melissa. "Citizenship as Agency within Communities of Shared Fate." In *Unsettled Legitimacy: Political Community, Power, and Authority in a Global Era*, edited by Steven D. Berenstein and William Coleman, 33–52. Vancouver, BC: UBC Press, 2010.

Wilson, Kerissa. "Nearly 80% of COVID-19 Cases in Toronto Were among Racializd Groups in November." *CTV News* (January 21, 2021). https://toronto.ctvnews.ca/nearly-80-of-covid-19-cases-in-toronto-were-among-racialized-groups-in-november-1.5276918.

Wonicki, Rafal. "Cosmopolitanism and Liberalism: Kant and Contemporary Liberal Cosmopolitanism." *Synthesis Philosophica* 48, no. 2 (2009): 271–80.

Yuval-Davis, Nira. "Intersectionality and Feminist Politics." *European Journal of Women's Studies* 13, no. 3 (2006): 193–209.

Conclusion and Future Directions

In this book we have considered immigration and the (re)making of Canadian citizenship from 2001–21. The time period is bookended by two events that had, and continue to have, global repercussions: the fallout from the September 11, 2001, attacks in the United States, which led to the global war on terrorism, and the World Health Organization declaring COVID-19 a global pandemic on March 11, 2020. We have shown how, in contrast to Canada's international image as an inclusive and tolerant country welcoming different groups of immigrants, the immigration system has in reality been focused on containing diversity and privileging a hierarchy of immigrants and would-be citizens. In the contemporary period, we argued that containing diversity takes place primarily through neoliberalism and criminalization. Although interrelated, these processes are paradoxical. Neoliberalism, in valuing global markets, has gone hand in hand with policy efforts to compete for select immigrants valued for their role in the economy. Unlike neoliberal valuing of global markets, criminalization tends towards closure, justified by positioning immigrants as dangerous threats to public safety and security and to national values. Linking immigrants with danger and threat is also a hallmark feature in the discourse of xenophobic populist movements, political parties, and politicians who engage in invidious us/them distinctions (see Schain 2018 for a discussion of the United States and Europe). We have also shown the ways in which health has re-emerged as more central to containing immigration in the wake of the COVID-19 pandemic.

In addressing the complex variation that characterizes global and Canadian immigration trends over close to two decades, our theoretical guideposts have come from three traditions. We have utilized a critical political economy approach, especially in considering Canada in a North American and global context (Abu-Laban et al. 2008; Clarkson 2002). We also have made use of an intersectional lens, developed out of critical race theory and anti-racist feminism, to illuminate how multiple points of difference intersect in creating disadvantage and/ or privilege as concerns the ability to move in a world of states, as well as to resettle and obtain citizenship (Cho et al. 2013; Yuval-Davis 2006). Finally, we have found a feminist care ethics approach useful for drawing attention to human and non-human interdependence, the importance of care and caring labour, and a stepping stone to considering the relevance of not merely asking "what is" but also "what ought to be," as well as in considering questions of justice in distinct ways (Engster 2007).

In this concluding chapter, we provide an overview of our findings and conclude briefly by considering future research directions, with the understanding that themes of migration and diversity will continue to be important in Canada and globally for the foreseeable future.

CONTAINING DIVERSITY: OVERVIEW OF FINDINGS

Our book is divided into three sections. The first section contextualized containing diversity, discussing the shifting landscape of international migration as well as historical and contemporary practices of containing diversity in Canada. As we established, there are three key trends characterizing contemporary migration internationally.

The first concerns the growth in the numbers of refugees worldwide who are primarily located in countries of the Global South and increasingly blocked by countries of the north from entering. When claiming asylum, refugees are also increasingly subjected to measures like detention or having their claims deemed inadmissible. A second trend is for wealthy states to prioritize economic considerations in immigration responses, which has corresponded with a move towards selectively targeting and competing for high-skilled immigrants. In this global competition, those selected for their high skills are favoured for citizenship, whereas growing numbers of temporary migrants, who may bring important skills and fill labour shortages, are excluded from permanent settlement. While skilled and temporary labour migration are increasing, a third evident trend is one of immigration restriction on family migration. Canada fits these three wider international trends, and as such exemplifies an approach to migration that we have termed "containing diversity." Our analysis of the Canadian government's efforts to contain diversity challenges the notion of Canada as a completely open multicultural community built on immigration and diversity. We instead reveal how the immigration system is gated against the supposed risks posed by "others" whose difference is variously marked by religion, race, ethnicity, country of origin, class, and gender.

Part two of the book discussed specific immigration pathways into Canada and how migrants and refugees have increasingly found it difficult to access these pathways because of efforts to contain diversity.

Chapter three focused on refugees, who are widely seen to be at the greatest disadvantage in navigating migration and settlement in a new state. As we noted, the majority of refugees reside in countries of the Global South, and female refugees in particular are less mobile than men, and therefore less able to exercise rights. Many refugees are also experiencing protracted situations in which they have been in exile from their home country for more than five years but are in limbo because they have not achieved resettlement or permanent residency elsewhere. We examined the unique ways that Canada has responded to refugees abroad, including through private sponsorship – a tradition that was also (re)activated when Justin Trudeau's newly elected government responded to Syrian refugees in 2015–16, admitting some 25,000 in his first months in office.

However, while officially part of Canada's "humanitarian" stream, refugees are also, in our estimation, the harbinger group in experiencing the full sweep of immigration controls fortified by rationales at the nexus of neoliberalism and criminalization. By placing Canada in a regional North American and global context, we illuminated how recent policy developments echo European trends. In particular the

Canada–US Safe Third Country Agreement, which came into force in 2004, has closed avenues to asylum in Canada at official entry points along the US–Canada border. In more recent years, this Safe Third Country Agreement encouraged larger numbers of people to cross irregularly and unsafely from the United States to Canada in order to make an asylum claim. In March 2020 the Trudeau Liberals, in the name of responding to COVID-19, further announced that asylum seekers entering irregularly from the United States would be placed in detention for fourteen days and/or immediately turned back to the United States. These developments raised serious questions for us about the extent to which Canada is meeting both the spirit and obligations of the United Nations refugee convention.

We also examined the way the 2018 United Nations Global Compact on Refugees has legitimated Canada's increasingly economic versus humanitarian approach to admitting refugees. We described how Canada is working with UNHCR in experimenting with a new program to facilitate the entry of high-skilled refugees who meet Canada's labour market needs. The Economic Mobility and Pathways Project brings humanitarian and economic considerations together by fast-tracking refugees who are highly skilled. This program, while experimental and small, reflects on the logic and biases of the larger immigration program, not simply humanitarianism. In light of such trends, as well as challenges to the spirit and/or obligations of refugee law, we made a case for considering normative frameworks, including a feminist care ethics, that might also guide practice.

In chapter four, we examined changes to Canada's economic immigration programs following the establishment of the Immigration and Refugee Protection Act (IRPA) in 2002. Our analysis revealed how these changes led to an amplification of neoliberal immigration trends in Canada. The federal government's decision to move from a human capital to an employment approach to immigration led decision-making to be downloaded onto private stakeholders, such as employers and private industry. Such downloading ensures that the most desirable citizens are those who not only have the requisite skills and qualifications but who also can prove that they are self-sufficient by already having job offers at hand. This fundamental belief in the value of "high skills" and high education was evident, we showed, in the streamlining of the Express Entry Program, under which exists the Federal Skilled Workers Program, the Federal Skilled Trades Program, and the Canadian Experience Class Programs, along with the more widespread use of Provincial Nominee Programs. Our analysis of these programs indicated how the mobilization of skill-based and education-based criteria ultimately devalued reproductive care work, whether paid or unpaid, and also produced discrimination based on gender, class, and national origin. As we noted, other "classes" of immigrants, such as family-class migrants, temporary foreign workers, refugees, and asylum seekers, were consequently deemed "not as worthy" because of the perceived insufficiency of their economic contributions.

Chapter five assessed Canada's growing reliance on temporary labour migration. Specifically, we examined how the tendencies towards neoliberalization and criminalization in the form of threat have led to the expansion of temporary labour migration policies. On the one hand, temporary labour migrants are seen as critical to Canada's labour market. Increased labour demands, which have grown deeper during the COVID-19 pandemic, have led the Canadian government to heavily recruit temporary foreign workers in fields such as caregiving, farming and meatpacking, which came to be deemed "essential" during the pandemic. On the other hand, temporary labour migrants are simultaneously seen as potential threats to public security and public health. As we noted, during the COVID-19 pandemic, seasonal agricultural workers and low-skilled temporary foreign workers reported encounters that scapegoated them for the spread of COVID-19. Particularly during times of economic duress, temporary foreign workers were immediately targeted for "stealing" jobs from citizens, despite the labour contributions they have made and the fact that they are working in industries that have a hard time recruiting Canadian workers. As such, temporary foreign workers have to grapple with the contradictions of being "essential" workers who are also deemed a threat to the nation.

Policy changes instituted by the Harper Conservatives to limit the ability of temporary foreign workers to gain permanent residency highlighted further the neoliberalization and criminalization of Canadian immigration policy. These changes have largely been left intact by the Trudeau Liberals. Indeed, the division made between the low-skilled Temporary Foreign Workers Program, where temporary foreign workers continue to have work permits tied to their employers, and the International Mobility Program, where most of the primarily medium- to high-skilled workers have open work permits and have more opportunities to transition to permanent residency, together exemplify how much more high-skilled workers are valued in Canada.

Chapter six examined how the trends of increased criminalization, which present immigrants as untrustworthy threats, and increased neoliberalism are in effect within Canada's family-class immigration policies. Although family reunification is an important component of Canada's immigration programs, the Harper government and, to a lesser extent, the Trudeau government, sought ways to restrict family immigration. To highlight the federal government's attempts to limit family immigration, we analysed a number of policies that attempted to ascertain the legitimacy of "real" family ties. These attempts to limit family migration were evident, for example, in the government's intensified use of DNA testing, which is inevitably biased towards biological kinship. Likewise, we analysed changes in sponsorship requirements and changes to parent and grandparent immigration as salient examples. The Harper Conservative government portrayed these changes *both* as a way to secure the country against fraudulent migrants *and* to protect Canada's welfare state from spurious claims. The latter in particular showed how family-class migrants, especially women, were seen as non-ideal citizens. Because they were coming into the country as dependents and were not evaluated on the basis of their skills or education, they were seen as being undesirable in comparison to economic migrants.

Chapter six also addressed how the Canadian government's policies prioritizing family reunification have led to massive inequities for some groups of migrants and not others, such as seasonal agricultural workers, caregivers, and "low-skilled" temporary foreign workers. Overall, our findings showed the human costs of increased criminalization and neoliberalization of immigration policy. In the final analysis, we illuminated how all groups of potential migrants have to demonstrate proof of their economic competitiveness in order to enter Canada, whether they are "skilled" migrants, family-class migrants, or temporary foreign workers. In effect, this waters down other values that have theoretically formed the basis for Canadian immigration, such as the rights of migrants to live with their families, the importance of a multicultural and anti-discriminatory ethos, and the need to meet international obligations towards refugees. At the same time, however, migrants have to constantly prove that they are not dangerous security threats and are not "taking advantage" of Canadian generosity. Put simply, migrants are asked to meet criteria that constantly evolves in order to justify their continued presence.

Part Three of the book addressed the larger question of membership, belonging, and normative questions of what the future should look like for Canada.

Chapter seven assessed internal debates and redefinitions of policy that have led to heightened restrictions to citizenship. Here, we examined the relationship between immigration, citizenship, and multiculturalism – or what Will Kymlicka has memorably characterized as a "three-legged stool" (2003). His analysis of the early 2000s in Canada found a pattern of strong support for both immigration and multiculturalism, which mitigated concerns with citizenship in evidence elsewhere like the United Kingdom (Kymlicka 2003, 202). Our analysis for the period 2002–20, however, illustrated that the naturalization of immigrants became a novel field of policy transformation and contestation in the 2010s in Canada. A series of changes presided over by the Harper Conservative government refashioned citizenship legislation and tested newcomers more rigorously via a new citizenship guide and higher requirements for passing the citizenship test. Overall, we argued, this policy transformation re-cast Canadian citizenship as a valuable resource that needed to be protected from the potential fraud, abuse, or criminality of immigrants. As a valuable resource, Canadian citizenship also became harder to acquire for immigrants and easier to lose for both naturalized Canadians as well as Canadians born abroad after the first generation.

Parallel to these developments in relation to citizenship and naturalization, symbolic shifts were happening with the federal policy of multiculturalism under the Harper Conservatives. As we noted, these symbolic shifts were tied implicitly to the stereotyped construction of Muslim immigrants and citizens as threats and were likewise reflective of the "multicultural backlash" expressed in many Western countries. Characteristic of expressions of anti-Muslim racism in the post-9/11 period, these stereotypes fed into gendered constructions of Muslim men as barbaric and Muslim women as in need of rescue from these men. In relation to multiculturalism policy, we showed how these symbolic shifts stressed "loyalty" to Canada and to liberal democratic norms and laws, as well as to secularism and gender equality. At the same time, efforts to fight racism in the "here and now" gave way to a new program of neoliberal heritage redress, aimed at offering select apologies and commemoration of historic wrongs, and showcasing how, by hard work and determination, minorities have thrived in Canada despite historic hardships (see also James 2013). This development comprised part of a trend in which anti-racist initiatives garnered less support, and forms of racialized inequality intensified.

While Canada has served as a model of successful immigrant integration and multiculturalism among states, as we noted in chapter six, naturalization rates for incoming were down significantly by the time of the most recent 2016 census, in comparison with the 1990s and mid-2000s. It is not clear that this will change significantly soon. After assuming office in late 2015, the Trudeau government did repeal and/or amend several features of the Harper-era citizenship legislation, including that citizenship could be revoked from naturalized dual citizens convicted of terrorism or treason. They also put renewed emphasis and funding into combating contemporary racism, a development that mirrors increased attention to racism in Canadian civil society, especially following the murder of George Floyd by Minneapolis police in 2020. However, notably, the Liberal government left intact the Harper-era provisions allowing for the revocation of citizenship on the basis of fraud, as well as limiting transmission of citizenship to those born abroad to the first generation. Additionally, the Trudeau Liberals have never questioned the orthodoxy of testing itself, even though this is an instrument which clearly demands competencies of naturalized citizens not required of birthright citizens. Indeed, as we highlighted, citizenship testing has emerged as a form of immigration management and control in many countries, including in Canada. Despite promises, a new guide to citizenship has proven sluggishly slow to be produced. As a result, the calls to action of the 2015 Truth and Reconciliation Commission have yet to be implemented, despite promises on the part of the Trudeau Liberals to incorporate newcomer education about the Indian residential school system and implementing an oath of citizenship that recognizes treaties.

In all these ways, our empirical analysis showcases nearly two decades of deeply racialized and exclusionary trends that characterize immigration and the politics of citizenship in twenty-first-century Canada. After examining troubling empirical trends that indicate to us the realities of containing diversity, we pivoted in chapter eight to reflect more fully on normative visions of what should be. We considered various theoretical approaches to the question of borders, ranging from approaches that endorse the status quo of closed borders, often espoused by communitarians, to liberal approaches to open borders and to abolitionist demands for no borders. We then discussed the emancipatory potential of Indigenous resurgence, which calls for a dismantling of unjust power structures *and* a centering of Indigenous knowledge and broader elements of relationality. For us, a critical feminist ethics of care would be one that draws from Indigenous resurgence, decentres embedded notions of Westphalian sovereignty, and takes seriously Indigenous approaches that foreground a greater complexity of "relationships and interdependencies" (Moreton-Robinson, as quoted in Bauder and Mueller 2021, 11). Such a radical ethics of care helps clarify what a more-just future looks like. We highlighted how the contemporary moment requires widening notions of care to include not just human beings but also non-humans and to the environment we live in. We unpacked moments of solidarity, whether across borders and between and within different communities, to illustrate how various struggles are interlinked. These moments show to us that despite the clear incompatibilities between different normative approaches, recognizing these instances of subversion and solidarity opens us to a more *relational* future that decentres and even eradicates settler colonialism.

FUTURE DIRECTIONS

In concluding this book, we recognize that there are other moments of containing diversity that present challenges to migrants, to refugees, and to various communities that will be even more pressing in the future. The following is a non-exhaustive list of these challenges that we believe merits further attention.

First, at the time of writing in the late summer of 2021, different variants of the COVID-19 pandemic have been discovered, leading to reversals in policies intended to re-open borders. Walia (2021) notes that many nation-states use COVID-19 as a "pretext" to further police the border *and* to police the actions of migrants and refugees within states, all under the guise of ensuring public health and safety (11). A number of questions occur based on this background context, as well as ever-increasing technological developments that strengthen border protection. *How are liberal immigrant-receiving states amending their border policies? Will there be a return to the pre-COVID-19 status quo ante? Are states selectively opening their borders to welcome* some *immigrants while simultaneously imposing more restrictions for others, and if so what are the consequences? How are states deploying AI in immigration and border enforcement?*

Second, global disparities in access to vaccines have exacerbated the public health and safety risks faced by Global South countries. While countries like the United States have made booster shots available for some of its citizens and debate how to increase vaccine uptake of unwilling citizens, many Global South countries have yet to access vaccines at all to meet the needs of citizens. Yet other countries only have access to vaccines that are less effective. *How is "vaccine nationalism" – defined as the tendency of states during the pandemic to hoard vaccines (Billky and Bown 2020) – affecting who gets to immigrate and to cross borders? What are the effects of uneven access to vaccines on prospective and current migrants? What is the future of health regulations in immigration, including "vaccine passports" and the use of quarantine?*

Third, Canada has not wavered on its commitment to continue accepting immigrants during the pandemic, declaring its intention to accept 400,000 immigrants in 2021 (Government of Canada 2021). However, it has been observed that a number of policy choices are implicated in these increasing numbers. The government moved quickly to modernize its application system through the use of online tools. Since 2021, it prioritized labour market needs and eased the entry of international students. Lastly, it raised permanent immigrant numbers by focusing on processing the citizenship applications of temporary residents who are already in Canada (Griffith 2022, 2–3). Yet we wonder about the specifics of this policy. *Will Canada continue prioritizing the entry of skilled economic immigrants, or will new opportunities for immigration for essential "low-skilled" or "unskilled" workers who are part of essential industries be prioritized? Will the latter be given access to Canadian citizenship, given recent Temporary Resident to Permanent Resident programs that were introduced in 2021? How will Canada fill its immigration targets in the face of border closures and travel restrictions?*

Fourth, in August 2021, the United States withdrew from Afghanistan, leading to an influx of Afghanis seeking refuge. In response, Prime Minister Trudeau issued a statement emphasizing that the Canadian government will not recognize the Taliban and will accordingly accept "thousands" of refugees fleeing the conflict (Aiello 2021). The urgent need for people to find places of refuge away from violence has increasingly intensified and will likely escalate in the years to come. The United Nations, in fact, declares that "conflict and violence are currently on the rise," with "more countries experiencing violent conflict" in 2016 than at any point in the previous thirty years (United Nations 2021). As a result, we expect that affluent countries will face mounting pressure to accept more refugees, especially in light of research that shows how Global South countries disproportionately accept the majority of the world's refugees. *What are the lived experiences of people who are escaping from violent situations? How will states accommodate ever-increasing demands for increased refugee intakes? What will "immigration diplomacy" – which rich blocs like the European Union deploy to contain asylum seekers within the borders of poor states in exchange for foreign aid – look like in the years to come? How will the needs of refugees, including those in protracted refugee situations be met? What will the impact of the global compacts on migration and refugees be, and what is the future for multilateral international cooperation on migration and refugees?*

Fifth, humans continue to be displaced for environmental reasons. Natural disasters, such as the August 2021 earthquake in Haiti and Typhoon Haiyan in November 2013 in Southeast Asia, create refugees. Similarly, climate change has also led to mass displacement. In 2017 climate emergencies led to the displacement of 68.5 million people (Podesta 2019), a figure that is expected to rise in the future. Understanding how to accommodate internal climate migrants is also increasingly becoming a challenge for rich states. For instance, within the Pacific Northwest in North America, we witnessed a heat wave that led to 486 sudden deaths in Vancouver, British Columbia, and that also led to people losing their homes. In British Columbia, for example, the village of Lytton was completely depleted (Cecco 2021). Although racist, anti-immigration arguments have long been a part of some segments of the environmental movement, with many seeing population control and closed immigration policies as "being essential to protecting the environment" (Salazar and Hewitt 2001, 295), the reality that climate change is creating more climate migrants makes clear that simplistic, bifurcated notions that one is either pro-environment or pro-immigration are simply untenable in the present day. *How will countries contend with the increased numbers of climate migrants? How will they manage internal migration wrought by climate emergencies? Can international legal definitions of "refugees" accommodate those fleeing their homes for environmental reasons? Can "special mobility rights" be given to climate migrants (Marshall 2015)?*

Sixth, the rise in far-right, xenophobic movements in liberal, immigrant-receiving states like Canada has led to an increase in anti-Muslim, anti-Asian, anti-Black, and anti-Indigenous hate crimes. These hate crimes include the mosque shootings in Quebec in 2017; murderous rampages in an area known as being the hub for Korean immigrants in Toronto in 2018 and against a Muslim family in London, Ontario, in 2019; and increased police brutality against Black and Indigenous people across Canada, to name but a few examples. *Will far-right, xenophobic movements shape Canadian politics and affect Canadian immigration policy? How do these far-right, xenophobic movements affect the everyday lives of Black, Indigenous, and People of Colour (BIPOC) in Canada? Have there been increases in these communities' experiences of xenophobia?*

Seventh, the establishment of grassroots social movements, such as the International League of People's Struggles (ILPS) and the Migrants Rights Network (MRN) – to name but a few movements – show that communities themselves are not waiting for policy elites to resolve the aforementioned challenges. These movements are engaged in on-the-ground work imagining alternative structures, providing support for underserved migrant communities in ways that governments cannot or will not (McNevin 2011; Nyers and Rygiel 2012). Importantly, these movements are also organizing with Black and Indigenous movements. *What do these coalitions look like? What happens when widespread demands for decolonization and Indigenization are brought alongside calls to abolish unjust systems of power? Will these movements continue flourishing? What sites of solidarity and tension exist among them? What visions of the future do these movements bring? Will there ever be a global consensus – seen not only in terms of state consensus but consensus among different grassroots communities – on migration?*

Some of the biggest economic, political, and social issues today relate to migration. Indeed, as Banting and Soroka observe, immigration has generated considerable "cultural anxiety" that has fuelled negative perceptions in many countries (2020, 824). In contrast, Canada is often lauded for its high levels of public support for immigration. But as their assessment of the evolution of Canadian attitudes towards immigration shows, Canadians share some of these same anxieties.

However, these perceptions are balanced by a belief that immigration is good for the Canadian economy. Banting and Soroka assert that Ministers of Immigration and Multiculturalism as well as Ministers of Finance and Economic Development all have a role to play in maintaining positive attitudes towards immigration. As they argued, "the ability of the government to preserve low levels of unemployment – and by extension – to foster Canadians' faith in the economic benefits of immigration is also critical" (2020, 834). As we showed in this book, states like Canada have tended to contain diversity in order to better manage migration and migration-related changes in relation to perceived national interests. How "national interest" is defined is thus a key political question.

As such, it becomes especially important to think more deeply about how to ethically confront the many questions and challenges that we have identified as lying ahead. We believe that an ethics of migration that prioritizes care and relationality provides a more humane starting point to resolving these challenges. After all, the migration-related challenges that we see as being the most urgent are those that require all of us to truly consider our ethical obligations to each other, to our immediate communities, to the rest of the world, and to the planet.

BIBLIOGRAPHY

Abu-Laban, Yasmeen, Radha Jhappan, and François Rocher. *Politics in North America: Redefining Continental Relations*. Peterborough, ON: Broadview Press, 2008.

Aiello, Rachel. "Trudeau Says Thousands of Afghans to Be Resettled in 'Coming Weeks' Amid 'Dire Situation.'" *CTV News* (August 16, 2021). www.ctvnews.ca/politics/federal-election-2021/trudeau-says-thousands-of-afghans-to-be-resettled-in-coming-weeks-amid-dire-situation-1.5548879.

Banting, Keith, and Stuart Soroka. "A Distinctive Culture? The Sources of Public Support for Immigration in Canada, 1980–2019." *Canadian Journal of Political Science* 53, no. 4 (2020): 821–38.

Bauder, Harald, and Rebecca Mueller. "Westphalian v. Indigenous Sovereignty: Challenging Colonial Territorial Governance." *Geopolitics* (2021). https://doi.org/10.1080/14650045.2021.1920577.

Bollyky, Thomas, and Chad P. Bown. "The Tragedy of Vaccine Nationalism." *Foreign Affairs* 99 (2020): 96–109.

Cecco, Leyland. "'Lytton Is Gone': Wildfire Tears through Village after Record-Breaking Heat." *The Guardian* (July 1, 2021). www.theguardian.com/world/2021/jul/01/lytton-wildfire-heatwave-british-columbia-canada.

Cho, Sumi, Kimberlé Williams Crenshaw, and Leslie McCall. "Toward a Field of Intersectionality Studies: Theory, Applications and Praxis." *Signs: Journal of Women in Culture and Society* 38, no. 4 (2013): 785–810.

Clarkson, Stephen. *Uncle Sam and Us: Globalization, Neoconservatism and the Canadian State*. Toronto: University of Toronto Press, 2002.

Engster, Daniel. *The Heart of Justice*. Oxford: Oxford University Press, 2007.

Government of Canada. *Supplementary Information for the 2021–2023 Immigration Levels Plan*. June 18, 2021. www.canada.ca/en/immigration-refugees-citizenship/news/notices/supplementary-immigration-levels-2021-2023.html.

Griffith, Andrew. "How the Government Used the Pandemic to Sharply Increase Immigration." *Policy Options*, April 2022. https://policyoptions.irpp.org/magazines/april-2022/immigration-increase-pandemic/.

James, Matt. "Neoliberal Heritage Redress." In *Reconciling Canada: Critical Perspectives on the Culture of Redress*, edited by Jennifer Henderson and Pauline Wakeham, 31–46. Toronto: University of Toronto Press, 2013.

Kymlicka, Will. "Immigration, Citizenship, Multiculturalism: Exploring the Links." *The Political Quarterly* 74, no. S1 (2003): 195–208.

Marshall, Nicole. "Toward Special Mobility Rights for Climate Migrants." *Environmental Ethics* 37, no. 3 (2015): 259–76.

McNevin, Anne. *Contesting Citizenship*. New York: Columbia University Press, 2011.

Nyers, Peter, and Kim Rygiel, eds. *Citizenship, Migrant Activism and the Politics of Movement*. Abingdon, UK: Routledge, 2011.

Podesta, John. "The Climate Crisis, Migration, and Refugees." *Brookings Blum Roundtable on Global Poverty* (July 25, 2019). www.brookings.edu/research/the-climate-crisis-migration-and-refugees/.

Salazar, Debra, and John Hewitt Jr. "Think Globally, Secure the Borders: The Oregon Environmental Movement and the Population/Immigration Debate." *Organization and Environment* 14, no. 3 (2001): 290–310.

Schain, Martin A. *Shifting Tides: Radical-Right Populism and Immigration Policy in Europe and the United States*. Washington, DC: Migration Policy Institute, 2018. www.migrationpolicy.org/research/radical-right-immigration-europe-united-states.

United Nations. "A New Era of Conflict and Violence." *UN Shaping Our Future Together*, 2021. www.un.org/sites/un2.un.org/files/un75_conflict_violence.pdf.

Walia, Harsha. *Border and Rule: Global Migration, Capitalism, and the Rise of Racist Nationalism*. Winnipeg: Fernwood, 2021.

Yuval-Davis, Nira. "Intersectionality and Feminist Politics." *European Journal of Women's Studies* 13, no. 3 (2006): 193–209.

Select Podcast and Documentary Suggestions

FAMILY IMMIGRATION

Podcast Episode Suggestions

1. Berena, M.E. "Mom, Let's Talk." *North York Community House* (2019). www.nych.ca/mom-lets-talk.

   Summary: The podcast talks about the challenges of family separation and the experiences of family reunification after years of separation.

Documentary Suggestions

1. Dai, D. *My First 150 Days*. TVO/Documentary Channel (2017). www.tvo.org/video/documentaries/my-first-150-days.

   Summary: The documentary follows the Banico family, a family of Filipino immigrants, as they move and adjust to a new land. Melona Banico came to Canada under the Caregiver Program and waited for nearly ten years to bring her family to Canada. The documentary captures the obstacles of having a transnational life and the hardships and joy of family reunification.

2. Fernando, R., T. Segura, and J. Simms. *Becoming Labrador*. National Film Board of Canada (2018). www.nfb.ca/film/becoming-labrador/.

Summary: A group of Filipinos, hopeful to give their families better opportunities but in the long run are experiencing the hardships of being away from their families.

REFUGEES & ASYLUM SEEKERS

Podcast Episode Suggestions

1. Brassard, C. "Trudeau's 'Welcome to Canada': Three Years Later." *The Big Story* (2019). https://thebigstorypodcast.ca/2019/04/23/refugees/.

   Summary: Guest speaker discusses the aspects of refugee immigration connected to Trudeau's stance on welcoming refugees in Canada. It also tackles whether Canada is indeed welcoming to refugees as well as loopholes in the immigration policies on refugees.

Documentary Suggestions

1. Nosheen, H. *After the Crossing: Refugees in Canada.* The Fifth State (2017). www.youtube.com/watch?v=8ba45eXFBW8.

   Summary: The documentary follows cases of individuals from El Salvador and Turkey who are seeking asylum in Canada. It focuses on their experiences, the process of seeking refuge, and the issues and challenges they faced.

2. Siad, A. and R. Siad. *19 Days.* National Film Board of Canada (2016). www.nfb.ca/film/19_days/.

   Summary: Features refugee families in Canada during their first nineteen days – following the timeline established by the federal government.

3. Horlor, S. and S. Adams. *Someone Like Me.* TVO Docs. National Film Board of Canada (2021). www-nfb-ca.ezproxy.library.yorku.ca/film/someone-like-me/.

   Summary: A group of queer people from Vancouver decided to sponsor and support Drake, a queer refugee from Uganda who seeks freedom in expressing their identity but was met with unexpected challenges during their resettlement.

TEMPORARY FOREIGN WORK

Podcast Episode Suggestions

1. Bowen, L.S. and F. Johnson. "The Nanny (Season 2)." *Secret Lives of Canada* (August 27, 2019). www.cbc.ca/radio/secretlifeofcanada/who-are-the-women-who-ve-looked-after-canada-s-children-1.5261955.

   Summary: Examines Canada's history of recruiting women (primarily from Global South countries) to come to Canada to work as care and domestic workers.

2. Brassard, C. "The Problem with Canada's Temporary Migrant Labour Program." *The Big Story* (2019). https://thebigstorypodcast.ca/2019/10/30/migrant-workers-canada/.

   Summary: Tackles the majors of Canada's Agricultural Workers Program and the exploitative experiences of Mexican farm workers as covered and shared by the guest speaker.

3. Hurley, S. "The Care Economy: What's at Stake if We Don't Make Change Now." *Spreaker* with the Canadian Centre for Policy Alternatives (August 24, 2021). www.spreaker.com/user/voicedradio/care-economy-what-s-at-stake-if-we-don-t.

   Summary: Talks about what policy changes need to be made to protect and compensate care workers for fair labour, especially since that federal election is coming.

4. Greene, S. "Stranded Servants: Nannies and Cleaners during Lockdown (Ep: 369)." *CANADALAND* (May 10, 2021). www.canadaland.com/podcast/369-stranded-servants-nannies-and-cleaners-during-lockdown/.

   Summary: Addresses the invisibility of women workers who do care work at the peak of the pandemic while exploring their experiences with the hopes of becoming permanent residents of Canada.

5. Hiebert, D. "Temporary Foreign Workers, Precarious Labour and the Politics of (in)Equality (Season 1, Episode 2)." *UBC Global Migration Podcast* (June 7, 2020). https://migration.ubc.ca/news/global-migration-podcast-season-1/.

Summary: Speaks on how the pandemic highlighted the importance of temporary foreign workers within the Canadian economy but at the same time, the inequalities that temporary foreign workers face when it comes to financial and health factors.

Documentary Suggestions

1. Lee, M.S. *Migrant Dreams*. TVO Docs (2019). www.youtube.com/watch?v=-_8bjt37xYo.

   Summary: Covers the stories of women working in Ontario's greenhouses under the Temporary Worker Program and have endured exploitative conditions because of their temporary status.

SKILLED ECONOMIC IMMIGRATION PROGRAMS

Podcast Episode Suggestions

1. Eitizaz, S. "Canada's One-Time Immigration Program Is a Doorway to Dreams but with a Deadline." *This Matters* (May 13, 2021). www.thestar.com/podcasts/thismatters/2021/05/13/canadas-special-one-time-immigration-program-opens-door-to-residency-and-dreams.html.

   Summary: Discusses the unique program announced in April 2021 that allowed a pathway to permanent residency for recent international graduates and temporary workers deemed essential during the COVID-19 pandemic.

2. Yeung, R. "Immigrants Need Not Apply, with Ali Ahmed." *Changing Lenses: Diversify Your Perspectives* (May 19, 2021). www.changinglenses.ca/podcast/episode/4b3df0ed/ep11-immigrants-need-not-apply-with-ali-ahmed.

   Summary: Covers the experiences and struggles of Ali Ahmed, an immigrant, in building his career in Canada. It discusses the additional barriers and issues faced by immigrants in the workplace.

MULTICULTURALISM

Podcast Episode Suggestions

1. Johnson, B. and L. Bowen. "The Indian Act (Season 2)." *The Secret Life of Canada* (October 24, 2019). https://curio.ca/en/audio/the-indian-act-22864/.

   Summary: Looks at the roots of the Indian Act during the late 1800s and how it is still embedded in Canadian policies, which has impacted Indigenous communities.

Documentary Suggestions

1. Mondesir, E. *The Banker Ladies*. Vimeo (2020). www.caroline-shenaz-hossein.com/projects-1.

   Summary: Racialized communities are often excluded from mainstream services such as banks, cooperatives, and community development are fundamental options for racialized communities to fend for themselves. *The Banker Ladies* explores the idea of community building to show up and support one another through the concept of ROSCAs (Rotating Savings and Credit Associations).

2. Bellange, T. *Doctors without Residency*. National Film Board of Canada (2010). www-nfb-ca.ezproxy.library.yorku.ca/film/doctors_without_residency.

   Summary: Shows systemic racism plays a role in the medical field. Foreign doctors are being refused to practise residency since it's insufficient to fit the "Canadian" standards.

3. Saäl, M. *Zero Tolerance*. National Film Board of Canada (2004). www-nfb-ca.ezproxy.library.yorku.ca/film/zero_tolerance-edu/.

   Summary: Shows the prejudices among marginalized groups in Montreal and how police use their power when it comes to minority youth.

Index

Note: Page numbers in *italics* indicate figures and tables.

Aas, Katja Franko, on good and bad mobilities, 20
Abolition: borders and 283; domestic worker programs, 286
Acadians, 31
Act Respecting Immigration and Immigrants (1869), 33
Act to Consolidate the Laws Relative to Emigrants and Quarantine (1853), 32
Act to Restrict and Regulate Chinese Immigration (1885), 38
adaptability elements, 109
Afghanistan, 14, 309
Agri-Food Pilot Program, 151
Aiken, Sharryn J., 80
Ajana, Btihaj, biometrics citizenship, 107
Alberta: immigration, 120; Provincial Nominee Programs (PNPs), 122, 124; recruitment tours for migrants, 142
Alboim, Naomi, 90, 110
Alexander, Chris: barbaric cultural practices, 241; Citizenship Act, 228; re-election of, 95; Venancio and, 137
Alicbusan, Luvvy, caregiver, 157
Amnesty International Canada, 89, 92, 93, 287
Anderson, Bridget, Canada's welfare state, 196
Andras-Bienvenue agreement (1975), 119
Angus Reid survey, 94, 179
anti-Asian racism, 36
anti-Muslim racism, 56, 240, 250
anti-racism: national plan, 253; politics of, 248–54; racism and, 249; redress politics, 251–2. *See also* racism
Arab Canadians, 22
Arbour, Louise, 59
Arendt, Hannah, 75, 95
arranged employment, 109
Association for Canadian Studies, 237
asylum seekers, 70; border of United States and Canada, 286–7
Atlantic High-Skilled Program, 128

Atlantic Immigration Pilot program (AIP), 128–9
Atlantic Intermediate-Skilled Program, 128
Atlantic International Graduate Program, 128
Augustine, Stephen, Mi'kmaq, 289–90
Australia, Expression of Interest (EOI), 16, 112

Balanced Refugee Reform Act, 90
Ban Ki Moon, 58
Banting, Keith, 233–4, 311
Bauder, Harald, border regulations, 283
BC Human Rights Tribunal, 163
Bee-Clean Building Maintenance, Inc., 162
Benhabib, Seyla: cosmopolitanism, 266, 274–5; porous borders concept, 274
Benitez, Mercedes, caregiver, 201
Bernhard, Judith, 207
Biden, Joseph, Global Compact for Migration, 15, 59
bilingualism, 52, 231
Bill C-6, "An Act to Amend the Citizenship Act" (2017), 229
Bill C-24, Strengthening Canadian Citizenship Act (2015), 23, 228
biological, word, 187
biometrics, 186; citizenship and neoliberals, 107
birthplace: citizenship, 226; nationality law, 226
Bissett, James, Safe Third Country Agreement, 88
Black, Indigenous and People of Colour (BIPOC), 310
Black Lives Matter, 254, 287
Black people: immigration of men, 35; stereotypes about women, 40–1
Black People and People of Colour, 289
Block, Ernst, no borders as "possibilia", 283
bloodline, nationality law, 226
bogus, term, 23, 182
bogus marriages, 181
border imperialism, Walia, 277
Bouchard, Gérard, usage of interculturalism, 237
Boucher, Anna, 55
bounded world, communitarian approach, 266–70
brain drain, term, 55
brain waste, term, 56
Brexit, 233, 254
British Columbia: immigration, 120; Provincial Nominee Programs (PNPs), 122, 124, 126–7
British Columbia Civil Liberties Union, 287
British North America Act (1867), 33. *See also* Constitution Act 1867
Brown, Black and Fierce! Collective, 289
Bush, George W., global war on terror, 4
Byrd, Jodi, 279

Cabot, John, 30
California Gold Rush, 36
Cameron, David, state multiculturalism, 233
Campbell, Kim, multiculturalism, 238
Canada: border between United States and, 6; citizens abroad, 1; citizenship status, 17; colonial past and present, 8; Confederation and nation building, 33–47; economic immigration, 106–8, 129–30; family migration, 7, 179–80; identity as immigrant-receiving state, 104; immigration, multiculturalism and citizenship, 3, 13–14;

immigration in pre-Confederation, 30–2; immigration policy, 5–6, 54–5; immigration restrictions, 17; Jewish refugees of Nazi violence, 73; as land of immigrants, 29; marketized immigration model, 106–7; membership inclusion/exclusion, 52–7; modern immigration environment, 47–52; multiculturalism in, 7–8, 222–4, 230–5; naturalization, 7–8, 222–4, 224–30; "non preferred" migrant groups, 36, 38; number of immigrants annually (1852–2014), 46; permanent residents admitted (2019), 51; points-based model, 49–50; private sponsorship of refugees, 74; provincial nominee system, 7, 122–8; refugee claimants, 70; selection system, 54–5; South Asians and Japanese immigrating to, 36, 38–9; Syrian refugees, 289

Canada Border Services Agency (CBSA), 23, 157, 165, 188

Canada-Manitoba Immigration Agreement, 121

Canada-Quebec immigration agreement, 119

Canada Revenue Agency, 193

Canada's Action Plan for Faster Family Reunification, 190–3

Canada-United States-Mexico Agreement (CUSMA), 96n1

Canada-US Safe Third Country Agreement, 302

Canadian Alliance Party (2000–3), 111, 238

Canadian Arab Institute, 229

Canadian Association of Refugee Lawyers, 287

Canadian Census, 33

Canadian Charter of Rights and Freedoms, 222, 230, 232

Canadian Citizenship Act (1947), 43, 227; Bill C-24 for strengthening, 23, 228

Canadian Civil Liberties Association, 240

Canadian Council for Refugees (CCR), 89, 92, 93, 185–6, 189, 194, 287

Canadian Council of Churches (CCC), 89, 93

Canadian Experience Class (CEC) program, 106, 112–16, 303

Canadian Immigration Act (1976), 182

"Canadian is a Canadian is a Canadian", refrain of, 221, 229

Canadian Multiculturalism Act (1988), 231, 236

Canadian Museum of Immigration, 73

Canadian Pacific Contract, 35

Canadian Pacific Railway (CPR), 34–5; deaths during construction, 37; immigration and settlement activities, 34–5

Canadian Race Relations Foundation, 236, 251

care ethics, 5, ; border restrictions, 265; feminist, 8, 281, 300, 302; immigration and, 77; vision of human beings, 284–6

Caregiver Action Centre (CAC), 159

Caregiver Connections Education and Support Organization (CCESO), 159

caregiver programs (CP), 144, 152–60; caregiver activism in relation to, 154–5, 157–9, Caribbean Domestics Scheme (CDS), *145*, 153; Foreign Domestics Movement (FDM), *145*, 154; Live-in Caregiver Program (LCP), *145*, 154–6, 158; nanny-cams for surveillance, 156; Non-Immigrant Employment Authorization Program (NIEAP), 51, *145*, 153, 160; nursemaids, 153; sponsorship, 198–202

Carens, Joseph: liberalism, 266; open borders of, 270–3
Cargill meatpacking plants, COVID-19, 139, 167–8
Caribbean Domestics Scheme (CDS), care/domestic work, 145, 153
Castles, Stephen, refugees and asylum seekers, 15
CCC. *See* Canadian Council of Churches (CCC)
CCESO. *See* Caregiver Connections Education and Support Organization (CCESO)
CCF. *See* Cooperative Commonwealth Federation (CCF)
CCR. *See* Canadian Council for Refugees (CCR)
CDWCR. *See* Committee of Domestic Workers and Caregivers Rights (CDWCR)
Chartrand, Tyler, temporary foreign workers program, 151
Chatterjee, Soma, settler colonialism, 280
cheapness, employers, 51
Chen, Xiaobei, parent and grandparent sponsorship, 191
children, immigration of dependent, 185–7
China: California Gold Rush and migrants, 36–7; Canada excluding migrants, 36, 38; migrants for CPR construction, 37; migration, 14
Chinese Canadians, 251, 252
"Chinese flu", 56
Chinese Immigration Act (1923), 38, 43
"Chinese virus", 2, 56
choice, 21
Chrétien, Jean: border after 9/11, 86; Liberal party's policies under, 111; Low Skilled Pilot Project, 160; multiculturalism, 238; neoliberalism, 238, 249
Christchurch attack at mosque, 56
Christian Democratic Party, Merkel, 83
CIC. *See* Citizenship and Immigration Canada (CIC)
citizenship: Canada, 17; definition, 221; guide, 241–8; nation-building, 221–2; naturalization, 222; naturalization process, 224–30; no-border advocates, 278; racism and anti-racism, 249
Citizenship Act (1947), 43, 227; Harper and, 222
Citizenship and Immigration Canada (CIC), 122, 138; agricultural work, 150; marriage fraud, 188; temporary foreign workers, 162, 164
Clement, Wally, political economy, 5
closed border: communitarian approach, 266–70; communitarian perspectives, 266–70
Cohl, Karen, 90
Cold War: Communists during, 43; homosexuals and national security, 45; refugees, 79–80
colonial gender systems, 281
Committee of Domestic Workers and Caregivers Rights (CDWCR), 159
communitarianism, 266
communitarian perspectives: immigration, 266–70; sanctity and boundedness of community, 282
communities: border of United States and Canada, 286–7; communities of character, 267
Community Historical Recognition Programme, 73, 252
Comprehensive Ranking Score (CRS), 128
Comprehensive Ranking System (CRS), 114

conditional permanent residence (CPR), sponsorships for spouses, 187–9
Confederation: history of Canadian immigration before, 29–47; nation building and, 33–47
Conquest of New France (1760), 31
Conservative government: economic immigration, 107–8; immigration policies, 110–13, 115–16. *See also* Harper, Stephen and Conservative government
Conservative Party of Canada, 111
Constitution Act (1867), defining immigration, 118
containing diversity: concept of, 30; family migration and, 180; hallmarks of, 8, 69, 96; immigration and, 299; intersectionality, 5; normative vision of, 265; politics of social and global justice, 282–91; political community, 230; process, 2, 3, 6, 13, 39, 128, 223–4, 247; term, 28, 61, 74, 255, 301; TFWs and, 170; trend of, 195, 221, 307
Continuous Journey Regulation, 39
Cooperative Commonwealth Federation (CCF), 34
Corntassel, Jeff, settlers and Indigenous people, 280
cosmopolitanism: Benhabib, 266; individuals as "citizens of world", 273–5
cosmopolitan justice, notions of, 285
Couillard, Philippe: legislation targeting Muslims, 253; religious neutrality, 239
Council for Canadians with Disabilities (CCD), excessive demand, 201
COVID-19: border closures, 54, 278; border of United States and Canada, 6, 287; borders and migration, 265–6; communitarian approach, 269–70; coronavirus, 1; economic immigrants, 123; ethic group fueled racism, 56–7; family migration, 210; First Nations, 290; global pandemic, 299–300; health and disease mitigation, 61; infection rates and deaths, 264; masking and vaccination, 265; outbreak in Canadian farms, 151; public health, 93; quarantine rules, 32; racism and, 249; repercussions, 4; seasonal workers, 151; social distancing and isolation measures, 21; straining health care systems, 285; temporary foreign workers, 7, 139, 167–8, 303; travel and border restrictions, 51–2, 92; Trudeau and inbound travel, 85; vaccine passports, 60–1; variants of, 308; violent acts at minorities, 254; vulnerability of caregivers, 159
CP. *See* caregiver programs (CP)
Crenshaw, Kimberlé, intersectionality 5
criminality, term, 87
criminalization: neoliberalism and, 6, 13–14, 18–24, 301–2; policy responses to, 19
crimmigration, term by Stumpf, 22
cross-border solidarity, United States and Canada, 286–7
Cullen-Couture agreement, 119
cultural anxiety, 311
Cultural Contribution of Other Ethnic Groups (Government of Canada), 242
cumulative duration rule, temporary foreign workers to, 163–4

Dauvergne, Catherine, citizenship law/migration law, 225–7
De Leon, Coney, reunification and settlement, 208–9

De Leon, Javier Alonzo, seasonal worker, 149
dependent children: family migration, 185–7; term, 187
deportation, 19; criminal activity and, 22; detention and, 19, 23, 69, 87, 277; domestic workers and, 154; formal measures, 33; medical care and, 198; nation building mechanism, 40; sexual morality as category, 41; seasonal agricultural workers and, 149–50; TFWs and, 127, 137, 163
Depression, immigration policy in, 41–2
Detention: migrant incarceration, 19, 23, 45, 69, 81, 87, 90, 92, 277–8, 300, 302
Dhalla, Ruby, caregivers for mother, 155
Dhamoon, Rita, settlers and Indigenous people, 280
Discover Canada (Harper Conservative's citizenship guide), 242–4
DNA testing, kinship determination, 186–7
Donald, Dwayne, 289
Drolet, Natalie, Migrant Workers Centre BC, 157
Dua, Ena: on Asian workers, 39–40; Indigenous communities, 279–80
Dublin Convention (1990), 82, 83

Economic and Skills Development Canada (ESDC), 165
economic immigration: Canada's programs, 106–8, 129–30; Conservative government, 107–8; employment-driven programs, 128–9
Economic Mobility and Pathways Project (EMPP), 21, 54, 91, 94, 302
entrepreneurship, 21

Environics, 105, 236; change pages to 104–205, 236
ethics: care, 284–8; refugees and, 77–8, 94–6
European Court of Justice, 83
European Union (EU), 14, 57
excessive demand provision, 138
Expedited Labour Market Opinion Pilot Project, 161
Express Entry (EE), 106, 107, 127–8; Canada, 16; market logics when seeking citizens, 110–18; program, 113–15, 302
Expression of Interest (EOI), Australia and New Zealand, 16

family class: caregivers, 195, 198–202; conditional permanent residence for spouses, 187–9; dependent children, 185–7; Immigration Act (1976), 50; low-skilled temporary foreign workers, 195, 203–4; parent and grandparent sponsorship, 190–5; seasonal agricultural workers, 195, 197–8; sponsorship in Canada, 184–209
family migration: Canada, 7, 179–80; gendered expectations, 207–8; immigration restrictions on, 17–18; migrant children, 208; neoliberalism and, 180–4; post-reunification reconciliation, 208–9; sponsorship, 182–4; staged migration process, 207
Fassbender, Peter, Talosig and, 138
federal immigration programs: Canadian Experience Class (CEC), 112–16; Express Entry (EE), 110–18, 113–15; Federal Skilled Workers Program (FSWP), 109–10, 112, 114–15; growing dominance of PNPs, 122–8; Immigration and Refugee Protection Act (IRPA), 109; from points system to Express

Entry, 108–18; Provincial Nominee Programs (PNPs), 112, 115, 117, 118
federal-provincial relationships, immigration and evolving, 118–22
Federal Skilled Trades Program (FSTP), 114, 303
Federal Skilled Workers Program (FSWP), 106, 109–10, 112, 114–15, 303
female genital mutilation (FGM), 243, 247
feudalism, 271
Filipino migrants: caregivers, 155; family reunification, 207; migrant work, 138–9; temporary foreign workers, 163, 167
Finnie, Ross, 110
First Nations, 53; COVID-19, 290
First World War, 41; Vimy Ridge battle, 243
Five Eyes, 93
Floyd, George, 254, 288, 306
Fogarty, Clare, 32
food services, temporary foreign workers, 165
Foreign Credential Recognition Program, 113
Foreign Domestics Movement (FDM), 116; care/domestic work, 145; caregiver program, 154; sponsorship and, 198
Fortier, Craig, 288; No One Is Illegal, 288
Fortress America, 86
France, passport of expertise, 16
Francophone Quebecers, 52
Fraser, Nancy, 285
Fraser Institute, 190
Fraud, 209–10, 222, 227–8; Fraud Prevention Month (2013), 188; fraudsters, term, 23; Fraud Tip Line, 188
free immigrants, contract labour, 44
Freedom Convoy, 61

Ganti, Tejaswini, neoliberalism, 18–19
gender-based violence, 243
Gentile, Patriza, homosexuals and national security, 45, 47
Gentlemen's Agreement (1908), 39
Germany: migration, 14; skilled foreign workers, 16
Ghebreyesus, Tedros Adhanom, 1
Ghiz, Robert, bribery scandal, 126
Gibney, Matthew J., 81
Girard, Philip, persons categorized as "homosexuals" in immigration, 45, 47
global apartheid regime, 278
Global Commission on International Migration, 17
Global Compact for Migration, 15, 59–60
Global Compact for Safe, Orderly and Regular Migration (GCM), 60
Global Compact on Refugees, 15, 60, 80, 91, 302
Global North: caregivers, 206; immigration policy, 223; migration politics, 14, 15; multiculturalism, 56; refugees, 80
Global South: caregivers, 206; lead immigration applications, 110; migration politics, 14, 15; migration scholars and citizens, 24; public health and safety, 308; refugees, 79, 300–1, 309
global war for talent, 111
Globe and Mail (newspaper), 168
Go, Avvy, 57
Goldring, Luin, 207
Gordo, Magdalene, caregiver, 155
grandparent sponsorship, family migration, 190–5
Guerrero, Ivan, seasonal worker, 150
guest worker programs, 43
Guterres, António, mega crisis of refugees, 71

Hanson, Pauline, One Nation political party, 233
Harper, Stephen and Conservative government, 6: anti-racism, 250; attention to caregivers, 156–7; Citizenship Act, 222; crime and security concerns, 22; *Discover Canada* guide, 242–4; discrimination, 251; economic immigration, 108; family-class sponsorship, 184–5; family migration, 180; fraudulent citizenship applications and, 23; immigration policymaking, 110–13, 115–16, 304; jobs, trade and military, 3–4; multiculturalism, 222, 238, 249, 252, 305–6; naturalization, 222; Parents and Grandparents Program (PGP), 190, 193; post-9/11 racism, 239; refugees, 90, 93; Syrian refugees and, 72, 72–3; temporary foreign workers, 161, 303
head tax, 38
health inspection, 32
High Medical Needs Stream/ In-home Childcare Stream, care/domestic work, *145*
Hinshaw, Deena, COVID-19 and meatpacking plants, 139
Hoffman, Sarah, 137; Venancio and, 137
Hollifield, James, 107
home childcare worker, 158, 202
home support worker, 158, 202
homosexuals, immigration legislation, 45, 47
honour killings, 243
HRSDC. *See* Human Resources and Skills Development Canada (HRSDC)
Hughes, Vanessa, Canada's welfare state, 196
Human Capital Approach to Immigration, Canada, 108, 112

humanitarian class, Immigration Act (1976), 50
Human Resources and Skills Development Canada (HRSDC), 162
Hussen, Ahmed: citizenship, 230; conditional permanent residency, 189; refugee claimants, 92

ILO. *See* International Labour Organization (ILO)
immigration: Canada's identity in, 104; Canadian, and diversity, 28–9; Canadian economy, 311; Canadians seeing, as favourable, 105; closed border perspective, 266–70; communitarian perspectives, 266–70; cosmopolitan perspective, 273–5; diplomacy, 309; evolving federal-provincial relationships, 118–22; fraud in family migration, 183–4; global governance and sovereignty, 57–61; Indigenous criticisms of open borders/no borders, 279–82; Irish landowners, 31–2; multiculturalism and, 2–3; in nineteenth-century Canada, 33–4; no borders perspectives, 275–8; "non preferred" groups for Canada, 36, 38; number of immigrants in Canada annually (1852–2014), 46, *46*; OECD member country policies, 15–16; open-borders approach, 270–3; policy during Depression, 41–2; restrictions on family migration, 17–18; White Canada policy, 48
Immigration, Refugees and Citizenship Canada (IRCC), 47, 92, 122, 165
Immigration Act (1902), amendments to, 38
Immigration Act (1910), 41, 44, 45
Immigration Act (1952), 44, 45, 47, 48

Immigration Act (1976), 50, 51
Immigration and Refugee Protection Act (IRPA), (2001) 21, 105, 157, 302; biological kin relationship, 186; caregivers, 200; economic priorities, 109; family migration, 182; skilled workers, 105
IMP. *See* International Mobility Program (IMP)
independent class, Immigration Act (1976), 50
India, 14
Indigenous Peoples, 52; colonial state, 288–9; criticisms of open borders/no borders, 279–82; opening or removing borders, 283; rights of, in Canada, 8; sovereignty and justice for migrants, 288; tribes, 31
individual freedom, Carens, 272
individual responsibility, 21
Industrial Workers of the World (IWW), 41
Ingram, David, bounded associations, 267
In-home Personal Support Work/ In-home Childcare Work, care/ domestic work, *145*
interculturalism, 237, 255
International Day for the Elimination of Racial Discrimination, 250
International Experience Canada, 166
International Labour Organization (ILO), 140–1
international law, political theory and refugees, 75–8
International League of People's Struggles (ILPS), 310
international migration, 6; international migration politics of, 14–18
International Mobility Program (IMP), 144, 165–7, 304; low-skilled, *145*; open work permits for high-skill workers, 150
intersectionality, containing diversity and, 5, 224
Inuit peoples, 53
Iraq, 14
IRCC. *See* Immigration, Refugees and Citizenship Canada (IRCC)
Ireland: immigration restrictions, 17; Irish landowners, 31–2; Irish migration, 31, 32
IRPA. *See* Immigration and Refugee Reform Protection Act (IRPA) (2002)
Islamic Cultural Centre, shootings of worshippers, 56
Islamophobia, 56, 240

Jamaican migrants: care workers under the Foreign Domestics Movement, 154; seasonal agricultural workers, 139
James, Matt, 252
Japan: immigrants coming to Canada, 39; Second World War, 22
Jewish Refugees, 42–3, 73, 252
Jhappan, Radha, immigration policy, 34; white settler construct, 29
jus solis principle, citizenship, 226
"Justice for Janitors" campaign, 162
"Justice for Vicky" campaign, 137
Justicia for Migrant Workers, social justice organization, 152

Kenney, Jason: bridge building, 250; Canada's Action Plan for Faster Family Reunification, 190–3; Canadian Experience Class (CEC), 113; caregiver program, 200; citizenship guide, 242, 244–5; immigration and multiculturalism, 111; immigration terms, 23; marriage fraud, 188; preventing fraud, 227–8; Provincial Nominee Programs (PNPs), 125

Khouri, Raja, Canadian Arab Institute, 72
King, Mackenzie, mass immigration, 42–3
Kinsman, Gary, homosexuals and national security, 45, 47
Kofman, Eleonore, 181
Korea, immigration restrictions, 17
Kosmopolites, individuals as "citizens of world", 273
Kurdi, Alan: crisis in Syria, 95; Syrian refugee, 72
Kurdi, Tima, Canadian aunt of Alan, 72
Kwan, Jenny, NDP immigration critic, 157
Kymlicka, Will: immigration, citizenship and multiculturalism, 2–3, 305; multiculturalism index, 233–5; naturalization, 224, place-based interests and rights, 284

labour brokerage states, 141
Labour Market Impact Assessments (LMIAs), 115, 165–6
labour migration, non-permanent, 142–3
Labour unions, 154, 162, 170
land of immigrants, Canada, 29
Landolt, Patricia, 207
Lang-Cloutier agreement (1971), 119
Larios, Lindsay, 107–8
"Last Best West" campaign, Sifton, 35
Laurier, Wilfrid, history of immigration, 35
Lawrence, Bonita, Indigenous communities, 279–80
Legault, François: Bill 21 by, 253; Coalition Avenir Québec, 240
Le Pen, Marine, 233, 253
Lewis, Nathaniel, Provincial Nominee Programs (PNPs), 124

LGBTQ2+: asylum, 87, 88; family migration, 183
liberalism: Carens, 266; open borders, 270–3
Liew, Jamie, definitions of 'family', 183–4
Live-in Caregiver Program (LCP), 116, 138, 154–6, 158; care/domestic work, *145*; excessive demand provision, 201; sponsorship and, 198
LMIAs. *See* Labour Market Impact Assessments (LMIAs)
Low Skill Pilot Project (LSPP), 160
Loyalists, 31

Maastricht Treaty (1993), 82
Macdonald, John A.: Chinese migrants for CPR construction, 37; National Policy initiatives, 34
McDougall/Gagnon-Tremblay Accord (1991), 119
McKay, Ian, rebranding Canada as "Warrior Nation", 242
Mackenzie, Sheldon, agricultural worker from Jamaica, 198
Macklin, Audrey, Syrian refugees, 72; Safe Third Country Agreement, 87
Marsden, Sarah, migrant work and liberal 'dilemma', 142
McNally, David, migrant acceptance, 277–8
McNevin, Anne, 289
Manitoba: immigration, 120–2; Provincial Nominee Programs (PNPs), 124
Marchetti, Raffaele, cosmopolitan citizenship, 274
marital status, nationality law, 226
marketized immigration model, Canada, 106–7
Martin, Paul: multiculturalism, 238; neoliberalism, 249

Martin, Paul Sr., citizenship, 43
Martin, Trayvon, 287
May, Theresa, multiculturalism, 233
membership: communitarian approach, 266–8; inclusion/exclusion, Canada, 52–7; liberal open borders, 270–3
Mendicino, Marco, mandate letter, 128
Meng, Ross, 110
Merkel, Angela, 83, 232
Metis, 53
Mexico, US southern border with, 19–20
Mexican migrants: racism against, 19; US immigration, 84–5; visitors, 81
migrant family, perception of, 181
Migrants Rights Network (MRN), 310
Migrant Workers Alliance for Change (MWAC), 159
Migrant Workers Centre BC, 157
migration: COVID-19 pandemic, 2; government policy, 1–2; shifting landscape of international politics, 14–18. *See also* immigration
Mi'kmaq, Augustine, 289–90
Milner, James, Canada and Global Compact on Refugees, 60
ministerial discretion, immigration policies, 105
Molinaro, Dennis, 40
mother country, 29
Mountz, Alison, death of asylum, 81
Mulroney, Brian, compensation for past injustices, 251
multicultiphobia, Ryan, 237
multicultural index, 233
multiculturalism, 52, 222; Canada, 7–8, 230–5; Canadian policy, 255; immigration and, 2–3; naturalization and, 222–3; Quebec, 236–40; term, 255; word, 235
multilateralism, 59
Municipal Nominee Program (MNP), 128–9

Muslims: global war on terror and, 4; Muslim Canadians, 22
MWAC. *See* Migrant Workers Alliance for Change (MWAC)

Nansen, Fridtjof, 73
National Council of Canadian Muslims, 240
national interest, 311
nationalism, Walia, 278
nationality law, elements of, 225–26
National Occupation Classification (NOC), 160
National Policy, Macdonald's initiative, 34
nation building, deportation as mechanism, 40
naturalization: Canada, 7–8, 224–30; citizenship by, 222; multiculturalism and, 222–23
neoliberalism, 299; administrative depoliticization, 105; biometrics of citizenship, 107; Chrétien on, 238; criminalization and, 6, 13–14, 18–24, 301–2; family forms and, 180–4
Netherlands, 17
Neve, Alex, Amnesty International, 92
New Brunswick: Loyalists, 31; Provincial Nominee Programs (PNPs), 122
Newfoundland: Cabot in, 30; Provincial Nominee Programs (PNPs), 122
New York Declaration on Migrants and Refugees, 58–9
New York Times (newspaper), 72
New Zealand: Expression of Interest (EOI), 16; two-step immigration, 112
NIEAP. *See* Non-Immigrant Employment Authorization Program (NIEAP)
no borders, 282–3; perspective on immigration, 275–8; Walia's work, 266

non-entry refugee regime, 80–1
Non-Immigrant Employment Authorization Program (NIEAP), 51, *145*, 153, 160
non-refoulement, 82; principle of, 76
No One Is Illegal, 288
North America, migration politics, 14
North American Free Trade Agreement (NAFTA), 79, 84, 85, 96n1
Norway, 17
Nova Scotia: Loyalists, 31; Provincial Nominee Programs (PNPs), 122, 124–5

One Nation party, 233
Ontario: immigration, 120; Ontario Human Rights Tribunal, 148
open borders, free movement, 76, 282; Liberal perspective 270–3
Orbán, Victor, Hungary, 83
Order-in-Council (1911), Negro race ban, 35
Orr, Frank, human trafficking charge, 155
Owen, David, pandemic spread and borders, 275

Palestine refugees, 45, 70
Parents and Grandparents Program (PGP), 190–5; Super Visa, 192, 195
parent sponsorship, family migration, 190–5
Paquet, Mireille, 107–8
Pavlich, Alex, 125
Peart, Ned Livingston, seasonal worker, 149
People of Color, 289
People's Party of Canada, 254
Peralta, Honorato, temporary foreign workers, 127
Philippines, recruitment tours for migrants, 142
Pickersgill, Jack, admission powers, 44

Pilot Project to Sponsor Undeclared Family Members, Trudeau government, 184
Plattsburgh Cares, 286
pluralism, Canada's, 250
PNPs. *See* Provincial Nominee Programs (PNPs)
points system, 48; Canada, 49–50, 112; FSWP and, 114, 115; program, 108–10, 112; university admission policy, 142
Poland, 14
political refugees, Loyalists, 31
political theory, international law and refugees, 75–8
porous borders, Benhabib's concept of, 274
Portugal, immigrants from, 232
positive arranged employment opinion, 109
Pratt, Anna, criminality, 87
Pratt, Geraldine: Filipina caregivers, 206; Filipino Canadian Youth Alliance, 208
Pratt, Minnie Bruce, 276
Preibisch, Kerry, 145
Prince Edward Island, Provincial Nominee Programs (PNPs), 122, 125–6
Progressive Conservative Party, 111
Project Guardian, Canadian Border Services Agency (CBSA), 157
Protecting Canada's Immigration System Act, 90
Provincial Nominee and Settlement Services Annex, 121
Provincial Nominee Programs (PNPs), 21, 106, 107, 112, 115, 117, 118, 303; growing dominance of, 122–8; temporary foreign workers to, 163, 203, 205
provincial nominee system, Canada, 7
public health: Canada's immigration legislation, 32; COVID-19, 93

quarantine: Canada's immigration legislation, 32; Chinese-origin passengers, 38; deportation, 40
Quebec: barbaric cultural practices, 244; immigration selection, 118–20; multiculturalism, 236, 236–40; politics of membership and belonging, 244; Provincial Nominee Programs (PNPs), 123; Quiet Revolution, 118
queue jumpers, term, 23
Quiet Revolution, 118

race: mass immigration, 42–3; racialization, 2. *See also* racism
race for talent, Shachar, 16
racism: anti-Muslim, 56; anti-racism and, 249; COVID-19 and, 249; cross-border solidarity, 287; denial of, 253–4; ethic group fueled, 56–7; political climate after 9/11, 248; post-9/11 racism, 239
Ramos, Howard, 193
RCMP: security vetting, 43; tip line for reporting on "barbaric cultural practices", 4
Reasonable accommodation, 239
Reform Party (1987–2000), 238
refugees: addressing ethics and, 94–6; Canada's private sponsorship system, 74; claimants, 70; communitarian approach, 268–9; cross-border solidarity, 287; description of, 69–70; growing numbers worldwide, 15; international law and political theory, 75–8; natural disasters, 309–10; resettled, 70; special obligation to, 78; treatment of, 77–8; United Nations High Commissioner for Refugees (UNHCR), 71; United Nations Nansen Medal, 73–4
Regulatory Impact Statement (2013), 185

Reid, Angus, 57
relationality, communities, 286
Rempel, Michelle, female genital mutilation (FGM), 247
residence, nationality law, 226
Rights of Others, The (Benhabib), 77
Romania, migration, 14
Royal Bank of Canada, 164
Royal Commission on Bilingualism and Biculturalism, (1963) 231
Royal Commission on Chinese Immigration, (1884) 36, 37
Royal Proclamation of 1763, 30, 31
Russia, invasion of Ukraine, 36, 58
Russia-Ukraine war (2022), 6, 58, 71
Ryan, Paul, multicultiphobia, 237

safe third country agreements, 74, 78; smart borders and, 84–94; US-Canada border, 302
safe third country principle, 81–2
Sandy Bay Anishinaabe First Nation, 290
Saranillio, Dean Itsuji, 279
Sarmineto, Letitia, migrant worker, 155
SARS, 56
Saskatchewan: Provincial Nominee Programs (PNPs), 122, 124; recruitment tours for migrants, 142
Satzewich, Vic, farm labour recruits, 44
SAWP. *See* Seasonal Agricultural Worker Program (SAWP)
Schengen Convention (1990), 82, 85, 86
Seasonal Agricultural Worker Program (SAWP), 17, 144; country surfing, 148; farm work, 145; gendered perceptions of, 148–9; racial abuse in, 148; routes for, 150–1; sponsorship, 197–8; win-win program, 145–6; worker vulnerability, 146–7

Second World War, 41, 57, 118, 252; humanitarian crisis, 83; Japanese Canadians, 22; Jewish refugees of, 73; refugees, 79
self-sufficiency, 21
Selling Diversity (Abu-Laban and Gabriel), 21
September 11, 2001: anti-Muslim racism after, 240; gender equality after, 243; multiculturalism policy in post-9/11 period, 223–4; political climate after, 248; refugees, 80; repercussions, 4; security and terrorism following, 234
Services Employees International Union (SEIU), 162
sexual morality, deportation category, 41
Shachar, Ayelet, race for talent, 16
Sharma, Nandita: open borders approach, 275–8; temporary foreign worker, 51
Sifton, Clifford: "Last Best West" campaign, 35; recruitment campaigns, 35–6
skilled workers, IRPA defining, 105
skills-based model, Canada, 49–50
slavery, 271
smart border agreements, safe third country agreements and, 84–94
Snelgrove, Corey, settlers and Indigenous people, 280
social relations, 5
Soennecken, Dagmar, 86
Somali-Jewish Canadian Mentorship Project, 250
Soroka, Stuart, 311
Spain, 14
Sparke, Mathew, neoliberalism, 20
sponsorship, 45; caregivers, 195, 198–202; comparing classes, 205–9; conditional permanent residence for spouses, 187–9; dependent children, 185–7; DNA testing for kinship, 186–7; family-class, in Canada, 184–209; family migration, 182–4; low-skilled temporary foreign workers, 195, 203–4; marriage fraud, 187–9; parent and grandparent, 190–5; seasonal agricultural workers, 195, 197–8. *See also* family class
Stasiulis, Daiva: immigration policy, 34; white settler construct, 29
Statistics Canada, 245; number of immigrants in Canada annually (1852–2014), *46*
Strangers within Our Gates (Wordsworth), 34
Stumpf, Juliet, "crimmigration" term, 22
Swift, Jaime, rebranding Canada as "Warrior Nation", 242
Syria, migration, 14
Syrian refugees: Canada and, 72–3; image of lifeless Alan Kurdi, 72

Talosig, Jazmin, medical status, 138
Talosig, Karen, 138, 139; application for residency, 157; Live-in Caregiver Program (LCP), 138
Tamondong, Vanessa, temporary foreign workers, 127
Temporary Foreign Worker Program (TFWP), 115, 137, 160–9; Canada, 7; cumulative duration rule, 163–4; family migration, 181; Harper Conservatives, 161; International Mobility Program (IMP), 165–7; low-skilled, *145*, 150–1; Low Skill Pilot Project (LSPP), 160; Non-Immigrant Employment Authorization Program (NIEAP), 160; permit holders, *144*
temporary foreign workers (TFWs), 126–7, 138–40; sponsorship of low-skilled, 203–4

temporary labour migration, 140–3; caregiver program, 152–60; low-skilled, in Canada, 143–69; migrant farm work, 144–52; Non-Immigrant Employment Authorization Program (NIEAP), *145*, 153, 160; Seasonal Agricultural Workers Program (SAWP), 144–52; Temporary Foreign Worker Program (TFWP), 160–9
territorial diffusion, border regimes, 277
terrorism, 61, 80, 222, 233
TFWP. *See* Temporary Foreign Worker Program (TFWP)
TFWs. *See* temporary foreign workers (TFWs)
Thompson, Debra, 287
Thorpe, Sherry Xiaohan, parent and grandparent sponsorship, 191
three-legged stool, immigration, citizenship and multiculturalism, 2–3, 305
Tim Hortons, 163
Tongson, Richelyn, caregiver, 155
TRC. *See* Truth and Reconciliation Commission of Canada (TRC)
Triadafilopoulos, Triadafilos, human rights after war, 48
Trudeau, Justin and Liberal government, 6; "a Canadian is a Canadian" mantra, 229–30, 241; caregivers, 202; COVID-19 response, 85, 302; diversity, 3, 91, 253; excessive demand provision, 201; family migration, 180, 184; government, 17; immigration policymaking, 3, 112, 115; leadership of, 221; multiculturalism, 222–3, 306; multilateral migration approach, 59; national anti-racism plan, 253; naturalization, 222–3; Pilot Project to Sponsor Undeclared Family Members, 184; Syrian refugees, 73, 90–1, 240, 301; Syrian refugees and, 73; temporary foreign workers, 204, 303
Trudeau, Pierre Elliott: bilingualism, 231; compensation for past injustices, 251
Trump, Donald, 253; immigrant attitudes, 19–20; inauguration of, 59, 84; merit based system, 49; multiculturalism, 233; protective measures, 92; refugees and, 15; travel ban, 91
Truth and Reconciliation Commission of Canada (TRC), 52, 246, 279, 290, 306
Turgeon, Luc, 240

Ukraine: diaspora in Canada, 36; Ukrainian-Canadians, 231; Russia-Ukraine war, 36, 58, 71
United Empire Loyalists, 73
United Kingdom, 14
United Nations (UN), 56, 57, 58; Ban Ki Moon, 58; General Assembly, 15; Global Compact for Migration, 15, 59–60; Global Compact for Safe, Orderly and Regular Migration (GCM), 60; Global Compact on Refugees, 15, 60, 80, 91, 302; International Day for the Elimination of Racial Discrimination, 250; Nansen Medal, 73–4; Secretary-General for International Migration, 60; Universal Declaration of Human Rights, 75
United Nations Convention on the Rights of Migrant Workers and Their Families, 197
United Nations Convention Relating to the Status of Refugees, 69, 70, 75
United Nations High Commissioner for Refugees (UNHCR), 54, 71, 302

United Nations Relief and Works Agency (UNRWA), 71
United States: border between Canada and, 6; citizens abroad, 1; United States-Mexico-Canada Agreement (USMCA), 96n1; US-Canada Smart Border Declaration, 79, 86
Universal Declaration on the Rights of Indigenous Peoples (UNDRIP), 279

Vaccines: global disparity in access 308; vaccine passport, Canada and COVID-19, 57, 60–1;
Vancouver Committee of Domestic Workers and Caregivers Rights (CDWCR), 159
VanderPlaat, Madine, 193
van Selm, Joanne, 82
Venancio, Vicky, 137–8, 139
venue shopping, 108
Vietnam: immigrants from, 14, 245; refugees from, 232, 268
voluntarism, 21
Vosko, Leah, deportability regime, 143, 146, temporary foreign workers program, 151

Walia, Harsha, no borders politics, 266, 277–8, 289
Waldman, Lorne, 167

Walsh, James, 50
Walzer, Michael, communitarian "closed border" perspectives, 266–70
War Measures Act, Quebec nationalists and separatists, 22
war on queers, term, 47
war on terror, term, 56
Whitaker, Reg, growth of ethnic groups, 45
White Canada immigration policy, 48
white supremacy, 281
Wilcox, Shelly, naturalization, 248
Williamson, John, temporary foreign workers, 164
Winnipeg Free Press (newspaper), 120
Winnipeg General Strike (1919), 41
Wordsworth, J.S., *Strangers within Our Gates*, 34
World Health Organization (WHO), 1, 299
World Refugee Day, 290
"Wuhan virus", 2

xenophobic movements, 310

Yoshida, Yoko, 193

Zero Tolerance for Barbaric Cultural Practices Act, 241
Zimmerman, George, 287

Milton Keynes UK
Ingram Content Group UK Ltd.
UKHW041707120324
439387UK00015B/130